THE BEST BED & BREAKFAST IN THE WORLD

ENGLAND, SCOTLAND & WALES

1987

Sigourney Welles
Jill Darbey
Joanna Mortimer

The finest Bed & Breakfast accommodation
in the British Isles.

Town Houses, Country Homes, Pretty Village Cottages
Manor Houses, Farmhouses.

In age the houses listed range over Nine Centuries

1084 to 1984

A   U.K.H.M./EAST WOODS PRESS PUBLICATION

U.K.H.M. - LONDON

EAST WOODS PRESS - CHARLOTTE NORTH CAROLINA

© U.K.H.M. PUBLISHING LIMITED 1987

U.K.H.M. Publishing Limited
P.O. Box 134,
15 Gledhow Gardens,
London,
SW5 0TX.
England.

Published in U.S. by

The East Woods Press
429 East Boulevard,
Charlotte
North Carolina 28203. U.S.A.
U.K. ISBN 0 907500 14 5
U.S.A. ISBN 0-88742-102-4

Distributed in Australia by:

Era Publications,
P.O.Box 231, Brooklyn Park,
South Australia 5032

Library of Congress Cataloging in Publication Data

Welles, Sigourney, 1946-
The Best Bed & Breakfast in The World.

1.Bed and breakfast accommodations -- Great Britain -- Directories. 2.Bed and breakfast
accommodations -- Ireland -- Directories. I.Darbey,Jill. II.Title. III.Title:Best bed and breakfast
in the world.
TX910.G7W365 1985 647'.94103 84-21203
ISBN 0-88742-102-4

Trades Description

The publishers have made every reasonable effort to ensure that the accommodations mentioned in
this guide are as stated, however the Publishers cannot accept any responsibility for any
inaccuracies, errors or omissions that may occur.

Typeset by— U.K.H.M. Publishing Ltd.
Printed by Redwood Web Offset, Trowbridge, Wiltshire

CONTENTS

FOREWORD

This book was created with the help of many hundreds of overseas visitors to Britain who took the time to write to us giving information about Bed and Breakfast establishments where they had stayed and enjoyed hospitality, comfortable accommodation and good cooking. In this way we have compiled a register of reputable establishments offering what we consider to be the Best Bed and Breakfast in the World.

They range from Tudor houses to country pubs, farmhouses to modern bungalows and are situated on the coast, in the countryside, in interesting towns and villages and have one thing in common - they have been "Personally Recommended" by previous visitors. We have endeavoured to convey the style and standards of each house combined with an idea of what the visitor can discover in the immediate area.

What is Bed and Breakfast

B. & B. is a warm welcome, a friendly atmosphere, a nights accommodation and breakfast. It means that you become a paying guest, usually, in someones home. It is important to remember that in general, B. & B. hosts do not offer hotel facilities or hotel service and these should not be expected. When staying at a B. & B., guests are not expected to arrive before 6 p.m. and to leave after breakfast the next morning by 10 a.m. If staying more than one night these arrangements are often flexible but check with your host. It is very important that you always contact your host to inform them of your estimated time of arrival.

Children, Animals and Evening Meals

You will be able to see at a glance those establishments which are happy to accept children, some though not all, offer special rates for children when sharing their parents' room.

Animals are also accepted by many establishments, however some hosts prefer that they remain in the car, so check before leaving home.

A full English breakfast is always served, except where stated. Most establishments also offer, at an additional charge, a well cooked substantial evening meal. Many hosts specialize in home cooking and baking, vegetarian meals, or Cordon Bleu cuisine. Advance notice (12 hours) is required if you wish an evening meal.

London Bed and Breakfast

You are strongly advised to book well in advance of your stay. Guests should always contact their host to inform them of their approximate time of arrival. Our London Homes are bookable ONLY through the W.W.B.B.A. reservation service. These homes, like all our others, have been personally inspected. They are all comfortable, spotlessly clean and well decorated, most offer private facilities, others have en-suite bathroom, very occasionally you may have to share a bathroom with one other. All these homes are located within 15 or 20 minutes of Central London (Knightsbridge), and are close to the underground, train stations or bus routes, so travelling by public transport is easy.

Prices and Payment

The prices quoted in this guide are minimum per person per night. These prices do, generally, increase during the summer months. It is therefore advisable to confirm the price with your host before or upon arrival. Payment should always be in English pounds.

Recommendations and Complaints

To maintain the standards in our book we are keen to hear your views on our establishments. If you have any comments, good or bad, about your accommodation, or if you would like to recommend a Bed and Breakfast establishment not in our book, please do so. You will find Recommendation and Complaint slips at the back

Reservation Information

Bed and Breakfast differs from hotel accommodation and your host needs certain advance information.

You will be staying in a family home and your host needs to plan his or her own day as well as giving you a warm welcome.

As a general guide you will not be expected to arrive before 6 p.m. and should leave after breakfast the next morning by 10 a.m. However these times vary at each home particularly if you will be staying for several nights. In most homes you will be able to drop off baggage earlier in the day.

Whether you book direct or through our reservation office the following details will be needed:-

    1) Your estimated time of arrival at each home.

    2) If you require an evening meal.

The prices that we show throughout the book are the minimum per person per night and do vary during the seasons.

If you book direct the host may require varying deposits. If you book through our office we shall require a deposit of £3 per person per night.

Booking Information

When making reservations through our office, either by phone or mail, we shall quote you the prices prevailing at the requested dates and make a provisional booking for you. We shall require a deposit of £3 ($4.50) per person per night to confirm the booking, this should be sent with your booking form by cheque or by quoting your VISA, AMEX, MASTERCARD or ACCESS number.

This deposit is deductable from the quoted price and the balance payable to your host will be shown on your deposit receipt.

You will also receive a confirmation slip with the name and address of your host and travel details about how to get there.

In the event of cancellation the deposit is non-refundable.

How to Book

If you are resident overseas, either; complete the reservation form overleaf and post it to:

W.W.B.B.A., P.O.BOX 134, 15 GLEDHOW GDNS, LONDON SW5 0TX U.K.

or;

Phone **01 370 7099** - (24 hour answer phone).

or;

Telex: **919942   W.W.B.B.A.G**

Giving full details.

We shall confirm as soon as possible and return the confirmation by registered mail.

If you need to make rapid bookings, particularly for London accommodation, we shall ask you to call again in one or two hours for confirmations. For confirmation of bookings outside London call again the following day. Our office hours are 9.30 a.m. to 6.30 p.m.

Payment

If you are resident in U.K. contact the homes yourself to make bookings outside London.

For bookings in London, please call our reservation office on 01 370 7099.

The deposit of £3 ($4.50) per person per night should be made out to W.W.B.B.A., would you please add £3 ($4.50) for bank charges if the cheque is in currencies other than Sterling (British Pounds).

Payment by VISA, AMEX, MASTERCARD or ACCESS is welcomed, it is also quicker for confirmation by phone and carries no bank exchange charges.

Booking Form

Remember the closer to the city centre the more expensive the accommodation

Name _____

Address _____

_____

_____

_____

Telephone:

No. in party: Childrens ages:

Date of departure from U.S.   Date of arrival U.K.

Arrival time at Heathrow/Gatwick airport   A.M./P.M.

Please send a deposit of £3.00 ($4.50) per person per night

All deposits are non refundable

	Expiry date
Access _____	_____
Amex _____	_____
Masterchage _____	_____
Visa _____	_____

Cheques payable to W.W.B.B.A. (plus $4.50 for non-sterling cheques)

Mail to: **W.W.B.B.A. P.O. Box 134, 15 Gledhow Gardens, London SW5 0TX. UK.**

Phone: **01 370 7099** (24 hr. phone) Telex: **919942 W.W.B.B.A.G**

London

Dates of stay in London: _____

No. of nights accommodation in London: _____

Preferred Location: (i.e. Knightsbridge, Kensington etc.) if available. _____

House No: _____

Accommodation required in London: Please book me the following rooms.

_____   single bedded room(s)

_____   twin bedded room(s)

_____   double bedded room(s)

U.K. Booking Form

Please reserve the following rooms:-

_____ single bedded room(s)
_____ twin bedded room(s)
_____ double bedded room(s)
_____ 3 bedded family room (if available)

for the nights of: _____

at   1st choice guest house _____
_____

2nd choice guest house _____
_____

3rd choice guest house _____
_____

Please reserve the following rooms:-

_____ single bedded room(s)
_____ twin bedded room(s)
_____ double bedded room(s)
_____ 3 bedded family room (if available)

for the nights of: _____

at   1st choice guest house _____
_____

2nd choice guest house _____
_____

3rd choice guest house _____
_____

Please reserve the following rooms:-

_____ single bedded room(s)
_____ twin bedded room(s)
_____ double bedded room(s)
_____ 3 bedded family room (if available)

for the nights of: _____

at   1st choice guest house _____
_____

2nd choice guest house _____
_____

3rd choice guest house _____
_____

Please reserve the following room(s):-

_____ single bedded room(s)
_____ twin bedded room(s)
_____ double bedded room(s)
_____ 3 bedded family room (if available)

for the nights of: _____

at 1st choice guest house _____

_____

2nd choice guest house _____

_____

3rd choice guest house _____

_____

Please reserve the following rooms:-

_____ single bedded room(s)
_____ twin bedded room(s)
_____ double bedded room(s)
_____ 3 bedded family room (if available)

for the nights of: _____

at 1st choice guest house _____

_____

2nd choice guest house _____

_____

3rd choice guest house _____

_____

Please reserve the following room(s):-

_____ single bedded room(s)
_____ twin bedded room(s)
_____ double bedded room(s)
_____ 3 bedded family room (if available)

for the nights of: _____

at 1st choice guest house _____

_____

2nd choice guest house _____

_____

3rd choice guest house _____

_____

Please reserve the following rooms:-

_____ single bedded room(s)
_____ twin bedded room(s)
_____ double bedded room(s)
_____ 3 bedded family room (if available)

for the nights of: _____

at   1st choice guest house_____

_____

2nd choice guest house_____

_____

3rd choice guest house_____

_____

Please reserve the following rooms:-

_____ single bedded room(s)
_____ twin bedded room(s)
_____ double bedded room(s)
_____ 3 bedded family room (if available)

for the nights of: _____

at   1st choice guest house_____

_____

2nd choice guest house_____

_____

3rd choice guest house_____

_____

Please reserve the following rooms:-

_____ single bedded room(s)
_____ twin bedded room(s)
_____ double bedded room(s)
_____ 3 bedded family room (if available)

for the nights of: _____

at   1st choice guest house_____

_____

2nd choice guest house_____

_____

3rd choice guest house_____

_____

Please reserve the following rooms:-

_____ single bedded room(s)
_____ twin bedded room(s)
_____ double bedded room(s)
_____ 3 bedded family room (if available)

for the nights of: _____

at   1st choice guest house_____
_____

2nd choice guest house_____
_____

3rd choice guest house_____
_____

Please reserve the following rooms:-

_____ single bedded room(s)
_____ twin bedded room(s)
_____ double bedded room(s)
_____ 3 bedded family room (if available)

for the nights of: _____

at   1st choice guest house_____
_____

2nd choice guest house_____
_____

3rd choice guest house_____
_____

Please reserve the following rooms:-

_____ single bedded room(s)
_____ twin bedded room(s)
_____ double bedded room(s)
_____ 3 bedded family room (if available)

for the nights of: _____

at   1st choice guest house_____
_____

2nd choice guest house_____
_____

3rd choice guest house_____
_____

Please reserve the following rooms:-

_____ single bedded room(s)
_____ twin bedded room(s)
_____ double bedded room(s)
_____ 3 bedded family room (if available)

for the nights of: _____

at   1st choice guest house _____
      _____

      2nd choice guest house _____
      _____

      3rd choice guest house _____
      _____

Please reserve the following rooms:-

_____ single bedded room(s)
_____ twin bedded room(s)
_____ double bedded room(s)
_____ 3 bedded family room (if available)

for the nights of: _____

at   1st choice guest house _____
      _____

      2nd choice guest house _____
      _____

      3rd choice guest house _____
      _____

Please reserve the following rooms:-

_____ single bedded room(s)
_____ twin bedded room(s)
_____ double bedded room(s)
_____ 3 bedded family room (if available)

for the nights of: _____

at   1st choice guest house _____
      _____

      2nd choice guest house _____
      _____

      3rd choice guest house _____
      _____

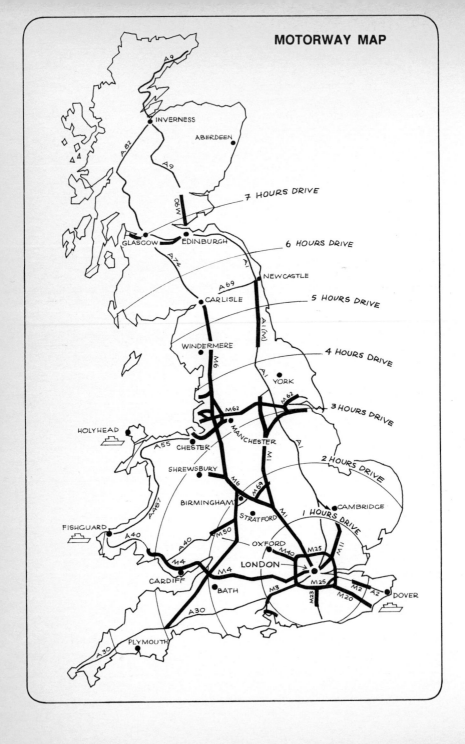

MOTORWAY MAP

General Information for Overseas Visitors

To help overseas guests get the most from their stay in the U.K. we have put together some basic information about the U.K.

Buses and Coaches

If you are travelling within a 5-10 mile radius you will probably need to use the local bus services. Timetables for these can be picked up at the local bus station or newsagents. If travelling more extensively you will want to use the National Coach Service. This is a regular fast service travelling the motorways between cities. These coaches are often full so it is advisable to book a seat ahead of time. There are also many day trips, sightseeing tours, special event excursions, etc., enquire at the bus and coach stations for full details. For mainline train services contact any British Rail station.

Car Hire

Prices do of course vary but generally it is very expensive. Mileage, V.A.T. and insurance are usually extra. A deposit is always required. You must be over 21 years and have held a license, valid for use in the U.K., for over 12 months.

Petrol/gas is also expensive. When travelling in rural areas, fill up. Petrol stations/garages can be difficult to find and they close early in the evening (5.30 - 6.00p.m.). The maximum speed limit on motorways is 70 m.p.h. (110 Kmph). In residential areas 30 m.p.h (45 Kmph) is the limit. Finally, remember to drive on the left and look for traffic lights on the side of the road not overhead.

Pubs

The licensing laws in the U.K. are very peculiar making pub opening times quite incomprehensible to most visitors. Monday-Saturday 11.00 a.m. - 3.00 p.m. and 5.00 p.m. - 11.00 p.m. Sunday 12.00 p.m. - 2.30 p.m. and 7.00 p.m. - 10.30 p.m. The same applies to wine bars and drinking in hotels etc. However you can buy alcohol in wine stores outside these hours. You must be over 18 years before you may buy or consume alcohol. 14 - 18 year olds may visit pubs accompanied by an adult but may not drink alcohol.

Telephones

Free calls: the operator dial 100, enquires 192, emergency services - police, fire, ambulance 999. These numbers are the same throughout the U.K. Public phone booths on the street come in many guises. The traditional red booth will only take exact coinage - 10p pieces - no change given, (only put your money in when you here the beeps). Modern call boxes take your money first, either 50p or 10p coins and give change. Booths showing a green phone card symbol don't take money at all. Only prepaid phone cards are accepted, (available from Post Offices and newsagents).

Hospital Services

All emergency services are free i.e., accidents. All other services are charged for - get insurance before leaving home.

Tipping

Is not obligatory anywhere, but when you do 12% is usual.

Please reserve the following room(s):-

_____ single bedded room(s)
_____ twin bedded room(s)
_____ double bedded room(s)
_____ 3 bedded family room

for the nights of: _____

at   1st choice guest house _____

2nd choice guest house _____

3rd choice guest house _____

Please reserve the following room(s):-

_____ single bedded room(s)
_____ twin bedded room(s)
_____ double bedded room(s)
_____ 3 bedded family room

for the nights of: _____

at   1st choice guest house _____

2nd choice guest house _____

3rd choice guest house _____

COUNTIES MAP

Each county has been assigned a number. This refers to the page where a detailed, full page map of the county is located.

SUTHERLAND

ISLE OF SKYE

ROSS-SHIRE

HIGHLAND

ABERDEENSHIRE
GRAMPIAN

INVERNESS

SCOTLAND 281

PERTHSHIRE

ISLE OF MULL

TAYSIDE

ARGYLL

CENTRAL

FIFESHIRE

EDINBURGH

LOTHIAN

DUMBARTON
LANARKSHIRE
AYRSHIRE
STRATHCLYDE

SELKIRK
PEEBLES
ROXBURGHSHIRE
BORDER

DUMFRIES
& GALLOWAY

NORTHUMBERLAND
DURHAM
TYNE & WEIR
179

52
CUMBRIA

YORKSHIRE &
HUMBERSIDE
261

151
LANCASHIRE

33
CHESHIRE &
MERSEY-
SIDE

65
DERBYSHIRE &
STAFFORDSHIRE

LINCOLN-
SHIRE
163

GWYNEDD

CLWYD

LEICESTERSHIRE &
NOTTINGHAMSHIRE

SHROPSHIRE
198

WARWICKSHIRE
239

156

NORFOLK
169

POWYS

HEREFORD &
WORCESTER
128

CAMBRIDGESHIRE &
NORTHAMPTON-
SHIRE
27

SUFFOLK
216

WALES
303

DYFED

GLOUCESTERSHIRE
107

186
OXFORD-
SHIRE

BEDS
BERKS
BUCKS &
HERTS
21

ESSEX
101

GLAMORGAN

GWENT

11
AVON

CARDIFF

WILT-
SHIRE
250

HAMP-
SHIRE
119

221
SURREY

LONDON

KENT 139

SOMERSET
205

DORSET
91

SUSSEX 227

DEVON
75

40
CORNWALL

xii

LONDON MAP

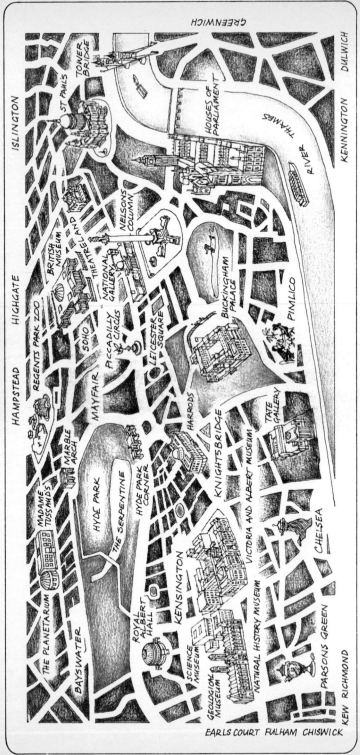

London

	minimum per person	children taken	evening meals taken	animals taken available
Home No. 1 W.W.B.B.A. Tel: 01-370 7099	A charming Georgian cottage situated in a very quiet leafy terrace. This beautifully furnished house has one double room with 4-poster bed and private bathroom plus one twin bedded room. The attractively decorated living room overlooks the garden. Perfectly situated for visiting St. Paul's and the theatres. Close to Kings Cross and Euston Stations. The West End and Knightsbridge only 15 minutes away. Superb breakfasts are served in a pretty country-style kitchen.	£23.00	■	■	■
Home No. 2 W.W.B.B.A. Tel: 01-370 7099	A comfortable Georgian terraced house situated close to Harrods, offering one double and two single rooms, one with a patio garden. The charming living room is attractively furnished and enhanced with many antiques. Within walking distance of Knightsbridge, Buckingham Palace and the museums.	£25.00	■	■	■
Home No. 3 W.W.B.B.A. Tel: 01-370 7099	Located less than two minutes walk from the underground, in a quiet and leafy street in Parsons Green. A comfortable Victorian terraced house which is delightfully furnished and decorated to a high standard. The charming hosts offer two twin-bedded rooms each having its own private bathroom.The enjoyment of your stay in London is the first consideration of the hosts who are always available should you require information and advice. This lovely house is only 10 minutes from the shops in Piccadilly, Knightsbridge, the museums and Buckingham Palace.	£18.00	■	■	■
Home No. 4 W.W.B.B.A. Tel: 01-370 7099	Located in one of the quietest streets in London within two minutes of the River Thames, this beautiful house offers a complete double-bedded suite with its own private bathroom and shower. Beautifully decorated to the highest of standards and very comfortable. Breakfast is served in the very attractive kitchen.The house has many Oriental antiques. Close to many antique shops - one specialising in old linen and embroidery. Situated within two minutes walk of the underground and only 20 minutes from Piccadilly and Knightsbridge.	£20.00	■	■	■
Home No. 5 W.W.B.B.A. Tel: 01-370 7099	Situated in lovely Parsons Green at the edge of Kensington, a charming house, superbly decorated which offers a twin room. The bedroom is large and attractive with many little touches that make guests feel special, including radio and colour T.V. A most pleasant and comfortable living room with antiques. A fabulous breakfast room overlooking a pretty garden. Knightsbridge only 10 minutes away. Tennis courts are just a few minutes away.	£23.00	○	■	■

○ yes ■ no

1

	Description	minimum per person	children taken	evening meals available	animals taken
Home No. 6 W.W.B.B.A. Tel: 01-370 7099	A delightful garden flat in the heart of Kensington offering a superb double bedroom, beautifully decorated. A huge comfortable living room looks out onto an attractive walled garden which guests will enjoy. The vivacious hostess has lived in both the United States and France and offers her guests guided tours of London at a little extra cost. This home is situated within 5 minutes walk of the museums and Knightsbridge. The hostess speaks fluent French.	£25.00	■	○	○
Home No. 7 W.W.B.B.A. Tel: 01-370 7099	Situated in a quiet residential area of London, only 15 minutes from Knightsbridge, this beautifully decorated and furnished home with many antiques, offers luxurious accommodation in two twin rooms, both with en-suite showers. A delightful lounge for guests to relax in and a charming dining room where Cordon Bleu evening meals are served. A good base for Windsor, Heathrow, Oxford and Bath.	£25.50	○	○	■
Home No. 8 W.W.B.B.A. Tel: 01-370 7099	An excellent family house in a quiet situation close to many antique shops and restaurants and only 10 minutes from Harrods. The hospitable hosts have an attractive twin-bedded room for guests. The house is decorated to a high standard and comfortably furnished. A charming living room for visitors to relax in and a huge kitchen/breakfast room overlooking the garden. The house is for animal lovers as there are 2 dogs and 2 cats.	£21.00	■	○	■
Home No. 9 W.W.B.B.A. Tel: 01-370 7099	A charming, self-contained flat, comfortably furnished and attractively decorated with double bedroom and bathroom, kitchen, sitting room/dining room. Available usually Friday, Saturday and Sunday nights, but occasionally extended stays are possible. Centrally situated in Bayswater, right by Hyde Park with Knightsbridge and Piccadilly only 10 minutes away by tube. The museums, and the Royal Albert Hall are just across the beautiful park and a slow walk would take about 20 minutes. Booking well in advance is advisable for this home.	£25.50	○	■	○
Home No. 10 W.W.B.B.A. Tel: 01-370 7099	Situated on the Embankment, a lovely modern town house on 3 floors overlooking the River Thames. Four excellent rooms are available, all most comfortable and attractively decorated. The pleasant modern living room overlooks the river and the dining room over a small garden. There is private parking for guests with car. Only minutes from Victoria Station and Buckingham Palace is within walking distance and so are the theatres.	£21.00	○	■	■

○ yes ■ no

	minimum per person	children taken	evening meals available	animals taken
Home No. 11 **W.W.B.B.A.** **Tel: 01-370 7099**	A very pretty town house in a private square, only two minutes walk from the underground and less than 7 minutes to Harrods. The charming hostess offers a most attractive single room. A comfortable lounge for guest use with antiques, china and many books. A cosy kitchen/dining room and small garden. Ideal for a single lady. The house is on the direct tube line from Heathrow.	£21.00	■	■	■
Home No. 12 **W.W.B.B.A.** **Tel: 01-370 7099**	Located right in the heart of Kensington, only minutes from the museums and Harrods in a quiet street. A delightful flat, very comfortably furnished and attractively decorated, enhanced with many antiques. A pretty and spacious double guest room is available. As the hostess is a busy professional working woman, guests have the whole flat during the day and make breakfast at any time they wish.	£20.00	○	○	○
Home No. 13 **W.W.B.B.A.** **Tel: 01-370 7099**	A quiet, lovely house standing in a quiet street only 10 minutes from Knightsbridge and Piccadilly. Here guests can relax in the very attractive living room and breakfast in a charming country cottage kitchen, overlooking the garden. The hostess offers one double room and one single, both very well-decorated, and both have a private bathroom. The hostess extends to guests the facilities of the famous Hurlington Club, where guests can play tennis, squash or just have luncheon by prior arrangement.	£23.00	■	■	■
Home No. 14 **W.W.B.B.A.** **Tel: 01-370 7099**	A very pleasant apartment close to Hyde Park, Baker Street and Oxford Street, so it's very central. One large and comfortable twin room with its own lounge area and T.V., most attractively decorated. Guests have their own private shower room. Breakfast is served in the light, spacious kitchen/dining room. An excellent base for the museums, Madame Tussauds and the Planetarium. Only 1 minute from the underground.	£21.00	○	■	■
Home No. 15 **W.W.B.B.A.** **Tel: 01-370 7099**	A charming flat situated in a quiet street hidden behind the Strand, in the heart of theatre-land. Furnished entirely with antiques and paintings, the comfortable lounge is most elegant. A large comfortable double bedroom is offered to guests. This apartment is only 2 minutes from Charing Cross Station, Trafalgar Square and Piccadilly.	£21.00	■	■	■

○ yes ■ no

	minimum per person	children taken	evening meals taken	animals taken available
Home No. 16 — W.W.B.B.A. — Tel: 01-370 7099 — Two very pleasant and sunny rooms, both attractively decorated and well furnished are offered in this most comfortable home. A large comfy lounge with plenty of books and T.V. for guests. A refectory dining room overlooking a pretty garden, where breakfast is served. The hostess is a professional cook and offers an evening meal if requested in advance. Close to the underground and only 10 minutes from Knightsbridge and museums.	£18.00	○	○	■
Home No. 17 — W.W.B.B.A. — Tel: 01-370 7099 — A superb house, delightfully furnished and prettily decorated, located in a lovely area close to the river, at the edge of Kensington. A beautiful lounge where visitors can relax overlooking a pretty garden. Two single rooms, with shower rooms adjacent. During August the whole house is available and includes a huge double master bedroom with en-suite facilities.	£18.00	○	■	■
Home No. 18 — W.W.B.B.A. — Tel: 01-370 7099 — An expensively furnished and decorated home in a quiet location in leafy Parsons Green. A light and airy twin room is available which has its own bathroom. There is also a pretty single room. Both overlook an attractive garden. Breakfasts are served in a formal dining room. Located a few minutes walk from the underground and only 10 minutes from museums and the shops of Knightsbridge and Piccadilly.	£18.00	■	■	■
Home No. 19 — W.W.B.B.A. — Tel: 01-370 7099 — Located in the quiet Parsons Green area of Kensington, a superb house offering 2 double suites with private bathroom. One room also has a private roof terrace where guests can relax in the evenings. Beautifully decorated and comfortably furnished, this is an ideal home for visitors to London. Buckingham Palace and Knightsbridge are only 15 minutes away.	£18.00	■	■	■
Home No. 20 — W.W.B.B.A. — Tel: 01-370 7099 — A Regency terraced house is a very quiet leafy street, close to Regents Park. A beautiful double room overlooking an indoor garden conservatory, with its own bathroom, is offered as well as two attractive single rooms. A charming living room where guests can relax. Only 3 minutes from the underground and 15 from Knightsbridge. From here guests could easily walk through the beautiful park to Regent Street and Piccadilly.	£18.00	○	■	■

○ yes ■ no

*Please mention **BEST BED & BREAKFAST IN THE WORLD** when booking your accommodation.*

4

	minimum per person	children taken	evening meals available	animals taken
Home No. 21 **W.W.B.B.A.** **Tel: 01-370 7099**	A comfortable house with an artistic atmosphere, only 15 minutes from Piccadilly and Buckingham Palace. One twin and one single room are offered to guests. Both rooms are comfortable and quiet. A pleasant country-style kitchen/dining room. Guests are made to feel very welcome by this outgoing hostess who is, by profession, a china restorer.	£18.00	O	■	■
Home No. 22 **W.W.B.B.A.** **Tel: 01-370 7099**	A very interesting Regency house, charmingly decorated and pleasantly furnished. Large, comfortable bedrooms which share a wonderful bathroom. An attractive dining area where a light breakfast only is served. A superb living room with antiques, books and some astounding Roman glass and Etruscan pottery. Situated in Bayswater, the house is only 15 minutes from Knightsbridge.	£18.00	O	■	■
Home No. 23 **W.W.B.B.A.** **Tel: 01-370 7099**	A large house situated at the end of a quiet cul-de-sac offering comfortable family atmosphere. There is one twin, one double and one family room and all are nicely decorated. A large comfortable living room for guests and a small garden. Only a short walk to the home of the 19th century painter, Hogarth, and the famous Dove Pub on the river. This is a house for non-smokers. Less than 20 minutes to Buckingham Palace and Knightsbridge.	£15.50	O	O	■
Home No. 24 **W.W.B.B.A.** **Tel: 01-370 7099**	A large, imposing house in a very quiet street less than 20 minutes from Knightsbridge and the museums. Only 1 minute from the underground. Two pleasantly decorated and comfortable twin rooms are available, one with shower en-suite, and two single rooms. All rooms have colour T.V., fridges and tea/coffee making facilities. Breakfast is served in the room. A twin-bedded self-contained flat, sleeping four, is also available. This house is perfect for visitors who will be driving to Bath or Oxford after their London stay as access to the M.4 is only minutes away.	£18.00	O	■	■
Home No. 25 **W.W.B.B.A.** **Tel: 01-370 7099**	A pleasant and comfortable house almost on Eel Brook Common, where the vivacious hostess offers an attractive twin room with its own bathroom situated right next door. The room has its own large patio overlooking the pretty garden where guests can relax. Breakfast is served in a pretty dining room overlooking the garden. Many antique shops locally and it is only 15 minutes from Piccadilly. Only 5 minutes from the underground.	£18.00	O	■	■

O yes ■ no

5

	minimum per person	children taken	evening meals available	animals taken
Home No. 26 W.W.B.B.A. Tel: 01-370 7099	Situated south of the River Thames with marvellous views over the city and St. Paul's Cathedral, yet only 20 minutes from Harrods. This large Victorian house is attractively decorated and furnished and offers one double and one twin room. The hostess goes out of her way to make her guests feel at home.	£18.00	○	○	■
Home No. 27 W.W.B.B.A. Tel: 01-370 7099	Situated in a quiet area close to the Oval cricket ground, just south of the river, yet only 10 minutes from The Houses of Parliament, offering 1 double room and 1 twin room for guests. Pleasantly furnished, this first floor apartment is very comfortable. The vivacious hostess provides a relaxed atmosphere and is very knowledgeable about London. The underground is only 4 minutes walk from the house.	£18.00	○	○	■
Home No. 28 W.W.B.B.A. Tel: 01-370 7099	Situated in a quiet leafy street, close to a pretty green, a comfortable Edwardian house, run like a small hotel with excellent facilities - many rooms having private shower. Rooms are cleverly planned to include a cosy lounge area and small kitchen for self-catering. A large dining room offering a wide choice of breakfasts and evening meals are available at pub prices. Only 15 minutes from Knightsbridge.	£18.00	○	○	○
Home No. 29 W.W.B.B.A. Tel: 01-370 7099	Situated in a quiet road, close to a main line station, this cosy house offers one twin and one single room with adjacent bathroom and shower. A comfortable living room with memorabilia of a lifetime of world travels. A pleasant dining room overlooks the garden. Only a few minutes walk from the Thames and famous riverside pubs and Kew Gardens close by. A good base for those driving into London from Heathrow - only 9 miles away, yet only 15 minutes from central London and Knightsbridge.	£18.00	○	○	■
Home No. 30 W.W.B.B.A. Tel: 01-370 7099	Situated only 2 minutes walk from the station, this cosy house offers comfortable accommodation in one double and two twin rooms, and one single, one en-suite. All rooms have wash basins and are spacious and pleasantly furnished. There is a large lounge where guests can relax. Only a few minutes walk from the world famous Greenwich Observatory, Maritime Museum and the tea clipper Cutty Sark. Your hostess offers guided tours of the area. Peaceful Greenwich is only 8 minutes from central London and theatres by train.	£15.50	○	○	■

○ yes ■ no

Home No. 31 **W.W.B.B.A.** **Tel: 01-370 7099**	Located only 3 minutes walk from the underground in a quiet and leafy road opposite Wimbledon Park. A charming and comfortable home offering a lovely twin bedded turret room to guests. The room is attractively decorated and furnished and has its private bathroom adjacent. Wimbledon tennis club is only 15 minutes walk through the park. Close to good restaurants and only 20 minutes to Knightsbridge and the theatres. This is a non-smoking house.	£18.00	O	■	■
Home No. 32 **W.W.B.B.A.** **Tel: 01-370 7099**	A superb house standing in a walled garden close to Wimbledon Lawn Tennis Club. The hosts have three delightful twin rooms, decorated to the highest standard, all with bathroom en-suite. Everyone will enjoy the beautiful lounge with its china and many antiques plus sporting memorabilia. The maid serves breakfast in a delightful dining room which has stained glass panels. The house is not available during Wimbledon fortnight. This lovely house is only 20 minutes to Knightsbridge and Piccadilly.	£36.00	■	■	■
Home No. 33 **W.W.B.B.A.** **Tel: 01-370 7099**	A pretty cottage situated on the banks of the River Thames. A beautiful garden runs down to the water. Guests have a charmingly decorated twin room with en-suite bathroom. Pretty chintzy living room with inglenook and beams. Breakfast is served on the terrace or in the sun lounge, overlooking the water. Close to Hampton Court, Kew, Richmond and Wisley. Windsor Castle is 30 minutes by car. This is a vegetarian house and non-smoking. Mrs. Brown collects guests from Heathrow.	£17.00	■	O	■
Home No. 34 **W.W.B.B.A.** **Tel: 01-370 7099**	A substantial Victorian house with verandah, quietly situated almost next to the River Thames. Beautifully furnished living and dining room with antiques and pictures. Two very attractive bedrooms each with its own private bathroom adjacent. A lovely large garden for guests with walks to the river. The French Lieutenant's Woman was partly filmed in this house. A tranquil setting yet only 30 minutes from Harrods. Close to Hampton Court, Kew, Chiswick and Richmond. Windsor Castle is 30 minutes by car.	£17.00	■	■	■
Home No. 35 **W.W.B.B.A.** **Tel: 01-370 7099**	Elegant twin bedded accommodation with bathroom en-suite, is offered in this pleasant Victorian house, situated in the fashionable Hurlingham area of London, close to the River Thames. Most attractive living room and dining room. The owners are delighted to share their knowledge of London with their guests. Free car parking. Close to the tube and Kings Road. Only 15 minutes from Knightsbridge.	£26.00	■	■	■

O yes ■ no

AVON

Avon is a new county which appeared in 1974 as a result of a rearrangement of the boundaries of Gloucestershire, Wiltshire and Somerset, but its newness is only on the surface, for the county holds a wealth of tradition and history. The rolling hills of the Cotswolds in the East and the Mendips in the South form a natural cradle of hills which hold at its centre the historic cities of Bristol and Bath. To the North is the attractive little town of Chipping Sodbury which retains a strong Cotswold flavour. To the west on the shores of the Bristol channel are the resort towns of Weston-Super-Mare and Clevedon. The manor house of Clevedon Court is a superb building of mellow, golden stone dating from the 14th century, and it houses a fine collection of Elton Ware pottery. The old church was built in 1142 on a hilltop site above the floods of the unpredictable River Severn and in a lovely isolated setting overlooks the river and the hills of Wales. Only at the extreme north of the county at Aust can the river be crossed and a magnificent and delicate suspension bridge forms the southern gateway to Wales.

Bath

Bath is certainly one of the most splendid and best loved historic cities in England. It owes its very existence to the hot springs which bubble up five hundred thousand gallons a day at a temperature of some 120oF. According to legend, in pre-christian times, King Bladud was the firstto appreciate the healing quality of the Bath waters and built a palace here and established his capital called Caerbren. The Romans were equally quick to see the possibilities. They renamed the place Aquae Sulis and built an elaborate healing and entertainment centre around the springs including reservoirs, bath and hypercaust rooms. The Roman baths, not uncovered until modern times,are on the lowest of three levels. Above them came the mediaeval city and on the top layer at modern street level is the elegant Georgian pump room.

During the middle ages the town prospered both through Royal patronage and through the development of the wool industry. Bath became a city of weavers and was the leading industrial town in the westof England. Edward was crowned the first King of all England in 973 in the original Saxon abbey butit was during the Tudor era that Henry VII commissioned the present abbey. Sometimes called the "lantern of the west" on account of its vast clerestories and large areas of glass, it is built in the graceful perpendicular style with elegant fan vaulting.

The spa town of Bath really boomed during the 17th and 18th centuries. Beau Nash was the celebratedleader of the glittering dancing and gambling society that gathered here and he turned the city intoa centre of fashion. Meanwhile an ambitious young achitect John Wood, was transforming the city with the elegant Georgian building we know today. He first laid out Queen Annes Square in the grandpalladian style and proceeded to produce his masterpiece of the Royal Crescent, generally regarded as the finest crescent in Europe. His scheme for the city was carried on by his son and a number ofother fine architects using the beautiful Bath stone. There are magnificent mansions like Prior Park and graceful curving streets like Landsdown Crescent and Somerset Place and the delightful old Bond Street is still a fine shopping centre.

Over the years the city has attracted many famous patrons including Gainsborough, Queen Victoria, Lord Nelson, Jane Austen and Charles Dickens and its cultural associations are still maintained in the summer festival of music and the arts. Its chief glory, however, remains in its superb architecture.

Bristol

Bristol can reasonably claim to be the Birthplace of America. In 1497 John and SebastianCabot sailed from the Bristol quayside and made landfall in Newfoundland. They named the new land Ameryke in honour of the King's agent in Bristol, Richard Ameryke. For more than a century before Cabots time Bristol had been a flourishing trading centre. The trade charter given to Bristols Merchant Venturers in 1552 can still be seen in the Hall of the Society of Merchant Venturers at Clifton Down. By the 18th century Bristol was the second city in the kingdom gaining enormous wealth from the slave triangle.

AVON GAZETEER

Areas of Outstanding Natural Beauty
The Cotswolds and the Mendip Hills.

Historic Houses and Castles

Badminton House -- Badminton
 Built in the reign of Charles II. Huge parkland where Horse Trials are held each year, Home of the Duke of Beaufort.

Clevedon Court -- Clevedon
 14th century manor house, 13th century hall, 12th century tower. Lovely garden with rare trees and shrubs.

Dodington House -- Chipping Sodbury
 Perfect 18th century house with superb staircase. Landscape by Capability Brown.

Dyrham Park -- Between Bristol and Bath
 17th century house -- fine panelled rooms, Dutch paintings, furniture.

Horton Court -- Horton
 Cotswold Manor house altered and restored in 19th century.

No. 1 Royal Crescent -- Bath
 An Unaltered Georgian House built1767.

Red Lodge -- Bristol
 16th century house -- period furniture and panelling.

St. Vincent's Priory -- Bristol
 Gothic revival house, built over caves which were sanctuary for Christians.

Blaise Castle House -- Henbury Nr. Bristol
 18th century house -- now folk museum, extensive woodlands.

Priory Park College -- Bath
 18th century, Georgian mansion, now Roman Catholic school

Claverton Manor -- Nr. Bath
 Greek revival house -- furnished 17th, 18th, 19th century American originals.

St. Catherine's Court -- Nr. Bath
 Small Tudor house -- associations with Henry VIII and Elizabeth I.

Cathedrals and Churches

Bristol Cathedral
 Mediaeval eastern halfnave Victorian. Chapterhouse richly ornamented. Unique vaulting over aisles.

Bristol -- Lord Mayor's Chapel
 13th century, 14th century perpendicular tower, 16th century fan vaulted chantry.

Bristol (St. Mary Redcliffe)
 Early perpendicular -- very large -- mediaeval tombs,brasses, baroque iron screen, 3 fonts Åairest parish church in all England

Bristol (St. Stephens')
 Perpendicular -- monuments, magnificent tower.

Backwell (St. Andrew)
 12th to 17th century, 15th century tower, repaired 17th century. 15th century tomb and chancel, 16th century screen, 18th century brass chandelier.

Bath Abbey
 Perpendicular -- monastic church. Nave finished 17th century, restorations in 1674 -- 73.

Iron Acton (St. James the Less)
 Perpendicular -- 15th century memorial cross. 19th century mosaic floors, Laudian altar rails, Jacobean pulpit, effigies.

Wrington (All Souls)
15th century aisles and nave; font, stone pulpit, notable screens.

Yate (St. Mary)
Splendid perpendicular tower.

Museums and Galleries

American Museum in Britain -- Claverton -- Nr. Bath
American decorative arts 17th to 19th century displayed in series of furnished rooms and Galleries of special exhibits. Paintings, furniture, glass wood and metal work, textiles, folk sculpture etc.

Holburne of Menstrie Museum -- Bath
Old Master paintings, silver, glass, porcelain, furniture and miniatures in 18th century building. Work of 20thcentury craftsmen.

Victoria Art Gallery -- Bath
Paintings, prints, drawings, glass, ceramics, watches, coins, etc. Bygones -- permanent and temporary exhibitions. Geology collections.

Roman Museum -- Bath
Material from remains of extensive Roman baths and other Roman sites.

Museum of Costume -- Bath
Collection of fashion from 17th century to present day.

St. Nicholas Church and City Museum -- Bristol
Mediaeval antiquities relating to local history, Church plate and vestments. Altarpiece by Hogarth.

City of Bristol Museum -- Bristol
Egyptology, archeology, ethnography, geology. Bristol ships.

Bristol Industrial Museum -- Bristol
Collections of transport items of land, sea and air. Many unique items.

City of Bristol Art Gallery -- Bristol
Permanent and loan collections of paintings, English and Oriental ceramics.

Chatterton House -- Bristol
Birth place of boy poet.

Historic Monuments

Kings Weston Roman Villa -- Lawrence Weston
3rd and 4th centuries -- mosaics of villa -- Some walls.

Hinton Priory -- Hinton Charterhouse
13th century -- ruins of Carthusian priory.

Temple Church -- Bristol
14th & 15th century ruins.

Stoney Littleton Barrow -- Nr. Bath
Neolithic burial chamber -- restoration work 1858.

Romans Baths -- Bath

Gardens

Clifton Zoological Gardens -- Bristol
Flourishing zoo with many exhibits -- beautiful gardens.

AVON
Recommended roadside restaurants

| 246 | A4/A36 | Bath, Avon
1 mile west of Bath |
| 278 | A39/A37 | Farrington Gurney, Avon
13 miles South of Bristol |

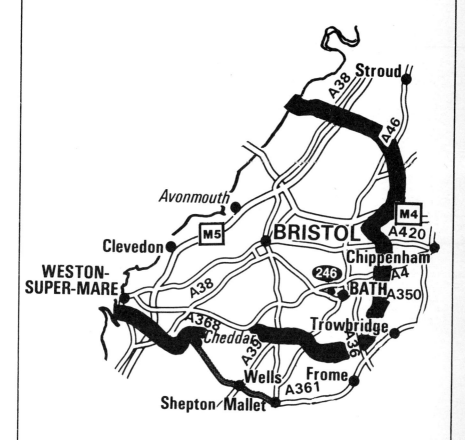

Avon

		minimum per person	children taken	evening meals available	animals taken
Elizabeth & Terence Tovey **Bathurst Guest House** **11 Walcot Parade** **London Road** **Bath BA1 5NF** **Tel: (0225) 21884** **OPEN: ALL YEAR** **(EXCL. XMAS)**	Nearest Road M.4 A.4 A pretty terraced Georgian house, with six spacious and very attractively decorated rooms for guests, all with colour T.V. and tea/coffee/hot chocolate making facilities. There is a comfortable and stylish lounge and a pleasant terraced garden. Exclusively for non-smokers. Next to the Hedgemead Park, the house is a stroll from the Roman Pump Rooms in the city centre and the antique shops. An excellent touring base.	£10.00	O	■	O
Mrs P.J. Rowe **"Abode"** **7 Widcombe Crescent** **Widcombe Hill** **Bath BA2 6AH** **Tel: (0225) 22726** **OPEN: JAN-NOV**	Nearest Roads A.367 A.36 A charming, Georgian residence located in a quiet, Georgian crescent only 10 minutes walk from the city centre. Accommodation is in five bedrooms with modern amenities with T.V. and tea/coffee making facilities. Well located for the city and the surrounding countryside.	£9.00	■	■	■
Dorothy & Cyril Burton **and Sue & John Burton** **Glenbeigh Hotel** **No.1 Upper Oldfield Park** **Bath BA2 3JX** **Tel: (0225) 26336** **OPEN: ALL YEAR** **(EXCL. XMAS)**	Nearest Roads A.367 A.4 A spacious Victorian house with lovely decorated ceilings. Offering comfortable accommodation in twelve pleasant, well decorated rooms with all modern amenities. Tea-making facilities in all rooms. Also a television lounge. Situated on the southern slopes overlooking the city, it offers panoramic views of Bath. The city centre is only 8 minutes walk. Friendly lounge with licensed bar for guests to meet and relax.	£17.00	O	■	O
Brian & Audrey Archer **The Tasburgh** **Warminster Road** **Bath BA2 6SH** **Tel: (0225) 25096/63842** **OPEN: ALL YEAR**	Nearest Roads A.36 M.4 A charming spacious Victorian House set in more than 1 acre of gardens within easy reach of many museums and places of interest in Bath and the surrounding countryside. Each room is individually and tastefully furnished, all with T.V. and tea/coffee making facilities, and en-suite facilities in some of the double and family rooms. A full English breakfast is served and a Residential Licence held. The proprietors offer a high standard of personal care and service to their visitors.	£14.00	O	O	O
Stephanie Weiss **Escobeck** **127 Wells Road** **Bath** **Tel: (0225) 310143** **OPEN: ALL YEAR**	Nearest Road A.367 A large Edwardian house offering five light airy bedrooms each with modern amenities. A residents lounge with colour T.V. is available throughout the day. Your host will provide tea/coffee at any reasonable time. Vegetarians are very well catered for at Escobeck. Conveniently located close to the city centre, only a 5 minute walk. A baby sitting service is also available.	£10.00	O	O	O

O yes ■ no

12

	minimum per person	children taken	evening meals available	animals taken
Rose Walton and Jeffrey Higgins Walton's Guest House 17 Crescent Gardens Upper Bristol Road Bath BA1 2NA Tel: (0225) 26528 OPEN: ALL YEAR	£12.00	O	O	O
Jenny King Oakleigh Guest House 19 Upper Oldfield Park Bath BA2 3JX Tel: (0225) 315698 OPEN: ALL YEAR	£15.00	■	■	■
A.L.C. & D.A. Thompson Grove Lodge Guest House 11 Lambridge London Road Bath BA1 6BJ Tel: (0225) 310860/29630 OPEN: ALL YEAR	£12.00	O	■	O
Mrs S.P. Drake Halfway House 130 Kelston Road Bath BA1 9AB Tel: (0225) 24119 OPEN: FEB-DEC	£22.00	O	■	O

Rose Walton — Nearest Roads M.4 A.46

A delightful house offering sixteen rooms with modern amenities. The rooms are well decorated and comfortable. They offer a licenced bar and packed lunches as well as a television lounge. There is much to see in the city. Roman Pump Room and Baths, Museum of Costume and the Botanical Gardens to name but three. Cots are provided.

Jenny King — Nearest Road A.367

Situated 10 minutes from the city centre this tastefully modernised pleasant house combines Victorian elegance with 20th century comfort. Four well decorated and comfortable rooms all with private bath/shower. Also tea/coffee making facilities and T.V. A lounge is available for guests. Apart from the charms of Bath there are the beautiful Cotswolds and Mendips to discover and also close by are historic Wells, Glastonbury and Cheddar Gorge. A warm welcome awaits the visitor.

A.L.C. & D.A. Thompson — Nearest Roads A.4 A.46 M.4

An extremely pleasant substantial Georgian house offering eight excellent rooms with modern amenities. Situated in attractive gardens it looks out onto the wooded hills surrounding the city. Apart from Bath's own attractions there are numerous beauty spots, walks and places of great historic interest close by. Two golf courses, fishing and tennis are well within one and a half miles. An excellent base for this region.

Mrs S.P. Drake — Nearest Road A.4

Price shown is for two people. This elegant family home, built in the 17th century, offers guests pleasant, comfortable accommodation. The three delightful bedrooms have modern amenities, colour T.V. and tea/coffee making facilities, as well as splendid views. Well located only a few minutes drive from the centre of historic Bath. A good base for touring the many rural villages in the area.

O yes ■ no

Why not use our fast efficient
RESERVATION SERVICE
to book all your accommodation.

	minimum per person	children taken	evening meals available	animals taken
Anthony & Nicole O'Flaherty **Oldfields** **102 Wells Road** **Bath BA2 3AL** **Tel: (0225) 317984** **OPEN: MID JAN-MID DEC** Nearest Road A.367 Price shown is for two people. A large Victorian house built in Bath stone overlooking the city towards Kelston Round Hill. Fourteen delightful bedrooms, most with T.V. and tea/coffee making facilities, eight with bath-/shower en-suite. Each room has recently been restored and completely refurnished. The character remains, but the Victorian elegance has been lightened by fresh Laura Ashley wallpapers and fabrics. Anthony and Nicole provide plenty of books, maps and delightful pictures and plants, and.....Mozart at breakfast.	£24.00	○	■	■
Geoffrey & Sylvia Alger **Wentworth House Hotel** **106 Bloomfield Road** **Bath BA2 2AP** **Tel: (0225) 339193** **OPEN: ALL YEAR** Nearest Road A.367 Situated only 1 mile from the city centre this imposing Victorian house is set in tranquil grounds. Twenty very comfortable large rooms. Ten with private bath/shower. All rooms have T.V. and tea/coffee making facilities. A comfortable and relaxed atmosphere combined with traditional home cooking, and licensed bar. The garden is delightful and guests can enjoy the outdoor swimming pool. An excellent base for touring the region. Winter bargain breaks.	£14.00	○	○	○
N.F. & P.E.K. Hunt **Amity Guest House** **42 King Edward Road** **Oldfield Park** **Bath BA2 3PB** **Tel: (0225) 318664** **OPEN: ALL YEAR** Nearest Road A.367 A friendly relaxed atmosphere is found in this pleasant Edwardian house. There are six pleasantly decorated bedrooms, all with modern amenities, colour T.V. and tea/coffee making facilities, three with shower en-suite. Your hosts provide a guest lounge for use throughout the day. Ironing facilities are also available. Only five minutes drive from the centre of Bath.	£9.00	○	■	■
Mrs Freda M. Brown **Highways House Hotel** **143 Wells Road** **Bath BA2 3AL** **Tel: (0225) 21238** **OPEN: ALL YEAR** **(EXCL. XMAS & NEW YEAR)** Nearest Road A.367 An elegant Victorian family run hotel offering superior accommodation in five bedrooms, each decorated in a tasteful and individual style. Lovely guest lounge with colour T.V. Varied English breakfast served with fresh-ground coffee. Good parking facilities. Situated close to the town centre.	£14.00	■	■	■
Linda & Robert Cooney **Charnwood House** **51 Upper Oldfield Park** **Bath BA2 3LB** **Tel: (0225) 334937** **OPEN: ALL YEAR** Nearest Road A.367 Charnwood House offers tastefully refurbished bedrooms in a prestigious Victorian home, with many luxuries usually only found in first-class hotels. Located in a quiet street only 12 minutes walk to the Roman Baths and city centre. Eight very comfortable rooms with modern facilities and most en-suite. Variety of traditional and vegetarian breakfast alternatives. Guests are encouraged to use the sauna and hydro-spa facilities.	£18.00	○	■	■

○ yes ■ no

14

	minimum per person	children taken	evening meals available	animals taken
Mrs Carrolle Sellick **Holly Lodge** **8 Upper Oldfield Park** **Bath BA2 3JZ** **Tel: (0225) 339187** **OPEN: ALL YEAR** Nearest Road A.367 Holly Lodge is set in its own grounds and located to the south of the city centre. This Victorian house offers guests a choice of six bedrooms, some with radio and T.V. A guests colour T.V. lounge is available. Ironing facilities are also provided. If advanced notice is given, packed lunches can be provided. A convenient base for exploring Bath and the surrounding area.	£20.00	O	■	■
Douglas & Lynne Johnson **Astor House** **14 Oldfield Road** **Bath BA2 3ND** **Tel: (0225) 29134** **OPEN: APRIL-OCT** Nearest Roads M.4 A.367 Here is a pleasant Victorian house, tastefully decorated in the style of the period whilst remaining light and airy in atmosphere. Very comfortable beds - provided with electric blankets. Hot/cold basins in all bedrooms and tea making facilities. Pretty dining room - nice gardens. Quiet situation, ten minutes walk from the centre of Bath. Very central for touring Cotswolds and Wales. Helpful hosts who really care that you enjoy your stay in this lovely city. 3 double and 4 twin bedded rooms. Several shower/bathrooms. Sound-proof T.V. lounge.	£10.00	O	■	■
Christina Gramellini **Haydon House** **9 Bloomfield Park** **Bath BA2 2BY** **Tel: (0225) 27351** **OPEN: FEB-DEC** Nearest Road This elegant Edwardian house is furnished with many antiques and is set in a quiet residential area on the southern slopes of the city. There is a choice of 4 comfortable Laura Ashley decorated bedrooms, each with private shower or bathroom, colour T.V. and tea/coffee making facilities. Continental or full English breakfast is accompanied by gentle classical music. Close by are The Abbey, Roman Baths and Pump Room - all within walking distance.	£20.00	O	■	O
Edward & Ida Mills **Brompton House Hotel** **St. Johns Road** **Bath BA2 6PT** **Tel: (0225) 20972** **OPEN: ALL YEAR** Nearest Road An elegant Georgian Rectory set in tranquil grounds close to the city centre. Built in 1777 as a Rectory it now offers guests a choice of 11 rooms each with modern amenities, T.V. and tea/coffee making facilities, some en-suite. T.V. snacks are also available upon request. A lounge is available throughout the day. In the dining room Continental, full English or a wholemeal breakfast is served.	£16.00	O	■	■

O yes ■ no

Please mention **BEST BED & BREAKFAST IN THE WORLD** *when booking your accommodation.*

	minimum per person	children taken	evening meals available	animals taken

Mr & Mrs K. Flower
Mrs Middleton
Fairhaven Guest House
19 Newbridge Road
Lower Weston
Bath BA1 3HE
Tel: (0225) 330239

OPEN: ALL YEAR

Nearest Road A.4

A pleasant Victorian family house offering three comfortable rooms and a warm welcome to visitors. It is a good base for touring the sights of Bath and also the West Country, with safe beaches at Weston-Super-Mare. There are numerous places to visit within a drive of an hour or two. No evening meals but snacks are offered. Rate shown for 2 people.

£18.00 | O | ■ | ■

Mrs Jean Thaxter
Esholt House
Mount Road
Lansdown
Bath BA1 5PW
Tel: (0225) 312553

OPEN: ALL YEAR

Nearest Road A.4

A friendly welcome and comfortable accommodation await the guests at Esholt. An attractive, Victorian Italianate detached villa located in a quiet residential street yet close to the famous Royal Crescent and Assembly Rooms. The accommodation is in five comfortable rooms all with modern amenities. T.V. and tea/coffee making facilities. There are delightful views across the city and there is also a pleasant garden for guests to use. This is an ideal base from which to explore the Roman City of Bath.

£15.00 | O | ■ | O

Mrs Olga London
The Orchard
80 High Street
Bathford
Bath BA1 7TG
Tel: (0225) 858765

OPEN: MAR-OCT

Nearest Road A.4

The Orchard is a listed grade II Georgian Country House situated in the delightful village of Bathford just three miles from Bath. The four spacious bedrooms have private facilities and are individually decorated and furnished to a high standard of comfort. The elegant drawing and dining rooms are filled with fine pieces of period furniture. Dinner, served at 7.15pm is delicious and fresh garden produce is used whenever possible. Guests are invited to bring their own wine. The Orchard is very conveniently located for visiting the ancient city of Bath and many historical sites in the area.

£16.50 | ■ | O | ■

John & Rosamund Napier
Eagle House
Church Street
Bathford
Bath BA1 7RS
Tel: (0225) 859946

OPEN: ALL YEAR

Nearest Roads M.4 A.4 A.46

Eagle House is a fine listed Georgian House in the heart of a conservation village on the edge of an area of outstanding natural beauty. Mr. & Mrs. Napier have six beautiful rooms, three having en-suite and tea/coffee makers and T.V. Each room has views over the 1½ acres of gardens or countryside. This is a delightful base for all visitors as Bath is only a matter of minutes away and in the area one can visit Wells, Glastonbury, Bradford on Avon, Lacock, Castle Combe, Longleat House, Durham Park, Stonehenge and Avebury. There are many excellent restaurants and pubs locally. The proprietors offer the highest of standards and warmly welcome all their guests.

£20.00 | O | O | O

O yes ■ no

16

	minimum per person	children taken	evening meals available	animals taken
Mr & Mrs R.J. Gillespie **The Wheelwrights Arms** **Monkton Combe** **Nr. Bath BA2 7HD** **Tel: (022122) 2287** **OPEN: ALL YEAR** Nearest Road A.36 A most attractive historic inn standing in the lovely Midford Valley yet only 3 miles from Bath. There are eight delightful rooms in the converted barn and stables, all with private shower, colour T.V. and tea/coffee making facilities. Home-made snacks, luncheons and steak dinners served in the beamed bar and breakfast is served in a really attractive room. Mr. & Mrs. Gillespie offer a most friendly welcome to their guests. A super base for walking, riding, fishing and touring generally. Bath is only a few minutes away. Children must be over 10 years of age.	£22.00	O	O	■
Ruth Shellard **Overbrook** **Stowey Bottom** **Bishop Sutton** **Nr. Bristol BS18 4TN** **Tel: (0272) 332648** **OPEN: ALL YEAR** Nearest Road A.368 A pleasant, wisteria covered house set in 3 acres of lovely garden with a stream crossing the land. The owners who breed a small flock of Suffolk sheep, offer comfort and hospitality to their visitors. There are 2 very comfortable bedrooms with modern amenities and tea/coffee makers and an attractive lounge with colour T.V. Excellent base for touring. Trout fishing on Chew Valley Lake just 5 minutes away.	£9.00	O	O	O
Mrs E. Rolls **Hillside** **Sutton Hill Road** **Bishop Sutton** **Nr. Bristol BS18 4UN** **Tel: (0272) 332208** **OPEN: ALL YEAR** Nearest Road A.368 Hillside is an attractive converted stone cottage located in quiet farmland with glorious views over the Chew Valley Lake. Accommodation is in two rooms. Careful attention by the owner. This makes an excellent base for touring and walking. It is within easy reach of Bath, Mendip Hills, Cheddar Gorge and Wells. Trout fishing and the Bird Sanctuary are close by.	£8.50	O	■	O
Mr & Mrs. G.R. Scoins **Downs View Guest House** **38 Upper Belgrave Road** **Clifton** **Bristol BS8 2XN** **Tel: (0272) 737046** **OPEN: ALL YEAR** Nearest Roads A.4176 M.5 Exit 17 A pleasant house offering most comfortable accommodation with modern amenities. Special rates are offered for families. Bristol offer a myriad of attractions, including superb museums, galleries, the Zoo and the Bristol Old Vic Theatre. Cots and highchairs provided. All rooms have colour T.V. Close to shops and buses.	£10.00	O	■	O
Delia Macdonald **Park House** **19 Richmond Hill** **Clifton** **Bristol BS8 1BA** **Tel: (0272) 736331** **OPEN: ALL YEAR** Nearest Roads A.4176 M.5 Exit 17 A friendly host and a warm welcome await guests at this large Georgian house. Offering a choice of four comfortable bedrooms with modern amenities, T.V. and tea/coffee making facilities. Located in the attractive residential area of Clifton. Close by are many restaurants and wine bars.	£19.00	O	■	■

O yes ■ no

17

	minimum per person	children taken	evening meals available	animals taken

Mr C.A. Seeley
Seeley's Hotel
17/27 St. Pauls Road
Clifton
Bristol BS8 1LX
Tel: (0272) 738544

OPEN: ALL YEAR

Nearest Road - Whiteladies Road

A most pleasant hotel with a very friendly atmosphere, centrally situated near all amenities and within walking distance of the Suspension Bridge and Clifton Downs. 63 centrally-heated bedrooms all with T.V., radio, tea-makers, hair dryers and some with private Jacuzzi baths. Sun terrace, sauna, solarium, steam baths, indoor heated pool. The food here is very good.

£18.00   ○   ○   ○

John & Daphne Paz
Dornden Guest House
Church Lane
Old Sodbury
Bristol BS17 6NB
Tel: (0454) 313325

OPEN: ALL YEAR
(EXCL. XMAS & NEW YEAR)

Nearest Road A.46

Dornden, former vicarage of Old Sodbury was built of local Cotswold stone and stands in a beautiful garden enjoying the peace of the countryside and magnificent views as far as the Welsh Hills. All rooms comfortably furnished and overlook the garden and countryside beyond. Meals are prepared as far as possible with home-grown produce and free-range eggs. Tennis court available to guests.

£13.50   ○   ○   ○

Mr & Mrs C.S.J. & A.D.Buck
Southmead Guest House
435 Locking Road
Weston-Super-Mare BS22 8QN
Tel: (0934) 29351

OPEN: ALL YEAR

Nearest Road A.370

A relaxed atmosphere and friendly hosts greet guests at this family run guest house. A choice of six rooms is available all with modern amenities. A residents colour T.V. lounge is also provided. Southmead is well located for visiting the sea front, shops, Cheddar Wells, Glastonbury as well as touring Somerset, Exmoor and Dunster Castle.

£8.00   ○   ○   ○

○ yes ■ no

Don't be disappointed. Book ahead.
Use our fast efficient
RESERVATION SERVICE
Be sure of your accommodation
Book Now!!
Call us on

01-370 7099   **01-370 7099**

BERKSHIRE

This county has always occupied an important place in history due to its strategic position commanding roads to and from Oxford and the North and Bath and the West. The natural gap in the downs has been utilised by all road builders from the Romans to modern motorway engineers. Inevitably it was the cause of many battles from the earliest times. Castles and forts were erectedand as often were destroyed or left unoccupied until they fell into ruins. The smaller houses - though large by our standards - were kept intact, being lived in by the same families for generations. This had a stabilising effect on the area and farms and villages grew and prospered. The Tudor period brought great development in the wool weaving trade and the wealthy wool merchants were able to buy large tracts of land, building wonderful houses. Some chose to build churches but it is curious that there is not one Cathedral in Berkshire.

Windsor Castle

Nothing can really fire imagination so well as this wonderful castle. It is the largest inhabited castle in the world and certainly is the best known. Begun by the Normans in the 11th century, it stands on top of a hill which gives it a commanding position and adds to the majesty of its appearance, although, to the people of Windsor, the massive walls rising up from the streets of the town are familiar and comfortable. The enormous yards, the vast interior and the spectacular treasures in the State Apartments make this Castle truly unforgettable. It is a perfect setting forthe pageantry constantly displayed there; the traditional ceremonies and the colourful mediaeval costume of the participants add to the splendour of the scene. It is no wonder that thousands upon thousands of people from all over the world gather to see this unique spectacle. When your eyes cannot appreciate one more wonder, try the simple pleasures. Walk along the quiet banks of the Thames, perhaps a few swans will glide past or a rowing eight will disturb the still waters for a moment or two. Find a country pub and rest there, contemplating the glory that is England.

HERTFORDSHIRE

First mentioned by name in 1011 by the Anglo Saxon Chronicles, there are recorded findings of tools and implements which bear witness to the presence of Paleolithic man and Iron Age forts and camp mark continuous settlement since that time. For example, the Roman invasion in 43 AD brought immense changes. With enormous power and influence the Romans annexed the whole of Eastern Britain to their Empire. At this time they were laying down a series of roads, all fanning out from London and traversing the country - the same roads or routes which we use still. Watling Street linked thenewly built city of Verulamium with Cirencester and Bath, Stane Street led to Colchester whilst Ermine Street led to Lincoln and York - important cities then as now. Christianity was forbidden then and Alban, a Roman himself, was martyred for his beliefs and the first church at St Albans was named for him, when some 600 years after his death the Abbey was re-established under the rule of St Benedict.

1066 brought the Norman Conquest and the Domesday Survey records that Hertfordshire was a flourishing region. The Normans rebuilt the Great Abbey Church, the present Cathedral, around the original building and there are wall murals of great age to be seen on the piers of the Norman nave.

The landscape varies from the chalk hills and rolling downlands of the Chilterns to the rivers, lakes and canals. Fine trees are an especially lovely feature of this pleasant county which remainslargely rural despite the presence of two New Towns and a fair amount of industrial development.

The Downs

The chalky Chiltern Hills of Hertfordshire stretch on unchanged into the tranquil Bedfordshire countryside. Here they form the heights of Dunstable Downs which include Ivinghoe Beacon the highest point in the county. Low in the valley between the rising chalk hills lies rich open farmland. Interestingly half the population of Bedfordshire live in just two towns, almost all the rest of the county is left to the farmers with small villages dotted across the countryside.

BERKSHIRE GAZETEER

Areas of outstanding natural beauty
North West Downs.

Historic Houses and Castles

Windsor Castle -- Royal Residence at Windsor
No. 25 The Cloisters, Windsor Chapel. Mediaeval house.

Basildon Park -- Nr. Pangbourne
18th century Bath stone building, massive portico and linked pavilions. Painted ceiling inOctagon Room, gilded pier glasses.

Cathedrals and Churches

Lambourn (St. Michael & All Saints)
Norman with 15th century chapel. 16th century brasses, glass & tombs.

Padworth (St. John the Baptist)
12th century Norman with plastered exterior, remains of wall paintings, 18th century monuments.

Warfield (St. Michael & All Angels)
14th century decorated style -- 15th century wood screen & loft.

Museums and Galleries

Stanley Spencer Gallery --' Cookham-on-Thames
Paintings, drawings and personal belongings of the artist.

Henry Reitlinger Bequest -- Maidenhead
Chinese,Italian, Persian & European pottery, paintings, sculpture.

Newbury Museum -- Newbury
Natural History and Archeology -- Paleolithic to Saxon & Mediaeval times.

Household Cavalry Museum -- Windsor

HERTFORDSHIRE GAZETEER

Areas of outstanding natural beauty
Chilterns (part)

Historic Houses and Castles

Hatfield House -- Hatfield
Home of Marquess of Salisbury. Tudor Palace and Jacobean House.

Knebworth House -- Knebworth
Delhi Durbar Exhibition

Shaw's Corner -- Ayot St. Lawrence
Home of G.B. Shaw -- relics.

Cathedrals and Churches

St. Albans Cathedral -- St. Albans
Imposing Norman tower -- splendid interior -- wooden painted roofs over choir -- reredos 1484, oak loft, stone rood screen.

Stanstead Abbots (St James)
12th century nave, 13th century chancel, 15th century tower and porch, 16th century North chapel, 18th century box pews and 3 decker pulpit.

Watford (St Mary)
13 - 15th century. Essex chapel. Tuscan arcade. Morryson tombs.

BEDS/BUCKS
BERKSHIRE/HERTS
Recommended roadside restaurants

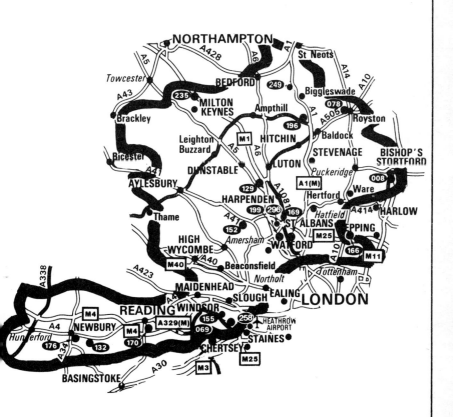

Berks/Bucks/Herts

	minimum per person	children taken	evening meals available	animals taken
Susan Dixon **Green Meadows** **Bucklebury** **Reading RG7 6NU** **Tel: (0734) 713353** **OPEN: ALL YEAR**	Nearest Roads A.4 M.4 A substantial private country house set in two acres of delightful grounds within a rural setting. There are 3 comfortable well decorated rooms with T.V. and tea/coffee facilities. The charming village of Bucklebury is ideally placed for touring Windsor, Oxford, Bath and London. Heathrow is within easy driving distance.	£12.50	O	■	O
Margaret Barr **St. Mary's House** **Kintbury RG15 0TR** **Tel: (0488) 58551** **OPEN: ALL YEAR**	Nearest Road A.4 Built in and situated next to Parish Church in a pleasantly rural area, this converted Victorian school makes a most unusual and attractive guest house. It offers five comfortable rooms most with private bath. Rooms on ground floor suitable for disabled. It is licenced and has a T.V. lounge. The River Kennet flows close to the house. It is a comfortable driving distance to Bath, Oxford, Salisbury, Stonehenge. Children over 10 years accepted.	£11.00	O	O	O
Mrs Madelaine Smith **Greenways** **Garden Close Lane** **Newbury RG14 6PP** **Tel: (0635) 40496** **OPEN: ALL YEAR**	Nearest Road A.343 This is a comfortable country house set in pleasant secluded parkland gardens. Offering a choice of two bedrooms with modern amenities including tea/coffee making facilities and colour T.V. There is also an outdoor swimming pool, a delightful garden, and guests lounge available. This house is ideally situated for London. Close by are Crookham Common 18 hole golf course, pony trekking and canal side walks. Donnington Castle and Littlecote House are within easy reach.	£10.50	■	■	■
Mrs Thornely **Bridge Cottage** **Station Road** **Woolhampton** **Reading RG7 5SF** **Tel: (0734) 713138** **OPEN: ALL YEAR**	Nearest Roads A.4 M.4 A warm welcome awaits the visitor to this delightful 275 year old riverside cottage. Offering 3 very pleasant bedrooms with beamed ceilings. It is surrounded by lovely countryside with many beautiful walks along the River Kennet. Close by is the local pub which serves excellent home cooked suppers. Very convenient for London which is 1 hour away.	£12.00	O	■	■
Mrs C.M. Wright **Centuries** **Midgham Green** **Nr. Woolhampton** **Reading RG7 5TT** **Tel: (0734) 712540** **OPEN: ALL YEAR**	Nearest Roads A.4 M.4 An absolutely beautiful 400 year old black and white half timbered country house set in its own delightful grounds. This lovely home with many exposed beams and inglenook fireplace creates an atmosphere of great comfort. The two bedrooms are extremely well furnished including T.V. radio and private bathrooms. Guests may also use the pleasant garden and the heated outdoor swimming pool. Locally there are many village pubs and excellent restaurants. London only 1 hour away. Children over 8 years	£15.00	O	■	■

O yes ■ no

22

Buckinghamshire

Column headers (diagonal): minimum per person · children taken · evening meals available · animals taken

	Nearest Roads	minimum per person	children taken	evening meals available	animals taken
Mrs F.A. Cooper Poletrees Farm Brill Nr. Aylesbury HP18 9TZ Tel: (0844) 238276 OPEN: ALL YEAR	Nearest Roads A.41 B.4011 Guests will receive a warm welcome from a friendly helpful host at this 500 year old farmhouse. Accommodation is in 2 rooms, sharing a bathroom. Tea/coffee making facilities. A T.V. lounge and garden are also available. Excellent farmhouse meals. 12 miles Oxford, 8 miles Blenheim Palace, 6 miles Waddesdon Manor.	£11.00	○	■	○
N.M.D. Hooper Foxhill Farm Foxhill Kingsey Aylesbury HP17 8LZ Tel: (0844) 291650 OPEN: FEB-NOV	Nearest Road A.4129 A delightful 17th Century white painted farmhouse situated in the Chiltern Vale with lovely views across the Chiltern Hills. This peaceful and comfortable oak beamed farmhouse offers accommodation in three twin or double bedded rooms with modern amenities, one with en-suite facilities. There is also a T.V. lounge/dining room, garden, heated swimming pool and a tennis court. Choice of restaurants nearby and London only 1 hour away.	£11.00	○	■	■
Mrs Corinne Berry 2 Hyde Green Marlow SL7 1QL Tel: (06284) 3526 OPEN: ALL YEAR	Nearest Roads M.40 M.4 Advance bookings only please. A warm welcome and a friendly atmosphere await guests at Mrs. Berry's home. The house is conveniently located only a few minutes walk from Marlow town centre and the River Thames. Accommodation is in one comfortable double bedroom with modern amenities, colour T.V., radio and tea/coffee making facilities. No single occupancy available.	£9.00	■	■	■
Mrs Patricia Rowe The Elms Country House The Elms Radnage Nr. Stockenchurch HP14 4DW Tel: (024026) 2175 OPEN: ALL YEAR	Nearest Roads A.40 M.40 The Elms is a delightful 17th century farmhouse standing in two acres of ground, set in an area of outstanding natural beauty. The house retains many original features including handmade roof tiles and many oak beams. There are 4 bedrooms, some with radio, T.V. and tea/coffee making facilities. A colour T.V. lounge is also available and guests may use the garden.	£12.50	○	○	○

Hertfordshire

	Nearest Roads	minimum per person	children taken	evening meals available	animals taken
Mrs Lesley Baldwin Venus Hill Farm Venus Hill Bovingdon HP3 0PG Tel: (0442) 833396 OPEN: APRIL-OCT	Nearest Road A.41 An absolutely delightful black and white 300 year old converted farmhouse standing in 2 acres of garden and surrounded by open farmland. Guests will receive a warm welcome and very comfortable accommodation. There is a choice of 2 bedrooms with modern amenities and radio in each. Guests may also like to use the tennis court, croquet lawn or outdoor heated swimming pool. This makes a good base from which to visit London. Heathrow is very easily accessible.	£12.00	■	○	■

○ yes ■ no

CAMBRIDGESHIRE

A county utterly different from any other, this is flat low-lying, fertile fen land, and to view the countryside it is only necessary to climb a high tower or the Gog Magog hills when the panorama spreads out like a carpet, the only interruption being the network of waterways, natural and man- made, which criss-cross the land.

It is immensely rich in architectural treasures from the wonderful colleges to the tiny village churches, so much has been written of its virtues that all the world must be as familiar with it as with their own home ground. But it exerts a fascination which draws everyone, sooner or later, into making the journey from however far to experience at first hand the joys of Cambridgeshire.

Architectural Splendours

Of all the splendours contained in this little county - surely the first must be the great Cathedral at Ely. Begun before the Domesday Book was written, it took the work of a full century before it was ready to have the timbered roof raised up. The Norman stonemasons worked with incredible skills which sets this Cathedral apart from any other, and their work was crowned by the addition of the glorious Octagon in the 14th century. This was, of itself, a most notable feat of architectural design.

The majestic Norman nave, exquisite in its simplicity, must be the finest of all England's fine Norman buildings. The massive piers of the main arcade carry the eye between great walls of stone towards the East windows which glitter like jewels. Above the painted ceiling glows with rich colours; the floor of the nave carries the rainbow of colours reflected from the windows adding to the glory of this wonderful nave. There are beautiful and elegant chapels, none lovelier than the Lady Chapel which is set a little apart. It must be near miraculous that stone can be made to appear as light and delicate as a spider's web and yet it is so, and carried by walls which appear to be half glass bringing the light showering on to the exquisite carving and sculpture.

Contrast with this magnificence the little church at Cottenham. It is mainly 15th century and has a tower which is quite a landmark. There is a gallery of gargoyles running around the walls of the church to keep off evil spirits. There is an old five lock chest - usually the five keys were kept by five men for security. The oak benches have carvings of local wild flowers, made in the last century by the village carpenter. There is recorded on the wall the story of the destruction of the steeple in 1617 by storm, and of the rebuilding under the patrongate of Katherine Pepys. Samuel Pepys records that in Cottenham in the time of Elizabeth I there were 26 families named Pepys living in that village.

Grantchester and Cambridge

Grantchester immediately comes to mind when speaking of Cambridge, and the immortal lines by Rupert Brooke who loved this area so well he made his home in the Old Vicarage here.

But of Cambridge itself, so much has been written and sung in its praise that the very mention of its name stirs something deep in the heart of so many people. For some it conjures up the names and qualities of the great men it knew; others think of the lovely "backs" and gracious colleges. For some it revives memories of precious youth whilst others can only long to be a part of the world it represents. Those who have visited this lovely place will already be enslaved by its beauty, but those who have not yet experienced this are to be envied - the first sight of this unbelievable city touches the heart and mind as no other ever can. For everyone, everywhere, Cambridge is the distillation of a magical spirit which cannot be found anywhere else in the world.

CAMBRIDGESHIRE GAZETEER

Areas of Outstanding Natural Beauty.

The Nene Valley.

Historic Houses and Castles

Anglesy Abbey -- Nr. Cambridge
Origins in reign of Henry I. Was re-designed into Elizabethan Manor by Fokes family. Houses the Fairhaven collection of Art treasures - stands in 100 acres of Grounds.

Hinchingbrooke House -- Huntingdon
13th century nunnery converted mid-16th century into Tudor house. Later additions in 17th and 19th centuries.

King's School -- Ely
12th and 14th centuries -- original stonework and vaulting in the undercroft, original timbering 14th century gateway and monastic barn.

Kimbolton Castle -- Kimbolton
Tudor Manor house -- has associations with Katherine of Aragon. Remodelled by Vanbrugh 1700's -- gatehouse by Robert Adam.

Longthorpe Tower -- Nr. Peterborough
13th and 14th century fortification -- rare wall paintings.

Peckover House -- Wisbech
18th century domestic architecture -- charming Victorian garden.

University of Cambridge Colleges

Peterhouse	1284
Clare College	1326
Pembroke College	1347
Gonville & Caius College	1348
Trinity Hall	1350
Corpus Christi College	1352
King's College	1441
Queens College	1448
St. Catherine's College	1473
Jesus College	1496
Christ's College	1505
St. John's College	1511
Magadalene College	1542
Trinity College	1546
Emmanuel College	1584
Sidney Sussex College	1596
Downing College	1800

Wimpole Hall -- Nr. Cambridge
18th and 19th century -- beautiful staterooms -- aristocratic house.

Cathedrals and Churches

Alconbury (St. Peter & St. Paul)
13th century chancel and 15th century roof. Broach spire.

Babraham (St. Peter)
13th century tower -- 17th century monuments.

Bottisham (Holy Trinity)
14th century -- famous brass indent -- stone screen -- wooden parcloses.

Chesterton (St. Micheal)
18th century-Roman chancel -- Jacobean monument.

Ely Cathedral
Rich arcading -- west front incomplete. Remarkable interior with Octagon -- unique in Gothic architecture.

Great Paxton (Holy Trinity)
12th century.

Harlton (Blessed Virgin Mary)
Perpendicular -- decorated transition. 17th century monuments.

Hildersham (Holy Trinity)
13th century -- effigies, brasses and glass.

Landwade (St. Nicholas)
15th century -- mediaeval fittings.

Peterborough Cathedral
Great Norman church fine example -- little altered. Painted wooden roof to nave -- remarkable west front -- Galilee Porch and spires later additions.

Ramsey (St. Thomas of Canterbury)
12th century arcades -- perpendicular nave. Late Norman chancel with Angevin vault.

St. Neots (St. Mary)
15th century.

Sutton (St. Andrew)
14th century.

Trumpington (St. Mary & St. Nicholas)
14th century. Famed brass of 1289 of Sir Roger de Trumpington.

Westley Waterless (St. Mary the Less)
Decorated. 14th century brass of Sir John and Lady Creke.

Wimpole (St. Andrew)
14th century rebuilt 1749 -- spendid heraldic glass.

Yaxley (St. Peter)
15th century chancel screen, wall paintings, fine steeple.

Museums and Galleries

Cromwell Museum -- Huntingdon
Exhibiting portraits, documents etc. of the Cromwellian period.

Fitzwilliam Museum -- Cambridge
Gallery of masters, old and modern, ceramics, applied arts, prints and drawing, mediaeval manuscripts, music an art library, antiquities.

Scott Polar Research Institute -- Cambridge
Relics of expeditions and the equipment used. Current scientific work in Arctic and Antarctic.

University Archives -- Cambridge
13th century manuscripts, Charters, Statutes, Royal letters and mandates. Wide variey of records of the University.

University Museum of Archeology and Anthropology -- Cambridge
Collections illustrative of Stone Age in Europe, Africa and Asia. Britain prehistoric to mediaeval times. Prehistoric America. Ethnographic material from South-east Asia, Africa and America.

University Museum of Classical Archeology -- Cambridge
Casts of Greek and Roman Sculpture -- representative collection.

Whipple Museum of the History of Science -- Cambridge
16th, 17th and 18th century scientific instruments -- historic collection.

NORTHANTS
CAMBRIDGESHIRE
Recommended roadside restaurants

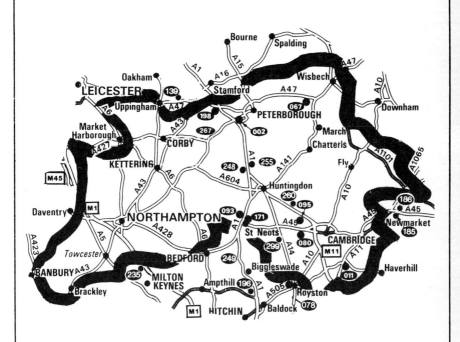

	minimum per person	children taken	evening meals available	animals taken
Mrs Jane Rowell **43 Norwich Street** **CB2 1ND** **Tel: (0223) 350446** **OPEN: ALL YEAR** Nearest Roads M.11 A.1 A friendly relaxed atmosphere is found at number 43. Mrs. Rowell has one room available for guests and does her best to make sure their stay is as comfortable as possible. English or Continental breakfast is provided and evening meals can be arranged with prior notice. This makes a good base for exploring the city of Cambridge.	£10.50	O	O	■
Mrs M. Northrop **Bon Accord House** **20 St. Margarets Square** **(Off Cherry Hinton Rd)** **CB1 4AP** **Tel: (0223) 246568** **OPEN: ALL YEAR** Nearest Road M.11 A warm welcome awaits the visitor to Bon Accord. A small family run guest house situated in a quiet cul-de-sac about a mile and a half to the south of this historic city. Accommodation is in twelve rooms with modern amenities. Radio, T.V. and tea/coffee making facilities. Children are always welcome here. A cot and high chair are available. A choice of full English breakfast and a three course evening meal are available.	£11.50	O	O	■
Julie Webb **Dykelands Guest House** **157 Mowbray Road** **CB1 4SP** **Tel: (0223) 244300** **OPEN: ALL YEAR** Nearest Roads M.11 A.10 Located on the south side of the city this pleasant guest house offers guests a choice of 7 rooms, most with private shower or bath, all have modern amenities, T.V. radio and tea/coffee making facilities. Dykelands is convenient for visiting the historic city of Cambridge and for exploring the surrounding countryside.	£14.00	O	O	■
A.R. & R.L. Setchell **Nyton Guest House** **7 Barton Road** **Ely CB7 4HZ** **Tel: (0353) 2459** **OPEN: ALL YEAR** Nearest Road A.10 Nyton Guest House is situated in a quiet, residential area in the city of Ely. Located in 2 acres of attractive grounds and adjoining an 18-hole golf course. There are uninterrupted views over a wide area of the Fenland Countryside. Offering comfortable accommodation in a homely atmosphere, there are 15 rooms with modern facilities, some with bath en-suite. There is much to visit locally including the Cathedral. Within a few miles there is Wicken Fen, Welney Bird Sanctuary, Denny Abbey and Haddenham Farm Museum.	£10.50	O	■	■
Mrs Beryl Taylor **Millside Cottage Guest House** **9 Mill Street** **Houghton PE17 2AZ** **Tel: (0480) 64456** **OPEN: ALL YEAR** Nearest Road A.1123 Houghton is a picturesque old village on the Bedford Ouse River, with many black and white buildings plus a famous water mill. Millside Cottage was once a pub and offers six pleasant rooms with modern amenities. A lounge and garden are available for guests. A short drive will take the visitor to the Cromwellian towns of Huntingdon and St. Ives. Cambridge and Ely are easily accessible and less than 1 hour away. London can also be reached by car or by train in under 1 hour.	£13.00	O	O	O

O yes ■ no

	Nearest Road / Description	minimum per person	children taken	evening meals available	animals taken
Mrs Sally Arnot **Church Farm Barn** **Horseware** **Over CB4 5NX** **Tel: (0954) 31494** **OPEN: MAR-DEC**	Nearest Road A.604 Situated in peaceful countryside this is a recent conversion of an 18th century barn and a 19th century addition. It now combines all the comforts of modern living with its original charm and character. Huge exposed beams and wood burning stove. Comfort and a friendly stay are assured here. Ideally situated for touring Cambridge and East Anglia. Stansted and Luton Airports are easily reached.	£13.00	O	■	■

Northamptonshire

	Nearest Road / Description	minimum per person	children taken	evening meals available	animals taken
Mr & Mrs R. Harrison **Walltree House Farm** **Steane** **Brackley NN13 5NS** **Tel: (0295) 811235** **OPEN: ALL YEAR**	Nearest Road A.422 This large Victorian farm house has been recently restored and now provides guests with spacious comfortable accommodation with delightful woodland and a garden to relax in. Offering a choice of seven bedrooms, some with private facilities, T.V. and radio. This makes an ideal base for touring the Cotswolds, Oxford, Blenheim and Stratford-on-Avon.	£12.00	O	O	O
Mrs Margaret Faulkner **The Maltings** **Aldwincle** **Kettering NN14 3EP** **Tel: (08015) 233** **OPEN: ALL YEAR**	Nearest Roads A.1 A.605 A.604 The Maltings is a 300 year old former farmhouse retaining much of its original character with inglenooks, beams, and antique furnishing. Located in the centre of the delightful village of Aldwincle, famous as the birthplace of John Dryden, the poet. Accommodation is in three rooms, all central heated. Tea/coffee served on request, T.V. and attractive flower garden. The house is conveniently located for touring the area and makes a good stop-over for those travelling north or south up the A.1. Good food, reasonably priced at local pubs.	£11.50	■	■	■

O yes ■ no

ADVANCE RESERVATIONS

Don't be disappointed. Book ahead.
Use our fast efficient

RESERVATION SERVICE

Be sure of your accommodation
Book Now!!
Call us on

01-370 7099   **01-370 7099**

CHESHIRE & MERSEYSIDE

This is not very well known, even to the neighbouring counties, except the Peak District with which it shares a border, but the people who have explored it from top to bottom are devoted to Cheshire. There are pretty villages with lanes and hedgerows, a profusion of wild flowers, prosperous farms, parks and gardens, fine towns, forests with herds of fallow deer. Canals and rivers thread their way across the landscape which is always green and pleasant. The Cheshire plain rising up to Alderley Edge which offers fine views of the district and then climbs dramatically to meet the splendid heights of the Peaks. IIn complete contrast to the Wirral Peninsula which has miles of sandy beaches and dunes. Elswhere there is motor racing, horse racing, golf, climbing, etc.

Chester

The county town is Chester and a walk through it streets is like walking through living history. The old city is encircled by two miles of city walls which takes the walker around a fine panorama of old and new. The gates and towers, arcaded streets with galleried buildings, the black and white architecture, even a Roman amphitheatre make the visitor feel that he has strayed into another period. Much of the historic architecture still stands and blends hand-somley with modern life. Chester was particularly important to the Romans and the Legions had a great fortress here and the museum in Grosvenor Street illustrates very well. Civil War also took its toll in Chester and that event is shown interesting in exhibits and diorama in the King Charles Tower in the City wall. There is a very popular Zoo, splendid shopping, pretty parks and it gives an interesting perspective to take a trip in a canal barge along the River Dee.

Architecture

The countryside shelters very beautiful houses, one of the most perfect imaginable being Little Moreton Hall near Congleton. It is a wonderful black and white "magpie" house and not one of its walls is perpendicular, yet it has withstood winds and weather for hundreds of years and still stands on the waterside, proudly gazing at its own reflection.

Tatton Hall at Knutsford is a complete contrast. Built in the 19th Century, it is large and imposing, splendidly furnished, with many fine objects displayed in the collection there. The parks and gardens are a delight and are especially renowned for the collection of azaleas and rhododendrons.

It is impossible to describe all the fine and historic buildings to be found in this interesting County. Surely the greatest of all wonders is the enormous radio telescope at Jodrell Bank. Here there is a planatarium giving an introduction to astronomy for interested visitors. So time has stretched from the Saxon stone crosses, through Roman acqeducts to reach outer space, in this quiet and gentle countryside.

Liverpool

The Mersey River has been the life blood of Liverpool ever since its northern shores were first inhabited in the 1st century A.D. From a small fishing village it grew rapidly and received its charter from King John in 1207. Commercial and slave trading with the West Indies lead to massive expansion in the 17th & 18th centuries. However, the Liverpool of today owes much to the introduction of the steam ship in the mid 1900s. At this time the great potato famine was at its height in Ireland. Thousands of Irish emigrated and came to Liverpool where many of their descendants still live today. This is a city with a reputation for patronage of art, music and sport. There are many art galleries, a Royal Philharmonic Orchestra and a constant stream of young innovative rock musicians who lead the world with their brand of contemporary music.

CHESHIRE GAZETEER

Area of Oustanding natural Beauty
Part of the Peaks National Park.

Historic Houses and Castles

Adlington Hall -- Macclesfield
15th century Elizabethan Black and White half timbered house.

Bishop Lloyd's House -- Chester
17th century half timbered house (restored) Fine carvings. Has associations with Yale University and New Haven, USA.

Chorley Old Hall -- Alderley Edge
14th century hall with 16th century Elizabeth wing.

Dorfold Hall -- Nantwich
17th century Jacobean country house, with fine panelling.

Gawsworth Hall -- Macclesfield
Fine Tudor half timbered Manor House. Tilting ground. Pictures, furniture, sculptures, etc.

Lyme Park -- Disley
Elizabethan with Palladian exterior by Leoni. Gibbons carvings. Beautiful park with herd of red deer.

Peover Hall -- Over Peover, Knutsford
16th century -- stables of Tudor period; has the famous magpie ceiling.

Tatton Park -- Knutsford
Beautifully decorated and funished Georgian House with a fine collection of glass, china and paintings including Van Dyke and Canaletto. Landscaping by Humphrey Repton.

Cathedrals and Churches

Acton (St. Mary)
13th century with stone seating around walls. 17th century effigies.

Bunbury (St. Boniface)
14th century collegiate church -- alabaster effigy.

Congleton (St. Peter)
18th century -- box pews, brass candelabrum, 18th century glass.

Chester Cathedral -- Chester
Subjected to restoration by Victorians -- 14th century choir stalls.

Malpas (St. Oswalds)
15th century -- fine screens, some old stalls, two family chapels.

Mobberley (St. Wilfred)
Mediaeval -- 15th century Rood Screen, wall paintings, very old glass.

Shotwick (St. Michael)
Twin nave -- box pews, 14th century quatre -- foil lights, 3 deck pulpit.

Winwick (St. Oswald)
14th century -- splendid roof. Pugin chancel.

Wrenbury (St. Margaret)
16th century -- west gallery, monuments and hatchments. Box pews.

Museums and Galleries

Grosvenor Museum -- Chester
Art, folk history, natural history, Roman antiquities including a special display of information about the Roman army.

Chester Heritage Centre -- Chester
Interesting exhibition of the architectural heritage of Chester.

Cheshire Military Museum -- Chester
The three local Regiments are commemorated here.

King Charles Tower -- Chester
Chester at the time of the Civil War Illustrated by dioramas.

Museum and Art Gallery -- Warrington
Anthropology, geology, ethnology, botany and natural history. Pottery, porcelain, glass, collection of early English watercolours.

West Park Museum and Art Gallery -- Macclesfield
Egyptian collection, oil paintings, watercolours, sketches by Landseer and Tunnicliffe.

Norton Priory Museum -- Runcorn
Remains of excavated mediaeval priory. Also wildlife display.

Quarry Bank Mill -- Styal
The Mill is a fine example of industrial building and houses an exhibition of the cotton industry: the various offices retain their original furnishing, and the turbine room has the transmission systems and two turbines of 1903.

Nether Alderley Mill -- Nether Alderley
15th century corn mill which was still in use in 1929. Now restored.

Historic Monuments

Chester Castle -- Chester
Huge square tower remaining.

Roman Amphitheatre -- Chester
12th Legion site -- half excavated.

Beeston Castle -- Beeston
Remains of a 13th century fort.

Sandbach Crosses -- Sandbach
Carved stone crosses dating from 9th century.

Gardens

Arley Hall -- Northwich
Walled Gardens, topiary, shrub roses, herbaceous borders, azaleas and rhododendrons.

Cholmondeley Castle Gardens -- Malpas
Gardens, lake, farm with rare breeds. Ancient chapel in Park.

Ness Gardens -- S. Wirral
Beautiful trees and shrubs, terraces, herbaceous borders, rose collection and herb garden.

Tatton Park -- Knutsford
Famed for azaleas and rhododendrons, an Italian terraced garden, a Japanese water garden, an orangery and a fernery.

MANCHESTER
CHESHIRE/MERSEYSIDE
Recommended roadside restaurants

Cheshire & Merseyside

		minimum per person	children taken	evening meals available	animals taken
Mrs Audrey O'Neill **Elizabethan Park Hotel** **78 Hoole Road** **Chester CH2 3NT** Tel: (0244) 310213 OPEN: ALL YEAR	Nearest Road - Hoole Road Elizabethan Park located approximately 1 mile from the city centre, is a large gabled house set in its own well tended grounds opposite a park. There is a choice of 7 bedrooms each with shower or bathroom en-suite, T.V. and tea/coffee making facilities. A very pleasant colour T.V. lounge is provided for guests and ironing facilities are available.	£18.00	O	O	O
Peter & Jayne Gregory **Curzon Hotel** **54 Hough Green** **Chester CH4 8JQ** Tel: (0244) 678581 OPEN: ALL YEAR	Nearest Roads A.55 A.549 Curzon Hotel is a large, pleasant 3 storey Victorian house standing in its own grounds on the A.549, 1 mile from the city centre. Accommodation is in 16 rooms, all en-suite with T.V., radio, telephone and tea/coffee making facilities. There is a licensed bar, dining room and meeting room. There is a choice of English or Continental breakfasts and early breakfasts can be arranged. Large private car park. This makes a good base from which to explore the area. ½ mile from the Race Course and Zoo. Good access for visiting North Wales.	£18.00	O	O	O
Mrs Beryl Minshull **Grange Farm** **Churton** **Chester CH3 6LA** Tel: (0244) 65259 OPEN: ALL YEAR	Nearest Road B.5130 Grange Farm stands in a 430 acre dairy and arable farm. There is a choice of four bedrooms with modern amenities, some with T.V., radio and tea/coffee making facilities. A colour T.V. lounge is available and guests may also use the garden. Evening meals are available in a family run restaurant close to the farm.	£9.00	O	■	O
Mrs M. Hurst **The Kings Guest House** **14 Eaton Road** **Handbridge** **Chester** Tel: (0244) 671249 OPEN: ALL YEAR	Nearest Road The Kings Guest House is a pleasant Victorian house located close to the River Dee and only a short distance from the city centre. Offering a choice of 10 bedrooms, all with modern amenities T.V. and tea/coffee making facilities. There is also a guests colour T.V. lounge and ironing facilities are provided. Guests also have access to their rooms throughout the day.	£8.00	O	■	O
P.G. & C.L. Maguire **Greenway's Guest House** **3 Eastern Pathway** **Queen's Park** **Handbridge** **Chester CH4 7AQ** Tel: (0244) 673308 OPEN: ALL YEAR	Nearest Road M.56 Greenway's is a pleasant family run guest house conveniently located within easy walking distance of the city and the River Dee. Accommodation is in 4 comfortable rooms with modern amenities, T.V. and tea/coffee making facilities. A residents colour T.V. lounge is also available. A good base for touring Cheshire and North Wales. No single occupancy available.	£9.00	O	O	■

O yes ■ no

	minimum per person	children taken	evening meals available	animals taken
Mrs A.J. Espie **Latymer House** **82 Hough Green** **Chester CH4 8JW** **Tel: (0244) 675074** **OPEN: ALL YEAR** Nearest Road A.549 A charming 1930's house with 1980's comfort where residents are welcomed as house guests. The accommodation is of a high standard, offering 12 rooms with en-suite bathrooms, colour T.V. and tea/coffee. Guests will also eat well, as one of the main interests of the hosts is food and wine. They cook for pleasure and don't mind if you bring your own wine. Guide dogs accepted.	£19.00	O	O	■
D.R. Bawn **The Gables Guest House** **5 Vicarage Road** **Hoole** **Chester CH2 3HZ** **Tel: (0244) 23969** **OPEN: ALL YEAR** Nearest Roads A.41 A.56 A warm welcome from Mr. Bawn awaits the visitor at the Gables. A pleasant, Victorian family house. Situated in a quiet residential area it is close to a park and tennis courts. Accommodation is in 7 rooms with modern amenities, a lounge and dining room. The price also includes a bedtime drink. Children over 2 years accepted.	£9.00	O	■	O
Mrs Joan Critchley **Roslyn Guest House** **8 Chester Street** **Nr. Saltney** **Chester CH4 8BJ** **Tel: (0244) 672306** **OPEN: ALL YEAR** **(EXCL. XMAS)** Nearest Roads A.549 A.55 A traditional guest house offering bright, cheerful and comfortable accommodation and home-cooked meals. There are 10 bedrooms all with modern amenities and television lounge available at all times. Situated within 1 mile of the city walls it is conveniently placed as a base for exploring Chester, Cheshire and the beautiful countryside of North Wales.	£8.50	O	O	O
Mrs Catherine Pratt **Stretton Lower Hall** **Tilston** **Malpas SY14 7HS** **Tel: (08298) 497** **OPEN: ALL YEAR** Nearest Roads A.41 A.534 A charming old farmhouse dating back to 1660, now a listed building being run as a small holding. Offering 4 spacious family rooms. Child rates apply up to 14. Situated in a quiet, unspoilt rural area, it is a perfect base for scenic walks along Cheshire's Sandstone Ridge. Chester is 10 miles. North Wales coast and mountains within easy reach. Animals by arrangement only. Cots provided.	£8.00	O	■	O
Mrs M. Winward **Stapleford Hall** **Tarvin** **Chester CH3 8HH** **Tel: (0829) 40202** **OPEN: ALL YEAR** Nearest Road A.51 Stapleford Hall is a beautiful Georgian farmhouse standing in large, well tended gardens in a peaceful, attractive countryside setting, with views across to Peckforton and Beeston Castles. The dining and drawing rooms are very attractively furnished. The 3 bedrooms are spacious and comfortable with 'phone, T.V. and tea/coffee making facilities. Within easy reach of North Wales.	£8.00	O	■	■

O yes ■ no

		minimum per person	children taken	evening meals available	animals taken
Anna & David Cohen **Anna's** **65 Dudlow Lane** **Calderstones** **Liverpool L18 2EY** **Tel: (051) 722 3708** **OPEN: ALL YEAR**	Nearest Road M.26 Anna's is a comfortable family home where every effort is made to ensure that visitors become one of the family. Eating well is of the utmost importance here and guests may bring their own wine if they choose. Accommodation is in three rooms all with modern amenities, radio and tea/coffee making facilities. A resident T.V. lounge is also available as is the garden. Anna's is right in the heart of "Beatle land" Penny Lane and Strawberry fields are moments away.	£9.00	○	○	○
Phil & Rita Corcoran **Walsingham Hotel** **25 Elgin Drive** **Wallasey L45 7PP** **Tel: (051639) 3074** **OPEN: ALL YEAR**	Nearest Road M.53 The Walsingham is a small family hotel, offering six bedrooms with modern amenities and residents lounge. Situated in a delightful position on promenade midway between Egremont and New Brighton. There are lovely views to sea and Liverpool pierhead. Set in a quiet, traffic free area making an ideal base for touring Liverpool, Wirral and Chester. Meals are available throughout the day in the coffee shop.	£10.35	○	○	○

○ yes ■ no

All the establishments in this book
are members of the
WORLDWIDE BED & BREAKFAST
ASSOCIATION

Look for this symbol

CORNWALL

Even the most casual visitor will acknowedge that there is something very special about Cornwall. It is not simply that it is bounded by sea on three sides, nor that the livelihood and history of its people are intimately bound up with the traditions of seafaring. It is not just the mild climate nor the profusion of primroses, foxgloves, rhododendrons and wild flowers that flourish here. Its secret is perhaps something to do with the windswept desolation of Bodmin Moor, the strange almost haunted atmosphere of the Zennor Moors and Lands End, the romance of the lost land of Lyonesse and the extraordinary clarity of light which has attracted so many artists to the area.

The Coast

To some extent the sea is Cornwall. The narrow granite peninsula reaches out to face the Atlantic to the west, the English Channel to the south and the Irish Sea and Bristol Channel to the north. It has over 300 miles of coastline of great variety. The cliffs are dotted with coves like Penberth, Porthgwana and St Levan where the waters are quite translucent and winding steps lead down to a world of caves and rockpools. Along the north coast and at St Ives there are splendid stretches of sand and at Newquay, Perranporth and Bude surfing is popular. The south coast holds magnificent estuaries like the Fal and Fowey and Helford River, where dense oak woodlands slope steeply to the waters edge. Then there are busy fishing ports such as Newlyn and Mevagissey where the slate hung cottages huddle in the steep valley. The headlands and cliff top paths offer a fine prospect of a restless glistening green sea from the dark cliffs of picturesque Boscastle to the green serpentine cliffs of the Lizard. Here the treacherous rocks have claimed countless vessels from tiny fishing boats to great sailing ships. The coast also has its legends. At Gwithian there is supposedly the "lost land of Langarrow" sleeping silently under the waves and legend has it that there was a splendid kingdom between the Scillies and Lands End which was inundated one night over 900 years ago. Fisherman say to this day that the roofs of houses are visible beneath the water. There is stronger evidence at Tintagel where the remains of a Celtic monastery and the ruins of King Arthur's Castle stand high on a headland above the thunder of the Atlantic rollers. Finally there is the monastery at St Michaels Mount, linked by a causeway to the mainland at Marazion and further along the coast is the Mynack theatre at Porthcurno.

Inland Cornwall

The landscape from Bodmin Moor to Lands End holds evidence of early settlement. There are numerous Celtic stone crosses (St Mowgan, St Kew, St Cleer) and prehistoric remains such as Lanyon and Trevethy Quoits, the remains of neolithic tombs, and the ritual stones at Madron near Lands End. Bodmin Moor holds its antiquities but most striking are the natural rock outcrops of the Tors like the Cheezening at St Cleer and the high summits like Brown Willy from which both coasts and most of the county can be surveyed. Daphne du Maurier provides some excellent descriptions of the moors in her novel "Jamaica Inn"; this lonely inn on the high moor can still be visited. The countryside is dotted with weird ruined buildings, the engine houses at the head of old tin mines. These carry romantic names like Wheal Treasure, Wheal Fortune and Botallack, which extends for miles under the sea. Strange place names like Twelve Heads and Seven Stamps also come from the days of mining and refer to the number of wooden piles used to crush the ore. Throughout the county are numerous delightful villages and small towns, some at the foot of the moors like Blisland with Georgian cottages of granite and the superb 15th century church of St Proctus and St Hyacynth. There are the delightful fishing ports like Falmouth. The deep inlets of the estuaries hold many attractive and peaceful villages in wooded and pastoral settings like Milbrook and Manaccan; elsewhere are rugged mining towns like St Just in Penwith and again there are the fine little resort towns of St Ives and Penzance. The variety and number of Cornish villages is bewildering and almost any turn of the luxuriant Cornish lanes will lead to a village well worth the finding. If the Cornish language was almost lost in the 18th century (happily there is now a revival) its customs and traditions have been maintained. In the charming village of Helston the famous tradition of the "Fleury Dance" is still maintained and at the ancient port of Padstow the May Day celebrations involve decorating the houses with green boughs and the "Hobby Horse" is paraded through the streets to the haunting tune of St Georges Song.

CORNWALL GAZETEER

Areas of Outstanding Natural Beauty.
Almost the entire county.

Historic Houses and Castles

Anthony House -- Torpoint
 18th century -- beautiful and quite unspoiled Queen Anne house, excellent panelling and fine period furnishings.

Cotehele House -- Calstock
 15th and 16th century house, still contains the original furniture, tapestry, armour, etc.

Ebbingford Manor -- Bude
 12th century Cornish manor house, with walled garden.

Godolphin House -- Helston
 Tudor -- 17th century colonnaded front.

Lanhydrock -- Bodmin
 17th century -- splendid plaster ceilings, picture gallery with family portraits 17th/20th centuries.

Mount Edgcumbe House -- Plymouth
 Tudor style mansion -- restored after destruction in 1941. Hepplewhite furniture and portrait by Joshua Reynolds.

St. Michael's Mount -- Penzance
 Mediaeval and 17th century with 18th and 19th century additiions.

Pencarrow House & Gardens -- Bodmin
 18th century Georgian Mansion -- collection of paintings, china and furniture -- mile long drive through fine woodlands and gardens.

Old Post Office -- Tintagel
 14th century manor house in miniature -- large hall used as Post Office for a period, hence the name.

Trewithen -- Probus. Nr. Truro
 Early Georgian house with lovely gardens.

Trerice -- St. Newlyn East
 16th century Elizabethan house, small with elaborate facade.
Excellent fireplaces, plaster ceilings, miniature gallery and minstrels' gallery.

Cathedrals and Churches

Altarnun (St. Nonna)
 15th century, Norman font, 16th century bench ends, fine rood screen.

Bisland (St. Protus & St. Hyacinth)
 15th century granite tower -- carved wagon roofs, slate floor. Georgian wine -- glass pulpit, fine screen.

Kilkhampton (St. James)
 16th century with fine Norman doorway, arcades and wagon roofs.

Laneast (St. Michael or St. Sedwell)
 13th century, 15th century enlargement, 16th century pulpit, some painted glass.

Lanteglos-by-Fowley (St. Willow)
 14th century, refashioned 15th century. 13th century font, 15th century brasses and altar tomb, 16thcentury bench ends.

Launcells (St. Andrew)
 Interior unrestored -- old plaster and ancient roofs remaining, fine Norman font with 17th century cover, box pews, pulpit, reredos, 3 sided altar rails.

Probus (St. Probus & St. Gren)
 16th century tower, splendid arcades, three great East windows.

St. Keverne (St. Keveran)
Fine tower and spire. Wall painting in 15th century interior.

St. Neot (St. Neot)
Decorated tower -- 16th century exterior, buttressed and double-aisled. Many windows of mediaeval glass renewed in 19th century.

Museums and Galleries

Museum of Witchcraft -- Boscastle
Relating to witches, implements and customs.

Millitary Museum -- Bodmin
History of Duke of Cornwall's Light Infantry.

Public Library and Museum -- Cambourne
Collections of mineralogy, archeology, local antiquities and history.

Cornish Museum -- East Looe
Collection of relics relating to witchcraft customs and superstitions. Folk life and culture of district.

Helson Borough Museum -- Helston
Folk life and culture of area around Lizard.

Museum of Nautical Art -- Penzance
Exhibition of salvaged gold and silver treasures from underwater wreck of 1700's.

Museum of Smuggling -- Polperro
Activities of smugglers, past and present.

Penlee House Museum -- Penlee, Penzance
Archeology and local history and tin mining exhibits.

Newlyn Art Gallery -- Newlyn
Collection of works by contemporary artists of West Country. Exhibition of paintings from the Newlyn School 1880 -- 1930.

Barbara Hepworth Museum -- St. Ives
Sculpture, letters, documents, photographs etc. exhibited in house where Barbara Hepworth lived.

Old Mariners Church -- St. Ives
St. Ives Society of Artists hold exhibitions here.

County Museum & Art Gallery -- Truro
Ceramics, art, local history and antiquities, Cornish mineralogy.

Historic Monuments

Cromwell's Castle -- Tresco (Scilly Isles)
17th century castle.

King Charles' Fort -- Tresco (Scilly Isles)
16th century fort.

Old Blockhouse -- Tresco (Scilly Isles)
16th century coastal battery.

Harry's Walls -- St. Mary's (Scilly Isles)
Tudor Coastal battery.

Ballowall Barrow -- St. Just.
Prehistoric barrow.

Pendennis Castle -- Falmouth
Fort from time of Henry VII

Restormel Castle -- Lostwithiel
13th century ruins.

St. Mawes Castle -- St.Mawes
16th century fortified castle.

CORNWALL
Recommended roadside restaurants

214   A38   *Trerulefoot Nr Saltash, Cornwall*
9 miles west of Plymouth toll bridge

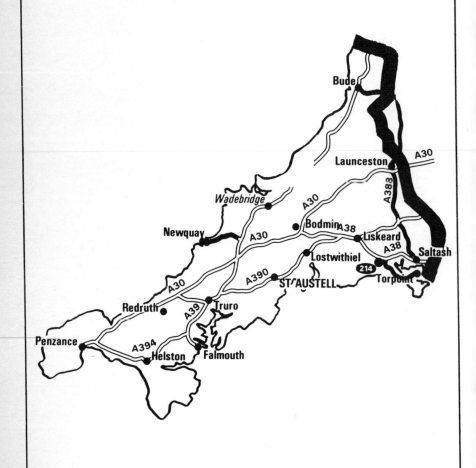

40

	minimum per person	children taken	evening meals available	animals taken
Mrs S.M. Mewton **'Hillcrest' Guest House** St. Teath Bodmin Tel: (0208) 850258 OPEN: ALL YEAR Nearest Road A.38 A pleasant house offering good accommodation for guests. All rooms overlook the countryside. Situated in the lovely area of St. Teath, this is a perfect base for sight-seeing, hiking or walking over the beautiful countryside of Bodmin Moor. The coast is not very far away. Homemade pasties, splits and soup. Really good home cooking. 4 miles from the beach.	£7.00	O	O	O
P.B. & Mrs A. Bowman **and S.G. & Mrs J. Piper** St. Christophers Country House Hotel High Street Boscastle PL35 0BD Tel: (08405) 412 OPEN: 1 MAR-1 NOV Nearest Roads A.39 B.3266 A superb Georgian house retaining its original character, providing excellent, comfortable accommodation in eight charming rooms with modern facilities. Here the welcome and standards are marvellous. The lovely harbour village is unspoilt. There is a wealth of history all around with plenty of interesting places to visit. Cots are provided. Meals are well prepared and delicious.	£10.50	O	O	O
Mrs Muriel Knight Manor Farm Crackington Haven Nr. Bude EX23 0JW Tel: (08403) 304 OPEN: ALL YEAR Nearest Road A.39 A really super 11th Century Manor house retaining all its former charm and elegance. Mentioned in the 1086 Doomsday book, it belonged to the Earl of Mortain, half brother to William the Conqueror. Delightfully located in a beautiful and secluded position it is surrounded by attractive gardens and 180 acres of farmland. All guest rooms have private facilities. There is a games room for guests' use. Log fires crackle in the hearth on winter evenings. Excellent home cooking. Only 1 mile from the beach. Non-smokers only.	£11.00	■	O	■
Mr & Mrs S. Goodwin **"Good-Winds" Guest House** 13 Stratton Terrace Falmouth TR11 2SY Tel: (0326) 313200 OPEN: ALL YEAR Nearest Road A.39 A large detached Georgian house in spacious gardens. Eleven charming rooms, eight with private bath. All rooms have tea/coffee makers and superb views of river and harbour. This pleasant house is situated close to the water between the new marina and the town. A T.V. lounge for guests' use. Packed lunches can be provided. Excellent value evening meals. A really good base for visitors to Falmouth. The area has plenty for everyone.	£8.75	O	O	O
Mrs Judy Ford Treviades Barton Constantine, Nr. Falmouth TR11 5RG Tel: (0326) 40524 OPEN: ALL YEAR (EXCL. XMAS & EASTER) Nearest Road This charming 16th century listed farmhouse stands in beautiful gardens close to the Helford River in the village of Traviades Barton. The farmhouse retains much of its former charm and original character. Offering 3 bedrooms with radio and tea/coffee making facilities. A colour T.V. lounge is provided and guests may play croquet and enjoy the garden. Home grown vegetables, soft fruit and local fish are used in the kitchen.	£12.50	O	O	O

O yes ■ no

	minimum per person	children taken	evening meals available	animals taken
Mrs Andrea Betty **High Massetts** **Cadgwith** **Ruan Minor** **Helston** **Tel: (0326) 290571** **OPEN: ALL YEAR** Nearest Road A.30 A warm welcome awaits visitors to High Massetts set in lovely gardens. The house is beautifully positioned and has lovely views over the cove. Accommodation is in four rooms, one en-suite. All have modern amenities and T.V. The cove itself offers safe bathing, fishing, skin-diving and boating. Mrs. Betty will do crab, lobster or steak suppers on request. Home grown fruit and vegetables, and fresh eggs are used here. Super cliff walks, tennis, golf and riding available locally.	£8.50	O	O	O
Mrs Peggy Peters **Gallen-Treath Guest House** **Porthallow** **St. Keverne** **Helston TR12 6PP** **Tel: (0326) 280400** **OPEN: JAN-NOV** Nearest Road B.3293 A warm, friendly welcome awaits you at Gallen-Treath. Bright and modern throughout, it is pleasantly situated with sea and country views, and only minutes from the beach. Accommodation is in seven rooms most with modern amenities. Lounge with colour T.V. and dining room. Children are especially welcome. Safe beaches, boating, cliff and coastal walks close by.	£8.50	O	O	O
Mrs Lindsay Pendray **Caduscott** **East Taphouse** **Liskeard PL14 4NG** **Tel: (0579) 20262** **OPEN: APRIL-SEPT** Nearest Roads A.390 A.38 Turn S. off A.390 An attractive traditional stone built Cornish farmhouse reputed to date back to the 17th century. Situated on a 500 acre working farm, the accommodation is comfortable offering 2 rooms. A large lounge/dining room with open log fire. Good farmhouse food is served.	£8.00	O	O	■
Mrs Carolyn Austin **The Mariners** **Church Cove** **The Lizard TR12 7PH** **Tel: (0326) 290988** **OPEN: APRIL-DEC** Nearest Road A.3083 The Mariners is a most attractive listed 17th century white washed thatched cottage, standing on the cliff overlooking the sea. Here Noel Coward wrote "Room with a View". Offering 2 delightful rooms with modern amenities, radio and tea/coffee making facilities. Evening meals are delicious with Cordon Bleu cooking, using fresh ingredients. Close by are marvellous cliff walks, and swimming in the cove below.	£12.00	O	O	O
Maureen & Dennis Childs **Fieldhead Hotel** **Portuan Road** **Hannafore** **West Looe PL13 2DR** **Tel: (05036) 2689** **OPEN: FEB-NOV** Nearest Roads M.5 A.30 A.38 A delightful hotel with a fine reputation; guests return year after year. Set in its own grounds with panoramic views of the sea, within 200 yards of the beach. Fourteen most attractive and comfortable rooms, thirteen with en-suite facilities. All have radio, T.V. and tea/coffee makers. An attractive residents lounge with super views. A games room, a heated outdoor pool and a lovely garden. The area is wonderful for all sports, riding, walking, fishing, sailing, golfing and the beaches are great. The Childs family make all visitors most welcome.	£16.00	O	O	■

O yes ■ no

42

		animals taken
	evening meals available	
children taken		
minimum per person		

	Nearest Road	minimum per person	children taken	evening meals available	animals taken
Mr & Mrs Michael Gilliat **Stallance** **The Crescent** **Hannafore** **West Looe, PL13 2DL** **Tel: (05036) 2363** **OPEN: ALL YEAR**	Nearest Road A.38 Stallance offers guests a friendly relaxed atmosphere and the personal attention of the proprietors. The house is located 100 yards from the sea and has superb south facing view to St. Georges Island. Offering 3 comfortable well furnished bedrooms with private bathroom, T.V. and tea/coffee making facilities. This is a perfect base for exploring the West country.	£12.00	O	■	■
Brian & Lynda Spring **Allhays Country House** **& Restaurant** **Talland Bay** **Looe PL13 2JB** **Tel: (0503) 72434** **OPEN: ALL YEAR**	Nearest Road A.387 Allhays Country House is set in delightful nature gardens and overlooks the beautiful Talland Bay. Guests have a choice of seven comfortable bedrooms, three with en-suite facilities. A comfortable dining room and spacious T.V. lounge are also available. This is an ideal base for touring the quaint fishing villages in the area. Horse riding, sailing, fishing, golf and tennis are close by.	£11.25	O	O	O
Colin & Margaret Blomeley **Harescombe Lodge** **Watergate** **Looe PL13 2NE** **Tel: (05036) 3158** **OPEN: ALL YEAR**	Nearest Road A.387 A delightful country cottage built in 1760. Formerly a shooting lodge, now completely modernised. It stands in its own charming gardens complete with waterfalls and stone bridges over the swiftly running trout stream. Offering four very pleasant bedrooms with bath or shower and toilet en-suite. Meals are excellent. Home grown/local produce when possible. Close by are fishing, golf and riding. Children over 12 years.	£8.25	O	O	O
Alexander Low **Coombe Farm** **Widegates** **Nr. Looe PL13 1QN** **Tel: (05034) 223** **OPEN: MAR-OCT**	Nearest Road B.3253 A lovely country house, beautifully furnished with antiques, set in 10 acres of lawns, meadows, woods, streams and ponds with superb views down a wooded valley to the sea. The atmosphere is delightful with open log fires, a candlelit dining room in which to enjoy delicious home cooking and an informal licensed bar. Two old barns have been converted for indoor games including snooker and table tennis. There is a croquet lawn, heated outdoor swimming pool and many birds and animals, including peacocks and horses. Nearby are golf, fishing, riding, tennis, beaches and glorious walks. Children over 5 years.	£15.00	O	O	O
Bettyann Baynes-Reid **The Slate House** **Bucklawren Farm** **St. Martin-by-Looe PL13 1NZ** **Tel: (05034) 481** **OPEN: MAR-OCT**	Nearest Road A.387 A mellow, old Cornish farmhouse, where guests are greeted by warm friendly hosts. Slate House has been carefully restored and offers visitors pleasant comfortable accommodation in a choice of 3 rooms. Facilities for golf, riding, fishing and tennis are nearby and a short drive will bring you to interesting old villages, coves and beauty spots.	£9.00	O	■	■

O yes ■ no

43

				minimum per person	children taken	evening meals available	animals taken

Mrs Diana Owens
Mevagissey House
Vicarage Hill
Mevagissey PL26 6SZ
Tel: (0726) 842427

OPEN: MAR-OCT
(PLUS XMAS)

Nearest Road A.390

Price shown is for two people. An elegant Georgian rectory standing in 4 acres of woodland, overlooking the beautiful woodland and valley to the harbour and sea beyond. Here guests can unwind and relax in pleasant comfortable surroundings. There is a choice of 6 rooms all with modern amenities, T.V. and tea/coffee making facilities. Snacks, morning coffee and Cornish cream teas are available on request. Evening meals are also served. Close by are fishing, beaches and golf courses.

£20.00 ○ ○ ■

Toyah Anne Richards
Goonhoskyn
Summer-Court
Newquay TR8 4PP
Tel: (087251) 226

OPEN: MAR-NOV

Nearest Road A.30

Goonhoskyn is a small working farm set in pleasant rural surroundings. Here guests will find comfortable accommodation and a quiet family atmosphere. Offering a choice of 3 rooms with T.V./radio. A T.V. lounge and delightful rose garden are also available. Good traditional Cornish cooking. An ideal base for touring. No children under 6 years please.

£7.50 ○ ○ ■

Trisha & Richard Hilder
Carnson House Hotel
East Terrace
Penzance TR18 2TD
Tel: (0736) 65589

OPEN: ALL YEAR

Nearest Road A.30

Carnson offers you a Cornish welcome and a friendly atmosphere. Eight modern and comfortable rooms all with heating and tea/coffee makers. Licensed with a pleasant lounge. Enjoying one of Penzance's most central positions close to railway and bus stations. A variety of coach, boat trips, car hire and bus tours are available all year round and can be arranged by the hotel. Add to this the international recommendations for food and it all adds up to make a happy and memorable visit.

£9.00 ○ ○ ■

Rosemary, John & Brenda
Knubley
Southern Comfort Hotel
Alexandra Terrace
The Seafront
Penzance TR18 4NX
Tel: (0736) 66333

OPEN: ALL YEAR

Nearest Road A.30

A very pleasant family run licensed hotel, offering a high standard of accommodation and excellent traditional cuisine in an informal friendly atmosphere. Twelve really comfortable and attractive rooms, six en-suite. Overlooking Mounts Bay, lovely sea views and only a few miles from Lands End.

£12.00 ○ ○ ■

○ yes ■ no

Don't be disappointed. Book ahead.
Use our fast efficient
RESERVATION SERVICE
Call us on
01-370 7099   01-370 7099

44

| --- | --- | --- | --- | --- | --- |
Mrs F.J. Wood **Lynwood Guest House** **41 Morrab Road** **Penzance TR18 4EX** **Tel: (0736) 65871** **OPEN: ALL YEAR**	Nearest Road A.30 A friendly relaxed atmosphere and a warm welcome await you at this Victorian house situated between promenade and town centre. Close to all amenities including sub-tropical Morrab Gardens. Offering six well decorated bedrooms all with modern facilities including tea/coffee makers. Comfortable colour T.V. lounge and large dining room. Own keys. Children welcome. A varied selection of restaurants within an easy walk. Ideal for visiting Lands End, Lizard, St. Michael's Mount and Isles of Scilly.	£8.50	O	■	O
Mr & Mrs David Green **Acton Vean** **Trevean Lane** **Rosudgeon** **Penzance TR20 9PT** **Tel: (0736) 762675** **OPEN: FEB-NOV**	Nearest Road A.394 On the edge of beyond, 6 miles from Penzance, Acton Vean is a gracious modern home of distinction on the southern coastal slope. It shares the unique privileged position of adjacent Acton Castle, with uninterrupted views over St. Michael's Mount and the bay, and access to the coastal footpath. Visitors welcomed and treated as houseguests. There are 2 comfortable sea-facing bedrooms, a barrel-ceiling sitting room and quiet, lovely gardens. Superb views, spectacular sunsets, lovely walks, together with a genuine welcome and excellent cuisine. Not suitable for children under 10.	£12.00	O	O	■
Mr & Mrs R. Jarratt **Kenython Country Guest House** **Kenython Lane** **St. Just** **Penzance TR19 7PT** **Tel: (0736) 788607** **OPEN: ALL YEAR**	Nearest Road B.3306 This attractive 90 year old modernised farmhouse stands in 3 secluded acres of ground on the Lands End Peninsula. The comfortable surroundings, friendly atmosphere and good food ensure a delightful stay. Accommodation is in 4 comfortable rooms, 2 with private facilities, all with modern amenities. Guests may also like to use the tennis court and the outdoor swimming pool. The home cooking is delicious and served with their own wine. The house is well located for visiting Penzance, Lands End, St. Ives and St. Michael's Mount. Superb views over countryside to Atlantic Ocean. Golf, riding and lovely beaches close by.	£9.00	O	O	O
Eddie & Mary Wood **Ednovean House** **Perranuthnoe** **Penzance TR20 9LZ** **Tel: (0736) 711071** **OPEN: ALL YEAR**	Nearest Road A.394 This really is a super place to stay - a 150 year old house offering 9 really delightful, comfortable rooms with modern facilities; most rooms have bath or shower en-suite. Situated in 1 acre of grounds and overlooking St. Michael's Mount and the entire bay. There is something for all ages here as Cornwall provides superb beaches and fine countryside. Plenty of sports available locally. Evening meals are excellent value. Vegetarian meals are available. No children under 7 please.	£13.75	O	O	O

O yes ■ no

45

	Nearest Road / Description	minimum per person	children taken	evening meals available	animals taken
Keith John Wooldridge **'Beach Dunes Hotel'** **Ramoth Way** **Reen Sands** **Perranporth TR6 0BY** **Tel: (0872) 572263** **OPEN: MAR-OCT**	Nearest Road Beach Dunes is a small friendly hotel pleasantly located next to Perranporth golf course, overlooking Perran Bay with its attractive 3 mile surfing beach. Offering 10 rooms, some en-suite, each with modern amenities, colour T.V. and tea/coffee making facilities. A well stocked bar and small dance floor. Guests may also enjoy use of the squash court, swimming pool and surf boards.	£11.50	O	O	O
Mr & Mrs K.G. Perkins **New House** **Talland Hill** **Polperro PL13 2RX** **Tel: (0503) 72206** **OPEN: ALL YEAR**	Nearest Road A.38 A delightful house with superb views overlooking Polperro harbour and out towards the Eddystone Light. Four charming and comfortable rooms, one with bath en-suite. All rooms have modern amenities. An attractive lounge with T.V. and a lovely garden for guests. Mr. & Mrs. Perkins make their visitors most welcome. This is a perfect base for exploring this beautiful area. Lovely beaches and walks, seafishing, sailing, golf tennis and riding. Many pretty villages.	£9.00	O	■	■
Ros & Tom Morey **Landaviddy Manor** **Landaviddy Lane** **Polperro PL13 2RT** **Tel: (0503) 72210** **OPEN: MAR-OCT**	Nearest Road Polperro/Looe This charming 200 year old manor house, built of traditional Cornish stone, stands in a peaceful and attractive setting next to the National Trust headlands. The house retains its former character while incorporating modern conveniences for guests' comfort. Accommodation is in 10 rooms, 4 with en-suite facilities, all with modern amenities and tea/coffee making facilities. The comfortable lounge with T.V. available and cosy bar, have delightful views over the garden towards Polperro and the bay. The food here is very good and freshly prepared each day.	£11.00	O	O	■
The Studley Family **Aviary Court** **Mary's Well** **Illogan** **Redruth** **Tel: (0209) 842256** **OPEN: ALL YEAR**	Nearest Road A.30 Aviary Court stands in 2½ acres of grounds on the edge of Illogan Woods. This charming 300 year old house offers guests a choice of six comfortable bedrooms, some with en-suite facilities, all have modern amenities; radio, colour T.V., tea/coffee making facilities and lovely views over the garden. The comfortable lounge has a bar and log fire for winter evenings. The restaurant serves delicious food and a selection of wine is available. Local amenities include golf, riding, walking, fishing.	£15.50	O	O	■

O yes ■ no

Please mention **BEST BED & BREAKFAST IN THE WORLD** *when booking your accommodation.*

	minimum per person	children taken	evening meals available	animals taken
Diana & Derek Mason "Kandahar" 11 The Warren St. Ives TR26 2EA Tel: (0736) 796183 **OPEN: ALL YEAR (EXCL. XMAS & NEW YEAR)** — Nearest Road A.3074. Kandahar has a most delightful and unique location, right on the water's edge with lovely views of the bay and harbour. The lounge, dining room and most of the bedrooms look directly out onto the harbour. 9 bedrooms are available all with modern amenities, some with T.V. and tea/coffee making facilities.	£9.00	○	■	○
Mrs A. Taylor Craigmeor Beach Road St. Ives TR26 1JY Tel: (0736) 796611 **OPEN: MAR-OCT** — Nearest Road A.30. An attractive 5 bedroom guest house for non-smokers, with uninterrupted views over Porthmeor Beach. All rooms have modern amenities, tea/coffee making facilities and are most comfortable and well decorated. A colour T.V. lounge with delightful views overlooking the sea. Close by are bowling and putting-greens and a level approach to shops and harbour. Good traditional English cooking and very good value. Vegetarian health food diets catered for. A very warm welcome is given by Mrs. Taylor to all her guests.	£10.00	○	■	○
John & Gillian Walkley Rosebud Cottage Bossiney Tintagel PL34 0AX Tel: (0840) 770861 **OPEN: ALL YEAR** — Nearest Roads A.39 B.3263. A picturesque stone Cornish cottage with secluded garden, within 10 minutes beautiful headland walk to Bossiney Cove which has a fine sandy beach and surfing. Four attractive comfortable rooms with modern facilities and tea/coffee makers. Good home cooking is the order of the day with vegetables from the garden. The evening meals are excellent value. The area has superb countryside for walking, fishing and riding and there are many ruined castles. Port Issac, Bodmin Moor and Boscastle are a short drive away.	£8.50	○	○	○
J.M. & C.A. Rayner The Old Borough House Bossiney Nr. Tintagel PL34 0AY Tel: (0840) 770475 **OPEN: ALL YEAR** — Nearest Road A.39. A delightful 17th century mellow stone house, formerly the home of J.B. Priestley. It is located between Tintagel and Boscastle in an area of outstanding natural beauty with National Trust property nearby. Offering 4 comfortable bedrooms with modern amenities and tea/coffee making facilities. The colour T.V. lounge and garden are also available for guests. Close by are safe bathing coves, caves and coastal walks.	£7.50	○	○	■
John Quinn & Bob Shenton The Driffold Hotel Devoran Lane Devoran Nr. Truro TR3 6PA Tel: (0872) 863314 **OPEN: ALL YEAR** — Nearest Road A.39. This small family run hotel is delightfully accommodated. Situated on the outskirts of Devoran village it overlooks Devoran Creek. If offers seven well decorated rooms with modern amenities. The cooking is of a high standard and special diets are catered for. Close by is boating, fishing, golf and scenic coastal walks. A good base for touring the Duchy of Cornwall. You can be assured of a relaxed stay here. Cots provided.	£11.00	○	○	■

○ yes ■ no

	minimum per person	children taken	evening meals available	animals taken
Mrs Bridget Dymond **Trevispian-Vean Farm House** **Trevispian-Vean** **St. Erme** **Truro TR4 9BL** **Tel: (0872) 79514** **OPEN: MAR-OCT** Nearest Road A.3076 A delightful farmhouse dating back over 300 years offering a very warm welcome and good accommodation in 7 pleasant, comfortable guest rooms. Situated only seven miles from the coast and surrounded by beautiful countryside it is a perfect base for everyone. Families will particularly enjoy it here as children can look around the farm and there are plenty of places to visit and things to do. There's even a donkey for the children.	£7.50	O	O	■
J.C. Gartner **Laniley House** **St. Clement** **Nr. Trispen** **Truro TR4 9AV** **Tel: (0872) 75201** **OPEN: ALL YEAR** **(EXCL. XMAS)** Nearest Road A.3076 Laniley House, formerly a gentleman's residence, was built in 1830. It stands in 2 acres of gardens amidst beautiful unspoilt country, yet only 3 miles from the Cathedral City of Truro. An ideal spot for a peaceful holiday discovering Cornwall. Accommodation consists of 3 airy double bedrooms furnished to a high standard, 1 with en-suite facilities. All with T.V. and tea/coffee making facilities. A large, extremely comfortable lounge with colour T.V. and a separate breakfast/dining room is provided. A relaxed comfortable stay is assured at Laniley House.	£12.50	■	O	■
Mrs Pat Walker **The Old Mill Country House** **Little Petherick** **Wadebridge PL27 7QT** **Tel: (0841) 540388** **OPEN: ALL YEAR** Nearest Road A.39 This delightful 16th century converted corn mill stands in its own attractive grounds with a stream meandering into the Camel Estuary. The lovely old mill offers guests a choice of 7 bedrooms with modern amenities. This makes a wonderful base for visiting the unspoilt villages, lovely beaches and beautiful countryside. Sailing, windsurfing and waterskiing available nearby.	£9.00	O	O	O

O yes ■ no

ADVANCE RESERVATIONS

Don't be disappointed. Book ahead.
Use our fast efficient

RESERVATION SERVICE

Be sure of your accommodation
Book Now!!
Call us on

01-3707099   *01-370 7099*

CUMBRIA

The Lake District National Park is deservedly famous as a tourist attraction. As well as the magnificent scenery of England's highest mountains, it has a wealth of tradition and history still alive today. There are village festivals that go back for generations and the traditional crafts and skills have not been lost. But there is more to Cumbria than the beautiful Lake District. It also has a splendid coastline, with a surprisingly mild climate and the advantage of accessibility from the main lakeland centres, as well as a fascinating border region where the Pennines, England's "backbone" reach their highest point, towering over the Eden Valley.

Central Lakeland

The dramatic lakeland scenery was formed in the far distant past. Earth movements in the Caledonian period raised and folded the already ancient rocks, then submerged the whole mass in seas, covering it with limestone. The massive glaciers of the ice age then carved out the lake beds and dales of today's landscape. There is tremendous variety in scenery from the craggy outcrops of the Borrowdale Volcanics, like Skiddaw at 3,054 feet, to the gentle dales and open moorlands and the lakes themselves. Each lake is distinctive; some with steep mountain slopes sliding straight to the water's edge and some more open with gently sloping wooded hillsides like Derwentwater or Ullswater, which inspired Wordsworth to write his famous poem "Daffodils" or Ellerwater, the enchanting "lake of the swans", surrounded by reeds and willows at the foot of Langdale. Some offer a range of water sports and others are deliberately left undisturbed so that peace and solitude can be easily found. The changeable weather of the highlands can produce sudden changes in the character of a lake from calm water mirroring the hills and light clouds above to a dark disturbed place where the wind raises choppy waves to skid across the surface and smash against the rocks along the shoreline. It is all part of the character of the region. Fell walking is perhaps the best way to appreciate the feel of the place. As well as the more gentle walks among the dales, it is possible in good weather to walk the tops of the ridges, an ideal way to experience the drama of the scenery. Pony trekking is another popular way to see the countryside and there are many centres, catering even for the inexperienced riders. Traditional crafts and skills are still carried on and there are craft centres at the Lakeland villages of Keswick, Ambleside and Grasmere. Once a year, the best of these crafts are brought together to create a superb exhibition, that of the Guild of Lakeland Craftsmen, held in Windermere from mid July to early September. There are numerous fairs and festivals held in the Lakes. The famous Appleby Horse Fair, held in June attracts a huge gypsy gathering and is the largest fair of its kind in the world. Gosforth holds a traditional agriculture show in August and there are numerous local sporting events such as the gruelling fell races. These can be watched in beautiful surroundings at the Grasmere Sports held every August. They also include Cumberland and Westmoreland wrestling, hound trials, pole leaping and many other events. Traditional customs such as "rush bearing" still survive as processions, originating from the old custom of strewing the church with rushes in the days when the floor was of beaten earth. These processions can be seen in Warcop, Ambleside, Grasmere, Urswick and many other villages during the summer months.

The Cumbrian Coast

The coast of Cumbria stretches from the estuaries of Grange over Sands and Barrow in Furness in the south, by way of the beautiful beaches between Bootle and Cardurnock, to the mouth of the Solway Firth. The fells behind Bootle contains a wealth of prehistoric cairns and stone circles, known as "Druids Circles" but undoubtedly predating the Druids. One of the largest and most impressive can be found at Swinside to the north east of Black Combe. Bootle itself has a mesolithic settlement and tradition says that Selker Bay hides the wrecks of Roman galleys sunk in a sea battle with the native Celts. The coastal areas, especially the estuaries are excellent for bird watching. The sand dunes north of the Esk are famous for their colony of black-headed gulls which can be visited with prior permission. At St Bees Head there is the largest colony of sea birds in Britain. Ravenglass is an attractive fishing village and the starting point for the narrow-gauge steam railway which climbs up to Eskdale in the heart of the fells, Muncaster Castle is not far north of Ravenglass and the beautiful grounds and thirteenth century castle are open all summer. Whitehaven port has an interesting history and architecture and at Harrington further up the coast a yachting centre and marina have been established in a restored harbour.

CUMBRIA GAZETEER

Area of outstanding natural beauty
National Park

Historic Houses and Castles

Carlisle Castle -- Carlisle
12th century. Massive Norman keep -- half-moon battery -- ramparts, portcullis and gatehouse.

Brough Castle -- Kirby Stephen
13th century -- on site of Roman Station between York and Carlisle.

Dacre Castle -- Penrith
14th century -- massive pele tower.

Sizergh Castle -- Kendal
14th century -- pele tower -- 15th century great hall. English and French furniture, silver and china -- Jacobean relics. 18th century gardens.

Belle Island -- Boweness-on-Windermere
18th century -- interior by Adams Brothers, portraits by Romney.

Swarthmoor Hall -- Ulverston
Elizabethan house, mullioned windows, oak staircase, panelled rooms. Home of George Fox -- birthplace of Quakerism -- belongs to Society of Friends.

Lorton Hall -- Cockermouth
15th century pele tower, priest·holes, oak panelling, Jacobean furniture.

Muncaster Castle -- Ravenglass
14th century with 15th and 19th century additions -- site of Roman tower.

Rusland Hall -- Ulveston
Georgian mansion with period panelling, sculpture, furniture, paintings.

Levens Hall -- Kendal
Elizabethan -- very fine panelling and plasterwork -- famous topiary garden.

Hill Top -- Sawtrey
17th century farmhouse, home of Beatrix Potter -- contains her furniture, china and some of original drawings for her children's books.

Dove Cottage -- Town End. Grasmere
William Wordsworth's cottage -- still contains his furnishing and his personal effects as in his lifetime.

Cathedrals and Churches

Carlisle Cathedral
1130. 15th century choir stalls with painted backs -- carved misericords 16th century screen, painted roof.

Cartmel Priory. (St. Mary Virgin)
15th century stalls, 17th century screen, large east window, curious central tower.

Lanercost Priory. (St. Mary Magdalene)
12th century -- Augustinian -- north aisle now forms Parish church.

Greystoke (St. Andrew)
14th/15th century. 19th century misericords. Lovely glass in chancel.

Brougham (St. Wilfred)
15th century carved altarpiece.

Furness Abbey
12th century monastery beautiful setting.

Shap Abbey.
12th century with 16th century tower.

Museums and Galleries

Abbot Hall -- Kendal
18th century, Georgian house with period furniture, procelain, silver, pictures, etc. Also contains modern galleries with contemporary paintings, sculptures and ceramics. Changing exhibitions on show.

Carlisle Museum and Art Gallery -- Carlisle
Archeological and natural history collections. National centre of studies of Roman Britian. Art galleryprincipally exhibiting paintings and porcelain.

Hawkshead Courthouse -- Kendal
Exhibition of domestic and working life housed in mediaeval building.

Helena Thompson Museum. Workington
Diplays Victorian family life and objects of the period.

Lakeland Motor Museum -- Holker Hall -- Grange-over-Sands
Exhibits cars, bicycles, tricycles, motor cycles etc. and model cars.

Millom Folk Museum -- St. George's Rd. Millom
Reconstructions of drift in iron ore mine, miner's cottage kitchen, blacksmith's forge and agriculturalrelics.

Ravenglass Railway Museum -- Ravenglass
History of railways -- relics, models, etc.

Wordsworth Museum -- Town End, Grasmere
Personal effects, first editions, manuscripts, and general exhibits from the time of William Wordsworth.

Border Regiment Museum -- The Castle. Carlisle
Collection of uniforms, weapons, trophies, documents, medals from 1702, to the present time.

Whitehaven Museum -- Whitehaven
History and development of area shown in geology, paleontology, archeology, natural history etc. Interesting maritime past.

Fitz Park Museum and Art Gallery -- Keswick
Collection of mauscripts -- Wordsworth, Walpole, Coleridge, Southey.

Historic Monuments

Arthur's Round Table -- Early Bronze age monument

Banks Burn Roman Wall -- fine stretch of Hadrian's Wall.

Gosforth Cross

Fine example of pre-Norman sculptured Stone Cross.

Hardknott Castle

Roman fort covering three acres, with bath block and parade ground.

Long Meg and Her Daughters

Tall block of red sandstone inscribed with concentric circles. Late Neolithic/Bronze age.

Pendragon Castle

Ruins and 12th Century -- Said to be home of father of King Arthur.

Furness Abbey

Ruins of 12th century Cistercian abbey.

Bewcastle Castle and Cross

Pre -- Norman sculpture -- Runic carvings.

CUMBRIA
Recommended roadside restaurants

073	A591	Staveley, Windermere, Westmorland 4 miles east of Windermere
160	A66	Appleby Westmorland 3 miles east of Appleby
191	A591	Ings, Cumbria 1½ miles east of Windermere
281	A595	Thursby, Cumbria 3 miles south of Carlisle
295	A590	Greystones Witherslack, Cumbria 3 miles west of Levens Bridge

Cumbria

minimum per person
children taken
evening meals taken
animals taken available

Mrs S. Harryman **Fell Foot Farm** **Little Langdale** **Ambleside LA22 9PE** **Tel: (09667) 294** **OPEN: APRIL-NOV**	Nearest Road A.598 Fell Foot Farm is a 200 year old farmhouse. It has oak beams and open fire places. It is also a National Trust property. Set on a 430 acre working beef farm, it offers accommodation in 3 rooms. Tea/coffee making facilities in all rooms. The cooking is plain but good and plentiful. The rates are for 2 people.	£16.00	○	○	■
Mr & Mrs P. Hart **Bracken Fell** **Outgate** **Ambleside LA22 0NH** **Tel: (09666) 289** **OPEN: ALL YEAR**	Nearest Road B.5286 Bracken Fell is situated in beautiful open countryside in the picturesque hamlet of Outgate. Located between Ambleside and Hawkshead this makes an ideal base for exploring the Lake District, Coniston, Windermere and Keswick. Accommodation in 5 comfortable rooms all with tea/coffee making facilities and outstanding views. There is also a comfortable lounge and dining room. All major outdoor activities are catered for nearby including sailing, fishing, windsurfing and pony trekking.	£9.00	○	■	■
Mrs N. Jex **Hare Hill Guest House** **Church Hill** **Arnside LA5 0DQ** **Tel: (0524) 761335** **OPEN: ALL YEAR**	Nearest Road A.6 M.6 A fine old house, built of local limestone with magnificent views of Lakeland hills and the estuary of the River Kent. A warm and friendly atmosphere welcomes guests, and children are very well catered for. Good home cooking with free tea, coffee and biscuits. Arnside is a beautiful seaside village with good shops. Many historic houses nearby. A touring base for both the Lakes and the Yorkshire Dales.	£10.00	○	○	○
Leslie & Joan Stewart **Hare & Hounds Inn** **Talkin Village** **Nr. Brampton CA8 1LE** **Tel: (06977) 3456 or 3457** **OPEN: ALL YEAR**	Nearest Roads M.6 A.69 A warm welcome and a happy cosy atmosphere are found at this 200 year old inn. It is situated in the picturesque village of Talkin in the heart of the beautiful Cumbrian Fells. Retaining all its former charm and character, this attractive inn boasts exposed beams, open hearths and log fires. Accommodation is in 4 rooms, all with private facilities and tea/coffee makers. There is also a T.V. lounge and games room. Excellent food and special "off the wood" brewed beer is served.	£12.50	○	○	■
Mrs Elizabeth Woodmass **Howard House Farm** **Gilsland** **Carlisle CA6 7AN** **Tel: (06972) 285** **OPEN: ALL YEAR**	Nearest Road A.69 Howard House is a 150 year old farmhouse situated on an elevated site overlooking Roman Wall country. 200 acre stock-rearing family run farm. A flock of Jacobs sheep is kept and their wool is spun on the farm. Visitors are assured of a warm welcome and friendly service in pleasant and comfortable surroundings. 2 rooms with modern amenities. Good home cooking. Private fishing.	£8.50	○	○	■

○ yes ■ no

	minimum per person	children taken	evening meals available	animals taken
Mrs P. Staff **'Holmhead' Guest House** **Hadrians Wall** **Greenhead** **Carlisle CA6 7HY** **Tel: (06972) 402** **OPEN: ALL YEAR** **(EXCL. XMAS & NEW YEAR)**	Nearest Roads A.69 B.6318 A traditional Northumberland farmhouse dating back 150 years, offering four really charming, comfortable rooms with modern amenities, plus a private lounge with T.V. Situated in 300 acres of ground with Hadrians Wall below the house, it offers excellent walking along the Pennine Way. The remains of a 14th century castle are very close. Many historic sites in the area, especially Roman. An ideal base, superb home cooking. Helicopter flights arranged from the house. Visits arranged to the Ancestral Research Centre. £12.00	O	O	■
Fred & Hazel Wilkinson **Riggs Cottage** **Routenbeck** **Bassenthwaite Lake** **Cockermouth CA13 9YN** **Tel: (059681) 580** **OPEN: MAR-NOV**	Nearest Road A.66 Riggs Cottage is a super 17th century house of great character and charm with many exposed oak beams, log burning inglenook fireplace and period furniture. The accommodation in 3 rooms, is comfortable and tastefully furnished with modern amenities. The cosy lounge is available throughout the day. In the nicely furnished dining room tasty home cooked meals are served using only the best ingredients. Oven fresh bread and home-made preserves are a speciality. This makes an ideal place to stay for a Lakeland holiday. £12.50	■	O	■
Brian & May Smith **Link House** **Bassenthwaite Lake** **Cockermouth CA13 9YD** **Tel: (059681) 291** **OPEN: APRIL-OCT**	Nearest Road A.66 Link House is a Victorian country house, situated at the head of Bassenthwaite Lake. There are superb views over the lake, forest and fell. Accommodation is in 7 rooms, 6 with en-suite facilities and T.V. In the evenings relax in the lounge in front of the log fire. £11.00	O	O	■
Angela & Martin Clark **Banerigg Guest House** **Lake Road** **Grasmere LA22 9PW** **Tel: (09665) 204** **OPEN: MAR-NOV**	Nearest Road A.591 Delightfully situated overlooking Grasmere Lake, is this small, friendly guest house. The informal hospitality and relaxing atmosphere make this a super base for a holiday. The accommodation is in a choice of six comfortable rooms all with modern amenities. There is a comfortable lounge with cosy log fire. Delicious, plentiful home cooking is served daily. The house is ideally located for fell walking, sailing, canoeing and fishing. Angela and Martin go out of their way to ensure that guests have a memorable Lakeland holiday. £11.25	O	O	O

O yes ■ no

		minimum per person	children taken	evening meals available	animals taken
N.K. & J.A. McGarr **Ivy House** **Cartmel** **Grange-over-Sands** **LA11 6HF** **Tel: (044854) 543** **OPEN: MAR-NOV**	Nearest Roads M.6 A.590 An attractive period house standing in its own grounds on the outskirts of this ancient village with its 12th century priory church. Six delightful rooms, all with private bath, T.V. and tea/coffee makers. There is one charming suite, formerly the music room, which has an ornate ceiling. A large comfortable lounge with open fire and pleasant gardens. This is a fine base from which to explore the Lake District. A warm welcome, good food and personal attention await all. No single occupancy.	£19.25	○	○	■
Mrs Elizabeth Watson **"Lightwood Farm"** **Cartmel Fell** **Grange-O-Sands LA11 6NP** **Tel: (0448) 31454** **OPEN: ALL YEAR**	Nearest Road A.590 A friendly relaxed atmosphere is found in this delightful 17th century renovated farmhouse. Offering very comfortable accommodation in a choice of 4 rooms. Each is individually decorated with pitch pine furniture, patchwork quilts and tea/coffoo making facilities. A colour T.V. lounge and large garden with patio, charming rockpool and waterfall. An ideal base for a Lakes holiday.	£9.00	○	○	○
Mrs K. Bell **Oxenholme Farm** **Oxenholme Road** **Kendal LA9 7HG** **Tel: (0539) 27226** **OPEN: ALL YEAR**	Nearest Road A.65 Guests to Oxenholme are warmly greeted and on arrival receive a cup of tea and home-made biscuits. This is a delightful 16th century farmhouse carefully renovated to retain all its character and charm, including many oak beams and inglenook fireplace. Accommodation is in 3 comfortable rooms with modern amenities. The colour T.V. lounge may be used throughout the day and tea/coffee making facilities are always available. This makes a good base for touring the area. Mrs. Bell will do her very best to ensure you have an enjoyable stay.	£7.50	○	■	■
Mrs M. Beresford **Wattsfield Farm House** **Wattsfield Lane** **(Off Wattsfield Rd)** **Kendal** **Tel: (0539) 27767** **OPEN: ALL YEAR**	Nearest Road A.6 A delightful 17th century house standing on the banks of the River Kent. The Beresford family have carefully restored the house, retaining all its "olde worlde" charm and character. There is a choice of 3 comfortable bedrooms with modern amenities, radio, T.V. and tea/coffee making facilities. Guests will enjoy the peaceful atmosphere and beautiful country surroundings.	£9.00	○	■	○

○ yes ■ no

		minimum per person	children taken	evening meals available	animals taken
Mr & Mrs A.R. Aitken **High Hundhowe Country** **Guest House** **Burneside** **Kendal LA8 9AB** **Tel: (0539) 22707** **OPEN: FEB-NOV**	Nearest Roads M.6 A.591 High Hundhowe is a small manor house built in the early 17th century. Overlooking the River Kent, amidst seven acres of pasture-land and gardens. The house is secluded, yet only 4 miles from the market town of Kendal and 5 miles from Windermere. Mr. & Mrs. Aitken offer five comfortable and attractive rooms all with modern amenities including colour T.V. and tea/coffee making facilities. A charming residents' lounge with log fire and full size billiard/snooker table. Ponies.	£12.00	○	○	■
Mrs S. Beaty **Garnett House Farm** **Burneside** **Kendal LA9 5SF** **Tel: (0539) 24542** **OPEN: ALL YEAR**	Nearest Road A.591 A 15th century farmhouse situated in 270 acres, only half a mile from the Kendal-Windermere road. Five delightful comfortable rooms with modern amenities and tea makers. All rooms have wonderful views towards Howgil Fells and Potter Fell. 16th century oak panelling, old beams, log fires. Wonderful five course evening meals, excellent value. Mr. & Mrs. Beaty provide a relaxed and comfortable atmosphere. The area provides many historic houses such as Levens Hall, Leighton Hall and Holker Hall.	£8.00	○	○	■
Michael & Irene Scales **"Greenbank Farmhouse"** **Chapel Lane** **Crook** **Nr. Kendal LA8 9HR** **Tel: (0539) 821216** **OPEN: FEB-NOV**	Nearest Road A.591 A small farmhouse looking down Lyth Valley, 3 miles from Kendal, Bowness and Windermere. 5 most comfortable rooms with modern amenities. The small restaurant is open to non-residents and the home cooked meals are fresh and interesting, with a change of menu each night and a wide selection of wines to compliment the food. Delightful base for touring. Children over 12 accepted.	£10.75	■	○	○
A. Wightman **The Glen** **Oxenholme** **Kendal LA9 7RF** **Tel: (0539) 26386** **OPEN: APRIL-OCT**	Nearest Roads A.65 M.6 A large modernised house set in its own grounds. The accommodation is in double and twin bedrooms with modern amenities. Close to Windermere, there are plenty of walks round about. Within easy reach are castles, historic houses and museums. Children over 12 years. Rooms not let for single occupation.	£9.00	■	○	■
Eileen Cornall & Jim Garnett **Low Jock Scar** **Selside** **Nr. Kendal LA8 9LE** **Tel: (053983) 259** **OPEN: ALL YEAR**	Nearest Road A.6 Low Jock Scar is set in a wonderfully secluded, peaceful riverside location. The house is delightful. Built with the local mellow-coloured stone, it is cosy and attractive. Offering three pleasant bedrooms all with countryside views. Each has modern amenities and tea/coffee making facilities. There is also a comfortable colour T.V. lounge, and guests may like to use the garden or walk by the river to which Eileen and Jim have private fishing rights. The house stands within the Lake District National Park.	£10.00	○	○	○

○ yes ■ no

		minimum per person	children taken	evening meals available	animals taken
Mrs Eileen Head **Thorny Bank House** **Skelsmergh** **Kendal LA8 9AW** **Tel: (0539) 83671** **OPEN: ALL YEAR**	Nearest Road A.6 Thorny Bank House is a large Victorian home set in an acre of well tended garden. The house is located in the beautiful Cumbrian countryside about 3 miles out of Kendal. Accommodation is in four pleasant bedrooms all with modern amenities, radio and tea/coffee making facilities. A comfortable colour T.V. lounge is also provided for guests'use. Children are most welcome at Thorny Bank House. Cots, highchairs and a baby listening service are available. This makes a most pleasant base for touring	£8.50	O	■	■
Fred Crozier **Red Hills** **Skelsmergh** **Kendal LA9 6NX** **Tel: (0539) 20885** **OPEN: ALL YEAR**	Nearest Road A.6 A relaxed and homely atmosphere awaits you in this attractive late Victorian home. Conveniently located only 9 miles from Lake Windermere, with lovely views across How Gill Fells and the Lakeland Hills. This is an ideal base for touring. Accommodation is in a choice of 3 rooms with modern amenities. A comfortably furnished colour T.V. lounge is also available. Tea/coffee are available when requested. No single occupancy	£10.00	■	O	O
James & Wendy Adamson **Thornleigh Guest House** **23 Bank Street** **Keswick CA12 5JZ** **Tel: (0596) 72863** **OPEN: ALL YEAR**	Nearest Road A.591 Thornleigh is a traditional Lakeland stone house with a happy blend of antique and modern furnishings. 7 charming bedrooms tastefully furnished and decorated with modern facilities and tea/coffee makers. A nice lounge with colour T.V. for guests use. Evening meal served at 7pm - last orders 5.30, £6.00 per head. Ideally situated for walking or touring. Thornleigh is conveniently located near the centre of Keswick with views of Skiddaw, Catbells, Latrigg, Borrowdale and Newlands Valley. A warm welcome	£9.50	■	O	■
Mr & Mrs W. Eyre **Sunnyside Guest House** **25 Southey Street** **Keswick CA12 4EF** **Tel: (0596) 72446** **OPEN: ALL YEAR** **(EXCL. NOV)**	Nearest Road A.591 Sunnyside is a comfortable friendly guest house located in a quiet residential street close to the town centre. Offering a choice of 8 bedrooms each with modern amenities, colour T.V. and tea/coffee making facilities. This makes a good base from which to tour the beautiful Lake District. Packed lunches can be provided, at a small additional charge.	£9.00	O	■	O
Mrs H. Mackerness **Claremont House** **Chestnut Hill** **Keswick CA12 4LT** **Tel: (07687) 72089** **OPEN: ALL YEAR**	Nearest Roads A.591 A.66 Situated in ¾ acre of woodland and gardens with superb views of the surrounding mountains and lakes. This well maintained 150 year old house has a friendly and homely atmosphere. The accommodation is comfortable; 4 bedrooms with modern amenities. Guests' bathroom and colour T.V. lounge. Good food; specialities are home produced soups, desserts and local fish. Vegetarians are catered for. Evening meals are a delight and should not be missed.	£11.00	O	O	O

O yes ■ no

		minimum per person	children taken	evening meals available	animals taken
Mrs M. Peat **Albany House** **38 Lake Road** **Keswick-on-Derwentwater** **CA12 5DQ** **Tel: (0596) 73105** **OPEN: ALL YEAR**	Nearest Road A.66 Pleasantly situated between Lake Derwentwater and the town centre, both only 3 minutes walk away. Mrs. Peat has 8 comfortable rooms with modern amenities including tea/coffee makers. Many rooms have lovely views of the mountains. An excellent lounge with colour T.V. Albany House is well known for its excellent cooking and evening meals are very good value. An ideal centre for walking, climbing or touring. Fishing, sailing, pony trekking can be arranged locally. A warm homely atmosphere.	£9.50	O	O	O
Jimmy & Jackie Dunn **Swinside Inn** **Newlands Valley** **Keswick CA12 5UE** **Tel: (059682) 253** **OPEN: ALL YEAR**	Nearest Road A.66 A charming inn dating back to the 16th century, offering a very warm welcome and 9 very comfortable rooms with modern facilities. Excellent bar meals with extensive choice. Free coffee/tea in residents' lounge. The inn is about 15 minutes walk from Lake Derwentwater in a beautiful valley. Ideal as a base for visitors touring this lovely region.	£11.50	O	O	O
Mrs J. Davis **The Mount** **Portinscale** **Keswick CA12 5RD** **Tel: (0596) 73070** **OPEN: MAR-NOV**	Nearest Road A.66 A large Victorian semi-detached house, tastefully decorated and maintaining original features, providing a friendly home-from-home atmosphere. Offering 4 bedrooms, 2 with private showers and w.c., all with tea/coffee making facilities. Lovely views over Lake Derwentwater. Good walking around Keswick and Portinscale, as well as boating, fishing, windsurfing and riding.	£10.50	O	O	O
Mrs Sheila Smith **Highgate Farm** **Penrith CA11 0SE** **Tel: (08533) 339** **OPEN: MAR-NOV**	Nearest Road A.66 A lovely stone built farmhouse dating back to 1730, offering a warm welcome, personal attention and good home cooking. Tastefully decorated with old beams and brasses, the 5 comfortable rooms have all modern amenities. An ideal base for fell-walking, riding, swimming and driving with Lake Ulswater just 4 miles away. No children under 10.	£10.00	O	O	■
Mrs Carole Tully **Brandelhow Guest House** **1 Portland Place** **Penrith CA11 7QN** **Tel: (0768) 64470** **OPEN: ALL YEAR**	Nearest Roads M.6 A.6 A very pleasant Victorian terraced house offering the warmest of welcomes and high standards of accommodation. Five tastefully decorated, bright and comfortable rooms, with modern amenities and tea/coffee makers. Evening meals very good value. This is an ideal base for visitors to discover this interesting region. A short drive takes you to unspoilt countryside with tiny bridges over streams. All the usual outdoor sporting activities locally. Mrs. Tully makes all her guests most welcome.	£9.00	O	O	O

O yes ■ no

		minimum per person	children taken	evening meals available	animals taken
Lesley & David White **Beckfoot Country** **Guest House** **Helton** **Nr. Penrith CA10 2QB** **Tel: (09313) 241** **OPEN: MAR-NOV**	Nearest Roads M.6 A.66 A fine old residence featuring a half-panelled hall and staircase, as well as an attractive panelled dining room. Set in 3 acres of grounds in the delightful Lake District, it is a quiet and peaceful retreat for a holiday base. It is also within easy reach of the many pleasure spots in the area. Offering 7 rooms, all with private shower/bathroom, and tea/coffee making facilities. A dining room, drawing and reading room. This is a delightful base for a touring holiday.	£13.50	○	○	○
Mrs C.A. Weightman **Near Howe** **Mungrisdale** **Penrith CA11 0SH** **Tel: (059683) 678** **OPEN: MAR-NOV**	Nearest Road A.66 A comfortable farmhouse set on a 360 acre farm. Accommodation is in 7 rooms; 3 doubles, 1 twin, all with modern amenities. There is also a games room for guests' use. Good farmhouse food is served. There is also a residential license. Central for all the lakes and Keswick is within easy reach.	£8.00	○	○	○
Joe & Val Varley **Cross Keys Hotel** **Cautley Road** **Sedbergh LA10 5NE** **Tel: (0587) 20284** **OPEN: APRIL-DEC**	Nearest Road M.6 Exit 37 A.683 Cross Keys is a 400 year old inn, now owned by the National Trust and run by Mr. & Mrs. Varley. The house has many of its original features including exposed beams, flag stone floors, open log fires, very low ceilings and a flying staircase. Accommodation is in 4 very pretty rooms, all with modern amenities. A comfortable lounge with period furnishings is also available. The hotel is conveniently placed for visiting lakes, dales and many ancient villages. Fell-walking, bird watching and fishing are also close by. Unlicensed, but guests are welcome to bring their own wine or spirits.	£13.00	○	○	■
Neville & Mavis Fowles **Rockside** **Ambleside Road** **Windermere LA23 1AQ** **Tel: (09662) 5343** **OPEN: ALL YEAR**	Nearest Road A.591 Every season in the Lake District has its own beauty, and Rockside offers warm hospitality to guests at all times of the year. 15 comfortable rooms with modern amenities. Tea/coffee always available. A pleasant lounge and a bar lounge both with colour T.V. Situated in the centre of the town. Neville and Mavis Fowles will help guests by planning routes by car, walks or climbs.	£9.00	○	■	■
Barry & Kitty Everett **The Royal Oak Hotel** **West Street** **Wigton CA7 9NP** **Tel: (0965) 42393** **OPEN: ALL YEAR**	Nearest Road A.596 The Royal Oak is an attractive 17th century coaching inn with its original cobbled courtyard. Located in the centre of this attractive market town of Wigton. It offers comfortable accommodation in 11 rooms with modern amenities, radio, T.V. & tea/coffee making facilities. This is an ideal base from which to explore the Solway Plain with its many interesting little villages and hamlets.	£9.50	○	○	○

○ yes ■ no

Mr & Mrs Hatley
South View
Cross Street
Windermere LA23 1AE
Tel: (09662) 2951

OPEN: FEB-NOV

Nearest Road A.591

A friendly welcome and a relaxed atmosphere is found at South View. This Victorian house offers six rooms with modern amenities and tea/coffee makers. A colour T.V. lounge is also available for guests' use. Guests are free to come and go as they please. Breakfast is cooked to order and evening meals are very good value. The house is quietly situated but handy for shops, transport and countryside walks.

£9.00 — ○ ○ ○

Mrs E.M. Graham
Brendan Chase Guest House
1 College Road
Windermere LA23 1BU
Tel: (09662) 5638

OPEN: ALL YEAR

Nearest Road A.591

A comfortable friendly family guest house, where visitors are made to feel at home. Located in the heart of the picturesque town of Windermere, it is close to all local amenities, as well as making an ideal base from which to tour the area. Accommodation is in a choice of nine rooms, some with private facilities, all with modern amenities. Tea/coffee are also available. There is also a residents lounge with colour T.V. Close by is riding, walking and sailing.

£9.50 — ○ ■ ○

David & Evelyne Limbrey
Glenburn
New Road
Windermere LA23 2EE
Tel: (09662) 2649

OPEN: ALL YEAR

Nearest Road A.591

Glenburn is a very attractive family run, 11 bedroom guest house, where every guest is assured of personal attention. The lounge is comfortable with open fireplace and T.V., just right for pre-dinner drinks. The bedrooms are tastefully decorated and well furnished. Some have bathroom en-suite and colour T.V. Located midway between the lake and Windermere, this is the perfect base for exploring the beautiful Lakeland.

£11.50 — ○ ○ ○

Sheila & Trevor Holmes
Boston House
The Terrace
Windermere LA23 1AJ
Tel: (09662) 3654

OPEN: MAR-NOV

Nearest Road A.591

A very attractive stone built Victorian house, set on the edge of Windermere. The accommodation is spacious and comfortable. 6 bedrooms, 2 with private shower, all with tea making facilities. A lounge with colour T.V. and dining room. The evening meal is very good value and the hospitality warm and relaxing.

£8.50 — ○ ○ ○

Irene & George Eastwood
Hilton House Hotel
New Road
Windermere LA23 2EE
Tel: (09662) 3934

OPEN: ALL YEAR

Nearest Roads M.6 A.591

Everything here is under the personal supervision of the Eastwoods. Situated between Windermere and Bowness, this Edwardian residence offers several rooms, all with modern amenities. Tea/coffee making facilities are available. There's an elegant colour T.V. lounge and excellent home cooking is a speciality here. It is licensed. Sailing, golf and walking are easily available, as is the entire Lake District. Cots provided.

£12.50 — ○ ○ ○

	minimum per person	children taken	evening meals available	animals taken
Robert & Barbara Tyson **Hawksmoor Guest House** **Lake Road** **Windermere LA23 2EQ** **Tel: (09662) 2110** **OPEN: FEB-NOV** Nearest Road A.591 Hawksmoor is situated halfway between the centres of Windermere and Bowness, just 10 minutes walk from the lake. Standing in lovely grounds, this creeper-clad house has ten charming rooms with modern facilities, all with garden views. Some with en-suite facilities and 4-poster beds, some strictly no smoking. A most comfortable residents' lounge with colour T.V., and garden for guests' enjoyment. The house has a residential license. A variety of maps and books with information on fell-walking and mountaineering.	£17.00	○	○	■
Mr & Mrs H.L. Wilde **and Family** **Ravensworth Hotel** **Ambleside Road** **Windermere LA23 1BA** **Tel: (09662) 3747** **OPEN: ALL YEAR** Nearest Roads M.6 Exit 36 A.591 A lovely stone built house dating back 120 years, with glorious views. Thirteen very comfortable rooms, all en-suite and full central heating, with radio, T.V., and tea/coffee making facilities. Candlelit dinners are on offer with an interesting variety of menus, generous portions and, special diets catered for, particularly vegetarians. A walker's paradise, but a car or local transport gives rapid access to all parts of the Lake District, particularly the less frequented Furness Fells.	£15.50	○	○	○
Milton Stills **Denehurst** **Queen's Drive** **Windermere LA23 3EL** **Tel: (09662) 4710** **OPEN: ALL YEAR** Nearest Roads M.6 A.591 Personal service and friendly hosts are found at Denehurst. Located within walking distance of the lake and village, this makes a pleasant base from which to discover beautiful Windermere. Offering 6 bedrooms, each with modern amenities, including radio, T.V. and tea/coffee making facilities. Nearby are pony trekking and the Windermere 18-hole golf course.	£9.00	○	○	○
Mr & Mrs G.S. Hilton **The Archway Guest House** **13 College Road** **Windermere LA23 1BY** **Tel: (09662) 5613** **OPEN: ALL YEAR** Nearest Road A.591 A traditional Lakeland stone built house. Situated in a quiet location with magnificent open mountain views, yet close to Windermere village centre and all transport and amenities. There are six well furnished bedrooms, all with modern amenities, a comfortable lounge with colour T.V., games room, and a dining room serving full English breakfast. Family run to a high standard. Excellent home cooking.	£8.50	○	○	○

○ yes ■ no

Why not use our fast efficient
RESERVATION SERVICE
to book all your accommodation.

		minimum per person	children taken	evening meals available	animals taken
Jim & Jan Bebbington **2 Holly Cottages** **Rayrigg Road** **Bowness-on-Windermere** **Tel: 09662) 4250** **OPEN: FEB-NOV**	Nearest Road Quietly situated in the lovely area of Bowness-on-Windermere, Holly Cottages have seven comfortable rooms, three with bath or shower en-suite. All rooms have modern amenities. A pleasant lounge with colour T.V. and a garden for guests. Mr. & Mrs. Bebbington cater for all types of diets and also offer packed lunches. This is a good base from which to discover the delights of the Lake District. A warm welcome awaits all guests.	£10.00	O	■	O
M.W. & C.A. Houghton **Birket Houses** **Winster** **Nr. Windermere LA23 3NU** **Tel: (09662) 3438** **OPEN: ALL YEAR**	Nearest Road A.5074 Set in 20 acres of beautifully tended grounds including woodlands, meadow, formal gardens, delightful rose garden, croquet lawn and topiary gardens, overlooked by the balustraded terraces of this Jacobean styled house. Traditional grace and elegance are emphasised in the decor with oak panelled walls, plaster relief ceilings, solid oak doors and open fireplace. Accommodation is in 5 very comfortable rooms some with private facilities and 4-poster beds. Good food is served in the delightful dining room. Candlelit dinners can be arranged. Close by are the lakes, fishing, watersports, riding, golf and tennis.	£30.00	O	O	■
Mrs Jones **Milton House Barn** **Milton** **Crooklands** **Nr. Milnthorpe LA7 7NL** **Tel: (04487) 628** **OPEN: ALL YEAR**	Nearest Roads A.65 M.6 Milton House Barn is a converted 18th century Westmorland barn located in the small village of Milton. Offering accommodation in three rooms, 2 doubles and a single with private shower/bath. A colour T.V. lounge is also available. This makes an ideal base for a Lakeland/Dales vacation or as a stop-over for those travelling to or from Scotland. Children over 10 years. A car is essential.	£7.00	O	O	■

O yes ■ no

All the establishments in this book
are members of the
WORLDWIDE BED & BREAKFAST
ASSOCIATION

DERBYSHIRE

A county with everything but the sea - this was the opinion of Lord Byron when he visited this fine countryside and who will disagree with him! It is the most lovely of our counties with a wide diversity of landscapes ranging from the high peaks of the Pennine Range of mountains to the deep valleys of the Dales. The Peak District is England's first National Park, noted for its outstanding beauty, and it offers spectacular climbing for the adventurous or wonderful hill walking for the less ambitious. With great craggy limestone outcrops, fast flowing rivers, wooded hills, steeply dropping down to the lush sheltered lowlands; here is unrivalled grandeur. Green hills and moorlands purple with blooming heather, great gorges with tumbling waters, meadows golden with buttercups, white limestone plateaux, and every-where dry stone walls enclosing the land.

Up on the Stanton Moor stand the Nine Ladies, a circle of standing stones which have been there since the Bronze Age and probably before that. There is at Birchover a remarkable museum which exhibits the excavations carried out in the area by the family who own the museum. Iron Age forts can still be seen - possibly they were built in order to hold back the Romans who were constantly pushing northwards, making their straight roads as they went (or were they just widening and surfacing existing tracks?). One of these roads led them to Buxton high in the hills where they enjoyed the warm springs - had they any idea of the popularity that Buxton was to enjoy and still does - witness its elegant crescent and opera house. The waters at Matlock were prized for their curative properties and in the last century an onormous Hydro was erected to give treatments to the hundreds of people who went there. Matlock stands at the gateway to the dales, and the River Derwent cuts through the limestone cliffs to make a great gorge. On one side of the river there is the High Tor which presents a constant challenge to rock-climbers. Looking up from the road they can be seen picking their way across the rock face, roped together, so high up that they look like flies on the window-pane. Across the other side are the Heights of Abraham where the huge Rutland and Masson Caverns are open to inspection. These caves were discovered during lead mining activities and are now opened up to show the enormous chambers and pillars and make a very interesting tour, especially for the student of geology. On the surface it is a gentle climb up to the top, through beech woods gloriously gold and green, and at the summit the Victoria Prospect Tower gives an excellent vantage point to view the breathtaking panorama of the hills and dales of Derbyshire and counties beyond.

Well Dressing is a custom still carried on throughout the summer in the villages and towns; one of the best being at Bakewell in the Wye Valley. It is a thanksgiving for the water and probably dates from pre-Christian days. Flower petals of every colour, leaves, moss, bark etc are gathered together in great quantities and pressed on to frames of wet clay - quite lovely effects are obtained and some of the pictures are very intricate. The frames are erected over the well and left for as long as a week staying fresh and colourful, proving a great attraction to the thousands of tourists who come to admire them. At Bakewell you can try the traditional "Bakewell Pudding" which originated there - although in other parts of the country it is described as a "tart". Try some, you will be pleasantly surprised.

The Dales

These are as lovely as their names - Dove Dale, Monk's Dale, Miller's Dale, Ravens Dale, Water-cum-Jolly Dale and many more. Each has its own particular beauty - some broad green lush valleys, wide open to the skies; others having steep hillsides, thickly wooded, with great crags of rock and appearing to be quite secret; but all having something special about them and have a loveliness unsurpassed. There are charming villages scattered throughout the Dales and in each of them, you'll find a nice old pub where you find rest and refreshment in the company of friendly people.

Architecture

The mining of lead and the prosperity of the farms brought great wealth to the landowning families who were able to employ the finest of architects and craftsmen to build and decorate their great houses. Through the centuries they collected art in all its forms and have left sumptuous collections behind them as their part in the heritage of England. These great houses and castles are, for the most part, open to the public for tours and inspection.

DERBYSHIRE GAZETEER

Areas of Outstanding Natural Beauty.
Peak National Park. The Dales.

Historic Houses and Castles

Chastsworth -- Bakewell
 17th Century, built for 1st. Duke of Devonshire. Furniture, paintings and drawings, books, etc. Fine Gardens and Parklands.

Haddon Hall -- Bakewell
 Mediaeval Manor House -- complete. Terraced rose gardens.

Hardwick Hall -- Nr. Chesterfield
 16th century -- said to be ore glass than wall. Fine furniture, tapestries and furnishings. Herb Garden.

Kedleston Hall -- Derby
 18th century -- built on site of 12th century manor house. Work of Robert Adam -- has world famous marble Hall. Old Master paintings. 11th century church nearby.

Melbourne Hall -- Nr. Derby
 12th century origins -- restored by Sir John Coke. Fine collection of Pictures and works of art. Magnificient gardens and famous wrought iron pergola.

Sudbury Hall -- Sudbury
 17th century -- has examples of work of greatest craftsmen of the day, such as Grinling Gibbons, Pierceand Laguerre.

Winster Market House -- Nr. Matlock
 17th century stone built market house.

Cathedrals and Churches

Chesterfield (St. Mary and All Saints)
 13th and 14th centuries. 4 chapels, polygonal apse, Mediaeval screens, Jacobean pulpit.

Derby (All Saints)
 Perpendicular tower -- classical style -- 17th century plate, 18th century screen.

Melbourne (St. Micheal and St. Mary)
 Norman with two West Towers and crossing tower. Splendid plate, 18th century screen.

Normbury (St. Mary and St. Barloke)
 14th century chancel -- original glass -- splendid windows, 2 Saxon cross shafts.

Tideswell (St. John the Baptist)
 14th century -- perpendicular tower. Wood carving and brasses.

Wirksworth (St. Mary)
 13th century, restored and enlarged. Norman font and 17th century font. Brasses, mediaeval sculpture -- 9th century coffin lid.

Museums and Galleries

Buxton Museum -- Buxton
 Local history, geology and mineralogy, including famous Blue John. Animal remains from Pleistocene period onwards.

Old House Museum -- Bakewell
 Early Tudor House with interior walls exposed to show wattle and daub, open-timber chamber. Kitchen implements, craftmen's tools, costumes.

Lecture Hall -- Chesterfield
 Exhibitions of photography, art, etc.

Museums and Art Gallery -- Derby
 Archeology, geology, local and natural history, model rail layout.

Industrial Museum -- Derby
 Rolls-Royce collection of historic aero-engines.

Regimental Museum -- Derby
 9th/12 Lancers.

STAFFS/DERBYSHIRE
Recommended roadside restaurants

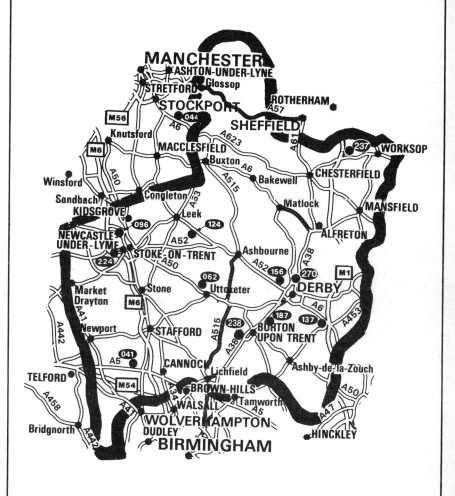

Derbyshire & Staffordshire

	minimum per person	children taken	evening meals available	animals taken
Mrs Barbara Challinor **The Old Orchard** **Stoney Lane** **Thorpe** **Nr. Ashbourne DE6 2AW** **Tel: (033529) 410** **OPEN: MAR-NOV** Nearest Road A.515 A relaxed and friendly atmosphere is found at The Old Orchard. A modern, split level bungalow, quietly situated in the Peak District National Park, in the heart of the Derbyshire Dales. The accommodation in 4 rooms is comfortable. Lots of walks, trails, bicycle routes and horse riding close by. An ideal centre for visiting stately homes; Chatsworth, Haddon Hall, Alton Towers, Matlock Bath, Cable Chair etc.	£9.00	O	■	O
Chris & Susan Harman **Cliffe House** **Monsal Head** **Nr. Bakewell DE4 1NL** **Tel: (062987) 376** **OPEN: ALL YEAR** Nearest Roads A.6 B.6465 Beautifully situated in the heart of the Peak District at the top of Monsal Dale. Cliffe House has seven pleasant and comfortable rooms with modern amenities and tea/coffee makers. Wonderful views from bedrooms. A large colour T.V. lounge. Centrally heated. A garden for guests. Excellent value evening meals - traditional home cooking. A walkers' paradise. Touring by car is wonderful with Bakewell, Buxton and the whole of the Peak District to explore.	£10.00	O	O	■
Philip & Phyllis Mathews **Shottle Hall Farm** ** Guest House** **Shottle** **Belper DE5 2EB** **Tel: (077389) 276 or 203** **OPEN: ALL YEAR** Nearest Roads A.517 B.5023 Shottle Hall Farm is set in the picturesque Ecclesbourne Valley on a 340 acre dairy farm. The homely welcome and personal attention will make your stay memorable. Accommodation is in 9 rooms with modern amenities. There's also a 2 acre garden for guests' use. Ideally situated for touring Derbyshire countryside and for visiting many of the famous houses.	£16.00	O	O	O
Derek & Norma Stephens **Westminster Hotel** **21 Broad Walk** **Buxton SK17 6JR** **Tel: (0298) 3929** **OPEN: FEB-NOV** **(PLUS XMAS)** Nearest Roads A.6 A.515 A lovely Victorian house set near a large park with a lake. Offering excellent accommodation in twelve rooms with modern facilities, plus tea making facilities. Buxton is a lovely spa town with much to discover. Plenty of superb walking and Stately Homes in the county. Child rates apply up to 14 and cots are provided.	£16.00	O	O	■
Mrs P.A. Green **Thorn Heyes Private Hotel** **137 London Road** **Buxton SK17 9NW** **Tel: (0298) 3539** **OPEN: ALL YEAR** Nearest Road A.515 A warm welcome awaits the guests in this pleasant Victorian house, which offers 8 rooms. All have tea makers and electric blankets. 7 rooms en-suite with shower/w.c. Colour T.V. and full central heating. Guided walks can be arranged for those who prefer to get away from the usual tourist trails. Extensive local knowledge is available to help visitors gain maximum enjoyment from their stay. Cooking is of high standard with daily menu changes. Home-made bread, pate and soup a speciality.	£14.50	O	O	O

O yes ■ no

	Nearest Road	minimum per person	children taken	evening meals available	animals taken
Mr & Mrs D.J.S. Smith **Hawthorn Farm** **Guest House** **Fairfield Road** **Buxton SK17 7ED** Tel: (0298) 3230 **OPEN: APRIL-OCT**	Nearest Road A.6 This beautiful 400 year old farmhouse offers 12 delightful rooms with modern facilities. It is only 10 minutes walk into the town, and countryside surrounding the house is magnificent. The proprietors are happy to assist in the planning of walks and tours. They have a comfortable lounge and large garden with masses of roses. Cots are provided. Wonderful four course dinners are great value.	£9.00	O	■	O
Mary MacKenzie **Staden Grange** **Staden Lane** **Staden** **Buxton SK17 9RZ** Tel: (0298) 4965 **OPEN: ALL YEAR**	Nearest Road A.515 A pleasant, spacious house in 250 acres enjoying uninterrupted views over open farmland. Four attractive and comfortable rooms, two with private bath. All rooms have modern amenities and tea/coffee makers. A comfortable lounge with colour T.V. and a large garden for guests. Mr. & Mrs. MacKenzie also have riding and shooting and there is a fine golf course nearby. Only 2 miles from Buxton, this is a wonderful base for touring, walking and riding in this magnificent scenic region. A warm welcome and good food await guests.	£14.00	O	O	O
Mrs M.A. Moffett **Biggin Hall** **Biggin-By-Hartington** **Buxton SK17 0DH** Tel: (029884) 451 **OPEN: ALL YEAR**	Nearest Road A.515 Dinner, bed and breakfast only. A really delightful 17th century stone house, completely restored keeping all the character of its origins, massive oak beams. There are 14 beautiful rooms, all charmingly furnished. 3 with 4-poster beds, 12 with en-suite facilities, all with modern amenities. Visitors have the choice of 2 sitting rooms, 1 with colour T.V. and a lovely garden. The house is beautifully furnished with many antiques. Evening meals are truly superb and great value. 10% service charge.	£15.00	O	O	O
Dawn & Miles Hutchinson **Nether Padley Farm** **Grindleford S30 1PH** Tel: (0433) 30073 **OPEN: FEB-NOV**	Nearest Road A.625 This lovely Georgian farmhouse, historically listed and formerly a coaching inn, stands in carefully tended gardens surrounded by farmland in the Peak District of Derbyshire. The delightful bedrooms have antique furniture and beautiful views. All have tea/coffee makers, fresh fruit, homemade biscuits and sweets. There is a charming sitting room for guests, with open fire and colour T.V. A games room with snooker, darts, etc., is also provided. The house is centrally heated throughout. A delicious and varied breakfast from the menu, is served in the original farmhouse kitchen or the more formal dining room.	£14.00	O	■	■

O yes ■ no

	minimum per person	children taken	evening meals available	animals taken
Mrs Marian Venning **"The Old Vicarage"** **Church Bank** **Hathersage** **Via Sheffield S30 1AB** **Tel: (0433) 51099** **OPEN: ALL YEAR**	Nearest Roads A.625 A.57 The Old Vicarage is an historic building dating back to the 1600's. Charlotte Bronte wrote 'Jane Eyre' after staying here in 1845. It has been recently modernised and a warm welcome awaits you. Set on a hill, only 5 minutes walk from the village and over-looking the glorious Hope Valley. Accommodation is in three centrally heated bedrooms. Caves, historic homes and reservoir nearby.	£8.00	O	O	O
Mr & Mrs T.C. Wain **Highlow Hall** **Hathersage** **Nr. Sheffield S30 1AX** **Tel: (0433) 50393** **OPEN: EASTER-OCT**	Nearest Road A.625 A delightful 16th century Manor House situated in the heart of the Peak District National Park. It is surrounded by spectacularly beautiful countryside. 6 large, comfortable rooms with modern amenities. Lovely views from the windows. Excellent farmhouse cooking, using their own produce when possible. Ideal walking country. Close by are Blue John Caverns, Welldressings, and Chatsworth House.	£12.50	O	O	O
Mrs Joyce Goodwin **Winstaff Guest House** **Derwent Ave** **Matlock DE4 3LX** **Tel: (0629) 2593** **OPEN: ALL YEAR**	Nearest Road M.1 An attractive stone built house set in extensive gardens which back onto the River Derwent. Seven pleasant and comfortable rooms with modern amenities, including T.V. and tea/coffee makers. A very nice lounge with colour T.V. and the garden is for guests to enjoy. Close to the house is Hall Leys Park with bowls, putting, tennis and a boating lake. Ideally situated for touring.	£13.00	O	O	■
Mrs Carolyn Partridge **Town Head Farmhouse** **70 High Street** **Bonsall** **Nr. Matlock DE4 2AR** **Tel: (062982) 3762** **OPEN: MAR-NOV**	Nearest Roads A.6 A.5012 A lovely 18th century stone built farmhouse and barns, tastefully converted to guest accommodation. All 6 well appointed bedrooms have modern amenities, some with private showers. Guests lounge and separate dining room. Ideally situated for touring the whole of Derbyshire. Close by are Matlock, Bakewell and Ashbourne. Children over 12 years.	£11.00	O	O	O
Mrs R.A. Groom **The Manor Farmhouse** **Dethick** **Matlock DE4 5GG** **Tel: (064982) 246** **OPEN: JAN-NOV**	Nearest Road M.1 Junction 28 This lovely stone built Elizabethan farmhouse is situated in unspoilt countryside and is the gateway to the Derbyshire Peak District. An ideal base for touring and walking; Haddon House, Hardwick House and Chatsworth House are close by. A comfortable, quiet service is offered.	£9.00	O	O	O

O yes ■ no

68

Staffordshire

Mrs Philomena Bunce **The White House** **Grindon** **Nr. Leek ST13 7TP** **Tel: (05388) 250** **OPEN: JAN-NOV**	Nearest Road A.523 The White House is a modernised 17th century village inn, offering all home comforts. Three centrally heated bedrooms with very pretty decor and modern facilities, T.V., and tea/coffee making facilities. An ideal centre for touring, walking or simply relaxing. Dovedale, Buxton, Matlock and Chatsworth are within easy reach. Children over 8 welcome. Price shown is for 2 people.	£18.00	○	■	■
William & Elaine Sutcliffe **"Choir Cottage &** ** Choir House"** **Ostlers Lane** **Cheddleton** **Nr. Leek ST13 7HS** **Tel: (0538) 360561** **OPEN: MAR-DEC**	Nearest Road A.520 Choir Cottage is a pretty 300 year old stone cottage, formerly a resting place for ostlers, later donated to the local church and used by the choir. Retains original tiny windows and doorway. Both bedrooms have private entrance, shower, toilet, colour T.V. and teasmade. One is a twin (ground floor), the other has a 4-poster bed and adjoining child's bed on landing. Meals are taken in adjoining Choir House. Garden for guests' use.	£12.95	○	○	■
Mrs L. Grey **The Old Vicarage** **Leek Road** **Endon** **Stoke-on-Trent ST9 9BH** **Tel: (0782) 503686** **OPEN: ALL YEAR**	Nearest Road A.53 A friendly family atmosphere is found at this delightful 70 year old former vicarage. It is situated in a quiet spot in the village of Endon, between the Staffordshire Moorlands and Stoke-on-Trent. Accommodation is in four rooms, all with modern amenities and tea/coffee making facilities. There is also a colour T.V. lounge. This makes a good base from which to visit the world famous potteries, the wonderful countryside and the National Garden Festival, museums and pleasure park.	£10.00	○	■	○
Mrs M.B. White **Micklea Farm** **Micklea Lane** **Longsdon** **Stoke-on-Trent ST9 9QA** **Tel: (0538) 385006** **OPEN: ALL YEAR**	Nearest Road A.53 Mrs. White offers bed, breakfast and evening meals in this substantial Staffordshire farmhouse. There are four bedrooms; two twin and two singles with cots available for children and baby-sitting arranged. Residents' lounge with colour T.V. Choice of English or Continental breakfast and packed lunches are available. A friendly welcome is assured.	£8.50	○	○	○
Mrs Jean C. Woods **Pales Corner Farmhouse** **Calton** **Waterhouses** **Stoke-on-Trent ST10 3JX** **Tel: (05386) 450** **OPEN: ALL YEAR**	Nearest Roads A.52 A.523 Personal attention is assured for the limited number of guests sharing the comfortable family home of Jean Woods. The traditional 18th century limestone farmhouse has been renovated to a high standard. Two bedrooms with modern amenities. Situated in a rural village in the Peak District National Park. Ideal for walking, cycling, visiting stately homes and the Staffordshire Potteries.	£10.00	○	■	■

○ yes ■ no

Mrs Barbara Jones **Hall End Hall** **Dordon** **Tamworth B78 1SZ** **Tel: (0827) 899200** **OPEN: ALL YEAR**	Nearest Roads A.5 M.42 The house exudes the elegance of a bygone era, with its low beams, stone floors and inglenook fireplaces. The dining room, where good home-cooked food is served, is furnished in antique oak. Five comfortable bedrooms with modern amenities. Sitting room, large attractive garden and courtyard area for parking. A unique and welcoming "home-from-home" atmosphere. No single availability.	£12.50	○	○	○
Mrs D.E. Moreton **Moors Farm & Country** **Restaurant** **Chillington Lane** **Codsall** **Nr. Wolverhampton WV8 1QH** **Tel: (09074) 2330** **OPEN: ALL YEAR**	Nearest Roads A.41 A.5 A 200 year old farmhouse, standing on a 100 acre farm within a beautiful and picturesque valley bordering the counties of Staffordshire and Shropshire. This comfortably furnished home has many oak beamed rooms, and the six bedrooms have wonderful views of the surrounding countryside. All have modern amenities and tea/coffee making facilities. There is also a colour T.V. lounge. The food here is absolutely delicious. Mrs. Moreton uses home produced lamb, poultry, eggs, milk and vegetables. All preserves, soups, pies and desserts are home made. Residential riding holidays are also available.	£15.00	○	○	■

○ yes ■ no

70

DEVON

Devon is a county of sharp contrast and tremendous variety. It could well be said that this is a county with two distinct faces, one belonging to the sea and the other to the land. There is green and rolling countryside and within whose gentle folds are secreted the tiny hamlets and small towns that have nestled here for hundreds of years. Village names bear witness to their past. Bovey Tracey takes its name from Sir Thomas Tracey who built the parish church as penitence for his part in the murder of Thomas Beckett and Barnstaple is one of the many Devon towns recorded in the 11th century Domesday Book. The seafaring traditions of Devon are well known, Sir Walter Raleigh was a Devon man and Drake fought the Spanish Armada off Plymouth Sound; the same harbour from which the Pilgrim Fathers sailed.

The Devon Landscape

The red soil and rich pasture of the low hills gives way to the open moorlands of Dartmoor. This is a perfect landscape for walking and riding. There are pleasant villages like Widecombe in-the-Moor and on higher ground the heather covered moorland is divided by deep wooded valleys and crowned with craggy rock outcrops knows as Tors. Alternatively the inland countryside offers shady wooded vales, golden cornfields strewn with poppies and lush green meadows. Further variety exists in Devon's two coastlines. The south coast with its soaring red cliffs is dotted with sunny bays and bright fishing villages together with popular resort towns such as Torquay and Paignton. At Brixham there is a busy fishing port famous for its lobster and crab. Salcombe has a setting of great natural beauty in the deep inlet of the Kingsbridge estuary and is a premiere sailing and boating centre. The Atlantic coast to the north of the county is more rugged with precipitous cliffs and small coves. The tiny village of Clovelly tumbles down cliffsides to the sea, along cobbled streets that can only be climbed on foot.

Traditional Devon

Devon has known many masters and from its earlier days, has had a chequered history. Successive waves of Saxon, Danes and Norman have each left their particular mark and brand of influence on the lives of Devonian people. The Flemish brought lace making skills to the county and in characteristics style the local people adopted the craft and made it their own, so that today Honiton lace ranks amongst the finest in the world. Legend and fable are inextricably mingled with historic fact to produce the rich folklore of the country. The story has it that during the 18th century wars with France, four French frigates were sighted off the coast of a virtually undefended village. Undaunted, the local women put on their traditional petticoats and marched up and down along the clifftops, convincing the French that they were redcoat soldiers and so foiled the raiding party. The tales of "wreckers" are well substantiated. Local fisherman would take lanterns to the clifftops in bad weather and use their misleading beacons to draw Spanish ships onto the rocks and then plunder the wrecks.

Towns and Villages

History has also left its mark on the fabric of Devon. The pretty village of Topsham contains Dutch fronted houses amidst the more English Tudor and Georgian styles. The Royal City of Exeter holds its title from the days when it was the personal property of Edward the Confessor. The city retains some of its mediaeval and Tudor buildings and has a number of fine old inns and churches. Its chief glory is the magnificent 14th century cathedral of St Mary and St Peter. It is of an unusual decorated gothic style with a notable west front covered with statues. The seafaring tradition of the city is commemorated in the excellent maritime museum located in converted riverside warehouses.

Plymouth is the second major city and has a magnificent setting in the great natural bowl of Plymouth Sound. The old dock area of the Barbican is fascinating but the town's most glorious sight is the gathering of wonderful old sailing ships for the Tall Ships Race. The estuary of the river Dart is guarded by the Tudor Castles of Dartmouth and Kingswear and has a long naval tradition. Dartmouth saw the crusaders set out for Europe in 1147 and was the point of departure for John David who sailed in search of the Northwest Passage. Up river, the Dart winds through dense woods, orchards, meadows and tiny villages and is undoubtedly one of the most beautiful rivers in England.

DEVON GAZETEER

Areas of Outstanding Natural Beauty.
North, South and East Devon.

Historic Houses and Castles

Arlington Court -- Barnstaple
Regency house, collection of shell, pewter and model ships.

Bickleigh Castle -- Nr. Tiverton
Thatched Jacobean wing. Great Hall and armoury. Early Norman chapel, gardens and moat.

Buckland Abbey -- Nr. Plymouth
13th Century Cistercian monastery -- 16th century alterations. Home of Drake -- contains his relics and folk gallery.

Bradley Manor -- Newton Abbot
15th Century Manor house with perpendicular chapel.

Cadhay -- Ottery St. Mary
16th Century Elizabethan Manor house.

Castle Drogo -- Nr. Chagford
Designed by Lutyens -- built of granite, standing over 900 feet above the gorge of the Teign river.

Chambercombe Manor -- Ilfracombe
14th-15th century manor house.

Castle Hill -- Nr. Barnstaple
18th century Palladian mansion -- fine furniture of period, pictures, pocelain and tapestries.

Hayes Barton -- Nr. Otterton
16th century plaster and thatch house. Birthplace of Walter Raleigh.

Oldway -- Paignton
19th century house having rooms designed to be replicas of rooms at Palace of Versailes.

Powderham Castle -- Nr. Exeter
14th century -- medieval castle much damaged in Civil war. Altered in 18th and 19th centuries. Fine music room by Wyatt.

Saltram House -- Plymouth
Some remnants of Tudor house built into George II house, with two rooms by Robert Adam. Excellent plasterwork and woodwork.

Shute Barn -- Nr. Axminster
Interesting architecturally -- built over several centuries and finished in 16th.

Tiverton Castle -- Nr. Tiverton
Fortress of Henry I. Chapel of St. Francis. Gallery of Joan of Arc.

Torre Abbey Mansion. -- Torquay
Abbey ruins, tithe barn. Mansion house with paintings and furniture.

Cathedrals and Churches

Atherington (St. Mary)
Perpendicular style -- mediaeval effigies and glass, original rood loft. Fine screens, 15th century bench ends.

Ashton (St. John the Baptist)
15th century -- mediaeval screens, glass and wall paintings. Elizabethan pulpit with canopy, 17th century altar railing.

Bere Ferrers (St. Andrew)
14th century rebuilding -- 14th century glass, 16th century benches, Norman font.

Bridford -- (St. Thomas a Becket)
Perpendicular style -- mediaeval glass and woodwork. Excellent rood screen c. 1530.

Cullompton (St. Andrew)
15th century perpendicular -- Jacobean west gallery -- fan tracery in roof, exterior carvings.

Exeter Cathedral
13th century decorated -- Norman towers. Interior tierceron ribbed vault (Gothic) carved corbels and bosses, moulded piers and arches. Original pulpitum c. 1320. Choir stalls with earliest misericords in England c. 1260.

Haccombe (St. Blaize)
13th century effigies, 14th century glass. 17th century brasses, 19th century screen, pulpit and reredos.

Kentisbeare (St. Mary)
Perpendicular style -- checkered tower. 16th century rood screen.

Ottery St. Mary (St. Mary)
13th century, 14th century clock, fan vaulted roof, tomb with canopy, minstrel's gallery, gileded wooden eagle. 18th century pulpit.

Parracombe (St. Petrock)
Unrestored Georgian -- 16th century benches. Mostly perpendicular, Early English chancel.

Sutcombe (St. Andrew)
15th century -- some part Norman. 16th century bench ends, restored rood screen, mediaeval glass and floor tiles.

Swimbridge (St. James)
14th century tower and spire -- mediaeval stone pulpit, 15th century rood screen, font cover of Renaissance period.

Tawstock (St. Peter)
14th century, Italian plasterwork ceiling, mediaeval glass Renaissance memorial pew, Bath monument.

Museums and Galleries

Bideford Museum -- Bideford
Geology, maps, prints, shipwright's tools, North Devon pottery.

Burton Art Gallery -- Bideford
Hubert Coop collection of paintings etc.

Butterwalk Museum -- Dartmouth
17th century row of half timbered buildings, nautical museum. 140 model ships.

Newcomen Engine House -- Nr. Butterwalk Museum
Original Newcomen atmospheric/pressure steam engine c. 1725.

Royal Albert Memorial Museum Art Gallery -- Exeter
Collections of English water colours, paintings, glass and ceramics, local silver, natural history and anthropology.

Rougemont House Museum -- Exeter
Collections of archeology and local history.

Guildhall -- Exeter
Mediaeval structure with Tudor frontage -- City regalia and silver.

Exeter Maritime Museum -- Exeter
Largest collection in the world of working boats, afloat, ashore and under cover.

The Steam and Countryside Museum -- Exmouth
Very large working lay-out -- hundreds of exhibits, including Victorian farm house -- farm yard pets for children.

Shebbear -- North Devon
Alcott Farm Museum with unique collections of agricultural implements and photographs etc.

The Elizabethan House -- Totnes
Period costumes and furnishings, tools, toys, domestic articles etc.

The Elizabethan House -- Plymouth
16th century house with period furnishings.

City Museum and Art Gallery -- Plymouth
Collections of pictures and porcelain, English and Italian drawing, Reynolds family portraits, early printed books, ship models.

Cookworthy Museum -- Kingsbridge
Story of china clay. Local history, shipbuilding tools, rural life.

Honiton and Allhallows Public Museum -- Honiton
Collection of Honiton lace, implements etc. Complete Devon Kitchen.

Lyn & Exmoor Museum -- Lynton
Life and history of Exmoor.

Torquay Natural History Society Museum -- Torquay
Collection illustrating Kent's Cavern and other caves -- natural history and folk culture.

Historic Monuments

Okehampton Castle -- Okehampton
11th-14th century Chapel, Keep and Hall.

Totnes Castle -- Totnes
13th-14th century ruins of Castle.

Blackbury Castle -- Southleigh
Hill fort -- well preserved.

Dartmouth Castle -- Dartmouth
15th century castle -- coastal defence.

Lydford Castle -- Lydford
12th century stone keep built upon site of Saxon fortess town.

Hound Tor -- Manaton
Ruins of mediaeval hamlet.

DEVON
Recommended roadside restaurants

119	A30	Lewdown, Devon 10 miles west of Okehampton
133	A30	Honiton Devon 2 miles east of Honiton
242	A38	Buckfastleigh, Devon 24 miles north east of Plymouth
243	A38	Smithaleigh, Devon 3 miles east of Plymouth
291	A35	Axminster, Devon 2 miles west of Axminster

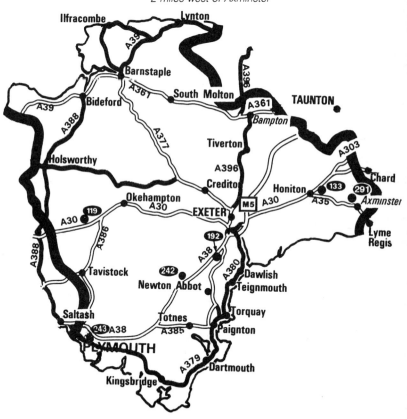

Devon

	Nearest Road	minimum per person	children taken	evening meals available	animals taken
Mr R. Pengilley & Mr I. Horner **Park House** **Western Road** **Ashburton TQ13 7ED** **Tel: (0364) 52158** **OPEN: MAR-NOV**	Nearest Road A.38 A pleasant modern house, surrounded by trees. Situated in 1½ acres in the Dartmoor Park. Superb views across the sweeping countryside. The country town of Ashburton is half a mile away. Park House offers three rooms, all with private bath or shower. Rooms have excellent views and tea/coffee making facilities. An outdoor heated swimming pool for guests. No smoking please.	£11.00	■	■	■
Sue Townsend **Wellpritton Farm** **Holne** **Ashburton TQ13 7RX** **Tel: (03643) 273** **OPEN: ALL YEAR** **(EXCL. XMAS)**	Nearest Roads M.5 A.38 A very pleasant Devon farmhouse offering modern facilities in pretty guest rooms. A friendly welcome and personal attention here, with excellent food using farm produce. Children over 6 are welcome and will love the donkeys, goats, rabbits etc. There is a swimming pool on the farm and riding, fishing and golf are available locally. Beautiful surrounding countryside for walking.	£9.00	O	O	O
M.J. Angseesing **Church House Inn** **Holne** **Nr. Ashburton TQ13 7SJ** **Tel: (03643) 208** **OPEN: ALL YEAR**	Nearest Roads B.3357 A.38 Oliver Cromwell is reputed to have stayed in this delightful 14th century inn. Full of character and charm, it has huge timbers and oak beams, walls 3-4 feet thick and inglenook fireplaces. The 8 bedrooms are comfortable and have modern amenities. Nearby are water skiing, sailing, sea fishing, riding, pony trekking, trout fishing.	£8.50	O	O	O
Mrs P. England **Mettaford Farm** **Hartland** **Bideford EX39 6AL** **Tel: (02374) 249** **OPEN: ALL YEAR**	Nearest Road A.39 A very quiet setting for this Georgian farmhouse situated in 18½ acres of its own unspoilt woodland. Nicely furnished with many antiques. Offering six Laura Ashley decorated bedrooms, one with en-suite facilities, and three bathrooms. A large lounge with wood burning fireplace. Separate T.V. room - on request. Children eat at 6.00 p.m., adults at 7.00 p.m. Cordon Bleu cooking.	£10.00	O	O	O
S. Christenson & K. Herschell **The Edelweiss Hotel** **and Restaurant** **Buttgarden Street** **Bideford EX39 2AU** **Tel: (02372) 72676** **OPEN: ALL YEAR**	Nearest Roads M.5 A.39 A.386 A charming white painted hotel situated in the centre of this most attractive small town. The Edelweiss has eight spacious and comfortable rooms, pleasantly decorated and well furnished. Each room has modern facilities and most rooms look over the rooftops and ancient winding streets, down to the Torridge Estuary. Three rooms have shower en-suite. A large T.V. lounge for guests. The hotel has a superb A la Carte restaurant and a cosy Austrian style bar. 400 yards from Lundy Island Ferry.	£11.50	O	O	O

O yes ■ no

	minimum per person	children taken	evening meals taken	animals taken available
Mrs M. Ogle **Lower Winsford** **Abbotsham Road** **Bideford EX39 3QP** **Tel: (02372) 75083** **OPEN: APRIL-OCT** Nearest Road A.39 The atmosphere at Lower Winsford farmhouse is welcoming and relaxing. The house, set in large gardens and a pretty courtyard, is comfortably furnished with a guests' sitting room with colour T.V., and a dining room serving good farmhouse cooking, two double and two twin bedrooms. Children over 5 welcome. Baby sitting arranged. A car is essential in this very pretty part of Devon.	£9.50	O	O	■
David & Flo Wallington **Whiteleaf at Croyde** **Croyde** **Braunton EX33 1PN** **Tel: (0271) 890266** **OPEN: ALL YEAR** Nearest Road A.361 David & Flo are experienced hosts, having kept a famous Herefordshire inn for many years. Accommodation is in 5 double rooms with private facilities; colour T.V., radio, and tea/coffee making and mini bars. Breakfast is a delight and dinner a nightly experience. Whiteleaf is an attractive 1930's house set in pretty gardens astride the North Devon coastal path.	£8.00	O	O	O
Mr & Mrs G.B. Thompson **Bly House Hotel** **Nattadon Hill** **Chagford TQ13 8BW** **Tel: (06473) 2404** **OPEN: JAN-OCT** Nearest Road A.30 A 100 year old residence situated in the Dartmoor National Park. There are sweeping lawns, woodland walks, elegant furnishing, many antiques and comfortable accommodation. Eight bedrooms, some with 4-poster beds and private bathrooms. Tea making facilities in all rooms. A pleasant quiet lounge and T.V. lounge. Good home cooked food using fresh produce.	£11.00	O	O	O
Mrs M. Stratton **Wheel Farm Country** ** Guest House** **Berry Down** **Nr. Combe Martin** **Tel: (027188) 2550** **OPEN: ALL YEAR** Nearest Road A.39 A really delightful old farm house in beautiful grounds on the edge of Exmoor. Offering seven spacious and comfortable rooms, three have bath en-suite. All have modern amenities. Each room has wonderful views. Excellent food with home grown produce and fresh baked bread. Wholefoods and vegetarian. Mr. Stratton is a chef. Pony trekking, riding and golf arranged and garden for guests use.	£9.50	O	O	O
Mrs Sylvia Frowd **Horselake Farm** **Cheriton Bishop** **Exeter EX6 6HD** **Tel: (064724) 220** **OPEN: ALL YEAR** Nearest Road A.30 An absolutely delightful thatched farmhouse deep in the Devon countryside. Set in 16 acres of attractive gardens, orchards and paddocks. Offering 4 rooms, 2 with antique 4-poster beds, all with en-suite or adjoining facilities, colour T.V. and tea/coffee making facilities. Home cooking is a speciality here and the food is delicious as all the fruit, vegetables and eggs served are produced on the farm. Convenient for Exeter, Dartmoor, Castle Drogo and Fingles Bridge.	£10.50	O	O	O

O yes ■ no

	Nearest Road	minimum per person	children taken	evening meals available	animals taken
Mrs Juliet Dymoke-Marr Venbridge House Cheriton Bishop Exeter EX6 6HD Tel: (064724) 415 OPEN: ALL YEAR	Nearest Road A.30 A most attractive large period country house, set in 16 acres with a courtyard and vinery, where guests are free to wander. A warm and lively family atmosphere to be enjoyed here. Two bedrooms available with tea/coffee making facilities. T.V., books and games in the family sitting room. Full English breakfast served or Continental alternative.	£11.00	O	■	■
Mrs Rosemary Christie Escotts 25 Higher Street Cullompton EX15 1AJ Tel: (0884) 38914 OPEN: MID MAY-MID SEPT	Nearest Road M.5 Escotts is an attractive 16th century weaver's cottage recently completely renovated by the owners. Conveniently located for touring the countryside including Exmoor, Dartmoor and the coast. Accommodation is in a choice of six rooms, beautifully decorated, some with private facilities. A guests colour T.V. lounge is also available. A good English breakfast is served each morning and other meals are catered for upon request.	£9.00	O	O	■
Mr R.C. Coleman Park View Hotel 8 Howell Road Exeter EX4 4LG Tel: (0392) 71772/53047 OPEN: ALL YEAR	Nearest Road B.3183 A very nicely appointed Georgian hotel, close to the centre of Exeter. Overlooking a park in an area noted for peace and quiet, handy for coach and rail stations. Fifteen very pleasant and comfortable bedrooms, five with en-suite facilities. Family rooms available. Pleasant dining room and T.V. lounge. A lovely garden for guests. A good base for touring the West country.	£12.00	O	O	O
Mr & Mrs K. Nicholson Westholme Hotel 85 Heavitree Road Exeter EX1 2ND Tel: (0392) 71878 OPEN: MID JAN-MID DEC	Nearest Road B.3183 A warm welcome and a friendly atmosphere are found at this delightful, creeper-clad, 100 year old house. There are seven comfortable bedrooms with modern amenities, three en-suite, radio and tea/coffee making facilities. There's a cosily furnished T.V. lounge and a small garden for guests to use. The house is conveniently placed for getting to and from the city centre, Exeter Airport and the M.5 motorway. Though evening meals are not available, sandwiches and light snacks are. There are several eating places close by.	£11.00	O	■	O
J.H. & G.M. Maskell Bridford Guest House Bridford Nr. Exeter EX6 7HS Tel: (0647) 52563 OPEN: APRIL-OCT (PLUS XMAS & NEW YEAR)	Nearest Road B.3193 A warm welcome awaits you at this 350 year old house in the centre of a charming village on Dartmoor. Five bedrooms with modern amenities, and tea/coffee making facilities. Lounge with colour T.V. has a large granite fireplace and there are lots of beamed ceilings. Plentiful home cooking, lovely Devon cream teas. Delicious 3-course evening meals are also available. Exeter 8 miles, Torbay and the coast 20 miles.	£9.00	O	O	O

O yes ■ no

	minimum per person	children taken	evening meals available	animals taken
Christopher & Karen Rogers **The LeaDene Guest House** **34 Alphington Road** **St. Thomas** **Exeter EX2 8HN** **Tel: (0392) 57257** **OPEN: ALL YEAR** **(EXCL. XMAS)** Nearest Roads A.377 M.5 Situated just outside the city centre, near to the Maritime Museum and new leisure centre, this large house has eight pleasant and comfortable rooms with modern amenities. All rooms have their own colour T.V. The spacious lounge also has colour T.V. A garden for guests. A large choice on the evening menu. There is one room on the ground floor suitable for the elderly or handicapped.	£11.00	○	○	■
Mr & Mrs E.J. Braund **Woodside** **Whimple** **Exeter EX5 2QR** **Tel: (0404) 822340** **OPEN: APRIL-OCT** Nearest Road A.30 Comfortable accommodation and personal attention are assured at Woodside. This delightful Edwardian house is set in a very attractive garden offering extensive views over Exeter to Dartmoor. The bedrooms are pleasant and very comfortable. There is also a flower lounge, T.V. lounge and dining room, where delicious home cooking is served. This makes an excellent base for a touring holiday.	£10.00	■	■	■
Mrs V.F.Jiggins **Down House** **Whimple EX5 2QR** **Tel: (0404) 822860** **OPEN: ALL YEAR** Nearest Road A.30 Down House offers peace, quiet and seclusion, being a lovely Edwardian farmhouse set in 5 acres of gardens and paddocks. Personal service, home produce and a family atmosphere are priorities. Five comfortable rooms are available and a spacious lounge leads on to a south facing terrace. Children welcome and well provided for. Most enjoyable meal times. Exeter and the coast 8 miles.	£7.50	○	○	■
Eric & Marion Cornish **Leworthy Farm** **Holsworthy EX22 6SJ** **Tel: (0409) 253488** **OPEN: ALL YEAR** Nearest Road - Holsworthy Leworthy Farm offers a happy blend of good food and fun, in congenial surroundings. A large house of Saxon origins, on a working farm, tastefully modernised and well equipped. Accommodation is in 20 rooms, en-suite available. Children made very welcome. Tasty traditional meals and a well stocked bar, where country singers entertain. Set in peaceful countryside yet central for touring. Many sporting facilities available.	£9.00	○	○	■

○ yes ■ no

	minimum per person	children taken	evening meals available	animals taken
Mrs I.E. Thorne **Wessington Cottage** **Awliscombe** **Nr. Honiton EX14 0N4** **Tel: (0404) 3860** **OPEN: APRIL-OCT** Nearest Roads A.30 A.373 to M.5 A friendly welcome and a relaxing atmosphere are found at Wessington Cottage. This is a comfortable guest house with garden, located one and a half miles from Honiton. Accommodation is in 3 rooms; 1 single, 1 double and 1 family room with modern amenities, some with radio and T.V. A colour T.V. lounge is also available. This guest house makes a good base for touring the Devon countryside.	£9.00	O	■	■
Mrs Jacqueline Yot **Colestocks House** **Colestocks** **Nr. Honiton EX14 0JR** **Tel: (0404) 850633** **OPEN: ALL YEAR** Nearest Road A.30 16th century thatched country residence, many antiques, huge inglenook fireplace, log fires, lovely gardens - almost 2 acres, with putting and croquet lawns. All home cooking using fresh local produce where possible. Tranquil rural setting well situated for touring Devon, Dorset and Somerset. Modern amenities in all rooms, one with 4-poster bed. No children under 10 years.	£13.75	O	O	■
Mrs Jill Balkwill **Court Barton Farmhouse** **Aveton Gifford** **Kingsbridge TQ7 4LE** **Tel: (0548) 550312** **OPEN: JAN-NOV** Nearest Road A.379 An absolutely delightful 16th century manor farmhouse situated on a 300 acre beef and cereal farm. Accommodation is in a choice of six bedrooms all comfortably furnished with modern amenities. A pleasant, well furnished T.V. lounge with books and tea/coffee making facilities. There is a swimming pool and games room with darts, snooker and table tennis. Early morning tea and a delicious full country farmhouse breakfast served.	£7.50	O	■	■
Mrs Muriel Paice **Trebles Cottage Private Hotel** **Kingston** **Nr. Kingsbridge TQ7 4PT** **Tel: (0548) 810268** **OPEN: MAR-OCT** Nearest Road A.379 A warm welcome and personal attention await you at this small, friendly hotel, set in large grounds on the edge of an attractive, unspoilt South Hams village, dotted with thatched cottages. An ideal touring centre, much of interest nearby, including golf. A picturesque beach is 1½ miles away and the area abounds in lovely walks. There are six comfortable bedrooms with wash basins and bathrooms en-suite, a bar and a dining room serving good food.	£11.50	O	O	■
Ellen & Ray Bidder **Lyncott** **56 St. Brannock's Road** **Ilfracombe EX34 8EQ** **Tel: (0271) 62425** **OPEN: MAR-OCT** Nearest Road A.361 A friendly family guest house situated only 200 yards from Bicclescombe Park. A most attractive rose garden at the front makes a welcoming sight. Ten nicely decorated and comfortable rooms with modern amenities. A T.V. lounge and garden for guests. This house is very suited to families and the evening meals are good value, with delicious home cooking and a varied menu. Children are well catered for and very welcome.	£7.50	O	O	O

	minimum per person	children taken	evening meals available	animals taken
Brian & Dorothy Murphy **Neubia House Hotel** **Lydiate Lane** **Lynton EX35 6AH** **Tel: (0598) 52309** **OPEN: FEB-NOV** Nearest Road A.39 A very charming former farmhouse, built in 1840, set in private courtyard/car park in Old Lynton. Twelve very comfortable bedrooms all with en-suite facilities, colour T.V., and tea/coffee making facilities. Proprietor-chef welcomes vegetarians. Situated in a very pleasant village, it is an ideal base for touring this lovely region. Riding, fishing and walking all superb and beaches are close by.	£15.00	O	O	O
June & Adrian Kamp **Southcliffe** **Lee Road** **Lynton EX35 6BS** **Tel: (0598) 53328** **OPEN: MAR-DEC** Nearest Road A.39 June and Adrian offer a homely relaxed atmosphere, in this comfortable, small hotel. The accommodation is nice and the atmosphere friendly. There's a modern lounge with colour T.V. and video for guests' use. Offering 8 well decorated bedrooms all en-suite with T.V., tea/coffee making facilities. In the licensed dining room you will enjoy good food. Children over 5 years.	£11.00	O	O	O
Mr & Mrs J.F. Travis **Gordon House** **31 Lee Road** **Lynton EX35 6BS** **Tel: (05985) 53203** **OPEN: MAR-NOV** Nearest Road A.39 A most attractive Victorian house, once a gentleman's residence, now sympathetically restored, marrying the charm of a bygone era to the facilities expected of a small modern hotel. There are seven bedrooms, all en-suite and centrally heated, some with 4-poster beds. Two luxurious lounges, one with books and games, one with colour T.V. The hotel is licensed and offers tempting meals.	£12.00	O	O	O
Mr D. & Mrs. A.M. Barratt **Gable Lodge** **35 Lee Road** **Lynton EX35 6BS** **Tel: (0598) 52367** **OPEN: FEB-NOV** Nearest Road A.39 A charming Victorian residence, built from local stone, facing south with pleasant views across the Lyn Valley to Countisbury Hill and Exmoor. The house has been modernised to retain many original features, in particular the natural pitch pine doors and staircases. Nine comfortable rooms, 6 en-suite, a sunny T.V. lounge, and licensed bar. Garden available for guests' use.	£9.00	O	O	■
Mr & Mrs Bassett **Sunnycliffe Hotel** **Chapel Hill** **Mortehoe-Woolacoombe** **EX34 7EB** **Tel: (0271) 870597** **OPEN: FEB-NOV** Nearest Road A.361 Sunnycliffe is a small, select hotel located on a hillside position with wonderful views of both coast and countryside. Accommodation is in 8 rooms, all with private facilities, T.V. and tea/coffee. All rooms have sea views. Traditional English food is prepared by Sunnycliffe's proprietor-chef. This makes a good base for any kind of holiday. Nearby are golden sands, safe swimming, surfing, riding and walking along the coastal paths. Sea fishing and boat trips. Potteries, market towns and stately homes are within easy reach.	£16.50	O	O	■

○ yes ■ no

animals taken
evening meals available
children taken
minimum per person

	minimum per person	children taken	evening meals available	animals taken
Mrs Candida Ker **The Old Farmhouse** **Fore Stoke** **Holne** **Newton Abbot TQ13 7SS** **Tel: (03643) 361** **OPEN: ALL YEAR** Nearest Road A.38 Guests are welcome to join in with life on this small sheep farm, to explore and help with the animals. Children are well provided for and there are pets and a farm pony for them to enjoy. Standing on Dartmoor, quiet and sheltered, with fantastic views, this old stone farmhouse offers cosy accommodation in four rooms, and a lounge with colour T.V. and open fire. Plenty of good food.	£8.50	O	O	O
Mrs H. Roberts **Willmead Farm** **Bovey Tracey** **Nr. Newton Abbot TQ13 9NP** **Tel: (06477) 214** **OPEN: FEB-NOV** Nearest Roads A.38 A.382 A superb 14th century thatched Dartmoor farmhouse offering the last word in luxury in three visitors' rooms. It has fabulous ing-lenook fireplaces, antiques and a minstrel gallery. Set in the centre of 31 acres of woodland this delightful house is the perfect base for touring the many local beauty spots. From Bovey Tracey take A.382 to Moreton Hampstead, take first left past Hawkmoor Hospital. Farm is half a mile.	£13.00	O	■	O
Margaret & John Tucker **Gate House** **North Bovey** **Moretonhampstead TQ13 8RB** **Tel: (0647) 40479** **OPEN: ALL YEAR** Nearest Roads A.30 M.5 Gate House is a mid-15th century thatched Devon longhouse with beamed ceilings and a huge sitting-room fireplace. Three double guest rooms are available, all en-suite with T.V. and tea/coffee making facilities. Vegetarian and wholefood meals are served alongside traditional meals, and produce is organically grown. Large swimming pool in a secluded garden, and uninterrupted views over Dartmoor.	£12.50	■	O	O
Mrs Judith Harvey **Budleigh Farm** **Moreton Hampstead** **Newton Abbot TQ13 8SB** **Tel: (0647) 40835** **OPEN: JAN-NOV** Nearest Road A.382 Budleigh, a delightful old thatched farm-house, nestles in a wooded valley in the Dartmoor National Park. All bedrooms have tea/coffee making facilities and handbasins. Two adjoining rooms with bathroom en-suite offer superb family accommodation. Board games, paperbacks and magazines, maps and books are available on loan. A delightful garden, with outdoor swimming pool and croquet, help make this the perfect touring base. Enjoy our own farm fresh free-range hen/duck eggs.	£8.50	O	O	■
Mr & Mrs M.C. Partridge **Cadditon Farm** **Cadditon Bondleigh** **North Tawton EX20 2AW** **Tel: (083782) 450** **OPEN: APRIL-OCT** Nearest Road A.30 Cadditon is at least 300 years old with ing-lenook fireplaces and oak beams. It is a lovely thatched house standing in 147 acres, and offers two delightful rooms with modern amenities. Tea makers in each room. A charming sitting room with colour T.V. and garden for guests. Evening meals are excellent and very good value indeed. An ideal base as Dartmoor is only 8 miles away. Pony trekking, golf, and swimming available locally. Children most welcome.	£8.00	O	O	■

O yes ■ no

	minimum per person	children taken	evening meals available	animals taken
Mr & Mrs John & Ellen Bryan **Lower Gorhuish Farm** **Northlew** **Okehampton EX20 3BU** **Tel: (0837) 810272** **OPEN: FEB-NOV**	Nearest Road A.30 A warm welcome is assured at Lower Gorhuish Farm, standing on a 160 acre mixed farm near a delightful wooded valley. Accommodation is in four comfortable rooms, all with modern amenities; radio, and tea/coffee making facilities, two with T.V. A colour T.V. lounge and garden are also available. Nearby is pony trekking/riding and they also have private fishing and shooting rights. Okehampton 18-hole golf course is also close by.	£10.00	O	O	■
Mrs J.S. Robinson **South Nethercott Farm** **South Nethercott** **Whiddon Down** **Okehampton EX20 2QZ** **Tel: (064723) 276** **OPEN: MAR-NOV**	Nearest Road A.30 Peace and tranquility, in a charming 400 year old farmhouse made of cob, offering two comfortable rooms, one with bath en-suite. It has low beamed ceilings and log fires. Dinner is by candlelight. Centrally located, it is an excellent base for the North and South coasts and Dartmoor. There are many places of immense interest in the vicinity apart from the local beauty spots. Children over 12 years.	£9.50	O	O	■
J.L. & B.R. Evans **Court Farm** **Heale** **Parracombe EX31 4QE** **Tel: (05983) 212** **OPEN: ALL YEAR**	Nearest Road A.39 Court Farm is a charming 350 year old traditional Devon long house. Situated in the Exmoor National Park it offers glorious views. Accommodation is in three well furnished rooms, all with private facilities and tea/coffee makers. The emphasis at this friendly house is on creating an enjoyable house party atmosphere, where every guest is made to feel welcome. Excellent food. Walking, riding, fishing and an 18-hole golf course close by.	£9.00	O	O	O
Pat & Malcolm Vaissiere **The Wood** **De Courcy Road** **Moult Hill** **Salcombe TQ8 8LQ** **Tel: (054884) 2778** **OPEN: ALL YEAR**	Nearest Roads A.38 A.381 A.379 The Wood is an 80 year old detached house standing in half an acre of wooded land high on Moult Hill, giving magnificent views. Accommodation is in five large, airy, comfortable rooms some with bathroom en-suite and balcony with modern amenities and tea/coffee making facilities. All have splendid views. The cooking is very good using local produce and serving home made soup and pies. A boat is available for hire. Beaches and golf courses nearby.	£11.00	O	O	O
Mr & Mrs G.C.J. Hunt **Three Horseshoes** **Branscombe** **Nr. Seaton EX12 3BR** **Tel: (029780) 251** **OPEN: ALL YEAR**	Nearest Road A.3052 Comfortable and pleasant, the Three Horseshoes is an "olde worlde" Devon inn with beams, brasses and open log fires. There are 12 bedrooms; 5 en-suite, all with radio, T.V., and tea/coffee making facilities. Meals A la Carte, or a choice from an extensive bar menu, served in a spacious dining room. There are two cosy bars. Well situated for touring.	£11.50	O	O	O

O yes ■ no

	minimum per person	children taken	evening meals available	animals taken
R.W. & G.A. Denton **Silver Howe** **Boughmore Road** **Bickwell Valley** **Sidmouth EX10 8SH** Tel: (03955) 78475 **OPEN: ALL YEAR** Nearest Road A.3502 Silver Howe is located in a quiet residential area, with lovely views to the sea. Built in 1908, in the grand traditional style, it offers accommodation in six very comfortable rooms, some with en-suite facilities and 4-poster beds, all with modern amenities and tea/coffee makers. The spacious T.V. lounge has delightful sea views. In the dining room good traditional English meals are served. Close by are tennis, croquet, putting, bowling, golf and concert hall.	£12.00	■	○	■
Mrs Theresa Ann Sampson **Kerscott Farm** **Bishopsnympton** **South Molton EX36 4QG** Tel: (07697) 262 **OPEN:** Nearest Road A.361 Kerscott Farm is delightfully located amid rolling farmland on the edge of Exmoor, 6 miles east of South Molton. This delightful 16th century house has a lovely "olde worlde" atmosphere where guests feel very much at home. There are 3 bedrooms with modern amenities, T.V. and tea/coffee making facilities. This is an ideal spot for those seeking a restful holiday in tranquil countryside surroundings. Kerscott is mentioned in the Domesday Book.	£8.00	○	○	■
Margaret Venner **West Down** **White Chapel** **South Molton EX36 3EQ** Tel: (07697) 373 **OPEN: ALL YEAR** Nearest Road A.361 West Down is a most attractive, creeper clad country house. Set in 25 acres of wooded countryside, with views of the River Yeo and beyond to Exmoor. This delightful house has cosy log burning fires and provides accommodation in three double bedrooms. A colour T.V. lounge is also available. The food here is excellent. Fresh vegetables and game in season. There's also golf, fishing and rough shooting nearby. Hunting by arrangment.	£14.00	○	○	○
J. & M. Chilcott **Moorland Hall** **Brentor Road** **Mary Tavy** **Tavistock PL19 9PY** Tel: (082281) 466 **OPEN: ALL YEAR** Nearest Road A.386 Moorland Hall is a delightful Victorian country house, standing in 4 acres of gardens and paddocks, in the relaxing and beautiful Dartmoor National Park. There are ten comfortably furnished bedrooms, most with private bathrooms. A pleasant lounge, small bar and a genuine 1930 bar billiards table. Tea or coffee and home-made scones are offered to each guest on arrival. The evening meals are delicious and excellent value.	£18.00	○	○	○
Mr & Mrs R.S.H. Cochrane **Bickleigh Cottage** **Guest House** **Bickleigh** **Nr. Tiverton EX16 8RJ** Tel: (08845) 230 **OPEN: APRIL-OCT** Nearest Road A.396 A gorgeous 17th century thatched cottage offering ten excellent rooms with modern facilities. Standing on the banks of the River Exe at one of Devon's most famous beauty spots, this lovely house is an ideal base for touring the county. Good home cooking. Cots are provided.	£11.50	○	○	■

○ yes ■ no

84

		minimum per person	children taken	evening meals available	animals taken
Mrs Ruth Hill-King **Little Holwell** **Collipriest** **Tiverton EX16 1PT** **Tel: (0884) 258741** **OPEN: ALL YEAR**	Nearest Road M.5 Little Holwell is a delightful "olde worlde" farmhouse standing in beautiful Devon countryside, surrounded by rolling hills and woodland. This 13th century home has many oak beams, inglenook fireplace and spiral staircase. Accommodation is in 3 rooms with tea/coffee making facilities. A lounge is also available. Home-made bread, fresh milk, eggs and vegetables are used whenever possible.This is a good base for touring as Tiverton, Exeter, Exmouth and Torbay are within easy reach.	£8.00	O	O	■
Mrs Hazel Ellis **Hill Rise Hotel** **Winterbourne Road** **Teignmouth TQ14 8JT** **Tel: (06267) 3108** **OPEN: ALL YEAR**	Nearest Road A.381 Hill Rise is an elegant Edwardian house located in a quiet residential area only a few minutes walk from the town centre. Accommodation is in eight rooms, some with shower en-suite, all with modern amenities and tea/coffee making facilities. Many rooms have sea views. A colour TV lounge and garden are also available for guests. This makes a good base for either a seaside or touring holiday as the coast, Dartmoor, Torquay, Exeter and Plymouth can be easily reached.	£8.00	O	O	O
Mrs Diana Ellis **Wood Grange Hotel** **18 Newton Road** **Torquay TQ2 5BZ** **Tel: (0803) 212619** **OPEN: ALL YEAR**	Nearest Road A.380 A friendly small hotel where the hosts will welcome you and ensure you have a pleasant stay. Twelve comfortable bedrooms are available, some en-suite, and a licensed bar, colour T.V. lounge, sun patio and garden are provided to help you have a relaxed holiday. The Wood Grange is close to all amenities and has a large car park.	£9.00	O	O	O
Michael & Sheila Edwards **Ford Farm Guest House** **Harberton** **Totnes TQ9 7SJ** **Tel: (0803) 863539** **OPEN: ALL YEAR**	Nearest Road A.381 Ford Farm Guest House - 16th century, is situated on the edge of a typical Devonshire village. No longer a working farm, it has a small, secluded, old world garden. Accommodation is very comfortable with antique furnishings, log fires and beamed ceilings. Offering 3 bedrooms, 1 with shower en-suite. Former restaurant owners. Professional home cooking and friendly service is offered.	£10.50	O	O	O

O yes ■ no

	minimum per person	children taken	evening meals available	animals taken
John & Susan Reynolds **Cherrybrook Hotel** **Two Bridges** **Yelverton PL20 6SP** **Tel: (0822) 88260** **OPEN: ALL YEAR**	Nearest Roads M.5 A.30 A.38 B.3357 Built early in the 19th century by one of the Prince Regent's friends, this most attractive house has beamed ceilings and slate floor. There are 7 nicely furnished rooms all en-suite. Also a comfortable lounge and bar. Excellent food with old English dishes. Personal service in a friendly, farmhouse atmosphere. Set on Dartmoor, with wide ranging views. Local pursuits include walking and pony trekking.	£15.00	O	O	O
Pam & Richard Kitchin **Overcombe Hotel** **Horrabridge** **Yelverton PL20 7RN** **Tel: (0822) 853501** **OPEN: ALL YEAR**	Nearest Roads A.386 A charming hotel offering 11 extremely comfortable rooms, with modern facilities, colour T.V. and tea/coffee makers. There is a lounge with open fires and a small bar. Overlooking beautiful countryside, it is set in Dartmoor National Park. Ideally situated for moorland walking, riding, golf, sea and river fishing and for exploring the North and South coast beaches. The lovely Cotehele House, Lydford Gorge and the Shirehorse Farm Centre are within a few miles. Cots are provided.	£13.50	O	O	O
Mr & Mrs M. Ward **Harrabeer Country House Hotel** **Harrowbeer Lane** **Yelverton PL20 6EA** **Tel: (0822) 853302** **OPEN: ALL YEAR**	Nearest Road. A.386 A small country house hotel in a quiet lane on the edge of beautiful Dartmoor, offering good food, warmth and comfort in a friendly atmosphere. Five of the seven bedrooms are en-suite, all have T.V. and tea/coffee making facilities. Delightful residents' lounge and licensed bar. Large secluded garden with panoramic views and swimming pool. Ideally situated for touring, walking and sports.	£14.75	O	O	■

O yes ■ no

*All the establishments in this book
are members of the*
**WORLDWIDE BED & BREAKFAST
ASSOCIATION**

Look for this symbol

DORSET

Dorset is a peaceful, rural county beautifully described in Thomas Hardy's novel "Far From The Madding Crowd". It is difficult to imagine that much has changed here since Hardy's day and outside the few towns there is an atmosphere of quiet and an inescapeable sense of history. Since man's earliest beginnings a fascinating blend of cultures have indelibly mapped their progress on the Dorset landscape and there can be few more pleasant areas in which to ponder their achievements. There are neolithic burial mounds, great earthworks, henge monuments, Roman encampments, Tudor mansions, Abbeys, Castles and Georgian Towns. This wealth of history is easily discovered in Dorset.

Landscape and Wildlife

Not only are man made monuments much in evidence but there is also great variety in the natural beauty of the landscape. In the heart of the county there are sandy heathlands and to the north the fox hunting hills reach down to the coast forming a natural barrier breached only at Corfe Castle where the Castle ruins stand as picturesque witness to the might of Cromwell during the Civil War.

The coastline is spectacular and much of it is now protected as an Area of Outstanding Natural Beauty, Poole Harbour is an enormous bay which forms an almost perfect circle pierced at its narrow entrance by the sea. It was an important harbour in medieval times and the town centre holds the fine 18th century house of Poole merchants. Further along the coast the notorious Chesil Beach is as perilous to shipping today as it was 1,000 years ago. Dorset building stone is well known for its variety and colour, Purbeck marble was used in Westminster Abbey and St Paul's Cathedral is constructed in Portland stone. Lyme Regis, a favourite Victorian resort, well known for its blue lias (a type of limestone) which is also found in hues of lilac, gold and green.

The different inland soils, coupled with the coastal variety has produced a haven for wildlife. Dorset has some of Britain's rarest birds within her boundaries, including the Osprey. There is a swannery at Abbotsbury where monks established a colony of mute swans some 600 years ago. Much of the wildlife can be seen by taking the well marked walking trails; especially good are the coastal and cliff top paths. Often these paths show off the county to its best advantage since views of both the countryside and the shoreline are excellent.

Historic Dorset

Dorset has many interesting archaeological features. The awesome fortified earthwork of Maiden Castle is a marvel of pre-historic engineering and it dominates the local landscape even today. The strange Badbury Rings wind round a wooded hilltop, like a coiled serpent and legend has it that King Arthur's soul in the form of a raven inhabited this "dread" wood. Then there is the strange Giant of Cerne Abbas, 180 feet in height and carved into the chalk hillside. Although long associated with fertility there has been much speculation as to who exactly was responsible for the creation and execution of the figure. One theory suggests it is a Romano-British depiction of Hercules.

The Romans first came to Dorset in 45 A.D. and ruled for over 300 years. During this time many towns were built, some of which still survive. Durnovaria, the modern Dorchester, has a Roman amphitheatre and the old Roman route to Weymouth is still followed by todays' roads. However, the visitor to Dorchester will find a quiet town, bustling on market days, with a largely Georgian city centre. This area was the heartland of the Saxon kingdom of Wessex as is evidenced by the Saxon place names. Fleet, for example comes from the Saxon word fleot, meaning estuary and the great pebble split on the south coast is called Chesil-the Saxon word for gravel. The Civil War brought bloody battles to the region as at Lyme Regis in 1685 and it was in Dorset that the Duke of Monmouth raised rebellion against James II. It ended disastrously for Monmouth and his friends at the hands of "Bloody Judge Jeffries" who held his Assize Court in Dorchester. At Beauminister Tower the rebels were hanged and quartered. There is a saying "stabbed with a Bridport dagger", a reference to the hangman's noose, made from Bridport hemp rope.

DORSET GAZETEER

Areas of Outstanding Natural Beauty
The Entire County.

Historic Houses and Castles

Athelthampton
Mediaeval house -- one of the finest in all England. Formal gardens.

Barneston Manor -- Nr. Church Knowle
13th-16th century stone built manor house.

Forde Abbey -- Nr. Chard
12th century Cisterican monastery -- noted Mortlake tapestries.

Manor House -- Sandford Orcas
Mansion of Tudor period, furnished with period furniture, antiques, silver, china, glass, paintings.

Hardy's Cottage -- Higher Bockampton
Birthplace of Thomas Hardy, author. (1840-1928).

Milton Abbey -- Nr. Blandford
18th century Georgian house built on original site of 15th century abbey.

Purse Caundle Manor -- Purse Caundle
Mediaeval manor -- furnished in style of period.

Parnham House   Beaminster
Tudor Manor -- some later work by Nash. Leaded windows and heraldic plasterwork.

Sherborne Castle -- Sherborne
16th century mansion -- continuously occupied by Digby family.

No. 3 Trinity Street -- Weymouth
Tudor cottages now converted into one house, furnished 17th century.

Smedmore -- Kimmeridge
18th century manor.

Wolfeton House -- Dorchester
Mediaeval and Elizabethan manor. Fine stonework, great stair. 17th century furniture -- Jacobean ceilings and fireplaces.

Cathedrals and Churches

Bere Regis (St. John the Baptist)
12th century foundation -- enlarged in 13th-and 15th centuries. Timber roof and nave, fine arcades, 16th century seating.

Blandford (St. Peter & St. Paul)
18th century -- ashlar -- Georgian design. Galleries, pulpit, box pews, font and mayoral seat.

Bradford Abbas (St. Mary)
14th century -- parapets and pinnacled tower, panelled roof. 15th century bench ends, stone rood screen. 17th century pulpit.

Cerne Abbas (St. Mary)
13th century -- rebuilt 15th & 16th century, 14th century wall paintings, 15th century tower, stone screen, pulpit possibly 11th century.

Chalbury (dedication unknown)
13th century origin -- 14th century east windows, Timber bellcote. Plastered walls, box pews, 3 deckerpulpit, west gallery.

Christchurch (Christ Church)
Norman nave -- ribbed plaster vaulting -- perpendicular spire. Tudor renaissance Salisbury chantry -- screen with Tree of Jesse: notable misericord seats.

Milton Abbey (Sts. Mary, Michael, Sampson & Branwaleder)
14th century pulpitum and sedilia, 15th century reredos and canopy, 16th century monument, Milton effigies 1775.

Sherborne (St. Mary)
 Largely Norman but some Saxon remains -- excellent fan vaulting, of nave and quire. 12th and 13th century effigies -- 15th century painted glass.

Studland (St. Nicholas)
 12th century -- best Norman church in the county. 12th century font, 13th century east windows.

Whitchurch Canonicorum (St. Candida and Holy Cross)
 12th and 13th century. 12th century font, relics of patroness in 13th century shrine, 15th century painted glass, 15th century tower.

Wimbourne Minster (St. Cuthberga)
 12th century central tower and arcade, otherwise 13th-15th century. Former collegiate church. Georgian glass, some Jacobean stalls & screen. Monuments and famed clock of 14th century.

Yetminster (St. Andrew)
 13th century chancel -- 15th century rebuilt with embattled parapets. 16th century brasses and seating.

Museums and Galleries

Abbey Ruins -- Shaftesbury
 Relics excavated from Benedictine Nunnery founded by Alfred the Great.

Russell-Cotes Art Gallery and Museum -- Bournemouth
 17th-20th century oil paintings, watercolours, sculptures, ceramics, miniatures, etc.

Rothesay Museum -- Bournemouth
 English porcelain, 17th century furniture, collection of early Italian paintings, arms and armour, ethnography, etc.

Bournemouth Natural Science Society's Museum
 Archeology and local natural history.

Brewery Farm Museum -- Milton Abbas
 Brewing and village bygones from Dorset.

Dorset County Museum -- Dorchester
 Geology, natural history, pre-history. Thomas Hardy memorabilia.

Philpot Museum -- Lymme Regis
 Old documents and prints, fossils, lace and old fire engine.

Guildhall Museum -- Poole
 Social and civic life of Poole during 18th and 19th centuries displayed in two storey Georgian market house.

Scapolen's Court -- Poole
 14th century house of local merchant exhibiting local and archeological history of town, also industrial archeology.

Sherborne Museum -- Sherborne
 Local history and geology -- abbey of AD 705, Sherborne missal AD 1400, 18th century local silk industry.

Gallery 24 -- Shaftesbury
 Art exhibitions -- paintings, pottery etc.

Red House Museum and Art Gallery - Christchurch
 Natural history and antiquities of the region. Georgian house with herb garden.

Priest's House Museum - Wimbourne Minster
 Tudor building in garden exhibiting local archeology and history.

DORSET
Recommended roadside restaurants

051	A35	Winterbourne Abbas Dorchester, Dorset 6 miles west of Dorchester
074	A31	St Leonards, Ringwood, Dorset 4 miles west of Ringwood (North-eastbound)
146	A31	Tricketts Cross Nr Ringwood, Dorset 9 miles east of Wimbourne 5 miles south-west of Ringwood (South-westbound)
240	A31	Wimborne, Dorset 2 miles west of Wimborne Opening May '84
265	A303	Sparkford, Somerset 1 mile west of Sparkford

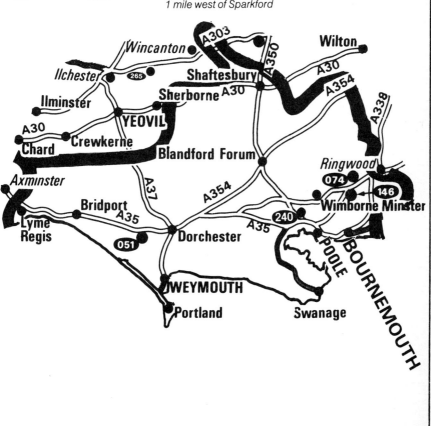

Dorset

minimum per person
children taken
evening meals available
animals taken

	Nearest Road	minimum per person	children taken	evening meals available	animals taken
Mrs Carolyn Anne Lighton **Long Hayes** **Stoke Abbott** **Beaminster DT8 3JN** **Tel: (0308) 862330** **OPEN: JAN-NOV**	Nearest Road A.3066 Long Hayes is a beautiful old house of great character, dating in parts back to the 16th century. It stands amongst trees and gardens from which produce is used for good, home-cooked meals. Personal attention is assured during your stay here. Four bedrooms; one single, one double, two twin. Children are well provided for. Stoke Abbott village is peaceful and picturesque.	£8.00	O	O	■
Mrs Rae Smith **Courtney Cottage** **Shroton** **Nr. Blandford Forum** **DT11 8QA** **Tel: (0258) 860033/860650** **OPEN: APRIL-NOV**	Nearest Road A.350 A charming 17th century house very nicely furnished, in a small pretty garden - set in beautiful countryside at the foot of Hambledon Hill. Access to house all day. Log fires in sitting room when needed. Baby sitter available. Ample parking. The local village shop, run by the owner's family, stock wines and spirits and will supply picnics to order.	£12.00	O	O	O
Mr & Mrs A.K. Bateman **"Mentieth Lodge"** **16 St. Augustins Road** **Bournemouth BH2 6NX** **Tel: (0202) 27804** **OPEN: ALL YEAR**	Nearest Road A.338 Every effort is made at Mentieth Lodge, to ensure the comfort and well being of guests in an informal and friendly atmosphere. A handsome, tastefully modernised character house in a peaceful location adjacent to Meyrick Park. Nine bedrooms are available, some with private facilities. Fresh grown vegetables and fruit are used to produce delicious meals and a full English breakfast is served.	£9.00	O	O	O
Capt. & Mrs L. Street **Freshfields Hotel** **55 Christchurch Road** **Bournemouth BH1 3PA** **Tel: (0202) 34023** **OPEN: ALL YEAR**	Nearest Road A.35 A family run small hotel of real quality. Offering eleven very pleasant and comfortable rooms, five with en-suite facilities. T.V. and tea/coffee makers in all rooms, plus a guest lounge and garden. Excellent home cooking and special diets catered for. Close to the beaches and shops. British hospitality at its best and a warm welcome make this an excellent base for the visitor.	£9.50	O	O	O
Mr & Mrs D. Spring **Fenn Lodge Hotel** **11 Rosemount Road** **(off Alumhurst Rd)** **Alum Chine** **Bournemouth BH4 8HB** **Tel: (0202) 761273** **OPEN: 1 MAR-MID OCT** **(Xmas prices on request)**	Nearest Road A.338 This is a comfortable small hotel with a happy, homely, relaxed atmosphere. Delightfully situated. Only a few minutes walk through charming Alum Chine to the sea. The accommodation is very comfortable, offering 13 rooms with modern amenities with access at all times. A colour T.V. lounge and dining room serving very nice food. Choice of menu with evening meal. Residents bar.	£9.50	O	O	O

O yes ■ no

Maureen & Albert Rabone **Wenmaur House Hotel** **14 Carysfort Road** **Boscombe** **Bournemouth BH1 4EJ** **Tel: (0202) 35081** **OPEN: ALL YEAR**	Nearest Road A.35 A comfortable house with a friendly atmosphere offering good accommodation in twelve rooms with modern facilities. It offers a games room, a license and T.V. lounge. Overlooking garden with patio, it is centrally placed for beaches and the usual sporting activities are all available locally. Cots are provided. They also have a covered table tennis area in the garden. Late night refreshments available.	£8.00	○	○	■
S.E. Mansbridge **Common Knapp House** **Coast Road** **Burton Bradstock DT6 4RJ** **Tel: (0308) 897428** **OPEN: ALL YEAR**	Nearest Road A.35 A quiet country guest house with extensive sea and country views, and direct access to the beach and Dorset Coast Path. Six pleasant bedrooms; double/twin, and one family room are available. Residents lounge with colour T.V. Fresh garden produce is used in the preparation of evening meals and there is a generous English breakfast.	£10.50	○	○	○
Mr & Mrs R.D. Jennings **The Old Pound Cottage** **Loders** **Nr. Bridport DT6 3SA** **Tel: (0308) 22779** **OPEN: ALL YEAR**	Nearest Road A.35 Old Pound Cottage is an absolutely delightful 17th century thatched stone cottage situated in the lovely and picturesque village of Loders. The cottage has lots of exposed oak beams, cosy rooms with low ceilings and glorious countryside views. Offering two pleasant bedrooms with modern amenities. Meals available in local inns and restaurants. Close by there is an equestrian centre and golf course.	£8.50	■	■	○
Mikki & Robert Hansowitz **Cranston Cottage** **25 Church Street** **Bridport DT6 3PS** **Tel: (0308) 56240** **OPEN: ALL YEAR**	Nearest Road A.35 A small Georgian house situated in a quiet cul-de-sac only 1½ miles from the beaches of West Bay. Three well decorated and comfortably furnished rooms, with modern amenities and tea/coffee makers. A pleasant lounge which has an original open fireplace with colour T.V. for guests. There is a small patio with sun loungers. Golf and riding locally for guests. The attractive Saxon market town is an excellent base for touring this unspoilt region. Lovely coastal walks, beaches, pretty villages and, of course, it is Hardy country.	£8.00	○	○	■
Roy & Dot Beckhelling **Britmead House Hotel** **154 Westbay Road** **Bridport DT6 4EG** **Tel: (0308) 22941** **OPEN: FEB-DEC**	Nearest Road A.35 Interesting house with individually decorated bedrooms, overlooking a river valley down to the sea. 10 minutes walk to harbour, beach and shops. All rooms have colour T.V., electric blankets, and tea/coffee making facilities. Private bathrooms available. Choice of menu at all meals. Pleasant location and ideally placed for touring, visiting beauty spots and places of interest.	£12.00	○	○	○

○ yes ■ no

93

		minimum per person	children taken	evening meals available	animals taken
Mrs G.M. Cocks **Uploders Place** **Uploders** **Bridport** **Tel: (030885) 228** **OPEN:**	Nearest Road A lovely white comfortable Regency house, in large gardens with the River Asker running through. The three bedrooms, all en-suite, are very spacious and so arranged that breakfast can be served there if desired. Uploders is a picturesque village at the foot of Eggardon Hill, an iron-age hill fort, 3 miles from the sea. Ideal for walking and riding. Stables in village.	£8.00	○	○	○
Mr S.J.C. & Mrs V.C. Connell **Matravers House** **Uploders** **Bridport** **Tel: (030885) 222** **OPEN: ALL YEAR**	Nearest Road A.35 Guests receive the warmest of welcomes at this wonderful 18th century thatched farmhouse. Set in the beautiful Dorset countryside made famous by Thomas Hardy. The house is a delight with open log fires and cosy rooms. Four bedrooms are available, some with T.V. and tea/coffee making facilities. There is also a guests' colour T.V. lounge and the garden is also available. The food here is very good and Mrs. Connell uses fresh produce from the small holding whenever possible. Guests will enjoy a family atmosphere here.	£9.50	○	○	■
Pat & Brian Marshall **Fairlight Hotel** **1 Golf Links Road** **Broadstone BH18 8BE** **Tel: (0202) 694316** **OPEN: ALL YEAR** **(EXCL. XMAS)**	Nearest Road A.349 Fairlight is a quiet, private, licensed hotel standing in it's own grounds with bridle path from the garden to the woods. Accommodation is in eleven comfortable rooms, all with modern amenities, some with en-suite facilities. There is also a sitting room, lounge and bar. The meals are delicious and prepared by the chef/proprietor. This is a super base for touring the region. Close by are Poole, Bournemouth, coast, rivers and lovely countryside and the golf course is only 200 yards away.	£14.00	○	○	○
Mrs Veronica Isobel Willis **Lamperts Cottage** **Sydling St.Nicholas** **Dorchester DT2 9NU** **Tel: (03003) 659** **OPEN: ALL YEAR**	Nearest Road A.37 Lamperts Cottage is a charming 16th century thatched cottage, standing in fields with streams running front and back, on the outskirts of the village. Roses climb around the windows and door. 3 bedrooms are available, equipped with tea/coffee making facilities. Full English breakfast is served, or Continental if preferred. Packed lunches can be prepared. Ideal for visiting Dorset's many beauty spots.	£12.50	○	○	○
Mrs Marian Tomblin **Lower Lewell Farmhouse** **West Stafford** **Dorchester DT2 8AP** **Tel: (0305) 67169** **OPEN: ALL YEAR**	Nearest Road A.35 A 17th century farmhouse situated in the delightful Frome Valley. The house is reputed to be the Talbuthayes Dairy in Hardy's novel Tess of the D'Urbervilles. Accommodation is in three bedrooms with modern amenities and tea/coffee making facilities in all rooms. Convenient for touring the Dorset coast. Nearby is Dorchester.	£10.00	○	■	■

○ yes ■ no

94

	minimum per person	children taken	evening meals available	animals taken
Mrs C. Walford **Rectory House** **Fore Street** **Evershot DT2 0JW** **Tel: (093583) 273** **OPEN: ALL YEAR** **(EXCL. XMAS)** Nearest Road A.37 A delightful 18th century listed building set in unspoilt Thomas Hardy countryside, with many beautiful walks and scenic views. Guests accommodated in three lovely bedrooms to suit families or couples, and there is a separate lounge and dining room. Superb home cooking will add to the pleasure of your stay. Children welcome. Fishing, riding or sailing nearby. Car not essential.	£10.00	O	O	■
John Budd **The Old Mill** **Halstock BA22 9SJ** **Tel: (093589) 278** **OPEN: MID MAR-OCT** Nearest Road A.37 Luxurious spacious accommodation in a lovely 17th century mill set in 10 peaceful acres, amidst beautiful countryside. Three bedrooms are offered, all en-suite, one with a 4-poster bed. Guest's own dining and sitting room. The emphasis is on 'real food' using fresh local produce, and the house is licensed. A very friendly welcome is extended from the Budd family. No single rooms available.	£14.00	O	O	O
Jill & Ken Hookham-Bassett **Stourcastle Lodge** **Goughs Close** **Sturminster Newton** **DT10 1BU** **Tel: (0258) 72320** **OPEN: ALL YEAR** Nearest Roads A30 A.303 Visitors to Stourcastle Lodge can expect a relaxing stay and a very warm welcome in a pleasant house built in 1739. Located in a quiet part of the town. There are four charming bedrooms with modern amenities and tea/coffee and soft drinks are available all day. Exposed beams throughout the house. A pretty lounge with open log fire and colour T.V. Super food here and good value. Regional Winners 1986.	£12.00	O	O	O
Mr & Mrs D.G. Marchington **Estyard House** **Fontmell Magna** **Shaftesbury SP7 0PB** **Tel: (0747) 811460** **OPEN: DEC-OCT** Nearest Road A.350 A very pleasant and comfortable house, approximately 100 years old offering six charming rooms to visitors. Shaftesbury is a superb place to begin touring Dorset as it holds so many places of interest in and around the town. It is centrally placed for touring by car. Animals are welcome. Dinner is offered at a good price. Fresh fruit and vegetables with home made brown bread. Prices reduced for stay of more than 1 night. Children over 8 years.	£11.75	O	O	O
Mr & Mrs A. de Crespigny **The Old Rectory** **St. James** **Shaftesbury SP7 8HG** **Tel: (0747) 2003** **OPEN: ALL YEAR** Nearest Road A.30 A delightful 18th century country house. The air of charm and elegance combine to create a most comfortable and relaxing place to stay. The accommodation, in two bedrooms, have en-suite facilities and tea/coffee making. A colour T.V. lounge is available for residents use. In the dining room guests are treated to excellent cordon bleu cuisine prepared by Mrs. de Crespigny. A games room is also available. Conveniently located ½ mile from the centre of Shaftesbury, this makes an ideal base for a holiday.	£16.00	O	O	O

O yes ■ no

		minimum per person	children taken	evening meals available	animals taken
Mrs J. Mayo **Almshouse Farm** **Hermitage** **Sherborne DT9 6HA** **Tel: (096 321) 296** **OPEN: MAR-OCT**	Nearest Road A.352 Almshouse farm is set on a 140 acre dairy farm, six miles from the old town of Sherborne with its Abbey and Castle. Accommodation is in three rooms with modern amenities. A colour T.V. lounge with log burning fire is also available. There is also a pleasant dining room with an attractive inglenook fire place. Each evening (except Sunday) a four course meal is available. Whenever possible local fresh produce is used.	£8.50	O	O	■
C. Woodard **Holway Mill** **The Vegetarian Guest House** **and Restaurant** **Sandford Orcas** **Nr. Sherborne DT9 4RZ** **Tel: (096322) 380** **OPEN: ALL YEAR**	Nearest Roads A.30 A.303 This is a delightful 200 year old farmhouse. Holway Mill has spacious accommodation, oak beams, log fires and period antique furniture. The bedrooms all have wonderful views across the beautiful surrounding countryside. All have modern amenities and tea/coffee can be served in guest's rooms. The licensed restaurant serves imaginative vegetarian home cooking with much of the produce grown organically in their own garden. In the summer, morning coffee, lunches and cream teas can be enjoyed on the terrace or by the heated swimming pool. Other facilities for guests include badminton, croquet and cycle hire.	£13.00	O	O	O
Ann & Eric Dick **Romaynes** **Lydlinch** **Sturminster Newton** **DT10 2HU** **Tel: (0258) 72508** **OPEN: ALL YEAR**	Nearest Road A.357 Romaynes is a spacious country house ideally situated for touring beautiful Dorset. Three doube, one twin, two single bedrooms. Residents lounge with colour T.V. and a sun-terrace. Children over 12 welcome. The cooking is good and homely, and accommodation is comfortable. Golf and riding nearby and some of the best coarse fishing in England.	£10.00	■	O	■
Mrs S.K. Lucas **Leyland** **Quarr Farm Lane** **Valley Road** **Swanage BH19 3DY** **Tel: (0929) 480573** **OPEN: 1 APRIL-31 OCT**	Nearest Road A.351 Good accommodation is offered in this large pleasant house which has a homely atmosphere. Mrs. Lucas offers an inclusive price with evening meal at a superb rate. An excellent area with much to interest everyone and plenty for children to do. The house is surrounded by fields and is only two and a half miles from the ancient village of Corfe Castle.	£8.00	O	O	■
Dorothy Harwood **Longmead** **Beach Road** **Studland BH19 3AQ** **Tel: (092944) 246** **OPEN: ALL YEAR**	Nearest Road A.351 This delightful Edwardian house is set in 1¼ acres of beautiful secluded gardens only 300 yards from Studland's safe and sandy beaches. Accommodation is in three rooms. The excellent family room includes sauna and sun roof and is suitable for five people. The 2 other rooms have en-suite bathroom and tea/coffee making facilities. A pleasant colour T.V. lounge is also available.	£13.00	O	O	O

O yes ■ no

animals taken
evening meals available
children taken
minimum per person

		minimum per person	children taken	evening meals available	animals taken
Mrs M.E. Elvins **1 The Quay** **Wareham BH20 4LP** **Tel: (09295) 3201** **OPEN: ALL YEAR**	Nearest Roads A.35 A.351 A lovely 200 year old residence. Situated on the banks of the River Frome, it overlooks the Purbeck Hills. The house is full of the most interesting antiques. Mrs. Elvins offers 6 rooms and does everything possible to help her guests in every way. Conveniently situated for the town and beaches. Fishing, riding, golf, walking available nearby. Also a separate holiday flat sleeping 2/3 people.	£12.00	○	■	○
Mr & Mrs P.G. Rudd **Bishops Cottage** **Lulworth Cove** **Wareham BH20 5RQ** **Tel: (092941) 261** **OPEN: MAR-OCT**	Nearest Roads A.354 A.352 An excellent small hotel offering accommodation in fourteen pleasant rooms some with private facilities. Situated in its own grounds on the edge of the cove, in a sunny sheltered position with beaches and cliffs only a short walk away, easily accessible via the coastal heritage Cliff Walk. The home cooking here is very good and excellent value. Dinner is also available. This makes an ideal base for touring. Heated outdoor swimming pool.	£12.65	○	○	○
Mrs Joyce Norman **Dingle Dell** **Osmington** **Nr. Weymouth DT3 6EW** **Tel: (0305) 832378** **OPEN: MAR-OCT**	Nearest Road A.353 A delightful rose covered house built of mellow local stone, standing in a secluded attractive garden of ancient apple trees and beautiful roses. The two spacious bedrooms, with modern amenities are comfortably and nicely furnished. The large windows give wide views of the garden and surrounding countryside, across to the White Horse hill. The house is conveniently located for visits to Weymouth, only 5 miles away and many historic sites. This makes a super base for a holiday.	£9.00	○	■	■
Mrs Melita Biggs **Heatherick** **Knights in the Bottom** **Weymouth DT3 4EA** **Tel: (0305) 786309** **OPEN: MAR-NOV**	Nearest Roads A.354 B.3157 A relaxed atmosphere is found at Heatherick. Quietly situated in the peaceful Dorset countryside, this is an ideal base for touring the many local beauty spots. The Bigg's offer a warm and friendly welcome, and a choice of 6 rooms all with modern amenities, T.V. and tea/coffee making facilities. There is also a garden for guests use. Ideal for exploration, diving, sailing, walking, birdwatching etc.	£10.00	○	■	○
Mrs M. Gregory **Ashton Lodge** **10 Oakley Hill** **Wimborne BH21 1QH** **Tel: (0202) 883423** **OPEN: ALL YEAR**	Nearest Roads A.31 A.349 A delightful house, offering excellent accommodation in 3 double rooms with modern facilities, one room with bath ensuite. It has a good size garden for use by guests. With the famous Minster close by and numerous attractions locally, this makes an ideal place to stay. Mrs. Gregory offers tour maps and helps with planning tours. Cots are provided.	£8.50	○	■	■

○ yes ■ no

97

		minimum per person	evening meals available	children taken	animals taken

Eveline Stimpson
Thorburn House
2 Oakley Road
Wimborne Minster
BH21 1QJ
Tel: (0202) 883958

OPEN: ALL YEAR

Nearest Road A.31 A.349

By the warmth of her welcome with tea and home-made cake, the high standard of decor and quality of full English breakfast, Eveline Stimpson ensures every visitor feels at home. Each of the three rooms have radio and tea/coffee making facilities, while colour T.V. is available if required. She will help folk to discover the beauties of Dorset. Thorburn House is situated on the Wimborne to Poole road, and provides a convenient centre for both the Isle of Purbeck and the New Forest. Close by is the acclaimed new acquisition of the National Trust, Kingston Lacey House.

£8.50 ○ ■ ■

○ yes ■ no

All the establishments in this book
are members of the
**WORLDWIDE BED & BREAKFAST
ASSOCIATION**

Look for this symbol

ESSEX

This is a county which encompasses three utterly different landscapes. In the East are lonely creeks, mud flats and huge reclaimed marshes which are a haven for wild fowl, seabirds, sailors and fisherman and of course, the "Colchester native" - the famous oysters.

The Coast

This coast has seen the Saxons, Romans, Danes, Vikings and Normans come creeping over the tide washed mud flats or sailing up the creeks in long boats to conquer, to burn and pillage and then to settle, adding their mark to the local culture, building roads and castles, becoming absorbed into the mysterious area and then to disappear. Today we still use the names of their settlements such as Wivenhoe, Layer-de-la-Haye, Colchester and Saffron Walden - Walden was the Saxon name but Saffron was added when the crocus was grown in 15th-18th centuries for dyes and flavourings etc. Stones from the great Roman fort at Othona were used to build a minute chapel in the 7th century and today, just a couple of miles away there stands a nuclear power station. Further along the coast there are little towns and fishing villages with harbours and boats, wooden houses and sailors' inns complete with tales of smuggling.

Inland

Inland the country changes to lush watermeadows and rivers fringed with willow trees; farming country, much admired by the great painter Constable who loved this area and who lived and worked close by. Going north to Colchester we find one of the greatest of the Roman fortress cities. Colchester also has one of the largest Norman Keeps in Europe; the remains of a huge castle built by the Normans on the site of the Roman temple. Some parts of the Roman wall still remain and their original street plan is the basis of much of modern Colchester. A great oyster feast is held annually to celebrate the famous "Native". There are charming sea-side towns, much loved by families for safe beaches and swimming - once crowded with "Nannies" and their charges. The islands and harbours are great favourites also with anglers, naturalists and yachtsmen alike. Ferries ply cross the North Sea to European ports as they have done for centuries past.

County Sights

At St Osyth there is a most important and imposing priory - founded in the 7th century, extended over the succeeding years; it has been lovingly restored and now has a magnificent Gatehouse which should not be missed on a tour of Essex. At Audley End, in a fine park, stands Audley End Mansion -Jacobean building par excellence - and in the surrounding towns and villages there are equally lovely half-timbered houses, manor houses and churches in settings which have changed little over the years. Eight villages are collectively known as "The Rodings", and get their name from the Old English "Hrothingas" (settlement of Hroth's people). The history of England can be read in the names of the towns and villages.

To the far West of the county, on the fringes of London lies Epping Forest which was the happy hunting ground for generations of monarchs. This is quite unlike any other part of the county and provides a much needed escape from London into peace and quiet among the heaths and glades under the huge ancient trees.

There are many fascinating villages and small towns to discover in the secret byways of this county. Burnham on Crouch with its attractive Quay and clapboard cottages. This pleasant town is most famous for Oysters and sailing. Ingatestone with its happy mix of Tudor, Georgian and Victorian buildings has a most interesting spired church. A path leads from here to the lovely Tudor house - Ingatestone Hall. Paglesham and its neighbouring hamlets of Churchend and Eastend are situated between two esturaries. There are some very interesting tudor farmhouses, cottages of clapboard - such a feature of the region - and several ancient inns.

ESSEX GAZETEER

Areas of outstanding Natural Beauty.
Dedham Vale (part), Epping Forest

Historic Houses and Castles

Audley End House -- Saffron Walden
1603 -- Jacobean mansion on site of Benedictine Abbey. State rooms and Hall.

Castle House -- Dedham
Home of the late Sir A. Munnings. President R.A. Paintings and other works.

Hedingham Castle -- Castle Hedingham
Norman Keep and Tudor Bridge.

Layer Marney Tower -- Nr. Colchester
1520 Tudor brick house. 8 storey gate tower. Formal yew hedges and lawns.

Payecock's -- Coggeshall
1500 -- richly ornamented -- merchant's house -- National Trust.

St. Osyth's Priory -- St. Osyth
Was Augustinian Abbey for 400 years until dissolution in 1537. 13th-18th century buildings. 13th century chapel. Wonderful gatehouse containing works of art including ceramics and Chinese Jade.

Spains Hall -- Finchingfield
Elizabethan Manor incorporating parts of earlier timber structure. Paintings, furniture and tapestries.

Cathedrals and Churches

Brightlingsea (All Saints)
15th century tower -- some mediaeval painting fragments. Brasses.

Castle Hedingham (St. Nicholas)
12th century doorways, 14th century rood screen, 15th century stalls, 16th century hammer beams, altar tomb.

Copford (St. Michael and All Angels)
12th century wall paints. Continuous vaulted nave and chancel.

Layer Marney (St. Mary)
Tudor brickwork, Renaissance monuments, mediaeval screens, wall paintings.

Little Maplestead (St. John The Baptist)
14th century, one of the five round churches in England, having hexagonal nave, circular aisle, 14th century arcade.

Newport (St. Mary The Virgin)
13th century. Interesting 13th century altar (portable) with top which becomes reredos when opened. 15th century chancel screen. Pre-Reformation Lectern. Some old glass.

Museums and Galleries

Dutch Cottage Museum -- Canvey Island
17th century thatched cottage of octagonal Dutch design. Exhibition of models of shipping used on the Thames through the ages.

Ingatestone Hall -- Ingatestone
Documents and pictures of Essex.

The Castle -- Colchester
Norman Keep now exhibiting archeological material from Essex and especially Roman Colchester.

Southchurch Hall -- Southend-on-Sea
14th century moated and timber framed manor house -- Tudor wing, furnished as mediaeval manor.

Thurrock -- Grays
Prehistoric, Romano-British and pagon Saxon archeology.

Finchingfield (St. John The Baptist)
Norman workmanship. 16th century tomb. 18th century tower and cupola.

ESSEX
Recommended roadside restaurants

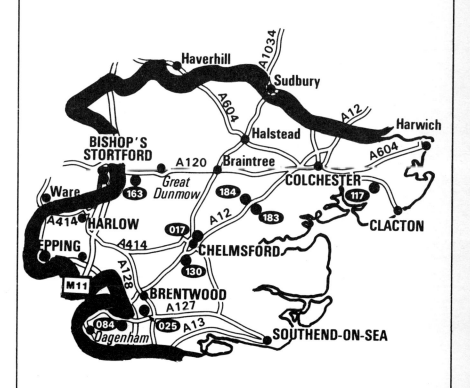

Essex

	minimum per person	children taken	evening meals available	animals taken
Mrs E.M. Watson **Upper Park** **Coles Oak Lane** **Dedham** **Nr. Colchester CO7 6DN** **Tel: (0206) 323197** **OPEN: APRIL-OCT** Nearest Roads A.134 A.12 A small country house set in 2 acres of garden, situated ½ mile from the centre of Dedham Village, offering four pleasant and comfortable rooms, one of which has private bath. All rooms have tea/coffee making facilities. Mrs. Watson has a pleasant T.V. lounge for guests' use. The house is surrounded by parkland where Constable is known to have painted, and there are lovely views towards the coast. An interesting area for touring and Cambridge is only 1 hour's drive.	£13.00	○	■	○
Mrs A.F. Bredin **Bovills Hall** **Ardleigh** **Colchester CO7 7RT** **Tel: (0206) 230217** **OPEN: ALL YEAR** Nearest Road A.137 A friendly host and a relaxing atmosphere are found at this delightful manor house. Listed in the Domesday Book, Bovills Hall offers interesting and comfortable accommodation in a choice of two rooms, both with modern amenities, T.V. and radio. There's a colour T V lounge for guests' use, open fires, and 14 acres of garden making a pleasant and delightful spot to relax in after a day's touring. This makes a perfect base for a holiday.	£12.00	○	○	■
M. Titmus **Boxley House** **The Street** **Ardleigh CO7 7NR** **Tel: (0206) 230981** **OPEN: ALL YEAR** Nearest Road A.137 Boxley House is a 17th century period cottage with a wealth of fine exposed beams, in the ancient village of Ardleigh on the edge of Dedham Vale. Ideal situation for touring town, country and coast. Three centrally heated bedrooms for guests, with colour T.V. and tea/coffee making facilities. Full English breakfast is served, using free-range eggs and local produce.	£10.00	○	■	○
Mrs C.A. Somerville **Rosebank** **Lower Street** **Stratford St.Mary** **Colchester CO7** **Tel: (0206) 322259** **OPEN: ALL YEAR** Nearest Roads A.12 An attractive part Tudor Manor House in the heart of Constable country, with gardens leading to river frontage, and an historic boathouse. Quietly situated in a pretty village in the Vale of Dedham, with Colchester and Ipswich 10 minutes drive. Aldeburgh and Felixstowe close by. Four pleasant and comfortable rooms with modern facilities. Full English breakfast. Inns in the village serve evening meals.	£11.00	○	■	○
Mrs Jacques **Hill House** **The Maltings** **Ramsey** **Harwich CO12 5LN** **Tel: (0255) 880324** **OPEN:** Nearest Road A.120 An attractive house and well situated for travellers to and from the Continent, being just off the main Colchester/Harwich Road and only minutes away from the harbour. There are rooms for six guests, with children catered for, a large garden and solar-heated outdoor swimming pool. Off the road car parking. Continental breakfast only.	£9.00	○	■	■

○ yes ■ no

		minimum per person	children taken	evening meals available	animals taken

Helen P. Mitchell
New Farm House
Spinnell's Lane
Wix
Manningtree CO11 2UJ
Tel: (025587) 365

OPEN: ALL YEAR

Nearest Road A.120

A comfortable, centrally-heated modern farmhouse, ideally situated for touring Constable country. All bedrooms have washbasins and optional T.V. guests' lounge with colour T.V. Small kitchen available for making hot drinks. Beverages and milk provided. Children welcome (reduced price). Cots, high chairs, babysitting. Large play area with swings etc. Games room, with table tennis etc. Convenient for Harwich.

£10.00 | ○ | ○ | ○

P.D. & J.A. Sloan
Stanford Rivers Hall
Stanford Rivers
Ongar CM5 9QG
Tel: (0277) 362997

OPEN: ALL YEAR

Nearest Road A.113

Stanford Rivers Hall is a very fine example of Georgian architecture, in a pleasant rural location yet within easy reach of London, Cambridge, Stansted, M.25 and M.11. Lovely accommodation in six characterful rooms all en-suite, and a friendly atmospheric lounge with oak beams and a wood burning stove. Spacious dining room where English or Continental breakfast is served.

£12.00 | ○ | ■ | ■

Mrs Susan Yates
The Stow
Great Sampford
Saffron Walden CB10 2RG
Tel: (079986) 354

OPEN: ALL YEAR

Nearest Road B.1053

The Stow is a lovely 16th century farmhouse, situated in the centre of the delightfully attractive village of Great Sampford. The house itself is a real treat featuring beamed ceilings, buttoned chairs, Persian rugs, patchwork and embroidered cushions. The kitchen is pinewood and delicious meals are prepared on the large Aga cooker. Accommodation is in two rooms with modern amenities and tea/coffee making facilities. There is also a residents' colour T.V. lounge and a super garden. Mrs. Yates makes all her guests most welcome and an enjoyable stay is assured.

£12.00 | ○ | ○ | ■

Mr & Mrs Sam Burls
Armigers
Thaxted CM6 2NN
Tel: (0371) 830618

OPEN: ALL YEAR

Nearest Road M.11

A beautiful 16th century Essex farmhouse, standing in 2 acres of grounds, including a hard tennis court and croquet lawn, which guests are encouraged to use. The house is a delight with many oak beams and inglenook fireplaces. Accommodation is in four rooms with modern amenities - some with T.V. A colour T.V. lounge is also available. Armigers is conveniently situated for Stansted Airport, Cambridge, Newmarket and the races as well as the many historic villages of Essex and Suffolk.

£12.00 | ■ | ○ | ■

○ yes ■ no

103

GLOUCESTERSHIRE

So varied is the landscape that people speak not of one Gloucestershire but of three; Cotswold, Vale and Forest. The rounded hills of the Cotswolds sweep and fold in graceful composition to form the most gentle, perhaps the most beautiful of English upland landscapes. The eastern hills offer magnificent views across the Vale of Berkley and Severn to the darkly wooded slopes of the Forest of Dean on the Welsh borders.

An Ancient Landscape

The hand of man has left its mark on the landscape since neolithic times. Hill forts, ancient trackways and long barrows with their dark passages & chambers charge the imagination and offer scope for speculation about the people who built them. Three centuries of Roman occupation have also left their print and the local saying goes "scratch Gloucestershire and find Rome". Three major Roman roads mark the path of invasion and settlement. Akeman Street leads to London, Ermine Street and the Fosse Way to the north east and west. A stretch of Roman road with original surface can be seen at Blackpool Bridge in the Forest Dean. Corinium (modern Cirencester) is at the crossroads of Roman Britain where these roadways intersect and the city's museum reflects its status as the second most important Roman city in the country. Many villas have been excavated in the area, some with intricate mosaic floors, as at Chedworth villa.

The Wealth of Wool

The Anglo-Saxon Kings of Mercia invaded in the wake of the Romans and threw up the 80 miles of bank and ditch that form Offa's Dyke on the boundary with Wales. The Anglo-Saxon tongue gave the name "Cotswolds" meaning "hills of the sheepcotes" but much of the character and scenery we have today has its origins in the wood industry that flourished in the middle ages. The fine Norman churches at Tewkesbury and Bishops Cleve were to be overshadowed as growing wealth enabled building in the perpendicular style. Handsome 15th century church towers crown many wool towns and villages as at Northleach, Chipping Camden, Cirencester and Gloucester with its splendid cathedral. The superb local stone, a mellow golden limestone, lends character and unity to the architecture of towns and villages. Detailing in church buildings gives recognition to the source of local wealth. Cloth workers' shears are depicted on the north west buttress of Grantham church tower and couchant rams decorate church buttresses at Compton Bedale. Wool and cloth weaving dominated life in the 14th and 15th centuries and most families were ultimately dependant on the industry. The cottage craft of weaving was gradually overtaken by larger looms and water power and many tranquil villages of today were early industrial centres. The water mill can still be seen in the beautiful village of Lower Slaughter and the charming cottages of Arlington Row at Bibury were a weaving factory. The growth of the Lancashire mills led to the decline of the Cotswold weaving but a few centres survive. At Witney for example you can still buy the locally made blankets for which the town is famous.

The Age of The Gentry

From the early 1500's the wealth of the gentry formed the basis for the building of parks and mansions, too numerous to the list here. Amongst the most notable is the Jacobean manor house at Stanway and the contrasting Palladian style mansion at Barnsley Park. Perhaps the most famous is the park and house at Badminton. The woods, avenues and rides designed by Capability Brown are a classic of English landscape architecture and form a perfect setting for the modern Badminton horse trials. On a smaller scale Elizabethan timber frame buildings can be seen at Didbrook, Dymock and Deerhurst but stone houses are more common and Chipping Camden provides excellent examples.

Regency Elegance

Cheltenham was only a village in 1716 when a local farmer noticed a flock of pigeons pecking at grains of salt around a saline spring in his fields. He began to bottle and sell the water and in 1748 his son-in-law, Henry Skillicorne, built a pump room and the place received the name of Cheltenham Spa. Physicians published treatise on the healing qualities of the waters and visitors began to flock there.

GLOUCESTERSHIRE GAZETEER

Areas of Outstanding Natural Beauty
The Costwolds, Malvern Hills and the Wye Valley.

Historic Houses and Castles

Ashleworth Court -- Ashleworth
15th century limestone Manor House. Stone newel staircase.

Berkeley Castle -- Berkeley
12th century castle -- still occupied by the Berkeley family. Magnificent collections of furniture, paintings, tapestries and carved timber work. Lovely terraced gardens and deer park.

Chavenage -- Tetbury
Elizabethan Cotswold Manor House, Cromwellian associations.

Clearwell Castle -- Nr. Coleford
A Georgian neo-Gothic house said to be oldest in Britain, recently restored.

Court House -- Painswick
Cotswold Manor House -- has original court room and bedchamber of Charles 1. Splendid panelling and antique furniture.

Kelmscott Manor -- Nr. Lechlade
16th century country house -- 17th century additions. Examples of work of William Morris, Rosetti and Burne-Jones

Owlpen Manor -- Nr. Dursley
Historic group of traditional cotswold stone buildings. Tudor manor house with church, barn, court house and a grist mill. Holds a rare set of 17th century painted cloth wall hangings.

Snowshill Manor - Broadway
Tudor house with 17th century facade. Unique collection of musical instruments and clocks, toys, etc. Formal garden.

Sudeley Castle -- Winchcombe
12th century -- home of Katherine Parr, is rich in historical associations, contains art treasures and relics of bygone days.

Cathedrals and Churches

Gloucester Cathedral
Birthplace of Perpendicular style in 14th century. Fan vaulting, East windows commemorate Battle of Crecy -- Norman Chapter House.

Prinknash Abbey -- Gloucester
14th and 16th century - Benedictine Abbey.

Tewkesbury Abbey - Tewkesbury
Dates back to Norman times, contains Romanesque and Gothic styles. 14th century monuments.

Bishops Cleeve (St. Michael & All Saints)
12th century with 17th century gallery. Magnificent Norman West front and South Porch. Decorated chancel -- fine window.

Bledington (St. Leonards)
15th century glass in this perpendicular church -- Norman bellcote, Early English east window.

Buckland (St. Michael)
13th century nave arcades. 17th century oak panelling, 15th century glass.

Cirencester (St. John The Baptist)
A Magnificent church - remarkable exterior, 3 storey porch, 2 storey oriel windows, traceries and pinnacles. Wine-glass pulpit c. 1450. 15th century glass in East window, monuments in Lady chapel.

Hailes Abbey -- Winchcombe
14th century wall paintings, 15th century tiles, glass and screen, 17th century pulpit. Elizabethan benches.

Newland (All Saints)
13th century, restored 18th century. Pinnacles west tower; effigies.

Museums and Galleries

Bishop Hooper's Lodgings -- Gloucester
3 Tudor timber frame buildings -- museum of domestic life and agriculture in Gloucester since 1500.

Bourton Motor Museum -- Bourton-on-the-Water
Collection of cars and motor cycles -- also vintage advertising.

Cheltenham Art Gallery -- Cheltenham
Gallery of Dutch paintings, collection of oils, watercolours, pottery, porcelain, English and Chinese; furniture.

City Wall and Bastion -- Gloucester
Roman and mediaeval city defences in an underground exhibition room.

Stroud Museum -- Cirencester
Depicts earlier settlements in the area and has a very fine collection of Roman antiquities.

Historic Monuments

Chedworth Roman villa -- Yanworth
Remains of Romano-British villa.

Belas Knap Long Barrow -- Charlton Abbots
Neolithic burial ground -- three burial chambers with external entrances.

Hailes Abbey -- Stanway
Ruins of beautiful mediaeval abbey built by son of King John, 1246.

Odda's Chapel - Deerhurst
Rare Saxon chapel dating back to 1056.

Witcombe Roman Villa -- Nr. Birdlip
Large Roman Villa -- Hypocaust and mosaic pavements preserved.

Hetty Pegler's Tump -- Uley
Long Barrow -- fairly complete, chamber is 120 feet long.

Ashleworth Tithe Barn -- Ashleworth
15th century tithe barn -- 120 feet long -- stone built, interesting roof timbering.

GLOUCESTERSHIRE
Recommended roadside restaurants

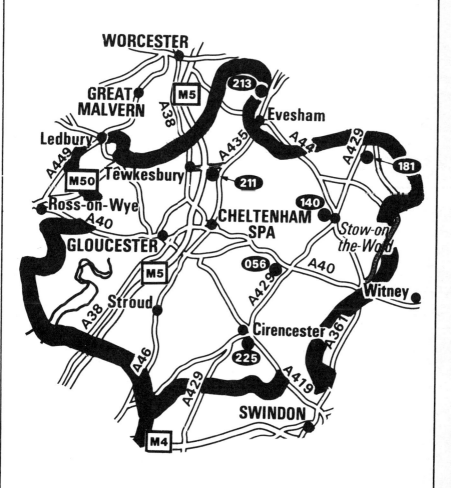

Gloucestershire

		minimum per person	children taken	evening meals available	animals taken
Mrs S. Campbell **Camalan House** **Station Road** **Bourton-on-the-Water** **GL54 3BY** **Tel: (0451) 21321** **OPEN: APRIL-OCT**	Nearest Road A.40 A very well appointed new house in a most attractive village in the Cotswolds. Mrs. Campbell makes her guests feel welcome and comfortable in her well managed house. There are five rooms with basins, the bathroom is only a step away. Vegetarians can be catered for at breakfast. No single occupancy available.	£8.50	○	■	■
Mrs Helen Adams **Upper Farm** **Clapton-on-the-Hill** **Bourton-on-the-Water** **Cheltenham GL54 2LG** **Tel: (0451) 20453** **OPEN: APRIL-OCT**	Nearest Roads A.429 A pleasant, peaceful atmosphere is found at Upper Farm, a 17th century Cotswold stone farmhouse. It is situated in the quiet, unspoilt village of Clapton. Upper Farm enjoys one of the best views of the Cotswolds from its hill position, only 2 miles above Bourton-on-the-Water. The house has been tastefully restored and offers exceptional accommodation, complemented with fresh farm produce and friendly service.	£10.00	○	■	■
M.B. & J.M. Wright **Farncombe** **Clapton-on-the-Hill** **Bourton-on-the-Water** **Nr. Cheltenham GL54 2LG** **Tel: (0451) 20120** **OPEN: APRIL-OCT**	Nearest Roads A.40 A.429 A large Cotswold family home, offering three guest rooms, situated in the small quiet hamlet of Clapton, with superb views over the Windrush Valley. Only 2½ miles from the enchanting village of Bourton-on-the-Water. Day trips can be made to Oxford, Blenheim Palace, Stratford-on-Avon and Berkley Castle. Approximately 1 hour's driving time to Heathrow.	£9.00	○	■	■
Mr & Mrs Minchin **The Ridge** **Whiteshoots** **Bourton-on-the-Water** **Cheltenham GL54 2LE** **Tel: (0451) 20660** **OPEN: FEB-NOV**	Nearest Road A.429 The Ridge stands in 2 acres of beautiful secluded grounds, just 1 mile from the centre of Bourton-on-the-Water. A large country house with five individually decorated bedrooms, it is an extremely pleasant and comfortable base for touring the Cotswolds. An excellent breakfast is served. Children over 6 welcome.	£10.00	○	■	■
Mr & Mrs Farley **Rooftrees** **Rissington Road** **Bourton-on-the-Water** **GL54 2EB** **Tel: (0451) 21943** **OPEN: ALL YEAR**	Nearest Road A.429 Warmth, comfort and hospitality are offered in the relaxed atmosphere of this detached Cotswold stone guest house, situated on the edge of the famous village of Bourton-on-the-Water. Three bedrooms available, one en-suite. Children well provided for. Traditional English home cooking using fresh produce. An enjoyable stay is assured here whilst visiting the Cotswolds.	£11.00	○	○	■

○ yes ■ no

	minimum per person	children taken	evening meals available	animals taken
Mrs Joan Lee **Hollington House Hotel** **115 Hales Road** **Cheltenham GL52 6ST** **Tel: (0242) 519718/570280** **OPEN: ALL YEAR** Nearest Road A.40 Hollington House is a distinctive detached house set in its own grounds. The accommodation is in a choice of seven rooms, all with colour T.V. and tea/coffee making facilities. Some rooms have en-suite facilities. There is also an attractive lounge and a garden for guests' use. The food here is very good. Guests will enjoy the pleasant, relaxed atmosphere, and the personal attention of their host.	£14.00	O	O	O
Stephanie & St.John Milton **Milton House** **12 Royal Parade** **Bayshill Road** **Cheltenham GL50 3AY** **Tel: (0242) 582601** **OPEN: ALL YEAR** Nearest Roads A.40 Comfort has been of prime importance in the planning of this elegant Regency family home, situated just a 4 minute stroll from the imposing promenade and Imperial Gardens in Cheltenham. Nine guest rooms available, many en-suite and all with modern facilities, colour T.V. and tea/coffee making facilities. A choice of healthy and generously portioned breakfasts are on offer.	£12.00	O	■	O
Eric & Kath Price **Stretton Lodge** **Western Road** **Cheltenham GL50 3RN** **Tel: (0242) 528724** **OPEN: ALL YEAR** Nearest Roads M.5 A.40 Situated in a quiet area, within easy walking distance of Cheltenham's famous Promenade, this attractive period house offers a friendly and informal atmosphere. Thirteen most comfortable and well decorated rooms, all with modern facilities. Five rooms have private bath. T.V. and tea/coffee making facilities in each room. A pleasant T.V. lounge and garden for guests' enjoyment. Mr. & Mrs. Price have masses of information on places and events in the area. A generous English breakfast assured.	£10.50	O	■	O
Michael G. Malloy **Eton House** **Wellington Street** **Cheltenham GL50 1XY** **Tel: (0242) 523272** **OPEN: ALL YEAR** Nearest Roads A.40 A.46 A listed Regency house in the centre of Cheltenham offering a friendly yet professional service. A relaxing stay at anytime of year in this beautifully decorated house, with comfortable, well appointed bedrooms. There is a delightful guests' sitting room. Perfectly placed for shops, restaurants and touring the Cotswolds. Children over 12 welcome.	£14.00	O	O	■
Mrs Sandra Sparrey **4 Pittville Crescent** **Cheltenham GL52 2QZ** **Tel: (0242) 575567** **OPEN: ALL YEAR** Nearest Road A.435 Mrs. Sparrey offers excellent bed and breakfast in a fine Regency house overlooking Pittville Park in Cheltenham's nicest area. Three rooms with tea-making facilities and a T.V. lounge for guests' enjoyment. Pittville Pump Room is venue for festivals of music and literature, while the race course and Cleeve golf course are close by. Prestbury, reputedly the most haunted village in England, is nearby, and guided tours of the Cotswold villages can be arranged from the door. Further off lie the charms of Tewkesbury, Stratford and the Malverns.	£10.00	O	O	O

O yes ■ no

		minimum per person	children taken	evening meals available	animals taken
Mrs E.A. Daniels **Bouchers Farmhouse** **Bentham** **Nr. Cheltenham GL51 5TZ** **Tel: (0452) 862373** **OPEN: ALL YEAR**	Nearest Roads A.46 A.417 Dating back to 1661, this lovely Cotswold stone house offers the peace and tranquility of unspoilt countryside. Set in 1 acre of garden, the house has been tastefully modernised and offers 2 double rooms. A roaring log fire awaits visitors in later season. It is only a few miles from the Cathedral city of Gloucester and Cheltenham.	£7.50	O	■	■
Mrs V. Walker **Redmans** **Cold Aston/Aston Blank** **Nr. Bourton-on-the-Water** **Nr. Cheltenham GL54 3BJ** **Tel: (0451) 20537** **OPEN: APRIL-OCT**	Nearest Road A.429 A delightfully attractive Cotswold stone farmhouse, located at the end of the lovely unspoilt village of Cold Aston. Guests are accommodated in their own self-contained part of this lovely, large, dark beamed house. There are three very pleasant comfortable bedrooms with private bathroom, modern amenities and tea/coffee making facilities. Guests may also like to use the very pleasant garden and the tennis court.	£10.00	O	■	■
Sue & Brian Silcock **Caramore Guest House** **16 St.Stephens Road** **Cheltenham GL51 5AA** **Tel: (0242) 526254** **OPEN: ALL YEAR**	Nearest Roads M.5 A.40 A Regency house situated 1 mile from Cheltenham city centre. Seven comfortable rooms with modern amenities, plus T.V. and tea/coffee making facilities. A pleasant T.V. lounge for guests. Good home cooking at a very reasonable cost. A warm welcome and personal service ensures a happy stay here. Very nicely situated for touring the Cotswolds, with pretty villages.	£10.00	O	O	■
Mrs Elizabeth J. Carey-Wilson **Halewell Close** **Withington** **Cheltenham GL54 4BN** **Tel: (024289) 238** **OPEN: ALL YEAR**	Nearest Road A.40 A lovely 15th century manor house situated in the centre of the Cotswolds. The house is extremely attractive with comfortable furnishings and many exposed beams. Accommodation is in six very comfortable bedrooms, all with private facilities, some with en-suite facilities, tea/coffee makers, radio and T.V. Guests also have a choice of two lounges. There are also tennis courts and a heated outdoor swimming pool.	£30.00	O	O	O
Mrs Pat Robinson **The Malt House** **Broad Campden** **Chipping Campden GL55 6UU** **Tel: (0386) 840295** **OPEN: ALL YEAR**	Nearest Road A.34 This delightful, original 16th century malt house, stands in its own traditional English garden with orchard and stream. Accommodation is in six comfortable rooms en-suite, T.V. and tea/coffee making facilities. One room with traditional 4-poster bed. There's also a lovely beamed dining room and drawing room with open log fire. Dinner - usually English or French dishes, is served table d'hote, with good wines. Guests sit around a large oak refectory table. Visitors may use the garden or play croquet on the lawn.	£18.00	O	O	■

O yes ■ no

	minimum per person	children taken	evening meals available	animals taken
Mrs A. Ingram **York Cottage** **Lower Chedworth** **Cirencester GL54 5AN** **Tel: (0285) 72523** **OPEN:** Nearest Road A.429 This is an especially lovely house set in a pretty garden in a small village. Lower Chedworth lies in an exquisite valley just off the ancient Fosse Way and is a haven of peace and quiet. Mrs. Ingram is a charming hostess and offers two very comfortable rooms and full English breakfast to guests at York Cottage.	£12.00	O	■	■
D. Gutsell **Warwick Cottage** **Guest House** **75 Victoria Road** **Cirencester GL7 1ES** **Tel: (0285) 66279** **OPEN: ALL YEAR** Nearest Road Warwick Cottage is a pleasant Victorian house where guest's receive a warm friendly welcome. Conveniently located only 5 minutes away from the town centre. Accommodation is in 3 rooms with modern amenities, radio, T.V. and tea/coffee making facilities. A colour T.V. lounge is also available throughout the day. This makes a good base for touring the Cotswolds. No single occupancy.	£10.00	O	O	■
Mrs Sheila Reid **Tudor Farm** **Clearwell** **Nr. Coleford GL16 8JS** **Tel: (0594) 33046** **OPEN: ALL YEAR** Nearest Road B.4228 Tudor Farm is a delightful 13th century building in old Clearwell. Mullioned windows, mediaeval wall panelling, exposed beams, open stonework, inglenook fireplace and an original oak spiral staircase add to its fascination. Seven guest rooms, three en-suite, all comfortably furnished with modern amenities. Excellent and imaginative cuisine and full English breakfast is served at a civilised hour. No single availability.	£11.50	O	O	O
Hugh & Crystal St.John Mildmay **Drakestone House** **Stinchcombe** **Nr. Dursley GL11 6AS** **Tel: (0453) 2140** **OPEN: MAR-OCT** Nearest Roads A.38 B.4060 A delightful country manor house where guests receive a warm, friendly welcome and personal attention from Hugh and Crystal. The house is beautifully located on the edge of beech woods surrounded by gardens, overlooking the Vale of Berkeley. This elegantly furnished and well maintained home offers most comfortable accommodation in three bedrooms with modern amenities. A cosy residents' lounge is also available. The formal Edwardian gardens are lovely and guests are welcome to use them. The house is conveniently situated for visiting Berkeley Castle, Bath, Bristol and Cheltenham. Golf and gliding facilities are nearby.	£12.00	O	O	O
Mrs Jane George **Hunters Moon** **Sherborne Street** **Lechlade** **Tel: (0367) 52985** **OPEN: APRIL-31 OCT** Nearest Road A.361 Hunters Moon is a 250 year old guest house with an interesting history. Originally three cottages, then for a brief time a public house, and now a small family run guest house. Accommodation in four rooms with modern amenities, radio and T.V. This makes a good base from which to explore the area.	£10.00	O	■	■

O yes ■ no

			animals taken
		evening meals available	
	children taken		
minimum per person			

	Nearest Road	minimum per person	children taken	evening meals available	animals taken
Colin & Sue Richardson **Stowe Court** **Nr. St.Briavels** **Lydney GL15 6QH** **Tel: (0594) 530214** **OPEN: ALL YEAR** **(EXCL. XMAS & NEW YEAR)**	Nearest Road A.466 A delightful 300 year old farmhouse, situated in the heart of the English countryside, between the beautiful Wye Valley and the Royal Forest of Dean. The whitewashed farmhouse stands in 3½ acres of orchard and paddocks, with a lovely walled garden. Sue is an excellent cook and a wonderful hostess. She makes everyone feel completely at home and ensures they have a memorable and happy stay. All rooms have modern amenities, some with en-suite shower facilities. Antique shop on the premises, and antique tours arranged.	£10.00	○	○	○
Caroline Harmer **Noxon Farm** **St.Briavels** **Nr. Lydney GL15 6QR** **Tel: (0594) 562236** **OPEN: MAR-NOV**	Nearest Road B.4231 A friendly relaxed atmosphere is found at Noxon Farm. Located in glorious countryside on the edge of the Forest of Dean, this delightful farmhouse built of traditional forest stone, has much of its original 17th century features still in evidence including many oak beams. The comfortable accommodation is in three rooms all with modern amenities. There is a colour T.V. lounge, with french windows to the 2½ acre garden, leading to the lake where coarse fishing is available. Guests are welcome to participate in farm activites.	£7.50	○	■	○
Mrs Shirley Carter **Severn Bank** **Minsterworth GL2 8JH** **Tel: (045275) 357** **OPEN: ALL YEAR**	Nearest Road A.48 Severn Bank is a large country house with residential license, in 6 acres of grounds alongside the River Severn. Extensive river frontage offers private fishing. A warm welcome is assured in spacious comfort with full central heating. The bedrooms have wash-basins, tea/coffee making facilities, colour T.V. and lovely views. Excellent restaurants and pubs nearby. Recommended viewpoint for the Severn Bore, with the Cotswolds, Forest of Dean, Wye Valley and Severn Vale close by.	£12.00	○	■	■
S.I. Billinger **Blue Cedar House** **Stow Road** **Moreton-in-Marsh GL56 0DW** **Tel: (0608) 50299** **OPEN: FEB-DEC**	Nearest Roads A.429 Blue Cedar House is a secluded property, standing in its own grounds, set back from the main road with trees all around. 4 charming and comfortable rooms with modern amenities, and tea/coffee making facilities. A pleasant lounge with colour T.V. The gardens are suitable for sunbathing, and garden furniture is provided. Moreton-in-Marsh is a lovely town and has a Tuesday market with 300 stalls. Blue Cedar House is an ideal touring centre covering the Cotswolds and beyond. Excellent golfing locally, also riding.	£9.00	○	○	■

○ yes ■ no

112

	minimum per person	children taken	evening meals available	animals taken

Mr & Mrs Dempster
Moreton House
High Street
Moreton-in-Marsh GL56 0LQ
Tel: (0608) 50747

OPEN: ALL YEAR

Nearest Roads A.429 A.44

A very pleasant guest house situated in the lovely village of Moreton-in-Marsh, offering very comfortable rooms with all modern amenities including T.V. and tea/coffee making facilities. There is a tea-shop, with an open log fire, serving morning coffee, lunches and afternoon teas, with home-baked cakes and pastries. This is a good base for touring the beautiful Cotswolds with its charming villages. Oxford and Stratford can be easily reached by car from here, as can Cheltenham and Gloucester.

£12.50 | ○ | ○ | ○

Helen Yeadon
Townend Cottage
** & Coach House**
High Street
Moreton-in-Marsh GL56 0AD
Tel: (0608) 50846

OPEN: ALL YEAR

Nearest Road A.429

Townend Cottage is a lovely 17th century house, built of mellow Cotswold stone, standing on the edge of a typical small Cotswold market town. The house has retained much of its original character, and the low beamed ceilings and inglenook fireplace create a lovely cosy atmosphere. Accommodation is in six rooms all with modern amenities, T.V. and tea/coffee making facilities. The food here is quite delicious, imaginatively prepared by the owner/chef.

£13.50 | ○ | ○ | ○

Mrs J. Wright
Twostones
Evenlode
Moreton-in-Marsh GL56 0NY
Tel: (0608) 51104

OPEN: APRIL-OCT

Nearest Road A.429 - Fosse Way

Twostones stands in 6 acres with uninterrupted views of lovely countryside, next to the village church. Built in Cotswold stone and said to be 500 years old, the house has a wealth of beams and an inglenook fireplace. 3 guest rooms with comfortable beds, good food and a friendly atmosphere make this an ideal base for touring the Cotswolds.

£8.50 | ○ | ■ | ○

Mrs M. Reece
Old Court
Church Street
Newent GL18 1AB
Tel: (0531) 820522

OPEN: ALL YEAR

Nearest Road A.40

An imposing and beautiful house. Old Court was originally the Priory to the church next door, and was rebuilt in the 17th century. Peacefully secluded in a walled garden in the heart of the village. Elegantly furnished, the house offers 3 guest rooms, two en-suite. Mrs. Reece serves excellent meals with produce from her large garden. Riding available by arrangement.

£10.00 | ○ | ○ | ○

Mrs Patricia Powell
Cotteswold House
Market Place
Northleach GL54 3EG
Tel: (0451) 60493

OPEN: ALL YEAR

Nearest Roads A.40 A.429

This is a delightful Cotswold stone house dating back some 300 years. It has been lovingly renovated to a high standard, offering three charming and comfortable rooms of individual character - with beams and modern facilities. Situated in a small market town it offers an excellent base for touring the many pleasant villages and surrounding countryside.

£10.75 | ○ | ■ | ■

○ yes ■ no

113

	Nearest Road	minimum per person	children taken	evening meals available	animals taken
Theresa & Mike Eastman **Market House** **The Square** **Northleach GL54 3EJ** **Tel: (0451) 60557** **OPEN: ALL YEAR**	Nearest Road A.40 A warm welcome and "olde worlde" atmosphere is to be found at Market House. This charming 16th century Cotswold stone house is situated in the centre of a small, unpoilt Cotswold town. Offering four pretty, comfortable rooms. A good base for touring the beautiful Cotswold countryside. Close by are Cheltenham and Gloucester.	£10.00	■	■	■
Mrs Patsy Spiers **The Green Farm** **Wainlodes Lane** **Bishops Norton** **Nr.Gloucester GL2 9LN** **Tel: (0452) 730252** **OPEN: MAR-NOV**	Nearest Road A.38 A very attractive 300 year old half-timbered farmhouse, standing on a 200 acre mixed farm. There are 3 beautifully decorated bedrooms with modern amenities. Exposed beams, inglenook fireplaces with brasses and very comfortably furnished rooms. There are most attractive lawns with masses of flowers. Ideal for touring Gloucester, Cheltenham, Tewkesbury, the Forest of Dean and the Cotswolds.	£8.50	○	○	■
Judith M. Price **Merrivale** **Tewkesbury Road** **Norton** **Nr.Gloucester GL2 9LQ** **Tel: (0452) 730412** **OPEN: ALL YEAR**	Nearest Roads M.5 A.38 A warm, friendly welcome awaits the visitor to Merrivale. This large homely guest house offers 6 charming, comfortable rooms. It has a nice garden for visitors to enjoy. It is well located for easy access to Gloucester and for touring the magnificent Cotswolds with their super historic villages and the surrounding countryside. Small dogs only, please. Cots provided.	£7.50	○	■	○
Mrs V Keyte **The Limes** **Tewkesbury Road** **Stow-on-the-Wold** **GL54 1EN** **Tel: (0451) 30034** **OPEN: ALL YEAR**	Nearest Roads A.424 B.4077 A very large family house offering excellent accommodation with six rooms, all having modern facilities. Situated only four minutes walk from the centre of the town, it overlooks the countryside in a quiet area. Large attractive garden with ornamental pool and waterfall. From here Bourton-on-the-Water, Broadway, Burford, Chipping Campden and Moreton-in-Marsh are just a short drive.	£9.00	○	■	○
Mrs Caroline Garrett **Lamfield** **Rodborough Common** **Stroud GL5 5DA** **Tel: (045387) 3452** **OPEN: ALL YEAR**	Nearest Roads A.46 A.419 A delightful gabled stone house dating back to 1730, modernised to a high standard and offering two double rooms with modern amenities. Guest lounge. Tea always available. Unrivalled views over the valley with the Welsh Mountains in the distance. This house of character is a super base for touring the whole region, with its wealth of sights and villages.	£9.00	■	■	■

		minimum per person	children taken	evening meals available	animals taken
Mrs J.G. Saunders **Great House** **Castle Street** **Winchcombe GL54 5JA** **Tel: (0242) 602490** **OPEN: ALL YEAR**	Nearest Roads A.46 A.40 A superb Jacobean house offering comfortable accommodation with modern facilities. A warm welcome awaits the visitor here. It is only ½ mile walking distance to Sudeley Castle, in the heart of the Cotswolds. Two rooms are available with T.V., and one with 4-poster bed. There is a garden for guests' use. Ideal touring centre.	£9.00	○	■	■
Mrs S. Simmonds **Gower House** **16 North Street** **Winchcombe GL54 5LH** **Tel: (0242) 602616** **OPEN: ALL YEAR**	Nearest Road A.46 Mick and Sally will welcome you to their handsome 17th century town house, situated centrally in Winchcombe, convenient for shops and restaurants. Car parking at rear of house. Three attractive bedrooms, one double, and two twin are available. Full English breakfast served, with Continental alternative if requested. Pretty garden for guests' use. Baby sitting can be arranged.	£9.00	○	■	■

○ yes ■ no

* * *ADVANCE RESERVATIONS* * *

Don't be disappointed. Book ahead.
Use our fast efficient
RESERVATION SERVICE
Reservation forms & Reservation Bureau
Be sure of your accommodation
Book Now!!
Call us on

01-370 7099   **01-370 7099**

HAMPSHIRE

Located in the centre of the south coast of England, this county possesses an almost magical quality. One visit is never enough, you will be lured back time and again, on each occasion previously undiscovered qualities are revealed. Hampshire has within its boundaries small towns and villages, great monuments to human endeavour, beautiful rivers, sweeping downs and deep woodlands. There is a splendid coastline with seaside resorts, the Cathedral City of Winchester and the "jewel" of the Isle of Wight.

The New Forest

The New Forest is probably the area most often frequented by the English visitor. It is an area of great character with pleasant villages of thatched cottages surrounded by glades and streams and yet it manages to retain a wild, romantic beauty, no doubt reminiscent of the scenes that must have existed in the days when Saxon Kings hunted here. There are the herds of wild deer and hardy New Forest ponies. It was a favourite hunting ground of William the Conqueror who instituted very strict laws governing hunting. Ancient penalties for poaching were blinding, mutilation or even death. To the northwest of Beaulieu are some of the most idyllic parts of the New Forest, with few villages and little streams that flow into the Avon. This area is less frequented than many other spots and offers some excellent walks. Lyndhurst can be said to be the capital of this area and has a most contentious 19th century church built by William White. Constructed in scarlet brickwork it has bands of yellow as well as quite unusual ornamental decoration with some interesting pre-raphaelite stained glass windows by William Morris.

Winchester and Environs

Treading in a northerly direction the landscape changes and wide, sweeping chalk downs become a familiar sight. In the midst of these hill lies the ancient Roman city of Winchester. Once the capital city of Saxon Wessex it is today the capital of Hampshire. The downs hold evidence of ancient settlement and discoveries at Quarley, Danebury and Haddlehill include neolithic burial mounds and iron age hill forts. Winchester is famous for its beautiful mediaeval cathedral built during the reign of William the Conquerer and his notorious son Rufus. With major rebuilding in the 13th and 14th century the cathedral adopts a long low form with an excellent Gothic roof supported by clusters of pillars and a superb nave. The city was of such importance that in 1194 Richard Coeur de Lion was crowned in the cathedral. The city boasts many mediaeval buildings especially around the peaceful cathedral close and was a great centre of learning during the time of Alfred the Great, when a school of calligraphy was established. It was at Winchester that William compiled the famous Domesday Book. The nearby castle was, at one time, the seat of Kings, but all that remains today is the great hall. Further north there are many small towns and villages with fine houses and churches and illustrious families whose names offer interesting glimpses back into history. In the wooded valley of the River Lodden is the Tudor mansion of Lyne, built by William Sandys often visited by Henry V111 in the company of Ann Bolyen. Jane Austen lived in the small village of Steventon for 25 years and from the surrounding villages and houses she was able to create some of her most memorable works. The first Marquess of Winchester, advisor to four out of five Tudor monarchs, built Basing House or, as it later became known, Loyalty House. His descendants fortified it against the Parliamentarians until finally Cromwell himself laid siege and eventually breeched it. A Hampshire saying goes "Clubs are trumps, as when Basing House was taken" - apparently the guards were playing cards when the house was stormed.

The Coast and The Isle of Wight

The Isle of Wight is separated from the mainland by the waters of the Solent. Guarded by Martello towers, this channel holds the major port of Southampton and numerous yachting centres such as Hamble, Yarmouth, Lymington and Bucklers Hard where a maritime museum has been established in honour of its ship building past. Cowes on the Isle of Wight is an international sailing centre and its regattas continue under the patronage of the Royal Family which the island has enjoyed since Queen Victoria came to live in the nearby Osborne House. There are excellent beaches and splendid bays, such as Alum Bay with its multi-coloured sands. There are unspoilt inland downs, historic towns and the famous chalk stacks.

HAMPSHIRE GAZETEER.

Areas of Outstanding Natural Beauty.
East and South Hampshire, North Wessex Downs and Chichester Harbour.

Historic Houses and Castles

Avington Park -- Winchester
 16th century red brick house, enlarged in 17th century by the addition of two wings and a classical portico. Stateroom, ballroom with wonderful ceiling, Red drawing Room, library etc.

Beaulieu Abbey & Palace House -- Beaulieu
 12th century Cistercian abbey -- the original gatehouse of abbey converted to palace house 1538. Houses historic car museum.

Breamore House -- Breamore
 16th century Elizabethan Manor House, tapestries, furniture, paintings. Also museum.

Jane Austen's Home -- Chawston
 Personal effects of the famous writer.

Broadlands -- Romsey
 16th century -- park and garden created by Capability Brown. Home of The Earl of Mountbatten of Burma.

Mottisfont Abbey -- Nr. Romsey
 12th century Augustinian Priory until Dissolution. Painting by Rex Whistler rompe l'oeil in Gothickmanner.

Stratfield Sayo House -- Reading
 17th century house -- presented to the Duke of Wellington 1817. Now contains his possessions -- also as wild fowl sanctuary.

Sandham Memorial Chapel -- Sandham -- Nr. Newbury
 Paintings by Stanley Spencer cover the walls.

The Vyne -- Sherborne St. John
 16th century red brick, chapel with Renaissance glass and rare linenfold panelling. Alterations made in 1654 -- classical portico. Palladian staircase dates from 1760.

West Green House -- Hartley Wintney
 18th century red brick house set in walled garden.

Cathedrals and Churches

Winchester Cathedral
 Largest Gothic church in Europe. Norman and perpendicular styles, three sets of medieval paintings, marble font c. 1180. Stalls c. 1320 with 60 misercords. Extensive mediaeval tiled floor.

Breamore (St. Mary) -- Breamore
 10th century. Saxon. Double splayed windows, stone rood.

East Meon (All Saints)
 15th century rebuilding of Norman fabric. Tournai marble font.

Idsworth (St. Hubert)
 16th century chapel -- 18th century bell turret. 14th century paintings in chancel.

Pamber -- (dedication unknown)
 Early English -- Norman central tower, 15th century pews, wooden effigy of knight c. 1270.

Romsey (St. Mary & St. Ethelfleda)
 Norman -- 13th century effigy of a lady -- Saxon rood and carving of crucifixion, 16th century painted reredos.

Silchester (St. Mary)
 Norman, perpendicular, 14th century effigy of a lady, 15th century screen, Early English chancel with painted patterns on South window splays, Jacobean pulpit with domed canopy.

Winchester (St. Cross)
 12th century. Original chapel to Hospital. Style changing from Norman at East to decorated West. Tiles, glass, wall painting.

Museums and Galleries

Browning Barracks -- Aldershot
Airborne Forces Exhibition of weapons from war, dioramas of battles, models, equipment, medals, photographs, etc.

Bargate Guildhall Museum -- Southampton
Former Hall of Guilds -- exhibition of local history etc.

Southsea Castle - Portsmouth
Local history and military history, archeology.

Cumberland House Museum and Aquarium -- Southsea
Natural history and geology of district.

Portsmouth Royal Naval Museum -- Portsmouth
Relics of Nelson, H.M.S. Victory, ship models, figureheads, etc.

Dickens Birthplace Museum. -- Portsmouth
House where the author was born in 1812.

Southampton Art Gallery -- Southampton
British and French paintings, particularly contemporary British.

Tudor House Museum -- Southampton
Tudor mansion -- historical antiquarian exhibits.

Westgate Museum -- Winchester
Mediaeval West Gate -- exhibition illustrating history of Winchester, collection of weights and measures from mediaeval time onwards.

Winchester Cathedral Treasury -- Winchester
Silver from churches and parishes etc. in Hampshire.

Winchester College Museum -- Winchester
English Watercolours -- collections of Greek pottery

Historic Monuments

Bishop Waltham's Palace -- Bishops Waltham
12th and 15th centuries. Flint ruins of the palace of the Bishops of Winchester.

Basing House -- Nr. Basingstoke
16th century -- ruined Tudor palace -- originally Saxon fortress, then Norman Castle.

Porchester Castle -- Porchester
4th century -- Saxon fort, 12th century Keep and Assheton's tower, 1368.

Netley Abbey -- Nr. Hamble
13th century -- remain of Cistercian abbey.

Hurst Castle -- Nr. Milford-on-Sea
Fortress built for Henry VIII -- restored in 1800's.

Mary Rose Museum -- Portsmouth
Almost complete Tudor Warship. Flagship of Henry VIII. Thousands of artifacts from the wreck including complete ship's surgeon's implements and the largest collection of Tudor arrows in the world. Possibly the most important archeological discovery of this century.

HAMPSHIRE
Recommended roadside restaurants

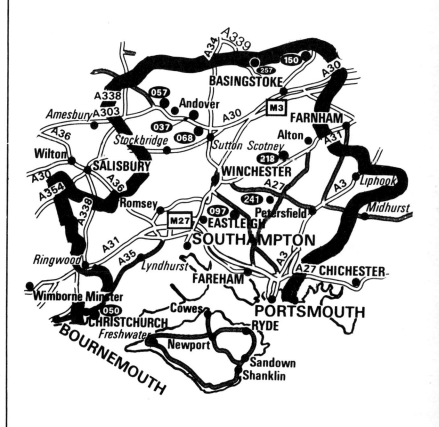

Hampshire

		minimum per person	children taken	evening meals available	animals taken
Mrs Margaret Moore **Wide Lane Cottage Hotel** **Sway Rd** **Brockenhurst SO42 7SH** **Tel: (0590) 22296** **OPEN: ALL YEAR**	Nearest Road A.337 A delightful 300 year old New Forest cottage, where guests receive a warm welcome and personal attention from the resident proprietors, Mr. & Mrs. Moore. There are five guest rooms with modern amenities. The heavily beamed, comfortable T.V. lounge has a cozy log burning fire and is full of "olde worlde" charm. In the pleasant dining room delicious four course meals are served by Mrs. Moore. This makes an ideal base for those seeking a restful holiday.	£19.00	O	O	■
Mr & Mrs M.D. Lancaster **Bentley** **Sway Road** **Brockenhurst SO42 7RX** **Tel: (0590) 22407** **OPEN: ALL YEAR**	Nearest Roads A.337 B.3055 This large Victorian house with garden, offers 6 delightful rooms to the visitor and a warm family welcome. Good home cooking - choice of menu. In the heart of the New Forest the house makes an ideal base for touring the immediate vicinity, with its delightful walks, or for going further afield to Lyndhurst, Lymington, Southampton etc.	£10.50	O	O	■
Mrs P.A. Mason **Crowd Hill Farm** **Winchester Road** **Fair Oak** **Tel: (0703) 692322** **OPEN: ALL YEAR**	Nearest Roads M.27 M.3 A very friendly family atmosphere may be found at Crowd Hill Farm. This comfortable 16th century farmhouse stands on 15½ acres of land, surrounded by farm and woodland. The lovely house retains all its original features including oak beams, oak panelling and Tudor inglenook fireplaces. Accommodation is in four comfortable bedrooms with modern amenities. There's also a garden and a games room for guests' use. Close by are many lovely walks along bridleways and footpaths through the woodland. A pleasant stay is assured.	£12.50	O	■	O
Nigel & Dawn Gussman **Little Uplands Country Motel** **Garrison Hill** **Droxford SO3 1QL** **Tel: (0489) 878507/877814** **Telex: 477046 ROBIN G** **OPEN: ALL YEAR** **(EXCL. XMAS)**	Nearest Road A.32 Little Uplands is a charming house, situated in 7½ acres of gardens in the picturesque Meon Valley, with sixteen most attractive rooms - eight with own shower. All rooms have colour T.V. and tea making facilities. Mr. & Mrs. Gussman also offer a large swimming pool, sauna, gym, trout fishing, tennis and snooker. Historic places abound in this area including Winchester, Broadlands, Portsmouth with Nelson's Flagship and The Mary Rose. The New Forest is not far.	£15.00	O	O	■
Mrs P.H. Hill **Priory Cottage** **Rockbourne** **Nr.Fordingbridge SP6 3NA** **Tel: (07253) 246** **OPEN: ALL YEAR**	Nearest Roads A.354 A.338 A charming house offering three delightful, comfortable rooms for guests. Mrs. Hill is well known for her hospitality and the house is very popular. Situated in a lovely village it is an ideal base for visiting the numerous stately homes, museums and beauty spots in the surrounding area. Evening meals are at a moderate price, offering good cooking and home produce. Children over 12 years.	£10.50	O	O	■

O yes ■ no

	Nearest Roads	min. per person	children taken	evening meals available	animals taken
Brigadier & Mrs A.C.D.Watts **Shearings** **Rockbourne** **Fordingbridge SP6 3NA** Tel: (07253) 256 **OPEN: MAR-OCT**	Nearest Roads A.354 A.338 Glorious 16th century thatched cottage fronting onto a stream, lovely gardens, great architectural interest, a photographer's dream. Delightfully furnished with great style. Charming hosts who enjoy sharing their beautiful home with guests who appreciate the cultured, elegant lifestyle offered. 1 single, 1 twin, 2 double rooms, (some en-suite costing a little extra), four course candlelit dinner £10 per person. For winter bookings or stay of 7 days, 10% reduction. Advance reservation essential.	£15.00	O	O	■
David & Diane Skelton **"Cockle Warren" Guest House** **36 Seafront** **Hayling Island PO11 9HL** Tel: (0705) 464961 **OPEN: ALL YEAR**	Nearest Roads A.27 M.27 A delightful house on Hayling sea-front overlooking the Solent and the Isle of Wight. Lovely garden with hens and ducks. Three attractive, very comfortable bedrooms, all with hand basins and colour T.V., one with 4-poster bed and en suite shower room. Pride is taken in good traditional English and Continental cookery with home-made bread and marmalade. Log burning stove in the comfortable lounge. Licensed. Riding on the beach by arrangement all year.	£15.00	O	O	O
Mrs Patricia Edwards **Wessex Guest House** **5 Palmerston Street** **Romsey SO51 8GF** Tel: (0794) 512038 **OPEN: ALL YEAR**	Nearest Roads M.27 A.27 This Georgian house is an excellent base for touring the region. Comfortable accommodation and a homely atmosphere are offered to the visitor. Romsey is a delightful area, with superb countryside for walking. Broadlands, home of the late Earl Mountbatten of Burma, is just a few minutes away. From here you can visit the New Forest or the coast. Salisbury and Shaftesbury are also within a comfortable drive.	£9.00	O	O	■
Mrs Jill Twine **100 Cedar Road** **Portswood** **Southampton SO2 1AH** Tel: (0703) 226761 **OPEN: ALL YEAR**	Nearest Road A.33 A pleasant town house built at the turn of the century, offering comfortable accommodation in four rooms. Southampton offers a wealth of places of interest to the visitor with many museums, galleries and sporting activities, especially sailing. From here one can drive to the New Forest in just about half an hour. It is also ideal as a base for day trips to the Isle of Wight. Cots are provided. Personal and friendly service.	£9.50	O	O	■
Douglas & Eileen Dawson **Nirvana Hotel** **384-386 Winchester Rd** **Bassett** **Southampton SO1 7DH** Tel: (0703) 760474 **OPEN: ALL YEAR**	Nearest Road A.33 Privately run family hotel, giving personal service in a large Victorian house. 21 comfortable rooms, some en-suite, some with telephones, fully centrally heated with tea/coffee making facilities, colour T.V. Excellent food and an attractive Tudor style bar with cosy log burning fire. Easy access to city centre and surrounding places of interest: New Forest, Winchester, Broadlands House.	£17.00	O	O	O

O yes ■ no

		minimum per person	children taken	evening meals available	animals taken
Mrs Rosamond M. Curtis 10c Edgar Road Winchester SO23 9SJ Tel: (0962) 54985 **OPEN: ALL YEAR**	Nearest Roads M.3 M.27 A pleasant welcome awaits the visitor to Mrs. Curtis' home. She offers accommodation in a choice of three rooms with modern amenities. Her home is located only a few minutes walk from the city and the Cathedral. It is a convenient base for touring.	£9.50	○	■	○
Mrs Heather Lawrence 67 St.Cross Road Winchester SO23 9RE Tel: (0962) 63002 **OPEN: ALL YEAR**	Nearest Road A.333 Two comfortable rooms are offered by Mrs. Lawrence for visitors. Situated in Winchester, it is not far from many of the museums, galleries and other places of historic interest. The cathedral which dominates the city, is a treasurehouse and should be visited. T.V., and teamakers in each room. Children over 3 welcome.	£9.00	○	■	■
Mrs A.D. Farrell 5 Ranelagh Road St.Cross Winchester SO23 9TA Tel: (0962) 69555 **OPEN: ALL YEAR**	Nearest Road A.33 A friendly atmosphere and warm welcome are found at number five. A pleasant Victorian house retaining many of its original features. Accommodation is in three rooms; 1 double, 1 twin and 1 family room, with modern amenities and tea/coffee making facilities. There is also a T.V. lounge for guests' to use. Conveniently located, only 15 minutes walk from the Cathedral.	£9.00	○	■	■
Mrs J.R. Talbot Church Farm House Barton Stacey Winchester SO21 3RR Tel: (0962) 760268 **OPEN: ALL YEAR**	Nearest Roads A.303 A.34 A.30 Church Farm House was a 15th century tythe barn, having Georgian and modern additions. With an adjacent coach house, recently converted, where guests may be totally self-contained or will be welcomed to the log fired family drawing room to dine on locally produced fresh food. Five beautiful bedrooms for guests, most with en-suite, T.V., tea/coffeee making facilities. Horses are kept. Swimming pool and croquet in the garden. Tennis court adjacent.	£20.00	○	○	○
Mrs M.J. Coombe Yew Tree Cottage Lower Baybridge Lane Baybridge Owslebury Nr. Winchester Tel: (096274) 254 **OPEN: ALL YEAR**	Nearest Road M.3 Yew Tree Cottage is an absolutely charming, rose covered 17th century thatched cottage, set in an attractive old fashioned English garden. Guests enjoy complete privacy and the two bedrooms have private facilities arranged so that the accommodation is suitable for families or friends sharing. The rooms also have T.V. and telephone. There is a private sitting and dining room. Mrs. Coombe is a professional cook and everything is home-made and fresh, providing excellent dinners.	£12.50	○	○	■

○ yes ■ no

		minimum per person	children taken	evening meals available	animals taken
Mr T.R. Lancaster **Alcester** **Colwell Road** **Colwell Bay** **Isle of Wight TO40 9SW** **Tel: (0983) 753201** **OPEN: ALL YEAR**	Nearest Road - Avenue Road A pleasant family run guest house, situated close to safe, sandy beaches and coastal walks. There is a golf club at Freshwater Bay which welcomes visitors and there are fishing trips from Yarmouth Harbour. Also riding stables close by. Three charming rooms, two en-suite. Comfortable T.V. lounge. Marvellous home cooked evening meals.	£11.50	O	O	O
Mr & Mrs Simmons **Shute Inn** **Clatterford Shute** **Carisbrooke** **Newport** **Isle of Wight PO30 1PD** **Tel: (0983) 523393** **OPEN: FEB-NOV**	Nearest Road B.3323 Shute Inn is a listed Georgian house located in a beautiful rural setting with unrivalled views of Carisbrooke Castle, where King Charles I was imprisoned, and the unspoilt Bowcombe Valley. Close by is a very pretty ford, crossing of the Lukeley Brook. Accommodation in three rooms with modern amenities and tea/coffee making facilities. English & Continental breakfasts are available with a wide choice of menu for lunch and dinner.	£10.95	O	O	■
John & Brenda Coyle **West Pines Guest House** **74 West Street** **Ryde** **Isle of Wight PO33 2QQ** **Tel: (0983) 67644** **OPEN: ALL YEAR**	Nearest Road - Queens Road A warm welcome awaits guests to this pleasant guest house. Accommodation is in six rooms with modern amenities. There is a comfortable colour T.V. lounge and pleasant dining room. The cooking is good and John and Brenda are personally responsible for the preparation and serving of all meals. Close by are sandy beaches, two swimming pools, two sports centres, riding, fishing, golf, tennis and canoe lakes.	£8.00	O	O	■
Mrs Maureen Wright **Littledene Lodge Private Hotel** **Granville Road** **Totland Bay** **Isle of Wight PO39 0AX** **Tel: (0983) 752453** **OPEN: ALL YEAR**	Nearest Road At Littledene Lodge guests are sure of a warm welcome, comfortable accommodation and good food. Located 500 yards from the beach on the West side of the island, this hotel makes a pleasant place to stay, whether on holiday or on business. Accommodation is in seven rooms, some with en-suite facilities, all with modern amenities and tea/coffee making facilities. There's also a comfortable lounge with colour T.V. In the spacious dining room good food is served by Mrs. Wright.	£10.50	O	O	O
Mr & Mrs Kevin Harris **The Nodes Country Hotel** **Alum Bay Old Road** **Totland Bay** **Isle of Wight PO39 0HZ** **Tel: (0983) 752859** **OPEN: ALL YEAR**	Nearest Road B.3322 Set in 2 acres of grounds at the foot of Tennyson Downs, this very pleasant country hotel offers 11 charming bedrooms, 8 with en-suite facilities. Totland Bay is well known for its beauty and from here one can visit the whole region by car. The walking and beaches around here are superb. Cots and highchairs are provided.	£12.00	O	O	O

		minimum per person	children taken	evening meals available	animals taken
Shirley Janes **Heather Cot Guest House** **77 St.Johns Road** **Sandown PO36 8HF** **Tel: (0983) 403890** **OPEN: ALL YEAR**	Nearest Road A.3055 A quiet and friendly Guest House, with tastefully furnished and spacious rooms, situated close to Sandown Bay and all the local amenities. A total of 5 bedrooms are available to guests, three of which are family rooms with children being well provided for. Highchairs, cots and baby sitting service available. All rooms have modern amenities and tea/coffee making facilities. Mrs. Janes takes pride in her home cooking. Licensed.	£10.00	O	O	■
Mrs S. Poulter **"Quinces"** **Cranmore Avenue** **Yarmouth** **Isle of Wight PO41 0XS** **Tel: (0983) 760080)** **OPEN: ALL YEAR**	Nearest Road - Yarmouth/Newport Rd. An attractive modern house set between a vineyard and a dairy farm, on a private road 2 miles from Yarmouth. Two delightful bedrooms, both with hand basins, heating and tea/coffee making facilities. It offers an ideal base for exploring the beautiful and varied countryside and coastline of West Wight. The delightful one acre garden with ponds, merges into a larger nature reserve where nightingales sing. The meals are very good and use is made of home grown produce. Children over 6 years.	£10.00	O	O	O

O yes ■ no

HEREFORD AND WORCESTER

Hereford

It is a beautiful and ancient city, standing on the banks of the river Wye, and is almost a crossroads between England and Wales. It certainly seems so on market days when it plays its role as market centre for the Marches, an area along the border with Wales which has a very particular history of its own. The Cathedral with its massive sandstone tower dominates the town, and makes a magnificent background for the Three Choirs Festival. This is a musical event which dates from 1727 and performances take place yearly in one or other of the great Cathedrals of Hereford, Worcester and Gloucester, providing music unsurpassed.

The county is fortunate in having so many historic buildings which have been well preserved. The charming "black and white" villages abound here, set in a hazy green dreamlike background, making it visually one of the most romantic of our counties. The landscape of the English plain alters dramatically as the land rises to merge with the Great Black Mountain range which rises up to 2660 feet. This is fine country for Pony-Trekking or walking and effort is well rewarded with unforgettable views. It is not possible to take cars everywhere - but there is a narrow mountain road, Gospel Pass, which takes traffic from Hay-on-Wye to Llanthony, and gives the most superb view of the Upper Wye Valley.

The Royal Forest of Dean is a dark and mysterious area, still having some twenty-two thousand acres of oak and beech trees. It must have been a truly enormous forest when the first men decided to make their lives and homes in the woodlands. There are rich deposits of coal and iron which have been mined for centuries by the Foresters and the trees have always been felled for making charcoal. There are in existence still, ancient courts where the Forest dwellers can and do claim their age old privileges and rights to mine in the forest and make charcoal.

The pre-Cambrian Malvern Hills form a natural boundary between Herefordshire and Worcester, the highest points commanding view is over fourteen counties. At their feet nestle the pretty little villages, such as Eastonor which has a 19th century castle built in Norman revival style and looking quite mediaeval amidst the parkland and gardens.

There are, in fact, five Malverns, the largest one, obviously known as Great Malvern, is noted for the purity of the water and it became very fashionable as a spa in the 19th century. It is still bottled and sold countrywide. The Priory at Malvern is particularly rich in 15th century stained glass and has a fine collection of mediaeval tiles which were made close by. William Ladgman, the 14th century author of "Piers the Ploughman" was educated at the Priory and it is said that he was sleeping on the Malvern Hills when he experienced the vision which inspired him to write the poem that became a landmark in English literature. Many famous names connected with music and the arts have sprung from this area - we remember particularly Sir Edward Elgar whose "Dream of Gerontius" had its first performance in Hereford Cathedral in 1902.

Worcester

Here is another glorious cathedral, begun before the Normans arrived in England. It stands beside the river Severn which appears to be a fairly lazy waterway, but in the past flood waters have reached quite astonishing heights. The river is well known because of the "Severn Bore".

It can a be very pleasant way of passing a day to take a cruise along the river when it is possible to see many more villages and churches and, of course, inns and pubs; seeing the county from a different perspective. But do not leave Worcester without visiting the College Close; a really lovely group of buildings, carefully preserved and so very English in character. To the south of the county lies Evesham in gently undulating vale, where you will find Broadway which is described as the show village of England and deservedly so. To the north and east of the county, there are the unmistakeable signs of man and progress. Heavy industry and the large towns and cities which support it - but there are many more delightful things and places to enjoy en route before reaching the borders of the next county.

HEREFORD AND WORCESTER GAZETEER

Areas of Outstanding Natural Beauty.
The Malvern Hills, The Cotswolds, The Wye Valley

Historic Houses and Castles

Berrington Hall -- Leominster
18th century -- painted and plastered ceilings. Landscape by Capability Brown.

Brilley -- Cwmmau Farmhouse -- Whitney-on-Wye
17th century timber framed and stone tiled farmhouse.

Burton Court -- Eardisland
14th century great hall. Exhibition of European and Oriental costume and curios. Model fairground.

Croft Castle -- Nr. Leominster
Castle on the Welsh border -- inhabited by Croft family for 900 years.

Dinmore Manor -- Nr. Hereford
14th century chapel and cloister.

Eastnor Castle -- Nr. Ledbury
19th century -- Castellated, containing pictures & armour. Arboretum.

Eye Manor -- Leominster
17th century Carolean manor house -- excellent plasterwork, paintings, costumes, books, secret passage. Collection of dolls.

Hanbury Hall -- Nr. Droitwich
18th century red brick house -- only two rooms and painted ceilings on exhibition.

Harvington Hall -- Kidderminster
Tudor manor house with moat, priest's hiding places.

The Greyfriars -- Worcester
15th century timber-framed building adjoins Franciscan Priory.

Hellen's -- Much Marcle
13th century manorial house of brick and stone. Contains the Great Hall with stone table -- bedroom of Queen ‹loody Mary· Much of the original furnishings remain.

Kentchurch Court -- Hereford
14th century fortified border manor house. Paintings & Carvings by Grinling Gibbons.

Moccas Court -- Moccas
18th century -- designed by Adam -- Parklands by Capability Brown -- under restoration.

Pembridge Castle -- Welsh Newton
17th century moated castle.

Sutton Court -- Mordiford
Palladian Mansion by Wyatt, watercolours, embroideries, china.

Cathedrals and Churches

Aymestry (St. John the Baptist & St. Alkmund)
16th century rood screen.

Abbey Dore (St. Mary & Holy Trinity)
17th century glass and great oak screen -- early English architecture.

Brinsop (St. George)
14th century, screen and glass, alabaster reredos, windows in memory of Wordsworth, carved Norman tympanum.

Bredon (St. Giles)
12th century -- central tower and spire. Mediaeval heraldic tiles, tombs, and early glass.

Brockhampton (St. Eadburgh)
1902. Central tower and thatched roof.

Castle Frome (St. Michael and All Angles)
12th century carved font, 17th century effigies in alabaster

Chaddesley Corbett (St. Cassian)
14th century monuments, 12th century font.

Elmley (St. Mary)
12th century and 15th century font, tower, gargoyles, mediaeval.

Great Witley (St. Michael)
Baroque - Plasterwork, painted ceiling, painted glass, very fine example.

Hereford (All Saints)
13th-14th centuries, spire, splendid choir stalls, chained library.

Hereford Cathedral
Small cathedral -- fine central tower c. 1325, splendid porch, brasses, early English Lady Chapel with lancet windows. Red Sandstone.

Kilpeck (St. mary & St. David)
Romanesque style -- mediaevel windows -- fine carvings.

Leominster (St. Peter & St. Paul)
12 century doorway, fine Norman arches, decorated windows.

Much Marcle (St. Bartholomew)
13th century. 14th & 17th century monuments.

Worcester Cathedral
11th to 16th century. Fine cloisters and crypt. Tomb of King John.

Worcester (St. Swithun)
18th century -- furnishings untouched. Ceiling vaulted in plaster.

Museums and Galleries

Hereford City Museum & Art Gallery
Collections of natural history and archeology, costumes, textiles, embroideries, toys, agricultural bygones. Paintings by local artists, examples of applied art, silver, pottery and porcelain.

The Old House -- Hereford
Jacobean period museum with furnishings of time.

Churchill Gardens Museum -- Hereford
Extensive costume collection, fine furniture, work by local artists.

Almonry Museum -- Evesham
Anglo-Saxon, Roman-British, mediaeval and monastic remains.

Avoncroft Museum of Buildings -- Stoke Heath
Open air museum showing buildings of reconstructed iron-age dwelling to 15th century merchant's homes.

City Museum and Art Gallery -- Worcester
Local history, archeology, natural history, environmental studies.

Dyson Perrins Museum of Worcester Porcelain -- Worcester
Most comprehensive collection of old Worcester in the world.

The Commandery - Sidbury
15th century timber-framed building, was originally a hospital. Royalist H.Q. during battle of Worcester, 1651.

HEREFORD & WORCESTER
Recommended roadside restaurants

200	A40	Whitchurch (North) Herefordshire 5 miles north of Monmouth
201	A40	Whitchurch (South) Hereford 7 miles south of Ross-on-Wye
216	A456/450	Hagley, Worcs. 4 miles east of kidderminster
262	A49	Dinmore, Herefordshire 7 miles north of Hereford at junct of A417
269	A449	Hartlebury, Herefordshire 4 miles south of Kidderminster

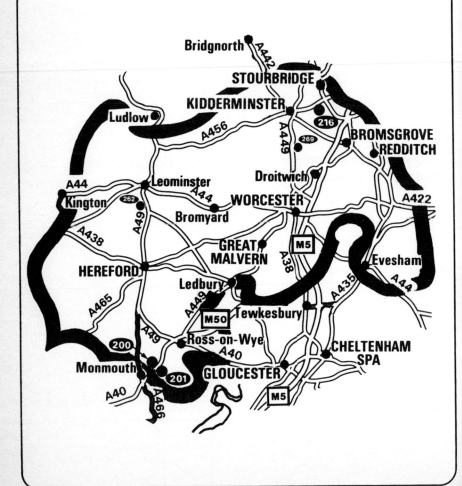

Hereford & Worcester

Madame Juliet Carro
"Cusack's Glebe"
Saintbury
Nr. Broadway WR12 7PX
Tel: (0386) 852210

OPEN: MAR-DEC 15

Nearest Road

Guests will enjoy the peace and quite of this delightful 15th century farmhouse, which stands in 5 acres of private paddocks, orchards and gardens. This medieval house is of great architectural interest retaining all of its former charm and character. The very comfortable, spacious accommodation in 3 rooms, have private shower or bathroom, colour T.V. and tea/coffee making facilities. Saintbury is an area of outstanding beauty, only 12 miles from Stratford upon Avon and 3 miles from Chipping Campden.

£28.00 ○ ■ ■

John & Helen Jones
The Old Rectory
Church Street
Willersey
Nr. Broadway WR12 7PM
Tel: (0386) 853729

OPEN: MOST OF YEAR

Nearest Road A.46

A delightful 17th century country house built in mellow Cotswold stone. The rectory retains its ancient beams and open fireplaces, creating a super atmosphere in which to relax. Delightfully located in a picturesque village with duck pond, village green, colourful cottages and ancient church. Accommodation is in 6 nicely decorated very comfortable rooms most with en-suite facilities all with radio, T.V. and tea/coffee makers. An attractive guests lounge overlooks the delightful walled garden. Ideally located for touring the Cotswolds. Prices shown are for 2 people.

£27.00 ■ ■ ■

Mrs Jacqueline Chugg
Little Lodge Farm
Broughton Green
Hanbury
Nr.Droitwich WR9 7EA
Tel: (052784) 305

OPEN: APRIL-OCT

Nearest Roads A.38 B.4090

This delightful 17th century black and white farmhouse is situated in a superb, secluded position in the heart of unspoilt Worcestershire. The accommodation is in three spacious, comfortably furnished and prettily decorated bedrooms. There is a unique oak beamed lounge with a beautiful inglenook fireplace. Glorious views from the large gardens. Excellent home cooking. Warm hospitality. Worcester 8 miles and Stratford on Avon 15 miles. Ideal base for visiting the Royal Worcester Porcelain Factory, Seconds Shop and Shakespeare's Country. Also ideal overnight stop en route North-/West country.

£10.00 ○ ■ ○

Michael & Veronica Shaw
Church House
Salford Priors
Nr. Evesham WR11 5UX
Tel: (0789) 773452

OPEN:

Nearest Roads A.439 A.435

A relaxed and pleasant atmosphere awaits guests at this beautiful Georgian/Tudor house. Many antiques, comfortable furnishings and log fires provide a delightful setting for a vacation. Bright cheery accommodation is offered in a choice of 5 rooms with modern amenities. A guests breakfast/lounge is also available. Michael & Veronica go out of their way to provide a super service and a memorable holiday. Conveniently located between Stratford-upon-Avon and Evesham.

£15.00 ○ ■ ■

○ yes ■ no

129

	Nearest Road	minimum per person	children taken	evening meals available	animals taken
Mrs Shirley E. Hickling **The Hermitage Manor** **Canon Pyon** **Hereford HR4 8NR** **Tel: (0432) 760317** **OPEN: ALL YEAR**	Nearest Road A.4110 Hermitage Manor in its extensive grounds, offers an enchanting combination of country house elegance and homely atmosphere. A peaceful, beautiful haven. Guests warmly welcomed in superb oak-panelled lounge and have exclusive use of this and separate T.V./dining rooms. The five delightfully furnished spacious rooms, all en-suite make for an unforgettable holiday in gentle Herefordshire. No single availability.	£12.50	○	■	■
Mrs Rosemary Price **Dinedor Court** **Dinedor** **Nr.Hereford HR2 6LG** **Tel: (043273) 481** **OPEN: MAR-NOV**	Nearest Road A.49 Peacefully situated on a 220 acre beef and arable farm, beside the River Wye, is this delightful 16th century farmhouse. Standing in an acre of garden the house offers 3 comfortable bedrooms with modern amenities. A colour T.V. lounge, table tennis room and marvellous oak panelled dining room. Traditional English food is served using local produce. Children are welcome. This is a super place to enjoy a quiet relaxing holiday, in a pleasant atmosphere.	£10.00	○	○	○
Mrs Carol Hart **The Bowens Farm Country** **Guest House** **Fownhope** **Hereford HR1 4PS** **Tel: (043277) 430** **OPEN: FEB-DEC**	Nearest Road M.50 A delightful early Georgian 17th century farmhouse, offering super accommodation in ten very comfortable, charming rooms, with modern facilities, including showers en-suite, and tea making facilities. Delightful inglenook fireplace and high standards of decor. A large garden and glorious views. Set in a beautiful village with an incredible amount to see close by, including Iron Age hill forts, Capler Hill and Cherry Hill. Children over 10 years.	£12.75	○	○	○
Freda Davies **Aberhall Farm** **St.Owen's Cross** **HR2 8LL** **Tel: (098987) 256** **OPEN: ALL YEAR**	Nearest Road A.49 All the peace and seclusion of the lovely Herefordshire countryside is to be found at Aberhall, a family run farm of 132 acres. Three bedrooms available with modern facilities. Full English breakfast served. Continental or special diets are available on request. Dining room and separate lounge with colour T.V. Games room in cellar with pool and table tennis. Garden with hard tennis court.	£10.00	○	○	■

○ yes ■ no

*Nominations for the 1987 awards for the **BEST BED & BREAKFAST** in the U.K. close on October 1st. Send your nominations now!!*

	minimum per person	children taken	evening meals available	animals taken
Henry & Tricia Howland **The Steppes Country** **House Hotel** **Ullingswick** **Nr. Hereford HR1 3JG** **Tel: (0432) 820424** **OPEN: ALL YEAR** Nearest Road A.417 The Steppes is an absolutely delightful 17th century country house, situated in the tiny hamlet of Ullingswick. It retains all its original character and atmosphere, including a wealth of exposed beams and antique furnishing. Accommodation is very comfortable with en-suite facilities, individually furnished rooms with T.V., clock/radio, tea/coffeee making facilities. The lounge is very comfortable and delightfully furnished. The dining room is charming with low beamed ceiling, inglenook fireplace and pretty windows. Gourmet cuisine and fine wines, accompanied by Renaissance music and candelight. No single occupancy.	£14.50	O	O	O
Amy & Graham Spencer **The Croft Country** **Guest House** **Vowchurch** **Hereford HR2 0QE** **Tel: (09816) 226** **OPEN: ALL YEAR** Nearest Roads A.465 B.4348 A spacious country home, set in delightful gardens and well planted grounds, with views to the Black Mountains, in the heart of the Golden Valley. Seven bedrooms all en-suite, with tea/coffee making facilities and colour T.V. The house is tastefully furnished throughout, with many period pieces, log fires and thoughtful extras. Excellent home cooking using own local produce. Personal attention assured.	£13.00	O	O	■
Catherine & **Marguerite Fothergill** **Highfield** **Ivington Road** **Newtown** **Leominster HR6 8QD** **Tel: (0568) 3216** **OPEN: ALL YEAR** Nearest Roads A.49 A.44 A warm welcome awaits you at this elegant Edwardian House. A most enjoyable country house atmosphere with modern facilities and first class service. Three large comfortable bedrooms, tastefully decorated, each with tea/coffee making facilities. The garden is a day-long suntrap where croquet can be played and barbeques can be provided. Excellent meals served in the well appointed dining room.	£12.50	■	O	■
Mrs Evelyn Mears **Ratefield Farm** **Kimbolton** **Leominster HR6 0JB** **Tel: (0568) 2507** **OPEN: ALL YEAR** Nearest Road A.49 Located in the heart of the beautiful unspoilt Herefordshire countryside, with 25 acres of pasture and woodland laid out by Capability Brown. This 200 year old house offers four bedrooms, all with modern amenities and tea/coffee making facilities. A comfortable colour T.V. lounge with log fire and comprehensive selection of tourist literature. In the dining room good home cooking is served, using farm produce including beef, lamb, eggs and vegetables. The home baked bread is super. Vegetarians specially catered for.	£8.50	O	O	O

O yes ■ no

	minimum per person	children taken	evening meals available	animals taken
Chris Saunders **Green Haven Guest House** **Green Haven** **Nr. Lucton** **Leominster HR6 9PN** **Tel: (056885) 276** **OPEN: ALL YEAR** Nearest Road Green Haven with its warm and welcoming atmosphere, is set in beautiful National Trust countryside with walks, views and many places of historical interest. Three bedrooms are available, dining room, T.V. lounge, games room and large attractive garden. Children well provided for. Evening meals by arrangement. Golf, fishing, flying and gliding all available locally for the active traveller.	£10.00	○	○	○
Martin S. Lockett **Mortimers Cross Inn** **Mortimers Cross** **Nr. Leominster HR6 9PD** **Tel: (056881) 238** **OPEN: ALL YEAR** Nearest Roads A.4110 B.4362 15th century black and white country inn, sturdily guarding crossroads on the old Roman Road, on the banks of the River Lugg. Site of a battle in 1461 during the Wars of the Roses. Accommodation is in 5 charming rooms. There is an aviary and a fishpool. Close by is Shobdon airfield offering flying, parachuting and microflight. Beautiful countryside with many historic castles and sites.	£9.50	○	○	○
Christopher & Anita **Syers-Gibson** **Bunns Croft Cottage** **Morton Eye** **Nr. Leominster** **Tel: (0568) 5836 or** ** Butterstone 215/216** **OPEN: MAR-SEPT** Nearest Road A.49 Dating from 1420, this beautiful mediaeval cottage is situated in beautiful unspoilt countryside only 4 miles from Leominster and 8 miles from Ludlow. Three charming rooms, one with private bath. All have modern amenities and tea/coffee makers. Evening meals are super value and based around traditional English cooking with home baked bread. This is an ideal base for discovering the delights of both Herefordshire and Shropshire with Ludlow castle, many National Trust properties, the famous black and white villages, beautiful rivers and totally unspoilt countryside.	£9.50	○	○	○
Grahame & Sian Belcher **Church Farm** **Castlemorton** **Nr. Malvern WR13 6BQ** **Tel: (068481) 361** **OPEN: ALL YEAR** Nearest Road M.50 A haven of comfort, hospitality and good food. Church Farm is a spacious Georgian farmhouse with views of the Malvern, Bredon and Cotswold Hills, close to the River Severn. Three rooms are available to guests, children being well provided for. Residents lounge with colour T.V., games room and garden to enjoy.	£9.00	○	○	○
Mr D. Tether ** and Mrs J. Harvey** **"One-eight-four"** **184 West Malvern Road** **West Malvern WR14 4AZ** **Tel: (06845) 66544** **OPEN: ALL YEAR** Nearest Road A.449 One-eight-four is a Victorian house built high on the western side of the Malvern Hills, looking towards the Welsh mountains, affording the most beautiful views and sunsets. Five bedrooms, doubles or twin, are available, all with beautiful and original decor and all en-suite. An atmosphere of warmth and hospitality has been created. Breakfast and dinner served in small panelled dining room.	£11.00	■	○	■

○ yes ■ no

132

		minimum per person	children taken	evening meals available	animals taken
Mrs Jill Jones **Elmbank Guest House** **52 Worcester Road** **Great Malvern WR14 4AB** **Tel: (06845) 66051** **OPEN: ALL YEAR**	Nearest Road A.449 A late Regency house with the attractive ironwork so typical of the period. 6 spacious, well decorated and comfortable rooms, 4 with private facilities, reached by a lovely curving staircase. All have tea/coffee makers and enjoy super views over the Severn Valley or Malvern Hills. A charming lounge with colour T.V. There is also a terrace and garden for guests. Evening meals are delicious and good value, with a choice of menu. Conveniently situated for the town centre with its priory, park, shops and theatre. Marvellous walks. A days touring can take you to Worcester, Hereford, Gloucester, Stratford, the Cotswolds or Wye valley.	£14.00	O	O	■
Mrs S. Williams **Moorend Court** **Mathon** **Nr. Malvern** **Tel: (088684) 205** **OPEN: ALL YEAR**	Nearest Roads B.4220 A.4103 Dating back to the 16th century this house offers seven charming, comfortable rooms with modern amenities and tea making facilities. Set in 120 acres overlooking the Malvern Hills it offers a small lake for fishing. This very impressive Manor house offers superb Cordon bleu cooking at excellent value. It has to be the ideal base for touring as it is within easy reach of Stratford, Cheltenham, Worcester. Special diets catered for.	£15.00	O	O	O
Margaret Thurnham **Pirton Court** **Pirton** **Worcester WR8 9EE** **Tel: (0905) 820691** **OPEN: ALL YEAR**	Nearest Roads A.44 M.5 Junction 7 A beautiful Elizabethan Manor house in 4½ acres offering four lovely rooms, all with shower en-suite, radio and tea/coffee makers. A delightful Jacobean panelled sitting room with colour T.V. and a garden for guests. This is a most relaxing house with panoramic views of the Malverns and Bredon Hill. An excellent centre for touring with the lovely Vale of Evesham, the Cotswolds and Stratford-on-Avon all easily accessible. Excellent home cooking and evening meals are tremendous value. A cot and babysitting arranged.	£10.50	O	O	O
Renate Van Gelderen **Edde Cross House** **Edde Cross Street** **Ross-on-Wye HR9 7BZ** **Tel: (0989) 65088** **OPEN: ALL YEAR** **(EXCL. XMAS & NEW YEAR)**	Nearest Roads A.40 M.50 This is a delightful period town house. Located in an area of outstanding natural beauty, and very centrally situated, it overlooks the Horseshoe bend of the River Wye. The accommodation, in 4 bedrooms, is very attractively furnished. All rooms have modern amenities. There is a comfortable guests lounge with colour T.V. The food here is excellent and evening meals are especially delicious. Mrs. Van Gelderen goes out of her way to make her guests welcome and she also helps to plan trips and routes. Close by are the Royal Forest of Dean, Goodrich Castle, Tintern Abbey. German spoken.	£11.00	O	O	■

O yes ■ no

133

		minimum per person	children taken	evening meals available	animals taken
Sylvia & Brian Adcock **Woodlea Guest House** **Symonds Yat West** **Ross-on-Wye HR9 6BL** **Tel: (0600) 890206** **OPEN: FEB-NOV**	Nearest Road A.40 A delightful family owned Victorian Guest House, set amid glorious scenery with wonderful valley views. The house also has a priviliged position and overlooks the famous Wye Rapids. Accommodation is in 10 rooms, with modern amenities and radio, some rooms have en-suite facilities. There is a colour T.V. lounge, reading lounge, and lounge bar where guests can relax comfortably with a drink. In the spacious dining room imaginative and delicious meals are served, accompanied by wine from the well stocked cellar. Guests may also like to use the outdoor swimming pool.	£13.00	O	O	O
Mrs Sian Watson **Trebandy House Farm** **Marstow** **Nr.Symonds Yat** **Ross-on-Wye HR9 6HD** **Tel: (098984) 230** **OPEN: APRIL-OCT**	Nearest Roads A.40 A.4137 An elegant Georgian family home, situated in a secluded valley overlooking the Garron stream, which meanders through the 237 acre farm. A games room is available with snooker and table tennis, as well as the drawing room with T.V. The 4-poster bed is recommended for a very comfortable night. A warm welcome is extended to all visitors and an opportunity for peaceful relaxation.	£9.00	O	■	O
Bernard & Jo Fowkes **Portland Guest House** **Whitchurch** **Nr.Ross-on-Wye HR9 6DB** **Tel: (0600) 890757** **OPEN: ALL YEAR**	Nearest Road A.40 A warm and welcoming atmosphere is found at this pleasant 17th century house. Situated in the centre of the village of Whitchurch, it is within easy reach of the Malvern Hills, Brecon Beacons, Black Mountains, Goodrich Castle and Tintern Abbey. Accommodation is in eight very comfortable bedrooms each with shower en-suite. Breakfast is a real treat. You choose from an A la Carte menu and eat as much as you like. Packed lunches are also available.	£11.00	O	O	O

O yes ■ no

Why not use our fast efficient
RESERVATION SERVICE
to book all your accommodation.
Booking forms at the back.

KENT

Kent is probably best known as the "garden of England" a tranquil landscape of fruit orchards and hopfields, of tidy villages and red roofed oast houses but there is more to it than this. There are empty downs, chalk sea cliffs, rich marshlands, sea ports, castles and the crowning glory of Canterbury Cathedral. Kentish men have known a romantic and turbulent history including Viking incursions, Roman and Norman invasion, Civil War and social unrest. The Peasants Revolt of 1381 was led by Wat Tyler of Kent.

The Pilgrims Way

The dramatic chalk ridgeway of the North Downs, links the famous white cliffs of Dover to the north of the county and so to London. This ancient roadway was a vital trade route in pre-historic times following the high downs well above the Kent Weald which was then dense forest. It can be followed today and offers fine views across the infinite landscape of the now agricultural weald. Delightful villages nestle in the folds of the hills, like Chilham, lying just above Canterbury. The village square is lined by the typical timber and white weatherboard cottages of Kent. The chequered flint church is beautifully restored; there is a fine Queen Anne rectory and the Jacobean Chilham Castle is set in pleasing gardens. It is probable that the Pilgrims who flocked to Canterbury between the 12th and 15th century did not follow the high ridgeway but rather used the path of Roman Watling Street. These events are colourfully chronicled in Chaucer's 14th century work - The Canterbury Tales.

Canterbury

Canterbury is the cradle of English christianity and is by tradition the seat of the Primate of All England. This site, on the River Stour, has been settled since the earliest times and became an important Saxon stronghold under King Ethelbert of Kent. He first established a church on the site of the present cathedral but it was in Norman times that the first great building work was carried out, to be continued in stages until the 15th century. The result is a subtle blending of styles, with early Norman work, a more delicate later Norman choir, a vaulted nave in Gothic style and the great tower of Tudor design. It was on the steps of this cathedral that Thomas Becket was murdered in 1170. The town retains much of its mediaeval character with half timbered weavers cottages, old churches and the splendid twin towers of the west gate but the cathedral soars above the roof tops and majestically dominates the city.

Houses and Castles

There are many grand buildings scattered throughout the county. Romantic castles have been restored, such as at Saltwood and Leeds and some are now private residences. There are excellent mediaeval manor houses like Ightham Moat, whose stone walls and squat tower rise straight from the waters of the moat and Old Soar at Plaxtol is a well preseved example of 13th century work. Perhaps most impresive is the huge Jacobean and Tudor manor of Knowle House. Its rough ragstone walls contain many quadrangles and the building covers some 3 acres of land in a glorious setting. It is open to the public and has excellent furniture and paintings. The attractive town of Tunbridge Wells with its famous paved parade called the Pantiles, is an excellent centre for the antique hunter. Nearby in the Eden Valley is Penshurst Palace, an elegant 16th century house and great hall, set in fine Italian gardens.

Village Architecture

Two main styles of house give the villages of Kent their special character. The Kentish Yeoman's house was the home of the wealthier farmers and is found thoughout the county. It is a timber frame building with white lath and plaster walls and a hipped roof of red tiles. Originally the centre room of the house was a high hall with central fireplace but most are now divided into two floors. Rather more modest in style is a small weatherboarded house, ususally painted white or cream but occasionally there are brick or tile buildings in similar style. It is this form of cottage with fresh white paintwork that gives Kent villages their unique charm; Rolvenden and Groombridge are good examples. The warm red tile roofs, often irregular with age also add great character and there are fine examples in Tenterden and Biddenden.

KENT GAZETEER

Areas of Outstanding Natural Beauty.
Kent Downs.

Historic Houses and Castles

Aylesford -- The Frairs -- Nr. Maidstone
13th century Friary and shrine of Our Lady, (much restored), 14th century cloisters -- original.

Allington Castle -- Nr. Maidstone
13th century. One time home of Tudor poet, Thomas Wyatt. Restored early 20th century. Icons and Renaissance paintings.

Black Charles -- Nr. Sevenoaks
14th century Hall house -- Tudor fireplaces, beautiful panelling.

Boughton Monchelsea Place -- Nr. Maidstone
Elizabethan Manor House -- grey stone and battlements -- 18th century landscaped park, wonderful views of Weald of Kent.

Chartwell -- Westerham
Home of Sir Winston Churchill.

Chiddingstone Castle -- Nr. Edenbridge
18th century Gothic revival building encasing old remains of original Manor House -- Royal Stuart and Jacobite collection. Ancient Egyptian collection -- Japanese netsuke etc.

Eyhorne Manor -- Hollingbourne
15th century Manor house with 17th century additions.

Cobham Hall -- Cobham
16th century house -- Gothic and Renaissance -- Wyatt interior. Now school for girls.

Fairfield -- Eastry -- Sandwich
13th-14th century aisled hall house.

Finchcocks -- Goudhurst
18th century baroque house -- excellent and interesting brickwork. Notable collection of musical instruments.

Hever Castle -- Nr. Edenbridge
13th and 14th centuries -- moated castle. Was home of Anne Boleyn. Beautiful gardens with unique collection of classical statuary.

Knole -- Sevenoaks
15th century -- splendid Jacobeain interior -- 17th and 18th century furniture. One of the largest private houses in England.

Leeds Castle -- Nr. Maidstone
Build in middle of the lake, it was the home of the mediaeval Queens of England.

Lullingstone Castle -- Eynsford
14th century mansion house -- Frequented by Henry VIII and Queen Anne. Still occupied by descendants of orignal owners.

Long Barn -- Sevenoaks
14th century house -- said to be home of William Caxton. Restored by Edwin Lutyens; 16th century barn added to enlarge house. Galleried hall - fine beaming and fireplaces. Lovely gardens created by Sir Harold Nicholson and his wife Vita Sackville-West.

Owletts - Cobham
Carolean house of red brick with plasterwork ceiling and fine staircase.

Owl House -- Lamberhurst
16th century cottage, tile hung, half timbered, said to be home of wool smuggler. Charming gardens.

Penshurst Place -- Tonbridge
14th century house with mediaeval Great Hall perfectly preserved.

English Gothic -- birthplace of Elizabethan poet, Sir Philip Sidney
 Fine staterooms, splendid picture gallery, famous toy museum. Tudor gardens and orchards.

Saltwood Castle -- Nr. Hythe
 Mediaeval -- very fine castle and is privately occupied. Was lived in by Sir Ralph de Broc, murderer of Thomas a Becket.

Squerryes Court -- Westerham
 Manor house of William and Mary period, with furniture, paintings and tapestries of time. Connections with General Wolfe.

Stoneacre -- Otham
 15th century yeoman's half timbered house.

Cathedrals and Churches

Brook (St. Mary)
 11th century paintings in this unaltered early Norman church.

Brookland (St. Augustine)
 13th century and some later part. Crown-post roofs, detached wooden belfry with conical cap. 12th century lead font.

Canterbury Cathedral
 12th century wall paintings, 12th and 13th century stained glass. Very fine Norman crypt. Early perpendicular nave and cloisters which have heraldic bosses. Wonderful central tower.

Charing (St. Peter & St. Paul)
 13th and 15th century interior with 15th century tower. 17th century restoration work.

Cobham (St. Mary)
 16th century carved and painted tombs.-- unequalled collection of brasses in county.

Elham (St. Mary the Virgin)
 Norman wall with 13th century arcades, perpendicular clerestory. Restored by Eden.

Lullingstone (St. Botolph)
 14th century mainly -- 16th century wood screen. Painted glass monuments.

Newington-on-the-Street (St. Mary the Virgin)
 13th and 14th century -- fine tower. 13th century tomb. Wall paintings.

Rochester Cathedral
 Norman facade and nave, otherwise early English. 12th century west door. 14th century doorway to Chapter room.

Stone (St. Mary)
 13th century -- decorated -- paintings, 15th century brass, 16th century tomb.

Woodchurch (All Saints)
 13th century, having late Norman font and Priest's brass of 1320. Arcades alternating octagonal and rounded columns. Triple lancets with banded marble shafting at East end.

Museums and Galleries

Royal Museums -- Canterbury
 Archeological, geological, mineralogical exhibits, natural history, pottery and porcelain. Engravings,prints and pictures.

Westgate -- Canterbury
 Museum of armour etc. in 14th century gatehouse of city.

Dartford District Museum, Dartford
 Roman, Saxon and natural history.

Deal Museum -- Deal
 Prehistoric and historic antiquities.

Dicken's House Musum -- Broadstairs
 Personalia of Dickens; prints, costume and Victoriana.

Dover Museum -- Dover
Roman pottery, ceramics, coins, zoology, geology, local history etc.

Faversham Heritage Society -- Faversham
1000 years of history and heritage.

Folkestone Museum and Art Gallery -- Folkstone
Archeology, local history and natural sciences.

Herne Bay Museum -- Herne Bay
Stone, Bronze and Early Iron Age specimens. Romans material from Reculver excavations. Items of local and Kentish interest.

Museum and Art Gallery -- Maidstone
16th century manor house exhibiting natural history and archeological collections. Costume Gallery, bygones, ceramics, 17th works by Dutch and Italian painters. Regimental museum.

Historic Monuments

Eynsford Castle -- Eynsford
12th century castle remains.

Rochester Castle -- Rochester
Storied keep -- 1126-39.

Roman Fort and Anglo-Saxon Church -- Reculver
Excavated remains of 3rd century fort and Saxon church.

Little Kit's Coty House -- Aylesford
Ruins of burial chambers from 2 long barrows.

Lullingstone Roman Villa -- Lullingstone
Roman farmstead excavations.

Roman Fort and Town -- Richborough
Roman 'Rutupiae' and fort.

Tonbridge Castle -- Tonbridge
12th century curtain walls, shell of keep and 14th century gatehouse.

Dover Castle - Dover
Keep built by Henry 11 in 1180-6. Outer curtain built 13th century.

KENT
Recommended roadside restaurants

018	*A2*	*Cobham (South) Kent* *5 miles west of Rochester (Northbound)*
019	*A2*	*Cobham (North) Kent* *5 miles west of Rochester (Southbound)*
052	*A21*	*Orpington Kent* *Farnborough Way* *3 miles south of Bromley* *12 miles north of Sevenoaks*
128	*A2*	*Rainham Kent* *London Road* *8 miles west of Sittingbourne* *5 miles east of Rochester*
135	*A225*	*Otford Kent* *Sevenoaks Road* *3 miles north of Sevenoaks* *10 miles south of Dartford Tunnel*
247	*A2*	*Gate, Kent* *5 miles west of Canterbury*
274	*A2*	*Harbledown, Kent* *5 miles west of Canterbury*
282	*A259*	*Hythe, Kent* *1 mile east of Hythe*
288	*A258*	*Richborough, Kent* *4 miles south of Ramsgate*

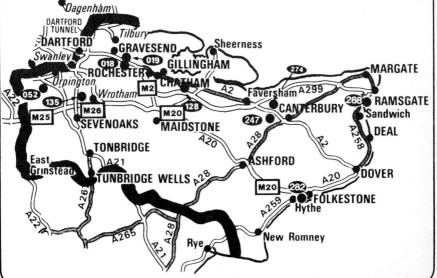

Kent

minimum per person
children taken
evening meals available
animals taken

Miss Erica Wallace **Little Hodgeham** **Bull Lane** **Bethersden TN26 3HE** **Tel: (023385) 323** **OPEN: MAR-OCT**	Nearest Road A.28 This is an absolutely delightful picture post-card cottage. This 500 year old house stands in beautiful gardens, fabulous blooms and blossoms create a wonderful setting. Low ceilings, masses of beams, ing-lenook fireplaces and wooden oak doors give the accommodation unique character and charm. Three attractive en-suite rooms. One room with 4-poster bed, has a fantastic vaulted beamed ceiling. Dinner is served by candlelight and the superb glass and silver sparkle wonderfully. Dinner, bed and break-fast only.	£25.00	O	O	O
Anne Swatland **Groome Farm** **Newland Green** **Egerton** **Ashford TN27 9EP** **Tel: (023376) 260** **OPEN: APRIL-OCT**	Nearest Road A.20 Groome Farm is a superb 15th century half timbered, black and white farmhouse. The rooms are quite delightful. Heavily beamed with inglenook fireplaces and decorated with many lovely antiques, creating a char-ming "olde worlde" atmosphere. Offering three rooms, a residents lounge and a fabu-lous garden. A plantsman's paradise beautifully tended with every kind of herb and shrub. A first class spot for a break.	£10.00	O	■	■
James Buss **The Dering Arms** **Station Approach** **Pluckley** **Nr.Ashford TN27 0RR** **Tel: (023384) 371** **OPEN: ALL YEAR**	Nearest Road A.20 This is a very unusual and attractive 17th century hunting lodge. Accommodation is in four rooms with modern amenities, some with radio, T.V. and tea/coffee making facili-ties. Friendly atmosphere, antique furniture and log fires. Good pub food is served 7 days a week and home made specialities, fresh fish and game dishes in season. Real ale and extensive wine list. Convenient for the Channel ferry ports, historic houses and gardens.	£14.00	O	O	■
Ian Turner **The Bell** **Bell Lane** **Smarden** **Tel: (023377) 283** **OPEN: ALL YEAR** **(EXCL. XMAS DAY)**	Nearest Road A.274 A warm welcome is extended to guests at this fine old Kentish Inn. The atmosphere is friendly and efficient. The four guest rooms are comfortable and tastefully furnished. Evening meals are good and reasonable. Three large bars, oak beamed and candlelit, with inglenook fireplaces, serving real ales and local wines. Pretty beer garden. Con-tinental breakfast is served.	£11.00	O	O	O
Mrs Rosemary Heathcote **Ash Farm** **Mill Lane** **Smarden TN27 8NW** **Tel: (023377) 282** **OPEN: ALL YEAR**	Nearest Roads A.20 B.2077 A lovely 14th century timber framed former Manor House. Situated on the outskirts of the beautiful village of Smarden amid the peace and tranquility of rural England. Accommodation is in two bedrooms with modern amenities, both en-suite. Conve-nient for Leeds Castle, Sissinghurst, Rye, old castles and old world inns. Rate shown is for two people.	£16.00	O	■	■

O yes ■ no

	Nearest Roads	minimum per person	children taken	evening meals available	animals taken
Frank Stevens **Chequers Inn** **Smarden** **Nr.Ashford TN27 8QA** **Tel: (023377) 217 or 623** **OPEN: ALL YEAR**	Nearest Roads B.2077 A.20 The Chequers has been an inn since 1450. It is much beamed and has a resident ghost. Mr. Stevens really cares for his guests in the true village inn tradition. Renowned for excellent breakfasts. Smarden is a beautiful village and surrounding it are many stately homes, castles and gardens. The area is beautiful and offers excellent walking and golfing. French and German spoken.	£11.95	O	O	O
Mrs S.M. Hodges **Wick Farm** **Biddenden Road** **Headcorn** **Nr. Ashford TN27 9HR** **Tel: (0622) 890260** **OPEN: APRIL-OCT**	Nearest Road A.274 A most attractive 15th century black and white Yeomans farmhouse. This delightful house retains many of its original features including the heavily oak beamed rooms, inglenook fireplace and polished oak flooring. The five guest bedrooms are comfortable and provide tea/coffee making facilities. There is also a pleasant colour T.V. lounge. Meals here are delicious, using home produce. Private fishing and shooting rights. London approximately 1 hour	£12.00	O	O	■
S.A. Boughton **Anchor Guest House &** **Restaurant** **25 North Lane** **Canterbury CT2 7EE** **Tel: (0227) 68105** **OPEN: ALL YEAR**	Nearest Road A.2 The Anchor Guest House is a charming old Hall House, with a Crown Post roof dating from around 1480. Formerly the Blue Anchor, this is one of the oldest coaching inns in Canterbury. Today it is a cozy restaurant and guest house, retaining all its former atmosphere with mediaeval beams and floors. Accommodation is in five rooms with modern amenities. There is a Georgian panelled bar with beamed ceilings, leading into the cottage style dining room where a varied A la Carte menu is available.	£9.00	O	O	■
Katrina Etheridge **Yorke Lodge Guest House** **50 London Road** **Canterbury CT2 8LF** **Tel: (0227) 451243** **OPEN: ALL YEAR**	Nearest Roads A.28 M.2 A spacious and comfortable Victorian house close to the city centre. Nine pleasant, well decorated rooms with modern amenities. Tea/coffee facilities in all rooms. A T.V. lounge, sun lounge and garden. Evening meals are good value and imaginative. Apart from the historic city itself the whole area has much to offer, including Leeds Castle and Chilham Castle. Guests are warmly welcomed. Rates shown are for two people.	£22.00	O	O	O
Mrs Elizabeth A. Clements **Anns Hotel** **63 London Road** **Canterbury CT2 8JZ** **Tel: (0227) 68767/63133** **OPEN: ALL YEAR**	Nearest Roads A.2 M.2 Set in the garden of England, this comfortable house offers nineteen excellent rooms all carefully decorated, four with 4-poster beds. The house is well known to tourists for its good value. There is much to visit in the town, and close by is Chilham Castle. Marvellous walks abound and the North Downs Way is superb. Guide dogs welcome. Facilities for disabled.	£14.00	O	■	■

O yes ■ no

141

minimum per person
children taken
evening meals available
animals taken

Derrick Blaikley & **Susan Mottershaw** **East Bridge Country** **Guest House** **Bridge Hill** **Bridge** **Canterbury CT4 5AS** **Tel: (0227) 830808** **OPEN: MAR-NOV**	Nearest Road A.2 A friendly, elegant and comfortable Georgian house in a pretty village. 5 minutes from Canterbury and 15 minutes from sea ports of Dover and Folkestone. Overlooking open countryside of outstanding beauty, the house offers accommodation in 8 rooms, all with modern amenities, some with private facilities. Ideal for walking, riding, fishing. Close to Kent's historic castles. Tasty English breakfasts. £12.50 per person in double room.	£16.00	○	■	○
Mrs Sheila Wilton **Walnut Tree Farm** **Lynsore Bottom** **Upper Hardres** **Nr. Canterbury CT4 6EG** **Tel: (022787) 375** **OPEN: ALL YEAR** **(EXCL. XMAS)**	Nearest Road A.2 Set in 6 acres of its own land, this delightful 14th century thatched farmhouse, offers peace and tranquility in unspoilt countryside. Offering family accommodation or friends wishing to share, in 4 double adjacent bedrooms with shower rooms and own toilet en-suite. Good farmhouse breakfast, homemade bread, marmalade preserves and fresh eggs. Ideal base for walking, birdwatching and en-route to Continent. Excellent pub food 2 miles away.	£12.00	○	■	■
Mrs Nicola Ellen **Crockshard Farmhouse** **Wingham** **Canterbury CT3 1NY** **Tel: (0227) 720464** **OPEN: ALL YEAR**	Nearest Roads A.2 B.20 An elegant traditional Georgian country farmhouse and family home, set in rural surroundings, within easy reach of Canterbury and the channel ports. Three double and two twin rooms are available, all large enough to be used as family accommodation. Residents lounge and beautiful gardens for guests use. Unique English language courses are on offer here, combining hard work, fun and relaxation.	£9.00	○	○	○
Mr & Mrs L. Robbins **Dell Guest House** **233 Folkstone Road** **Dover CT17 9SL** **Tel: (0304) 202422** **OPEN: ALL YEAR**	Nearest Roads A.20 A.2 A friendly welcome is extended to all guests, together with comfort and cleanliness, at this pleasant Victorian house. Offering a choice of 6 bedrooms with modern amenities. The Robbins' serve breakfast from 6 a.m. every morning so that those catching the early morning cross channel ferries get a good early start. Private parking.	£8.00	○	■	■
Doreen Wraight **Tower Guest House** **98 Priory Hill** **Dover CT17 0AD** **Tel: (0304) 208212** **OPEN: ALL YEAR**	Nearest Roads A.20 A.2 An old converted water tower making an unusual and interesting place to stay. Five comfortable pleasant rooms, with modern amenities, one with private bath. T.V. lounge and garden for guests. Centrally heated. Situated in a quiet position within easy reach of the town centre and port facilities. Mrs. Wraight will welcome you most warmly. Rates shown are for two people.	£19.00	○	■	○

○ yes ■ no

142

	Nearest Roads	minimum per person	children taken	evening meals available	animals taken
Mrs K.A.C. Morriss **St. Martins Guest House** **17 Castle Hill Road** **Dover CT16 1QW** **Tel: (0304) 205938** **OPEN: ALL YEAR**	Nearest Roads A.2 A.20 M.2 M.20 A comfortable Victorian house offering 9 pleasant rooms with modern facilities, 5 with shower. Some of the rooms offer excellent views of Dover Harbour. Behind the house is the ruin of St. James the Apostle Church c.1070. The Dover sports centre is close at hand. Dover is steeped in history and there are numerous sites close by.	£12.00	○	■	■
Mr L. Morriss **Ardmore Private Hotel** **18 Castle Hill Road** **Dover CT16 1QW** **Tel: (0304) 205895** **OPEN: ALL YEAR**	Nearest Roads A.2 A.20 Ardmore house is an attractive 17th century home, where a warm welcome, and courteous helpful hosts are to be found. Accommodation is in a choice of four pleasant bedrooms, all with modern amenities, T.V. and tea/coffee making facilities. A comfortable colour T.V. lounge for guests is available throughout the day. Children are also welcome at Ardmore, cots and highchairs are provided. A good base for a touring/sightseeing holiday as the house is conveniently situated for the many historical sites.	£20.00	○	■	■
Mrs Adeline Reidy **Number One Guest House** **1 Castle Street** **Dover CT16 1QH** **Tel: (0304) 202007** **OPEN: ALL YEAR**	Nearest Road - Town Centre An attractive house dating back to 1800 and is one of Dover's oldest homes. Dominated by the imposing Castle it is ideally situated for both town and ferries. Six very comfortable rooms all with bath or shower en-suite, colour T.V. and tea/coffee makers. Breakfast is a real pleasure as it is served in your room. A pleasant lounge for guests and a high walled garden - a perfect sun trap on summer evenings.	£11.00	○	■	○
Pamela Frances McAllister **Broad Street Lodge** **89 Broad Street** **Canterbury CT1 2LU** **Tel: (02273) 470185** **OPEN: ALL YEAR**	Nearest Road M.2 Caring personal service is the hall mark of a stay at Broad Street Lodge, a Georgian family residence beside the ancient city wall. Furnished to a high standard, the house accommodates guests in two bedrooms, with bathrooms en-suite, and radio, T.V., and tea/coffee making facilities. Residents lounge. Wholesome English breakfast served. 2 minutes walk from cathedral and restaurants catering for all tastes.	£10.00	○	■	○
Mrs Maggie Chocqueel-Mangan **Ashton House** **129 Whitstable Road** **Canterbury CT2 8EQ** **Tel: (0227) 65237** **OPEN: FEB-NOV**	Nearest Roads A.2 A.290 A beautiful restored and modernised Victorian house, within walking distance of the Cathedral, city centre and University. Warm and friendly hospitality in spacious and comfortable accommodation. Three bedrooms, all en-suite. Lovely garden room for guests to relax in. A traditional English breakfast is served, Continental alternative if requested. Vegetarians catered for and wine with meals can be arranged. Car parking. No single availability.	£15.00	○	○	■

○ yes ■ no

143

minimum per person
children taken
evening meals available
animals taken

A. & K. McPherson **Pennyfarthing Guest House** **109 Maison Dieu Road** **Dover CT16 1RT** **Tel: (0304) 205563** **OPEN: ALL YEAR**	Nearest Roads A.2 A.20 Pennyfarthing Guest House is a really convenient place to stay if you are going to the continent, as the port and hovercraft terminal are only 2 minutes away. The town centre is easily reached from here. This makes an excellent overnight stop or short stay base. Accommodation is in six rooms, some with private facilities, all with modern amenities and tea/coffee making facilities. A residents colour T.V. lounge is also available for guests to use throughout the day.	£12.00	○	■	■
Chris & Lea Oakley **Walletts Court Manor** **West Cliffe** **Dover CT15 6EW** **Tel: (0304) 852424** **OPEN: ALL YEAR**	Nearest Roads A.258 B.2058 A wonderful 17th century Manor House. Home of William Pitt the younger, situated in countryside above the White Cliffs of Dover. Seven luxury bedrooms, all en-suite. Oak beams and inglenook fireplaces. True 17th century atmosphere. Homemade produce for breakfast and Saturday is 'Gourmet Evening' in the restaurant. Kingsdown golf course close by. A very warm welcome awaits all visitors to this lovely house.	£18.00	○	○	■
Mrs E. Bowles **"Linden Guest House"** **231 Folkestone Road** **Dover CT17 9SL** **Tel: (0304) 205449** **OPEN: ALL YEAR** **(EXCL. XMAS)**	Nearest Road A.20 A friendly welcome is always extended to guests at Linden Guest House. There are four bedrooms with modern facilities and tea/coffee making facilities. The house is elegantly decorated, comfortable, warm and quiet, yet only 5 minutes by car from the Docks. Early breakfasts will be catered for and children under 14 charged at reduced rates in family rooms. Residents lounge with colour T.V.	£9.50	○	■	■
Mrs L. West **"The Moorings"** **5 Wear Bay Road** **Folkestone CT19 6AT** **Tel: (0303) 51198** **OPEN: ALL YEAR**	Nearest Road M.20 Guests will find a friendly family atmosphere at The Moorings. This pleasant house is situated on the East Cliff overlooking the English Channel. Accommodation is in three comfortable rooms, with modern amenities and tea/coffee making facilities. Beaches, tennis courts, town centre and the continental ferry terminal, are all within easy reach. This is an ideal base for exploring Kent.	£8.50	○	■	■
Jacqueline M. Berry **Davy's Locker** **4 Wear Bay Road** **Folkestone CT19 6AT** **Tel: (0303) 42525** **OPEN: ALL YEAR**	Nearest Road A.20 Davy's Locker is a small, family run guest house, where guests are sure to receive a warm and friendly welcome. The house is well located for the continental ferry terminal, harbour, beaches and the famous old high street. Accommodation is in three comfortable bedrooms all with modern amenities, T.V. and tea/coffee making facilities. A lounge with colour T.V. and garden are also available. This makes a good base for touring many of the interesting historical sites, Canterbury Cathedral and Leeds Castle. Close by are tennis, bowls, pitch and putt and the Sports Centre	£8.50	○	■	■

144

○ yes ■ no

	minimum per person	children taken	evening meals available	animals taken
Mrs Dorothy Hutchinson **Seacliffe Guest House** **3 Wear Bay Road** **Folkestone CT19 6AT** **Tel: (0303) 54592** **OPEN: APRIL-OCT** Nearest Roads A.20 M.20 A warm welcome and a homely atmosphere is found at Seacliffe. This guest house has lovely views across the harbour and out to sea. Accommodation is in six rooms, with modern amenities and tea/coffee making facilities. All rooms have nice sea views. A residents T.V. lounge is available throughout the day. Seacliffe is centrally situated, only 10 minutes walk from the town centre. Close by are nice cliff top walks. A pleasant base from which to tour this area.	£9.00	○	○	○
J.E. Larssen **"Ramsey House"** **228a Barnsole Road** **Gillingham ME7 4JB** **Tel: (0634) 54193** **OPEN: ALL YEAR** Nearest Road A.2 Everything possible will be done here to make guests feel at home and at ease. "Ramsey House" is a modern detached house in residential Gillingham with good access to A.2/M.2. Three bedrooms, one en-suite all with modern facilities and T.V. English or Continental breakfast served. The guests lounge/dining room looks out onto a pleasant secluded garden.	£12.00	○	■	■
Mrs B.L. Penn **178 Bredhurst Road** **Wigmore** **Gillingham ME8 0QX** **Tel: (0634) 33267** **OPEN: ALL YEAR** Nearest Roads M.2 A.2 An attractive bungalow offering homely accommodation, and a very warm welcome. Mrs. Penn offers two separate suites, each with its own sitting room and private facilities. A lounge with T.V. for guests and also a garden. Children are welcome and there is a cot and highchair for baby. Situated just a few minutes from the M.2 motorway. Evening meals are not offered as there are many good restaurants with reasonable prices close by. Close to the North Downs and several castles.	£8.50	○	■	■
Mrs Veronica Loynes **The Lookout** **Spa Esplanade** **Hampton Pier** **Herne Bay CT6 8EP** **Tel: (0227) 365365** **OPEN: ALL YEAR** Nearest Road 'The Lookout' is a light and airy house with a friendly atmosphere, sited at beach level just a few steps from the sea with wide grassy banks either side. Quiet, with uninterrupted views over the Estuary, yet within easy reach of the town. Three guest rooms, large sun room and patio. Children welcome. Table tennis. Fishing rods available, also rowing boat.	£10.00	○	■	■
Mrs Arbuthnott **The Old Cottage** **Church Green** **Hollingbourne** **Maidstone ME17 1UJ** **Tel: (062780) 287** **OPEN: APRIL-NOV** Nearest Roads B.2163 M.20 By the church on the outskirts of the village, stands The Old Cottage, an attractive 18th century house. Mrs. Arbuthnott offers two guest rooms with modern amenities and her Cordon Bleu cookery skills ensure enticing meals. Vegetarian/special diets catered for. The Pilgrims Way is close by. Leeds Castle, Canterbury, Sissinghurst, Knole and Penshurst Place just a few of the interesting places to visit.	£11.00	■	○	■

○ yes ■ no

	minimum per person	children taken	evening meals available	animals taken
Mrs Lisa Coleman **Warwick House** **64 Tonbridge Road** **Maidstone ME16 8SE** **Tel: (0622) 56096** **OPEN: ALL YEAR**	Nearest Road A.20 A marvellous 1620 Jacobean House set in huge garden. Four super rooms with modern facilities. The proprietors extend a warm welcome and arrange theatres, outings, restaurants, plus a guided car tour to many interesting places. Leeds Castle, Knowle Castle, Hever Castle, Sissinghurst and Canterbury within comfortable driving distance. French and German spoken. No babies please. Hostess is accredited guide to Leeds Castle and area.	£11.00	○	■	■
Stella Galwey **Gates House** **5 Lower Green Road** **Pembury TN2 4DZ** **Tel: (089282) 2866** **OPEN: ALL YEAR**	Nearest Road A.21 Gates House is a Georgian house standing on the village green. Offering accommodation in one twin room, with modern amenities, private shower and tea/coffee making facilities. Guests may choose either a full English or Continental breakfast. This makes a good base from which to tour the area. No single occupancy.	£8.50	○	■	■
Amanda Webb **Pond Cottage** **Eggpie Lane** **Weald** **Sevenoaks TN14 6NP** **Tel: (0732) 463773** **OPEN: ALL YEAR**	Nearest Road A.21 The Webb family extend an extremely warm welcome to their beautiful 16th century farmhouse home. The house, with oak beams and huge inglenook fire, is set in 4 acres with a large (safely fenced) lake where Kingfishers and wild duck visit. Guests welcomed with afternoon tea. Three lovely rooms. Children provided for. Pub and restaurant meals available locally. London 30 minutes by train.	£16.00	○	■	■
Mrs Pat Stearns **Sissinghurst Castle Farm** **Sissinghurst** **Cranbrook TN17 2AB** **Tel: (0580) 712885** **OPEN: ALL YEAR** **(EXCL. XMAS)**	Nearest Road A.229 This Victorian farmhouse is delightfully located in the grounds of Sissinghurst Castle. Accommodation is in 3 rooms, all with modern amenities and tea/coffee making facilities. All the bedrooms have beautiful views. A guests colour T.V. lounge, and garden is also available. Evening meals can be provided if one day's notice is given. Vegetarian meals are also available. This makes a good base for touring the many historic sites of Kent.	£10.00	○	○	○
Mrs Josephine Lindsay **Jordans** **Sheet Hill** **Plaxtol** **Sevenoaks TN15 0PU** **Tel: (0732) 810379** **OPEN: ALL YEAR**	Nearest Road M.25 A magnificent 16th century Tudor house with beams, leaded windows and inglenook fireplaces. Rambler roses grace the exterior and the beautiful garden makes for an idyllic scene. Plaxtol is a picturesque Kentish village abounding in orchards and fields. Three guest rooms, two en-suite are available and a residents sitting room with colour T.V. Your hostess here is a professional Tourist Guide.	£18.00	■	■	■

○ yes ■ no

	Nearest Road	minimum per person	children taken	evening meals taken	animals taken available
Mr & Mrs G.T.R. Scott **Herons Court** **Wittersham** **Nr. Tenterden TN30 7EJ** **Tel: (07977) 272** **OPEN: FEB-DEC**	Nearest Road B.2082 Herons Court is a lovely old farmhouse dating in part to the 15th century, with many period features, oak beams, panelling and floors throughout, and oven fireplaces. Four bedrooms are available for guests and children of any age welcome. Full English breakfast. Ample parking. On the outskirts of the village, the house has lovely views over Kent and Sussex countryside.	£10.00	O	■	O
Maureen Rawlinson **Brattle House** **Cranbrook Road** **Tenterden TN30 6UL** **Tel: (05806) 3565** **OPEN: APRIL-DEC**	Nearest Road A.28 A handsome listed building, dating from the 17th century. The house offers views of the surrounding Kentish countryside from all its rooms. Guests are accommodated in five bedrooms with modern amenities, T.V., radio, tea/coffee making facilities. Unique Wealden town of Tenterden is close by, as are Canterbury, Leeds Castle and many other sites of historic interest.	£10.50	O	O	■
Cynthia Dakin **Old Swaylands** **Poundsbridge Lane** **Penshurst** **Nr. Tonbridge TN11 8AH** **Tel: (0892) 870738** **OPEN: ALL YEAR**	Nearest Road A.26 Old Swaylands is one of the oldest houses in Kent, 13th century manor house. This lovely black and white timbered house offers five beautiful rooms, all with en-suite facilities. Fine antique furniture throughout. An excellent evening meal at reasonable prices. Standing in 25 acres, the grounds have a large lake and three quarter mile of the river Medway with fishing rights. The gardens are magnificent. There is also good stabling offered for horses. From here one can visit Penshurst, Chartwell, Hever Castle and Knowle Park. Mrs. Dakin makes all her guests most welcome.	£16.00	O	■	O
Mrs A. Emanuel **Little Pagehurst** **Staplehurst** **Tonbridge** **Tel: (0580) 891486** **OPEN: ALL YEAR**	Nearest Road A.20 Situated near Staplehurst, in the Weald of Kent, this fine period house offers pleasant surroundings, including mature gardens, and a high standard of decor. Excellent English home cooking is produced with service in an atmosphere conducive to an enjoyable break. Five guest rooms with all modern facilities, one with 4-poster bed. Outdoor pool. Good access by rail and road. Children over 10 years.	£10.00	O	O	O
Mrs C.M.Carrell **Rowden House Farm** **Frant** **Tunbridge Wells TN3 9HS** **Tel: (089275) 259** **OPEN: APRIL-OCT**	Nearest Road A.267 A most delightful Elizabethan house standing on a 15 acre smallholding with sheep, horses and chickens. It is surrounded by the beautiful rolling wooded countryside of Sussex. The house is perfectly placed for visiting the counties of Kent, Sussex and the coast. There are many National Trust Properties nearby, including Leeds and Hever Castles. Accommodation is in 1 twin bedded room, with radio and tea/coffee making facilities. Gatwick is only 1 hour and London 1½ hours drive.	£12.00	■	■	■

O yes ■ no

		minimum per person	children taken	evening meals available	animals taken
Mrs Nanette Fitchie "Windyridge" Wraik Hill Whitstable CT5 3BY Tel: (0227) 263506 **OPEN: ALL YEAR**	Nearest Road A.299 Windyridge is a family run guest house, in rural surroundings with panoramic sea views. Of architectural interest, the house is comfortably furnished with a wealth of exposed beams. Full central heating. Lounge with colour T.V. Guests are accommodated in family, double or single rooms, all with modern amenities. Good home-cooked meals. Vegetarians catered for. Children over 10 years.	£9.00	O	O	■

○ yes ■ no

All the establishments in this book
are members of the
**WORLDWIDE BED & BREAKFAST
ASSOCIATION**

Look for this symbol

148

LANCASHIRE

Lancashire can prove a surprisingly beautiful county. Despite its link with the cotton industry there is a magnificent landscape and many fine towns and villages. Its history, its connections with the crown and the clashes of the houses of Lancaster and York have left a rich heritage of houses, churches, castles, towns and villages and variety of architecture. There are villages of stone cottages, superb stone farmhouses, barns and fine Georgian buildings. It also has some of the finest countryside in England with the sweeping hills of Bowland, the beautiful Ribble Valley and the moors of Rossendale.

The Forest of Bowland

The Royal Forest of Bowland is a forest or "Foris" without trees, which has provided rich hunting grounds since Saxon times. An old windswept pass, where many travellers have perished in the past, runs over the high hills of Salter Fell and High Cross Fell from Slaidburn, once linking Lancaster to Clitheroe. Slaidburn's Inn was once a courtroom where the strict forest laws were enforced, prohibiting poaching, trespass, tree felling or the cutting of rushes for thatch. The Inn is now called the "Hark to Bounty" after the noisiest hound in the squire's pack and is set in a village of pleasant cobble edged streets and stone cottages. Further south, the trough of Bowland provides an easier route through the hills from the delightful village of Newton-in-Bowland, passing the 1,000 foot summit and the Trough Stone where the gibbet once stood. Within the trough, set amongst trees, is the beautiful village of Abbeystead in Wynoedale, where monks once farmed the land. The church has stained glass windows portraying shepherds and their flocks and in the porch are pegs where shepherds crooks were hung. There are many other pleasant villages amongst the hills and valleys of Bowland each with it's own character. Chiping is known for chair making and its markets and festivals. It has seventeenth century houses, the ancient church of St Batholomew containing many antiquities and the Grammer School and Alms Houses founded in the seventeenth century by John Brabbin, a local boy who made good.

The Ribble Valley

Below the dramatic hills of Bowland, the green valley of the Ribble climbs from Preston to the Yorkshire Dales. At the beginning of the valley is Hangridge Fell where the legends of witches are almost as numerous as those of Pendle Hill. At Halloween a procession carrying lighted candles used to cross the dark windy ridge of the Fell. The old village of Hangridge has stone cottages rising along the steep main street to the Fells above. Below Hangridge lies Ribchester with its fine Georgian architecture. An eighteenth century triple arched bridge now spans the old Roman ford where the fort of Bremetennacum once stood. It extended over some five acres and was an important cavalry station for legions in transit to the wall.

Some of the original Roman stones have since been incorporated into the houses and the porch pillars of the village pub, the White Bull, are Roman. Further up the valley, the ancient market town of Clitheroe lies amongst beautiful countryside. The twelfth century castle of the De Laceys towers above the houses, providing an excellent viewing point for the hills of Bowland, the valley and the mysterious Pendle Hill to the south. Pendle Hill can be reached via the unspoilt village of Downham, one of the prettiest in England with its Tudor, Jacobean and Georgian houses, the village stocks and the old Inn. Old Pendle rises abruptly above Downham to 1,831 feet and has a history going back to prehistoric man. A strange land formation, it is shrouded in legend and is still believed by many to be the haunt of witches. Between Pendle Hill and the moors of Rossendale Forest are the textile towns of Nelson, Colne, Burnley, Accrington and Blackburn. The textile industry was well established in the east of Lancashire in early Tudor times and the towns grew up as markets for the trading of cloth woven in the Piece Halls. At Helmshaw, south of Accrington, is the Higher Mill Museum, built in 1789 and one of the oldest wool textile finishing mills left in Lancashire. The museum includes early examples of spinning wheels, Hargreave's spinning jenny, several of Arkwright's machines and a twenty foot water wheel. The moors which descend to the very edge of the textile towns are wild and beautiful and have a wealth of prehistoric tumuli and earthworks. Through the towns and through gentle countyside, the Liverpool to Leeds canal winds and climbs its way, providing an excellent footpath for seeing the area.

LANCASHIRE GAZETEER

Areas of Outstanding Natural Beauty.
The Forest of Bowland, Parts of Arnside and Silverdale.

Historic Houses and Castles

Rufford Old Hall -- Rufford
15th century screen in half timbered hall of note. Collection of relics of Lancashire life.

Chingle Hall -- Nr. Preston
13th century -- small manor house with moat. Rose gardens. Haunted!

Astley Hall -- Chorley
Elizabethan house reconstructed in 17th century. Houses pictures, tapestries, pottery and furniture.

Gawthorpe Hall -- Padiham
17th century manor house, with 19th century restoration. Moulded ceilings and some fine panelling. A collection of lace & embroidery.

Bramall Hall -- Bramhall
Fine example of half-timbered (black & white) manor house built in 14th century and added to in Elizabethan times. Fine grounds.

Lancaster Castle -- Lancaster
Largest of English castles -- dates back to Norman era.

Astley Hall -- Chorley
16th century half timbered grouped around central court. Rebuilt in the Jacobean manner with long gallery. Unique furniture.

Hoghton Tower. Nr. Preston
16th century -- fortified hill top mansion -- magnificent banquet hall. Dramatic building -- walled gardens and rose gardens.

Thurnham Hall -- Lancaster
13th century origins. 16th century additions and 19th century facade. Beautiful plasterwork of Elizabethan period. Jacobean staircase.

Cathedrals and Churches

Lancaster (St. Mary)
15th century with 18th century tower. Restored chapel -- fine stalls.

Whalley (St. Mary)
13th century with 15th century tower, clerestory and aisle windows. Fine wood carving of 15th century canopied stalls.

Halsall (St. Cuthbert)
14th century chancel, 15th century perpendicular spire. 14th century tomb. Original doors, brasses and effigies. 19th century restoration.

Tarleton (St. Mary)
18th century part 19th century. Glass is clear -- gallery.

Great Mitton (All Hallows)
15th century rood screen, 16th century font cover, 17th century pulpit.

Museums and Galleries

Blackburn Museum -- Blackburn
Extensive collections relating to local history, archeology, ceramics, geology and natural history. Oneof finest collection of coins and fine collection of mediaeval illuminated manuscripts and early printed books.

Bury Museum & Art Gallery -- Bury
Houses fine Victorian oil and watercolours. Turner, Constable, Landseer, de Wint.

City Gallery -- Manchester
Pre-Raphaelites, Old Masters, Impressionists, modern painters all represented in this fine gallery; also silver & pottery collections.

Dinting Railway Centre. Glossop
Steam locomotives -- famous trains.

LANCASHIRE
Recommended roadside restaurants

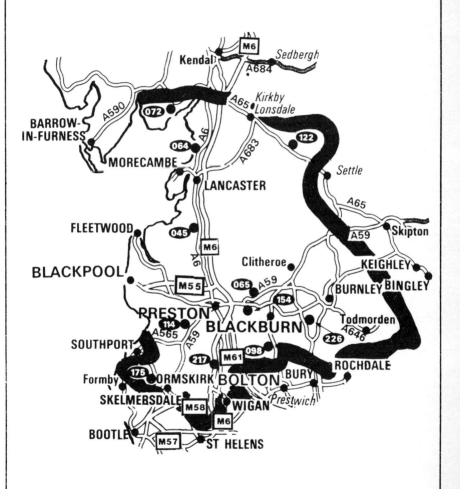

Lancashire

minimum per person
children taken
evening meals available
animals taken

Mr & Mrs Robert Owen **Mains Hall Hotel** **Mains Lane** **Singleton** **Nr. Blackpool FY6 7LE** **Tel: (0253) 885130** **OPEN: ALL YEAR**	Nearest Roads M.55 A.585 A most attractive 16th century manor house, with carved oak panelling and a splendid staircase, set in secluded gardens on the bank of the River Wyre. Run by Bob and Beryl, in a friendly and informal way, but with every comfort. Delicious, interesting home cooked food. Only 10 miles from the M.55 for those travelling north.	£16.50	○	○	○
Jim & Doreen Shearer **Lynstead Private Hotel** **40 King Edward Avenue** **Blackpool FY2 9TA** **Tel: (0253) 51050** **OPEN: ALL YEAR**	Nearest Road A.584 Situated in the quieter North Shore area, adjacent to the cliffs, boating pool, golf course, and convenient for the Town Centre and public transport (buses/trams). Good food, service and comfort is assured in a pleasant atmosphere. All rooms with showers en-suite. A unique Tramcar lounge bar, full of memorabilia, an extraordinary collection of postcards and tram signs.	£11.35	○	○	■
Mrs A. Ireland **Thwaite End Farm** **Bolton-le-Sands** **Carnforth LA5 9TN** **Tel: (0524) 732551** **OPEN: MAR-NOV**	Nearest Roads A.6 M.6 Exit 35 Guests will find a comfortable, friendly atmosphere in this delightful 17th century farmhouse. Situated on a small sheep and beef rearing farm of 52 acres, it is conveniently located between Carnforth and Bolton-le-Sands. Accommodation is in three pleasant rooms with modern amenities and tea/coffee making facilities. There are two comfortable lounges, one with colour T.V. Tea and biscuits are served each morning. Breakfast is served in the attractive dining room.	£10.00	■	■	■
Mrs Sally Townend **New Capernwray Farm** **Capernwray** **Carnforth LA6 1AD** **Tel: (0524) 734 284** **OPEN: ALL YEAR**	Nearest Roads M.6 A.6 An immensely attractive white 17th century stone built house set in a beautiful but little known area. There are three very charming bedrooms, all with en-suite facilities. The house has a wealth of ancient oak beams. A delightful lounge for guests and a garden. Sally Townend is well known for her superb cuisine which is most imaginative and excellent value. Please bring your own wine, the house is not licensed. A super base for touring the Lake District and the Yorkshire Dales. N.W. Regional Winners. Kelloggs Award for Excellence 1985.	£15.00	○	○	○
Dr & Mrs M.C. Cobb **Thie-Ne-Shee** **Moor Close Lane** **Over Kellet** **Carnforth LA6 1DF** **Tel: (0524) 735882** **OPEN: JAN-MID DEC**	Nearest Roads B.6254 M.6 A.6 Thie-ne-shee is a most attractive modern chalet bungalow in a hillside garden offering superb views towards Morecambe Bay and South Lakeland Hills. Two bedrooms for guests, one family and one twin, both on the ground floor. A wide choice for breakfast is available. A good selection of brochures on places of interest will be found. All easy day excursions from here.	£8.00	○	■	■

○ yes ■ no

LEICESTERSHIRE

This is ancient England where the landscape has barely changed since the earliest times. Great houses, village churches, thatched cottages set in green countryside - some of it hedged about, making a patchwork of the land, but in other places it has rough and ragged appearance. It is a quiet and secret county, not revealing itself instantly, but waiting to be discovered at your leisure. Many places have a deserted look. Villages seem to have disappeared and though the houses and parks still stand in their glory there is little around them. This is largely due to the fact that many of the people were cleared off their little farms and small holdings to make pasture land for the great landowners. Wool was a very profitable commodity then. Communities were broken up and the families had to move elsewhere to make their living and the houses they left behind, little more than shelters for the most part, were allowed to fall into decay and eventually vanished, leaving the curiously empty impression one has of rural Leicestershire. Even so, the rich grazing land remains and at Market Harborough there is still a weekly cattle market as there has been for centuries past.

The Waterways

The rivers break up the landscape of open endless fields and there is a branch of the Grand Union Canal. This was once a very important waterway for the carriage of industrial goods from the factories of the Midlands to London and the docks. It passes through an interesting series of multiple locks at Foxton where the spectators love to watch the water go uphill or down. Today the decorative canal barges, the "narrow boats" are pleasure craft rather than working boats and afford pleasant holidays, passing through lovely countryside, stopping off at the canalside "pubs" which once got their trade from the passing "boat people" who were almost a closed community due to their lifestyle of living and working solely on the canals.

NOTTINGHAMSHIRE

This is one of the group of North Midland Counties having a diversity of landscape, from forestry to farming and through mining to industry. The novels of D.H. Lawrence sprang from the coal mining areas where he drew his background and characters. The principle river of the county is the Trent which flows through the peaceful Vale of Belvoir. This is a broad valley, rich and fertil affording lovely scenery, far removed from the industrial towns which also benefit from the Trent river before it flows into the Humber Estuary.

County Town

Nottingham was recorded in Domesday Book as a thriving community. Before that time it had been an important area and the Saxons, Romans, Vikings and Normans all left their mark upon it. Robin Hood and Sherwood Forest spring to mind whenever the county is mentioned, but here it was that Arkwright perfected his cotton spinning machinery and then went on to develop steam as a power source - founding an industrial era which continues to this day. Textiles, shoes, bicycles and tobacco are all produced here. The famous Castle was built and destroyed and rebuilt many times through its history - now it houses the Art Gallery and Museum. Close by its walls is the oddly named Inn, "The Trip to Jerusalem" said to be named after the Crusaders who stopped to drink there on their way to fight in the Holy Land.

LEICESTERSHIRE GAZETEER

Areas of outstanding Natural Beauty.
Charnwood Forest, Rutland Water.

Historic Houses and Castles

Belvoir Castle -- Nr. Grantham
Home of the Duke of Rutland since Henry VIII -- rebuilt 1816. Paintings, furniture, historic armoury, military museums, magnificent staterooms.

Belgrave Hall -- Leicester
18th century Queen Anne house -- furnishing of 18th and 19th centuries.

Langton Hall -- Nr. Market Harborough
Privately occupied -- perfect English country house from mediaeval times -- drawing rooms have 18th century Venetian lace.

Stanford hall -- Lutterworth
17th century William and Mary House -- collection of Stuart relics and pictures, antiques and costumes of family from Elizabeth I onward.

Stapleford Park -- Nr. Melton Mowbray
Old wing dated 1500, restored 1663. Extended to mansion in 1670. Collection of pictures, tapestries, funiture and Balston's Staffordshire protrait figures of Victorian age.

Cathedrals and Churches

Breedon-on-the-Hill (St. Mary and St. Hardulph)
Norman and 13th century, Jacobean canopied pew, 18th century carvings.

Empingham (St. Peter)
14th century west tower, front and crocketed spire. Early English interior-double piscina, triple sedilia.

Lyddington (St. Andrew)
Perpendicular in tho main -- medieval wall paintings and brasses.

Staunton Harold (Holy Trinity)
17th century -- quite unique Cromwellian church -- painted ceilings.

Museums and Galleries

Bosworth Field Exhibition -- Sutton Cheney
Relating to the Battle of Bosworth Field (Death of Richard III) 1485

Leicester Museum & Gallery
Painting collection. 18th, 19th century, watercolours and drawings, 20th century French paintings, Old Master and modern prints, English silver and ceramics.

Jewry Wall Museum - Leicester
Huge Roman Wall with arches - built about 130 AD - later became part of the Roman Baths. Archeology from prehistoric times to 1500.

Historic Monuments

The Castle -- Ashby-de-la-Zouch
14th century with tower added in 15th century.

Kirby Muxloe Castle -- Kirby Muxloe
15th century fortified manor house with moat ruins.

NOTTINGHAMSHIRE GAZETEER

Historic Houses and Castles

Holme Pierrepont Hall -- Radcliffe-on-Trent
Medieval brick Manor House. 19th century formal courtyard garden.

Newstead Abbey
Originally a priory -- converted into house 1540. Bryon relics etc.

Wollaton Hall -- Nottingham
Late Elizabethan Renaissance architecture.

Cathedrals and Churches

Egmanton (St. Mary)
Magnificent interior by Comper. Norman doorway & font. Canopied rood screen, 17th century altar.

Newark (St. Mary Magdalene)
15th century. 2 painted panels of "Dance of Death", Reredos by Comper.

Southwell Cathedral
Norman nave, unvaulted, fine early English choir. Decorated pulpitum 6 canopied stalls, fine misericords. Octagonal chapter house.

Teresval (St. Catherine)
12th century -- interior 17th century unrestored

Museums and Galleries

Castlegate Museum -- Nottingham
Row of Georgian terraced houses showing costume & textile collection. Lace making equipment and lace collection.

Nottingham Castle Museum -- Nottingham
Collections of ceramics, glass and silver. Alabaster carvings.

LEICESTERSHIRE
NOTTINGHAMSHIRE
Recommended roadside restaurants

Bawtry

A159

A631

141

Gainsborough

WORKSOP

A57

A1

219

LINCOLN

MANSFIELD

009

A46

088

A617

A612

A15

075

NEWARK-ON-TRENT

212

M1

A17

172

205

NOTTINGHAM

GRANTHAM

A52

A453

A46

A607

LOUGHBOROUGH

189

Melton Mowbray

A50

A1

Oakham

A47

LEICESTER

139

092

A47

HINCKLEY

A6

Uppingham

NUNEATON

Market
Harborough

A43

A5

CORBY

A427

Leicestershire & Nottinghamshire

Mrs Ruth Miller **The Old Vicarage** **Plumgar Road** **Barkestone le Vale** **Nr. Belvoir NH13 0JA** **Tel: (0949) 42258** **OPEN: APRIL-OCT**	Nearest Roads A.1 A.52 A warm welcome and a relaxed atmosphere await the visitor to this lovely old Georgian house. This former vicarage is now part of a 600 acre dairy farm. Surrounded by open countryside, it has delightful views across to Belvoir Castle. Three rooms are available, some with radio, T.V. and tea/coffee making facilities. A guests' colour T.V. lounge is available. Pony trekking and golf nearby.	£10.00	○	○	○
Mrs D.E. Renner **Belton Country Home** **The Old Rectory** **Belton-in-Rutland LE15 9LE** **Tel: (057286) 279** **OPEN: ALL YEAR**	Nearest Road A.47 A superior establishment set in beautiful, pastoral Rutland, with easy access to major roads. A very hospitable, happy traditional farm atmosphere prevails here with many interesting activities, country craft centre, miniature farm, country bygones etc. Very elegant rooms with marble fireplaces. Four guest rooms with all modern amenities, one en-suite, one with 4-poster bed. Children are well provided for.	£9.00	○	■	○
Mr & Mrs B. Brotherhood **Beechcroft & Stable Cottage** **Church Lane** **Asfordby** **Melton Mowbray LE14 3RU** **Tel: (0664) 812314** **OPEN: ALL YEAR**	Nearest Road A.6006 A Georgian residence (circa 1800) and cottage situated in 2 acres of gardens and lawns with river frontage. Melton Mowbray is a bustling market town noted for Stilton Cheese and Pork Pies. This is the heart of fox hunting country. In easy reach of Belvoir Castle, Stapleford Park and Rutland Water. Ideal for day excursions to Stratford-on-Avon, Lincoln, Leicester and Nottingham. To find the house look for the church spire - it's behind the church.	£8.50	○	○	○
Mrs S. Goodwin **Hillside House** **Burton Road** **Burton Lazars** **Melton Mowbray LE14 2UR** **Tel: (0664) 66312** **OPEN: ALL YEAR**	Nearest Road A.606 Charming converted farmhouse with superb views of countryside. Burton Lazars is a small village in the midst of fox hunting country. Mrs. Goodwin offers a warm welcome to her visitors and charming, comfortable accommodation. Cots available. Rutland Water, Burghley House, Belvoir Castle and other interesting and historic locations within easy reach.	£8.50	○	■	○
Mrs Valerie Anderson **Home Farm** **Church Lane** **Old Dalby** **Nr. Melton Mowbray LE14 3LB** **Tel: (0664) 822622** **OPEN: ALL YEAR**	Nearest Road A.606 A comfortable Victorian farmhouse in a quiet lane on the edge of Old Dalby, an attractive village in the rural vale of Belvoir. Three bedrooms are available, one family, two twin. Residents' lounge with colour T.V. and garden available for guests. Children welcome, cots are provided and baby sitting can be arranged. Full English or Continental breakfast served.	£12.00	○	○	■

○ yes ■ no

		children taken	evening meals available	animals taken

Mrs J.C. Hitchen
Rutland House
61 High Street
Uppingham LE15 9PY
Tel: (0572) 822497

OPEN: ALL YEAR

Nearest Road A.47

Rutland House offers excellent accommodation in four guest rooms. Double, single and twin rooms are available, all with private bathrooms, central heating, colour T.V. and tea making facilities. Being a small establishment, the rooms are quiet and homely. Children are well provided for. Full English breakfast, or Continental alternative is served. Packed lunches can be prepared.

£15.00 | O | ■ | O

Mrs Sylvia Smart
The Paddocks
Barkestone-le-Vale
NG13 0HH
Tel: (0949) 42208

OPEN: ALL YEAR

Nearest Roads A.1 A.52

Visitors to the Paddocks can expect a very warm welcome from Mrs. Smart, Mathilda the goose, Jemima the donkey and the peacock. A spacious farmhouse set on 150 acre sheep farm, with a large garden and a heated swimming pool. Accommodation is comfortable, offering five rooms with modern amenities and guest bathroom, colour T.V. lounge and games room. Super home cooking. They also offer horse riding.

£8.50 | O | O | ■

June Ibbotson
Blue Barn Farm
Langwith
Mansfield NG20 9JD
Tel: (0623) 742248

OPEN: ALL YEAR

Nearest Roads A.616 A.1 M.1

Blue Barn is a family run, 250 acre arable farm. It is situated in the quiet countryside, on the edge of the famous Sherwood Forest. Accommodation is in four bedrooms with shower, bathroom and toilet separate. A dining room and lounge with colour T.V. Many places of interest close by including Clumber Park, Creswell Crags, Hardwick Hall, Thoresby Hall and Rufford Park.

£8.00 | O | ■ | O

Mrs B. Hinchley
Titchfield House
300/302 Chesterfield Rd North
Mansfield NG19 7QU
Tel: (0623) 810356

OPEN: ALL YEAR

Nearest Roads M.1 A.617

This is two houses, converted into one family run guest house, offering eight comfortable rooms, lounge with T.V., kitchen for guests' use, bathroom and showers. It also has an adjoining garage. Near to Mansfield which is a busy market town. Sherwood Forest and the Peak District easily accessible. Very handy for touring this lovely area and onward travel. A warm and friendly welcome is assured here.

£12.00 | O | O | ■

Peter & Marjorie Need
Peacock Farm Country
Restaurant & Guest House
Redmile NG1 30GQ
Tel: (0949) 42475

OPEN: ALL YEAR

Nearest Road A.1

Peacock Farm is a 250 year old house situated within sight of Belvoir Castle. The house is surrounded by glorious open countryside, with views of the nearby village across to the wooded hillside. Accommodation is in six rooms, some with en-suite facilities, tea/coffee making facilities and T.V. The small licensed restaurant provides delicious food, using fresh local produce and special meals can be arranged. Guests receive personal attention from their hosts who provide a homely friendly atmosphere for the whole family. There is also a swimming pool available for guests use.

£10.50 | O | O | O

O yes ■ no

		minimum per person	children taken	evening meals taken	animals taken	available

Mrs Sheila A. Woodhull
Upton Fields House
Southwell NG25 0QA
Tel: (0636) 812303

OPEN: ALL YEAR

Nearest Road A.612

A delightful friendly host and a welcoming atmosphere await the visitor to Upton Fields House. This large family house stands in 1½ acres of garden, just off the A.612. The house boasts a magnificent inlaid galleried staircase and beautiful stained glass windows. Accommodation is in four rooms, two with private facilities and all with modern amenities. There is also a guests T.V. lounge available throughout the day. This makes a comfortable base for visiting the many interesting places in both Leicestershire and Nottingham.

£10.00 ○ ■ ■

○ yes ■ no

LINCOLNSHIRE

An intriguing mixture of coast and country, flat fens and gently rising wolds, castles and cathedrals, farmers and sailors - these are all typical of this county.

The city of Lincoln may well boast of its glorious cathedral which must be the most beautiful in Europe, with the triple towers soaring upwards and dominating the landscape, surpassing the ancient castle of William the Conqueror which stands nearby. It is floodlit by night and presents a breathtaking spectacle. If architecture is "frozen music" then Lincoln Cathedral is a symphony of Beauty. It has a great 17th Century library by Wren which holds among its treasures one of the four original copies of the Magna Carta.

History

This area has always attracted travellers and adventurers - the Roman Legions were here in A.D. 48 and the North Gate which they built in the 3rd Century is still in use today. Then the Normans came with William the Conqueror and left us fine churches and houses; an outstanding example of these is Steep Hill in Lincoln and there are 16th century half timbered shops on the High Bridge which spans the Witham.

Great Houses

Elizabethan spendour is shown at its finest in Burghley House, set in lovely parklands, famous now for the annual horse trials. There is a spendid collection of art treasures gathered by discerning patrons over hundreds of years and preserved with love and care for future generations. Close by Burghley, is the town of Stamford which is a little gem in itself, said by many to be the finest and most beautiful small town in England.

Horncastle, Spilsby and Louth are attractive market towns. Alford has a thatched Manor House - quite rare - and a windmill. There is a famous race course at Market Rasen, and for the golfer there is a championship course at Woodhall Spa. Incidentally this course is crossed by the Viking Way, another reminder of the many invaders who came, stayed for a time and left their mark on the county and the people, becoming part of the immensely rich and complex history of Britain. There is hardly an acre of ground that has not felt the tread of invading armies and even today we still find traces of their occupation. Every year, in some part of the land, there is someone ploughing, or making a new road or just digging over his garden who turns up a few coins or pieces of jewellery or a sword, or maybe even a mosaic floor from a Roman villa - all of them invaluable indications of the life and times of the owners.

Coast

Not all our "guests" have been hostile armies - many brought skills and trades which they taught to the local people. For example, go to Spalding in May and see the Tulip parade - how alike that is to Holland. This exchange of ideas and people was not just one way. In Boston you will find the history of early Pilgrim Fathers who tried to sail from the little port to find religious freedom, but alas, they were caught and brought back to spend some time in prison cells which can still be seen at the Guildhall. Later they were released and sailed to the Netherlands and onwards to America. Boston also has a famous "Stump" church; that is, a lantern tower, which is a famous landmark.

Navigating the waters of the Wash can be very tricky, as King John discovered when he lost his ships, treasures and his Crown to the angry seas long, long ago. Every child spending a holiday here, building his sandcastles on the lovely golden beaches hopes to find just a little bit of that treasure washed up along the shore. The quiet fens, the beaches and the sand-dunes offer abundant food and shelter to birds which flock here. There are two large nature reserves at Gibraltar Point and Saltfleetby which attract bird-watchers and naturalists from many countries. There are many lovely historic houses with very well kept gardens, such as Doddington Hall Manor which is a charming Elizabethan house.

Harrington Hall gardens are those referred to by Alfred, Lord Tennyson, in his poem "Maud" (she actually lived in the Hall). The great poet was born in the tiny village of Somerby and was, no doubt, influenced by the gentle country life around him.

LINCOLNSHIRE GAZETEER

Areas of Outstanding Natural Beauty.
Lincolnshire Wolds.

Historic Houses and Castles

Auborn Hall -- Nr. Lincoln
16th century house with imposing carved staircase and panelled rooms.

Belton House -- Grantham
17th century -- said to be by Christopher Wren -- work by Grinling Gibbons and Wyatt also. A great English house with formal gardens and extensive grounds with orangery.

Doddington Hall -- Doddington -- Nr. Lincoln
16th century Elizabethan mansion -- gabled Tudor gatehouse. Fine furniture, paintings, pocelain, etc. Walled rose gardens.

Burghley House -- Stamford
Elizabethan -- England's largest and grandest house of the era -- famous for its beautiful painted ceilings, silver fireplace and art treasures.

Gumby hall -- Burgh-le-Marsh
17th century house built by Sir William Massingberd. Lovely walled gardens.

Marston Hall -- Grantham
16th century Manor house. Ancient gardens

Harrington Hall -- Spilsby
Mentioned in Domesday Book -- has mediaeval stone base -- Carolinean Manor House in red brick. Some alterations in 1678 to mullioned windows. Panelling, furnishings of 17th and 18th century.

The Old Hall -- Gainsborough
15th & 16th century Manor house with mediaeval kitchen rebuilt after original hall destoryed during Wars of the Roses. It was the first meeting place of the "Dissenters" later known as the Pilgrim Fathers.

Woolsthorpe Manor -- Grantham
17th century house. Birthplace of Sir Isaac Newton.

Fydell House   Boston
18th century house now Pilgrim College.

Cathedrals and Churches

Addlethorpe (St. Nicholas)
15th century -- mediaeval stained glass -- original woodwork.

Boston (St. Botolph)
14th century decorated -- very large parish church. Beautiful south porch, carved stalls.

Brant Broughton (St. Helens)
13th century arcades -- decorated tower & spire -- perpendicular clerestory. Exterior decoration.

Ewerby (St. Andrew)
Decorated -- splendid example of period -- very fine spire. 14th century effigy.

Fleet (St. Mary Magdalene)
14th century -- early English arcades -- perpendicular windows -- detached tower and spire.

Folkingham (St. Andrew)
14th century arcades -- 15th century windows -- perpendicular tower -- early English chancel.

Gedney (St. Mary Magdalene)
Perpendicular spire (unfinished) Early English tower. 13th-14th century monuments, 14th-15th century stained glass.

Grantham (St. Wulfram)
14th century tower and spire -- Norman pillars -- perpendicular chantry -- 14th century vaulted crypt.

Lincoln Cathedral
13th century -- some 14th century additions. Norman work from 1072. Angel choir -- carved and decorated pulpitum -- 13th century chapter house -- 17th century library by Wren (containing one of the four original copies of Magna Carta).

Long Sutton (St. Mary)
15th century south porch, mediaeval brass lectern, very fine early English spire.

Louth (St. James)
Early 16th century -- mediaeval Gothic -- wonderful spire.

Scotter (St. Peter)
Saxon to perpendicular -- early English nave -- 15th century rood screen.

Stow (St. Mary)
Norman -- very fine example, particulary west door. Wall painting.

Silk Willoughby (St. Denis)
14th century -- tower with spire and flying buttresses. 15th century-17th century pulpit.

Stainfield (St.Andrew)
Queen Anne -- mediaeval armour and early needlework.

Theddlethorpe (All Saints)
14th century -- 15th century and reredos of 15th century, 16th century parcloses, 15th century brasses-,some mediaeval glass.

Wrangle (St. Mary the Virgin and St. Nicholas)
Early English -- decorated -- perpendicular -- Elizabethan pulpit. 14th century east window and glass.

Museums and Galleries

Alford Manor House -- Alford
Tudor manor house -- thatched -- folk museum. Nearby windmill.

Boston Museum -- Boston
15th century building -- archeology -- local history -- associated with Pilgrim Fathers.

Lincoln Cathedral Library
Built by Wren housing early printed books and mediaeval manuscripts.

Lincoln Cathedral Treasury
Diocesan gold and silver plate.

Lincoln City and Country Museum
Prehistoric, Roman and mediaeval antiquities with local associations. Armour and local history.

Usher Gallery -- Lincoln
Tennyson Collection. Works of English watercolourist Peter de Wint. Usher collection of antique watches, porcelain and miniatures.

Museum -- Grantham
Archeology, prehistoric, Saxon and Roman, local history.

LINCOLNSHIRE
Recommended roadside restaurants

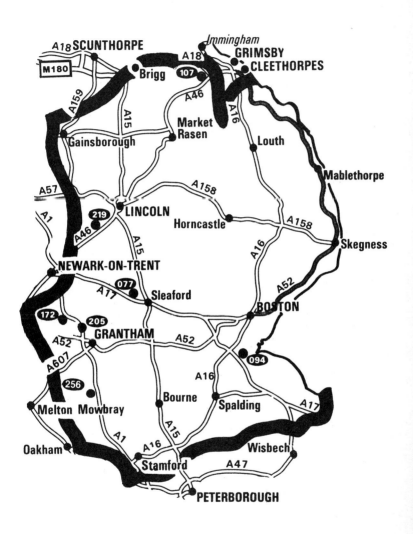

Lincolnshire

	minimum per person	children taken	evening meals available	animals taken

Dr & Mrs G.D. Bishop **Bourne Eau House** **South St** **Bourne PE10 9LY** **Tel: (0778) 423621** **OPEN: ALL YEAR**	Nearest Roads A.1 A.15 Enjoy warm hospitality and superb accommodation in lovely Bourne Eau House, a country home with Elizabethan/Georgian origins, combining modern comforts with 16th century oak beams and inglenooks. Standing by a 12th century abbey, with its gardens bordered by a stream. The house offers four excellent guest rooms, all en-suite with radio, T.V., tea/coffee making facilities, and central heating. Jacobean sitting room with log fire.	£20.00	■	○	■
Mrs Ann Higginbottom **Dunston Manor** **Dunston** **Lincoln LN4 2EN** **Tel: (0526) 20463** **OPEN: JAN-NOV**	Nearest Roads B.1188 A.15 A delightful old manor house dating back to 1750. The oldest house in the small, unspoilt village of Dunston. The house, built of local stone, has huge walls up to 32 inches thick. Accommodation is in 2 comfortable rooms with separate bathroom. Private lounge and dining room. Good home cooked Lincolnshire food. Excellent for an overnight stop or for touring. Golf and coarse fishing nearby. Children over 12 years. No smoking.	£11.50	○	○	■
Mrs Peter Gosse **Rookery Farm** **Castle Carlton** **Nr. Louth LN11 8JF** **Tel: (0521) 50357** **OPEN: ALL YEAR**	Nearest Road A.157 Rookery Farm is a delightful, traditional, late 18th century farmhouse. The owners have sympathetically restored it to a high standard of comfort and convenience, while maintaining many of the original features, including the low beamed ceilings and original interior brick walls. The main features outside are the old fashioned shrub roses and herb garden. Accommodation is in 3 nice rooms with modern amenities. A residents' lounge is also available. The food here is delicious, mainly whole food with organically grown vegetables from the garden. Homemade bread is a speciality. Louth, Alford, The Wolds and Rimac Nature Reserve are all easily accessible from here.	£9.00	○	○	■
Mr & Mrs P.H.G. Wilkins **Corner Cottage** **"Hare & Hounds"** **Greatford** **Nr. Stamford PE9 4QA** **Tel: (077836) 332** **OPEN: ALL YEAR**	Nearest Road A.16 Excellent accommodation in an 18th century stone built cottage modernised to a very high standard. Three bedrooms for guests, one with private bathroom, all with tea/coffee making facilities. Breakfast, English or Continental, is served in the cottage while evening meals if required are served in the "Hare & Hounds opposite, an inn of repute. Garden for guests. Children over 10 years.	£10.00	○	○	■

○ yes ■ no

		minimum per person	children taken	evening meals available	animals taken
Brian & Mary Shillaker **Washingborough Hall** **Country House Hotel** **Church Hill** **Washingborough LN4 1BE** **Tel: (0522) 790340** **OPEN: ALL YEAR**	Nearest Road B.1190 A pleasant 200 year old manor house, now a Grade II listed building, is situated in three acres of grounds, giving a quiet secluded atmosphere. It offers twelve comfortable rooms all with en-suite facilities and has an outdoor swimming pool. Historic Lincoln is nearby. Superb food on an A la Carte menu. Log fires in winter. Bar serving real ale.	£22.00	○	○	○
Mr & Mrs R. Miller **Dunn's Guest House** **The Broadway** **Woodhall Spa, LN10 6SQ** **Tel: (0526) 52969** **OPEN: ALL YEAR**	Nearest Road A.1 This is a solid Victorian house with large airy rooms. All bedrooms are nicely furnished and have hand basins. There are six comfortable rooms: singles, twins and doubles. The lounge is very pleasant and is available all day for guests. The dining room is bright and you will enjoy Mrs. Miller's good home cooking - well recommended by all who have stayed here. Woodhall is a pretty spa town, in a wooded area, having access to Horncastle market town and Lincoln Cathedral City.	£9.00	○	○	■

○ yes ■ no

Don't be disappointed. Book ahead.
Use our fast efficient
RESERVATION SERVICE
Reservation forms & Reservation Bureau
Be sure of your accommodation
Book Now!!
Call us on

01-370 7099   ***01-370 7099***

165

NORFOLK

One of the largest of the old counties, it is divided by rivers from neighbouring counties and it pushes out into the sea on the Northern and Eastern sides. This is old East Anglia - it has a style all of its own - whether countryside or seaside there is something quite distinctive about the people and the lifestyle. It is amazingly involved with water, and yet it appears to be mostly rural. There are lovely country houses and castles to be visited; churches of immense age and beauty; market towns; fishing villages and all these so different it seems hardly possible they belong to the same county.

Norwich

The County town is a history lesson in itself and overflows with riches to delight the heart and eye. The Cathedral and Castle dominate the landscape as the Normans intended they should. The interior of the cathedral is magnificent, especially the cloisters which have fine decorated work from the 13th century. The choir stalls of the 15th century are canopied with splendid carving. The Cathedral Close is quite lovely - so gentle and elegant, perfectly preserved as is Elm Hill, a cobbled street from the mediaeval era. The great keep of the castle is hugh; now a museum of great interest and houses the wonderful paintings of the Norwich School. The town has had a chequered history - it suffered from a series of disastrous fires and was decimated by the Plague when that horror spread through the town as fast as the fires. (There is a reputed burial pit where the victims were thrown - now known as Tombland Alley). The main trade was weaving, particularly worsted made from the local wool; however this almost died out leaving great poverty behind, and the trade did not revive until the arrival of refugees from Holland, just across the sea, who bought new methods of weaving finer cloth. Prosperity returned to the town, but during the bleak period there were no patrons to build fine houses etc. and the gaps in the architectural history are quite marked.

Country and Broads

Driving through the countryside it is surprising to encounter long deserted villages such as Egmere or a completely isolated church as at Hardingham - can these be reminders of a difficult and troubled past? Standing in such a village one longs for an explanation - all too quickly supplied by vivid imagination. There is a great concentration on agriculture, the land hedged about for miles with Hawthorn bushes which make a very pretty sight when they bloom like snow in summer. There is a great deal of land drainage required and the area is criss crossed with dykes and ditches - some of them going back to the Roman times. Marl and peat were dug from enormous pits which flooded and became vast stretches of water known as the famous Norfolk Broads. Miles and miles and miles of inland waterways, navigable and safe make this one of the happiest of holiday centres, not only for those who love to sail but also for the naturalist and bird watcher - the wild life is quite fascinating. On a bright summer day, with the boats drifting lazily along, the Broads seem like a paradise.

Coast

Contrasting with the still quiet inland waters is the boisterous coastline which takes in a host of towns and villages as it arcs round into the Wash, that unpredictable stretch of water. But here are all the joys of the seaside at its best. Miles of golden beaches, safe and sandy, delighting the children. There are dunes and salt marshes where bird life flourishes and many areas have been set aside as nature reserves or bird sanctuaries. The busy ports; fishing villages with pink washed cottages tumbling down to the shore, pretty villages gay with flowers; all offer something of interest for everyone. The brisk and invigorating sea air blows right across the county and can be very chilling in the winter. But for summer holidays here you will find this area marvellously rewarding. The sailing is superb, there is fishing, golfing, trekking, walking and everywhere a warm welcome from the East Anglians. It is a county much loved by our Royal Family and the Queen has her Norfolk home at Sandringham, which is a lovely area. Not far away is the busy town of King's Lynn which stands a little way inland on the River Ouse and provides a deep water shelter from the stormy Wash. It was made prosperous by the trade between England and Europe, particularly with the Hanseatic League. Accordingly, fine building and churches were erected and make the town extremely handsome, and there is some of the finest mediaeval domestic architecture in England.

NORFOLK GAZETEER

Areas of Outstanding Beauty.
Norfolk coast (part)

Historic Houses and Castles

Anna Sewell House -- Great Yarmouth
17th century Tudor frontage. Birthplace of writer Anna Sewell.

Blicking Hall -- Aylsham
Great Jacobean house. Fine Russian tapestry, long gallery with exceptional ceiling. Formal garden.

Felbrigg Hall -- Nr. Cromer
17th century, good Georgian interior. Set in wooded parklands.

Holkham Hall -- Wells
Fine Palladian mansion of 1734. Paintings, statuary, tapestries, furnishings and formal garden by Berry.

Houghton Hall -- King's Lynn
18th century mansion. Pictures, china and state rooms.

Oxburgh Hall -- Swaffham
Late 15th century moated house. Fined gatehouse tower. Needlework by Mary Queen of Scots.

Wolterton Hall -- Nr. Norwich
Built 1741 contains tapestries, porcelain, furniture.

Trinity Hospital -- Castle Rising
17th century, nine brick and tile almshouses, court, chapel & treasury.

Cathedrals and Churches

Attleborough (St. Mary)
Norman with late 14th century. Fine rood screen and frescoes.

Barton Turf (St. Michael and all Angels)
Magnificent screen with paintings of the Nine Orders of Angels.

Beeston-next-Mileham (St. Mary)
14th century. Perpendicular clerestory tower and spire. Hammer Beam roof, parclose screens, benches, font cover. Tracery in nave and chancel windows.

Cawston (St. Agnes)
Tower faced with freestone. Painted screens, wall paintings, tower, screen and gallery. 15th century angel roof.

East Harding (St. Peter & St. Paul)
14th century, some 15th century alterations. Monuments of 15/17th century. Splendid mediaeval glass.

Erpingham (St. Mary)
14th century military brass to John de Erpingham, 16th century Rhenish glass. Fine tower.

Gunton (St. Andrew)
18th century. Robert Adam -- classical interior in dark wood -- gilded.

King's Lynn (St. Margaret)
Norman foundation. Two fine 14th century Flemish brasses, 14th century screens, reredos by Bodley, interesting Georgian pulpit with sounding board.

Norwich Cathedral
Romanesque and late Gothic with late 15th century spire. Perpendicular lierne vaults in nave, transeptsand presbytery.

Ranworth (St. Helens)
15th century screen, very fine example. Sarum Antiphoner, 14th century illuminated manuscript -- East Anglian work.

Salle (St. Peter & St. Paul)
15th century. Highly decorated west tower and porches. Mediaeval glass, pulpit with 15th century panels and Jacobean tester. Stalls, misericords, brasses & monuments, sacrament font.

Terrington (St. Clement)
Detached perpendicular tower. Western front has fire-light window and canopied niches. Georgian panelling west of nave. 17th century painted font cover, Jacobean commandment boards.

Trunch (St. Botolph)
15th century screen with painted panels, mediaeval glass, famous font canopy with fine carving and painting, ringer's gallery, Elizbethan monument.

Wiggenhall (St. Germans)
17th century pulpit, table, clerk's desk & chair, bench ends 15th century.

Wymondham (St. Mary & St. Thomas of Canterbury)
Norman origins including arcades and triforium windows, 13th century font fragments, complete 15th century font. 15th century clerestory and roof. Comper reredos, famous Corporas Case, rare example of 13th century Opus Anglicanum.

Museums and Galleries

Norwich Castle Museum
Art collection, local and natural history, ceramic display.

Strangers Hall -- Norwich
Mediaeval mansion furnished as museum of urban domestic life in 16th-19th centuries.

St. Peter Hungate Church Museum -- Norwich
15th century church for the exhibition of ecclesiastical art and East Anglian antiquities.

Sainsbury Centre for Visual Arts -- University -- Norwich
Collection of modern art, ancient, classical and mediaeval art, Art Nouveau, 20th century constructivist art.

Bridewell Museum of Local Industries -- Norwich
Crafts, industries and aspects of city life.

Museum of Social History -- King's Lynn
Exhibition of domestic life and dress etc. noted glass collection.

Bishop Bonner's Cottages
Restored cottages with coloured East Anglian pargetting, c. 1502, museum of archeological discoveries, exhibition of rural crafts.

The Guildhall -- Thetford
Duleep Singh Collection of Norfolk and Suffolk portraits.

Shirehall Museum -- Walsingham
18th century court room having original fittings, illustrating Walsingham life.

Historic Monuments

Binham Priory & Cross -- Binham
12th century ruins of Benedictine foundation.

Caister Castle -- Great Yarmouth
15th century moated castle -- ruins. Now motor museum.

The Castle -- Burgh Castle
3rd century Saxon fort -- walls -- ruin.

Mannington Hall -- Saxthorpe
Saxon church ruin in gardens of 15th century moated house.

Castle Rising -- Castle Rising
Splendid Norman keep and earthworks.

Castle Acre Priory and Castle Gate -- Swaffham

NORFOLK
Recommended roadside restaurants

024	A47/ A1067	Norwich Norfolk Sweet Briar Road Norwich Ring Road between A47 and A1067
105	A47	Swaffham Norfolk 2 miles west of Swaffham
113	A140	Tasburgh Long Stratton, Norwich, Norfolk 2 miles north of Long Stratton 6 miles south of Norwich
121	A47	Acle, Norfolk 8 miles west of Great Yarmouth
131	A11	Snetterton, Norfolk 19 miles south of Norwich 10 miles north of Thetford

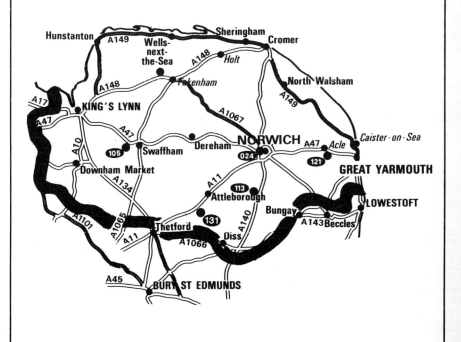

Norfolk

minimum per person
children taken
evening meals available
animals taken

		minimum per person	children taken	evening meals available	animals taken
Mr & Mrs N.J. Brown **Sherbourne Country House** **Norwich Road** **Attleborough NR17 2JX** **Tel: (0953) 452129** **OPEN: ALL YEAR**	Nearest Road A.11 Set in an acre of mature grounds, this delightful 17th century house has a friendly atmosphere with open fires, period furnishings and candlelit dining. Six beautiful rooms, four en-suite with T.V. and tea/coffee makers, three with 4-poster beds. A charming lounge with colour T.V. and superb garden for guests. The evening meals are super and great value. The house has a fine reputation for cuisine. This is an excellent base for touring. Attleborough is a most interesting town. Norwich and the Broads are not far. Riding is available locally. For bird watchers and walkers this area is superb.	£14.00	○	○	○
Mrs P.A. Morfoot **Church Cottage** **Breckles** **Attleborough NR17 1EW** **Tel: (095382) 286** **OPEN: ALL YEAR** **(EXCL. XMAS & NEW YEAR)**	Nearest Road A.11 A charming 18th century house situated in beautiful Breckland, looking out over typical Norfolk farmland. Convenient for touring - East Anglia being central. Two double, two single bedrooms. Good home cooking, using own produce, bread, eggs, etc. Visitors own sitting/dining room with colour T.V. Heated outdoor swimming pool. Own coarse fishing. Children over 10 years.	£9.50	○	○	■
Connie & Doug Atkins **Ingleneuk Guest House** **Hopton Road** **Garboldisham** **Diss IP22 2RQ** **Tel: (095381) 541** **OPEN: ALL YEAR**	Nearest Road A.1066 A warm welcome is extended to visitors at Ingleneuk, a large modern family run bungalow, in quiet wooded countryside with riverside walks. A variety of rooms, most en-suite, all centrally heated, double glazed, with colour T.V., telephone, and hot drink facilities. Children well provided for. Residents' lounge, licensed bar and dining room. Wildlife Park, Steam Museum, Forest nature trails and zoo nearby.	£12.00	○	○	○
Mrs B. Wells **"Spindrift" Private Hotel** **36 Wellesley Road** **Great Yarmouth NR30 1EU** **Tel: (0493) 858674** **OPEN: ALL YEAR**	Nearest Road - Marine Parade/North Dr. Good food and comfortable accommodation are the by-words at "Spindrift". Attractively situated adjacent to the sea front, the Golden Mile. Bowling greens, tennis courts and the Waterways. Easy going atmosphere with keys provided for access at all times. A selection of eight bedrooms, some with excellent sea views, all with modern amenities, T.V., and tea/coffee making facilities. Good parking. Coach station close by.	£8.50	○	○	■
Mr & Mrs Adrian Taunton **The Old Barn House** **Kelling** **Holt NR25 7EF** **Tel: (026370) 543** **OPEN: ALL YEAR**	Nearest Road A.149 Guests will enjoy individual attention at the Old Barn House. An 18th century traditional flint and brick farmhouse, with extensive barns and gardens, in rural Norfolk village within sight of the sea. One twin bedded room is available, looking south over the garden, with private bathroom looking out to sea. Dining room exclusively for guests at breakfast. Dinner with hosts, enjoying 'haute cuisine'.	£10.00	■	○	○

○ yes ■ no

		minimum per person	children taken	evening meals available	animals taken
Mrs Sheila Tweedy Smith **Fieldsend House** **Homefields Road** **Hunstanton PE36 5HL** **Tel: (04853) 2593** **OPEN: ALL YEAR**	Nearest Road A.149 Fieldsend is a large carrstone house, built at the turn of the century by a timber merchant, as his seaside residence. Set in ½ acre of walled garden within easy walking distance of the town centre. Three attractive and comfortable country style rooms with canopied beds. All have sea views. Mrs. Tweedy Smith serves a full English breakfast in the oak panelled dining room. Special diets can be served but prior warning is requested. Guests have their own sitting room and are free to come and go as they please. Tea/coffee is served on request.	£12.00	O	■	O
Mr & Mrs R.D. Moody **Stuart House Hotel** **35 Goodwins Rd** **King's Lynn PE30 5QX** **Tel: (0553) 772169/774788** **OPEN: ALL YEAR** **(EXCL. XMAS & NEW YEAR)**	Nearest Roads A.47 A.17 An attractive detached Georgian house, standing in its own quiet grounds. Located close to the Queen's home at Sandringham. This hotel is well placed for visiting both coast and countryside. Accommodation is in 21 pleasant bedrooms, most with private facilities. All have modern amenities, telephone, radio, T.V. and tea/coffee makers. There's also a guests' T.V. lounge and dining room. The food here is delicious. Dinner is as important a part of the service as breakfast. All food is freshly prepared using only the best fresh meats and vegetables. A la Carte or Table d'hote menus are available.	£19.00	O	O	O
Dawn Nightingale **The White House** **44 Hunstanton Road** **Dersingham** **King's Lynn PE31 6HQ** **Tel: (0485) 41895** **OPEN: ALL YEAR**	Nearest Road A.149 This comfortable detached house offers guests a warm welcome and a friendly atmosphere. Built on land once owned by Edward VII it is only 1½ miles from the Queen's home at Sandringham. Guests have a choice of five rooms with modern amenities and tea/coffee making facilities. Nearby are beautiful sandy beaches, golf course, bird reserve, Wedgwood and crystal glass factories. Houghton, Oxburgh, Holkham Halls and Peckover House, as well as many interesting museums.	£10.00	O	■	O
Eddie & Margaret Lovatt **Edmar Lodge** **64 Earlham Road** **Norwich NR2 3DF** **Tel: (0603) 615599** **OPEN: ALL YEAR**	Nearest Road A.47 A large corner house with parking for guests, situated in a quiet area, only 10 minutes walk from the city centre. There are four very attractive, comfortable rooms with every modern amenity, including tea/coffee makers and T.V. Mrs. Lovatt makes all her guests very welcome and serves wonderful breakfasts in a pretty dining room. There is an area set aside for literature and maps of places to visit in the region and Mrs. Lovatt will help with tour planning and advice on Norwich. There are many good restaurants within a few minutes drive and a theatre. This is a happy house with a relaxed atmosphere. An excellent base for touring.	£9.50	O	■	O

O yes ■ no

171

	minimum per person	children taken	evening meals available	animals taken
Mrs Ruth Hemsted 35 Mount Pleasant Norwich NR2 2DH Tel: (0603) 53638 **OPEN: MAR-DEC** Nearest Road A.11 An attractive Victorian house standing in large gardens, set back a good distance from the road. Offering four very large, comfortable and well decorated rooms with antique furniture. Rooms have modern amenities, tea/coffee makers and all look out over beautifully landscaped gardens. There is a lounge with T.V. for guests. Situated only 1 mile from the city centre, in a quiet side road. A very pleasant base for visitors to historic Norwich.	£10.00	○	■	■
Mrs S.M. Greenslade 24 Eaton Road Norwich NR4 6PZ Tel: (0603) 57115 **OPEN: ALL YEAR** Nearest Road A.11 A comfortable Edwardian house, quietly situated just 1 mile from the centre of Norwich. Convenient for the A.11, the University and the golf course. Mrs. Greenslade offers 3 rooms, one single, one twin and one family room, with modern amenities, radio, T.V. and tea/coffee making. Children are well provided for with cots, high chairs and baby sitting. Lounge and garden.	£10.50	○	■	○
Mrs Daphne Vivian-Neal Welbeck House Brooke Nr. Norwich NR15 1AT Tel: (0508) 50292 **OPEN: ALL YEAR** Nearest Road B.1332 Three twin bedrooms are available to guests in this delightful pink Georgian farmhouse, set in its own spacious gardens surrounded by trees. Situated ¼ mile north of Brooke Church, 7 miles south of Norwich, a restful base for touring and enjoying the riches of Norwich, the Broads and the Norfolk coast, Blakeney Point, and Minsmere Nature Reserve. Historic houses nearby. Children over 12 years.	£8.50	■	■	○
Mrs H.M. Grimsdale Sandegate Norwich Road Horstead Norwich NR12 7LA Tel: (0603) 737390 **OPEN: APRIL-OCT** Nearest Road B.1150 Sandegate is a large, modern, centrally heated family house, offering guests accommodation in four bedrooms, one double, one twin, one single and one family room, with modern amenities, and tea/coffee making facilities. Cots can be provided and baby sitting arranged. 7 miles from Norwich, 3 miles from Wroxham, the centre for the Norfolk Broads. Coast within easy reach.	£9.50	○	■	■
W.R. & A.E. Parker Elm Farm Chalet Hotel St.Faith Norwich NR10 3HH Tel: (0603) 898366 & 897129 **OPEN: ALL YEAR** Nearest Road A.140 A 17th century farmhouse with chalet accommodation which is extremely comfortable in 15 rooms, all with modern facilities, some with bathroom en-suite, and tea making amenities. T.V. lounge. Situated in the attractive village of St.Faith and only 4 miles from Norwich, within easy reach of the Norfolk and Suffolk coasts, this is an attractive base for touring. Cots are provided.	£16.50	○	○	■

○ yes ■ no

		minimum per person	children taken	evening meals available	animals taken
Mrs Patricia Wayre **Hawks Hill** **Gt.Witchingham** **Norwich NR9 5QS** **Tel: (0603) 872552** **OPEN: ALL YEAR**	Nearest Road A.140 Hawks Hill is a small 300 year old country house. Built of mellow red brick it stands in its own extensive gardens surrounded by the beautiful Norfolk countryside. The house is most attractively furnished and has oak beams and inglenook fireplaces. Accommodation is in two very comfortable rooms with modern amenities, attractive private bathrooms, radio and tea/coffee making facilities. The guests' lounge has colour T.V. and is well furnished with comfortable chairs, sofas, paintings and personal treasures. Meals are prepared to very high standards using only fresh food and vegetables from the owners garden. Wines and spirits are available.	£12.00	■	○	○
Mrs Philippa Earp **Staitheway House** **Staitheway Road** **The Avenue** **Wroxham** **Norwich NR12 8TH** **Tel: (06053) 3347** **OPEN: ALL YEAR**	Nearest Road A.1151 Visitors will receive a warm welcome in a relaxed atmosphere, in this charming house. Three pleasant and comfortable rooms with modern facilities, overlooking the garden. Good evening meals available on request. Staitheway House is quietly situated within a few minutes walk of the village, the Broads and the river. This is an ideal holiday centre for boat lovers, hikers and naturalists. 7 miles from historic Norwich.	£10.00	○	○	■
Mrs V. O'Hara **Geoffrey the Dyer House** **Church Plain** **Worstead** **North Walsham** **Tel: (069260) 562** **OPEN: ALL YEAR**	Nearest Road Enjoy the peace and tranquility of Norfolk's heartland in the excellent accommodation offered at this 17th century weavers residence. A carefully restored building, full of character and comfort, the house has four guest rooms, some with private bathroom, all with modern facilities, interesting residents' lounge and garden. The home of Worstead cloth, this conservation village is dominated by its famous 13th century church.	£10.50	○	○	○
R.W. & D.F. Johnson **Pound Green Guest House** **Pound Green Lane** **Shipdham** **Thetford IP25 7LS** **Tel: (0362) 820165** **OPEN: ALL YEAR**	Nearest Road A.47 An attractive three storey modern house set in 1 acre of garden. They have 16 very comfortable rooms with modern amenities, 7 with private shower. A pleasant T.V. lounge and a games room for guests. Also a large heated swimming pool which guests can use. This is a very good base for touring. Large restaurant with A la Carte menu. The proprietors will assist guests in route planning as there is so much to see in the area.	£14.65	○	○	○

○ yes ■ no

173

		minimum per person	children taken	evening meals available	animals taken
Mrs Lavender Garnier College Farm Thompson Thetford IP24 1QG Tel: (095383) 318 **OPEN: ALL YEAR**	Nearest Roads B.1075 A.1075 This attractive 600 year old farmhouse, formerly a college of priests, is located in the peace and quiet of the countryside. Recently modernised, it now offers comfortable accommodation in four large bedrooms with colour T.V. and armchairs. A charming panelled dining room where a substantial breakfast is served. An ideal centre for touring East Anglia. Super old thatched pubs in the village serving excellent evening meals.	£10.00	O	■	■
Mrs Molly Castlo The Well House Standard Road Wells-Next-The-Sea NR23 1JY Tel: (0328) 710443 **OPEN: ALL YEAR (EXCL. XMAS)**	Nearest Road A.148 A charming 16th century manor house, overlooking the salt marshes, only 1 mile from the beach. Four most attractive rooms, two with en-suite facilities. All have modern amenities including T.V. A comfortable lounge with T.V. for guests. A very good base for bird watching, sailing, water skiing and walks. Many outstanding historic houses and museums within a reasonable driving distance. Mrs Castlo makes all visitors most welcome and will give advice on places of interest locally. Prices quoted are for 2 people.	£19.00	O	■	O

O yes ■ no

ADVANCE RESERVATIONS

Don't be disappointed. Book ahead.
Use our fast efficient
RESERVATION SERVICE
Reservation forms & Reservation Bureau
Be sure of your accommodation
Book Now!!
Call us on

01-370 7099   *01-370 7099*

NORTHUMBRIA

Mountains and moors, hills and fells, coast and country - all these are to be found in this Northern region which embraces four counties: Northumberland, Durham, Cleveland and Tyne and Wear.

Saxons, Celts, Vikings, Romans; all fought to control what was then a great wasteland between the Humber and Scotland. All left their marks on the people and the landscape - none more dramatically than the Romans. Deere Street, for example (part of the length of Watling Street) was begun by Petrilius Ceralis and completed by Agricola between AD 78-85, and is still a main road to the North today. It crosses Hadrian's Wall, which was built as the permanent Northern frontier of the Roman Empire in AD 122, stretching from Wallsend near the Tyne mouth in the East to Bowness on the Solway Firth in the West. Excavations along the wall have brought to light many archeological treasures. To follow the Wall on foot takes the traveller through a history of Roman building and engineering for which they were renowned. They left a network of roads which made it easy for them to move their men to maintain discipline among the wild tribes. 300 fortified sites are recorded and the area is dotted with ruined forts, castles and pele towers, telling the story of centuries of struggling to defend the area. Berwick on Tweed, the most northerly English town changed hands between England and Scotland 13 times. Coastal fortresses defended the region from seaborne invaders.

Local Geography

The Cheviot Hills make a northern boundary, the great Pennine Chain (backbone of England) lies to the West and the Southern edge is bounded by the River Tees and parts of Cleveland.

The region has some of the least spoiled of the English countryside and provides magnificent walking upon the dales and fells or the moors. There are 4 magnificent National Parks and a Border Forest Park. Historic ruins of castles and monastic foundations abound - again signs of the times when the Vikings destroyed and plundered the churches and monasteries - fearing the influence of the new religion of Christianity. A monastery was built for St. Aidan of Iona on the Holy Island of Lindesfarne off the coast of Northumberland but the Danes destroyed it. However a new monastery was built on the site on 1082 by the monks of Durham. It was in the Norman style and its remains are part of our great architectural heritage. Holy Island is completely cut off from the mainland for several hours each day at high tide - but at low tide the causeway can be crossed on foot. Beware the rising waters. The Cathedral of Durham took 40 years to build 1093 to 1133 and stands today as a masterpiece of mediaeval building - quite breathtaking in its grandeur.

Developement

Tyne & Wear take their names from the rivers running through the area. George Stephenson - the railway engineer was born in this county which holds Wall Village, so called because it was built with stone plundered from Hadrian's Wall. Weardale lies in a beautiful valley - wild, bleak moors and fells surround it, peaceful now, but there was a thriving industry there 100 years ago, mining coal and silver, zinc and lead. Now nature trails and recreational areas have been created among the villages and market towns built of local stone.

Cleveland county has moorland and coast and heavy industrialized towns, but it has beautiful contryside and it is a delight to climb Roseberry Topping. It is the birthplace of Captain James Cook the great explorer who was born in Marton in Cleveland in 1728 and sailed in colliers built in Whitby - a little town in North Yorkshire facing the North Sea. His great voyages of discovery changed world history.

Teesdale, one of the Pennine Dales, has many faces. The Tees rises high up in the rugged fells and gathers force as it falls down some 2000 feet of rapids and cascades on its way down to the valley. The villages have lovely names like Widdybush Fell and Fairy Dell or Cotherstone where the regional cheeses are made. Gentle country, busy market towns, Barnard Castle and the famous Bowes Museum nearby with its great galleries exhibiting European paintings together with a variety of other exhibits.

NORTHUMBRIA GAZETEER

Historic Houses and Castles

Alnwick Castle -- Alnwick
A superb mediaeval castle of the 12th century.

Bamburgh Castle -- Bamburgh
A resorted 12th century castle with Norman keep.

Callaly Castle -- Whittingham
A 13th century Pele tower with 17th century Mansion. Georgian additions.

Durham Castle -- Durham
Part of the University of Durham -- a Norman castle.

Lindesfarne Castle -- Holy Island
An interesting 14th century castle.

Ormesby Hall -- Nr. Middlesbrough
A mid 18th century house.

Raby Castle -- Staindrop, Darlington
14th century with some later alteration. Fine art and furniture. Large gardens.

Wallington Hall -- Cambo
A 17th century house with much alteration and addition.

Washington Old Hall -- Washington
Jacobean Manor House parts of which date back to 12th century.

Cathedrals and Churches

Brancepeth (St. Brandon)
12th century with superb 17th century woodwork. Part of 2 mediaeval screens, Flemish carved chest.

Durham Cathedral
A superb Norman cathedral. A unique Galilee chapel and early 12th century vaults.

Escombe
An interesting Saxon Church with sundial.

Hartlepool (St. Hilda)
Early English with fine tower and buttresses.

Hexham (St. Andrews)
Remains of a 17th century church with Roman dressing. A unique night staircase and very early stool. Painted screens.

Jarrow (St. Pauls)
Bede worshipped here. Strange in that it was originally 2 churches until 11th century. Mediaeval chair.

Newcastle (St. Nicholas)
14th century with an interesting lantern tower. Heraldic font. Roundel of 14th century glass.

Morpeth (St. Mary the Virgin)
Fine mediaeval glass in east window -- 14th century.

Pittington (St. Lawrence)
Late Norman nave with wall paintings. Carved tombstone -- 13th century.

Skelton (St. Giles)
Early 13th century with noteable font, gable crosses, bell-cote and buttresses.

Staindrop (St. Mary)
A fine Saxon window. Priests dwelling, Neville tombs and effigies.

Museums and Galleries

Arbiea Roman Fort Museum -- South Shields
Interesting objects found on site.

Berwick on Tweed Museum -- Berwick
Special exhibition of interesting local finds.

Bowes Museum -- Barnard Castle
European art from mediaeval to 19th century.

Captain Cook Birthplace Museum -- Middlesbrough
Cook's life and natural history relating to his travels.

Clayton Collection -- Chollerford
A collection of Roman sculpture, weapons and tools from forts.

Corbridge Roman Station -- Corbridge
Roman pottery and sculpture.

Dormitory Museum -- Durham Cathedral
Relics of St. Cuthbert. Mediaeval seats and manuscripts.

Gray Art Gallery -- Hartlepool
19th-20th century art and oriental antiquities.

Gulbenkian Museum of Oriental Art -- University of Durham
Chinese pottery and porcelain, Chinese jade and stone carvings, Chinese ivories, Chinese textiles, Japanese and Tibetan art. Egyptian and mesopotamian antiquities.

Jarrow Hall -- Jarrow
Excavation finds of Saxon and mediaeval monastery. Fascinating information room dealing with early Christian sites in England.

Keep Museum -- Newcastle upon Tyne
Mediaeval collection.

Laing Art Gallery -- Newcastle upon Tyne
17th-19th century British art, porcelain, glass and silver.

National Music Hall Museum -- Sunderland
19th-20th century costume and artefacts associated with the halls.

Preston hall Museum -- Stockton on Tees
Armour and arms, toys, ivory period rooms.

University of Newcastle upon Tyne
The Greek museum -- a superb collection. The Hatton Gallery -- Housing a fine collection of Italian paintings.

Museum of Antiquities
Prehistoric, Roman and Saxon collection with an interesting reconstruction of a temple.

Historic Monuments

Arbiea Roman Fort -- South Shields
Remains which include the gateways and headquarters.

Barnard Castle -- Barnard Castle
17th century ruin with interesting keep.

Bowes Castle -- Bowes
Roman Fort with Norman keep.

The Castle & Town Walls -- Berwick on Tweed
12th century remains, reconstructed later.

Dunstanburgh Castle -- Alnwick
14th century remains.

Egglestone Abbey -- Barnard Castle
Remains of a Poor House.

Finchdale Priory -- Durham
13th century church with much remaining.

Guisborough Priory -- Guisborough
Remains of 14th century church.

Hadrian's Wall -- Housesteads
Several miles of the wall including castles and site museum.

Mithraic Temple -- Carrawbrough
Mithraic temple dating back to the 3rd century.

Norham Castle -- Norham
The partial remains of a 12th century castle.

Prudhoe Castle -- Prudhoe
Dating from the 12th century with additions. Bailey and gatehouse well preserved.

The Roman Fort -- Chesters
Extensive remains of a Roman bath house.

Tynemouth Priory & Castle -- Tynemouth
11th century priory -- ruin -- with 16th century towers and keep.

Vindolanda -- Barton Mill
Roman Fort dating from 3rd century.

Warkworth Castle -- Warkworth
Dating from the 11th century with additions -- a great keep and gatehouse.

Warkworth Hermitage -- Warkworth
An interesting 14th century Hermitage.

NORTHUMBERLAND
DURHAM/TYNE & WEAR
Recommended roadside restaurants

091	A1	Stannington Northumberland 12 miles north of Newcastle-on-Tyne 5 miles south of Morpeth
123	A1	Skeeby Nr Richmond, Yorks ½ mile south of Scotch Corner (Northbound)
126	A1	North Charlton, Alnwick, Northumberland 5 miles north of Alnwick
197	A69	Bardon Mill Northumberland 5 miles east of Haltwhistle
294	A66	Sadberge County Durham 2 miles east of Darlington

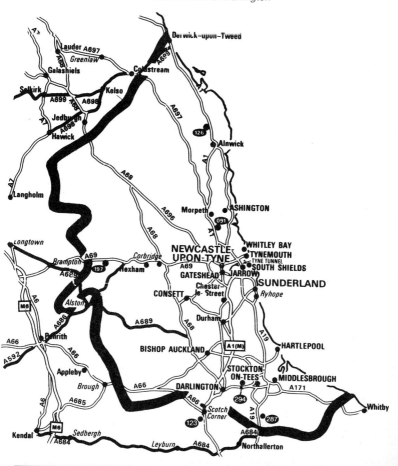

Northumberland
Durham & Tyne & Wear

		minimum per person	children taken	evening meals available	animals taken
T.L.A. & J.A. Robson **Dunstanburgh Castle Hotel** **Embleton** **Nr. Alnwick NE66 3UN** **Tel: (066576) 203** **OPEN: ALL YEAR**	Nearest Road A.1 Dunstanburgh is a small, friendly hotel. The Robson's have been running this establishment for the past forty years and know exactly how to make their guests feel at home. The Hotel offers a choice of seventeen comfortable rooms with modern amenities and tea/coffee making facilities. There is a residents' colour T.V. lounge and a garden for guests' use. Close by is the 18 hole Dunstanburgh golf course. This makes an ideal base for a touring holiday or for a one night stop over.	£14.50	O	O	O
Mrs P. Staff **'Holmhead' Guest House** **Hadrians Wall** **Greenhead** **Carlisle CA6 7HY** **Tel: (06972) 402** **OPEN: ALL YEAR** **(EXCL. XMAS & NEW YEAR)**	Nearest Roads A.69 B.6318 A traditional Northumberland farmhouse dating back 150 years offering four really charming, comfortable rooms with modern amenities, plus a private lounge with T.V. Situated in 300 acres of ground with Hadrians Wall below the house, it offers excellent walking along the Pennine Way. The remains of a 14th century castle are very close. Many historic sites in the area, especially Roman. An ideal base, superb home cooking. Helicopter flights arranged from the house. Visits arranged to the Ancestral Research Centre.	£12.00	O	O	■
Mrs Dorothy Wilson **Town Barns** **Off Trinity Terrace** **Corbridge NE45 5HP** **Tel: (043471) 3345** **OPEN: FEB-NOV**	Nearest Roads A.69 A.68 A delightful modern stone house, once the home of authoress Catherine Cookson. Luxurious accommodation in three beautiful rooms, one with private facilities, all have modern amenities, and tea/coffee makers. Downstairs is a gallery with an unusual double staircase. A superb lounge for guests, with colour T.V. A wonderful seasonal heated indoor swimming pool with private changing rooms. A beautiful garden with a series of lawns and a patio. Wonderful views of the peaceful Tyne Valley. This is an ideal base for exploring this historic region.	£11.00	O	■	O
Mrs Edith M. Clarke **Clive House** **Appletree Lane** **Corbridge NE45 5DN** **Tel: (043471) 2617** **OPEN: ALL YEAR** **KELLOGGS NATIONAL** **AWARD WINNER 1986**	Nearest Roads A.68 A.69 A lovely house dating back 150 years, offering delightful accommodation in comfortable rooms with bathrooms on suite. Two rooms have 4-poster bed and all rooms have tea/coffee facilities, hair dryers, electric blankets and T.V. Residents' lounge also has colour T.V. The breakfast room has exposed beams, a gallery and log fires. The warm welcome given by Mrs. Clarke extends to small touches like fresh flowers in the bedrooms. No children under 12 years. Price shown is for 2 people.	£25.00	O	■	■

O yes ■ no

180

		minimum per person	children taken	evening meals available	animals taken
Mrs E.J. Mark **Low Hills** **Carrsfield** **Corbridge NE45 5LJ** **Tel: (043471) 2460** **OPEN: ALL YEAR**	Nearest Road A.69 A pleasant modern house offering three well appointed rooms situated on the edge of the village only 10 minutes gentle walk from the restaurants, shops etc. Mrs. Mark will provide packed lunches for guests. A comfortable lounge with T.V. and baby listening service. Plenty of interesting pubs and eateries locally. Plenty of places to visit in the locality such as Roman remains and museums.	£9.00	O	■	■
Mrs M.P. Henderson **Ashcroft Guest House** **Ashcroft** **Haltwhistle NE49 0DA** **Tel: (0498) 20213** **OPEN: ALL YEAR** **(EXCL. XMAS & NEW YEAR)**	Nearest Road A.69 Formerly a Victorian vicarage, this elegant house stands in its own private grounds with terraced gardens. Facing south it overlooks the Tyne Valley. Accommodation is in a choice of eight rooms all with modern amenities. Tea/coffee are available most of the time. The colour T.V. lounge is available throughout the day. This makes an ideal base for touring the whole of Northumbria, Lake District and The Roman Wall. Close by are fishing, bowling, climbing, golf, tennis and swimming.	£9.00	O	O	■
Mrs J. Roberts **Lilac Mount** **Catton** **Nr. Allendale** **Hexham NE47 9QR** **Tel: (043483) 553** **OPEN: ALL YEAR**	Nearest Road B.6295 An attractive luxurious bungalow offering excellent accommodation and a warm welcome. Set in a delightful North Pennines village surrounded by beautiful countryside. Good base for walking and touring. Close to Hadrian's Wall, Kielder Forest, Durham and coast and border country. Golf course and stables within 1 mile. Good cooking a speciality. Ideal overnight stop between York and Scotland.	£11.00	O	O	O

Durham

		minimum per person	children taken	evening meals available	animals taken
Mrs H.P. Close **Grove House** **Hamsterley Forest** **Nr.Bishop Auckland DL13 3NL** **Tel: (038888) 203** **OPEN: ALL YEAR**	Nearest Road A.68 A wonderful country house in the heart of Hamsterley Forest, with large comfortable reception rooms, dining room with log fire, separate T.V. lounge. Plenty of room to find peace and quiet. The evening meal is an experience in itself, beautifully cooked and candlelit. Bedrooms are comfortable, all with tea/coffee making. Ideal situation for children with rivers, walks, long garden, birdwatching from bedroom windows.	£13.50	O	O	O

O yes ■ no

		minimum per person	children taken	evening meals available	animals taken
Una Cranston **Wharmley Burn** **Castleside** **Consett DH8 9AY** **Tel: (0207) 508374** **OPEN: ALL YEAR**	Nearest Road A.68 A delightful 14th century farmhouse, retaining all of its former charm and character, including its original low beamed ceilings and very low doorways. It is located in the beautiful Derwent Valley on the borders of County Durham and Northumberland. The Cranston's offer 3 delightful rooms, 1 twin, 1 with en-suite shower facilities and 1 single with tea/coffee making facilities. A comfortable colour T.V. lounge is available throughout the day. Guests dine together at a large antique oak table. Whenever possible local or home grown produce is used. Home made bread, cakes, biscuits and preserves are a speciality.	£8.00	○	○	○
Col D.A. Brown **Trevelyan College** **Elvet Hill Road** **Durham DH1 3LN** **Tel: (0385) 61133** **OPEN:-** **MID DEC-MID JAN** **MID MAR-MID APRIL** **JULY/AUG/SEPT**	Nearest Roads A.167 A.1M Trevelyan College is set in parkland within one mile of the beautiful city centre. It offers 241 rooms, as it is part of the University of Durham, giving excellent facilities and accommodation. It is adjacent to the Gulbenkian Museum of Oriental Art which is a treasurehouse. The botanical gardens are a walk away. The coastline of Northumbria, wild moorlands of North Yorkshire and Teesdale abound with old castles, cathedrals and super little villages all within driving distance - there is something for everyone. This is an excellent base for touring this part of the country. Good food is always available here. Open during University vacations only.	£8.50	○	○	■

Tyne & Wear

		minimum per person	children taken	evening meals available	animals taken
Capt K.J. Hagerty **Chirton House Hotel** **46 Clifton Road** **Newcastle upon Tyne** **NE4 6XH** **Tel: (091) 2730407** **OPEN: ALL YEAR**	Nearest Roads A.1 A.69 An imposing elegant house standing in its own pleasant grounds, offering eleven very comfortable rooms with modern facilities, a T.V. lounge and cocktail bar - a friendly countryhouse atmosphere. Situated within a few minutes of the city centre it is a good base for touring the region. Walkers, riders and golfers will like it. The beaches are not too far away and there are many places of great interest close by. One self-contained flat for disabled.	£18.00	○	○	○

○ yes ■ no

Be sure of your accommodation
Book Now!!
Call us on

01-370 7099   **01-370 7099**

OXFORDSHIRE

Oxfordshire must surely be one of the most fascinating counties in England with a wealth of prehistoric monuments and a wide diversity of architecture. It has early Norman churches, 15th century coaching inns, Regency residences and distinctive cottages of black and white chalk flints. From this county have sprung an abundance of marvellous historical characters, both real and fictional, like King Arthur, Thomas Hardy's Jude the Obscure and John Milton and of course, it has "Old Father Thames" meandering gently across the countryside to Henley-upon-Thames, home of the famous regatta. The countryside ranges from lush meadows with willow edged river banks, scattered with small villages of thatched cottages, to the hills of the Oxfordshire Cotswolds in the west, wooded Chilterns to the east and the distinctive ridge of the Berkshire Downs to the south.

The Great Ridgeway

Through the county along the Berkshire Downs runs the ancient trackway known as the Great Ridgeway, which stretches for 85 miles from Ivinghoe Beacon in Buckinghamshire to Avebury in Wiltshire.

A walk along any part of its length gives visible evidence of our distant past including barrows, tumuli, hill forts and stone circles, a unique experience for anyone with a sense of history. It was originally used as a trading route and followed the tops of the ridge line to give the traveller easier passage than the marshy and forested lowlands. To the east of the village of Ashbury the paths run by a remarkably well preserved long barrow, some 5,000 years old, known as Wayland's Smithy. It stands in open country but surrounded by a circle of beech trees. When the only sound is the wind sweeping over the downs and the rustling of leaves it is not difficult to believe that you are standing at the "Anvil of Wayland", blacksmith to the horses of the gods. The old Saxon legend says that a rider who leaves his horse and places a coin on the anvil, will return to find the horse shod and the coin gone. The horse figures in many of Oxfordshire's legends and further east along the trackway can be found the famous Uffington Horse, which is over 2,000 years old. This great white horse is cut into the chalk of the hillside below the ancient hill fort of Uffington Castle, and is some 360 feet in length and 160 feet in height.

It can best be viewed in total from the Wantage to Swindon Road below and is a very stylised rendering of a horse - indeed many believe that it is not a horse at all but a dragon. The small hill below the carving, known locally as Dragon Hill, is believed to be where St. George killed the dragon. Legend tells that no grass will grow where the dragon's blood was spilled and there is still a patch of bare earth on top of Dragon Hill, to convince anyone who doubts it.

Many of Oxfordshire's towns and villages have legends associated with either their names or locations and there is a wealth of history to be found in a study of place names. To mention just a few:
Banbury is sung about in the nursery rhyme "Ride a cock horse to Banbury Cross", which is believed to be associated with pre-Christian pagan religion. Brampton-in-the-Bush is so called because the only way to reach it was by using the church steeple as a guide, since the village was otherwise hidden in the middle of woodland. Charney Bassett received its name from "Charn", the old Celtic name for the river which runs through the area and "Bassett", the name of Norman lord who owned the land. Stanford-in-the-Vale means stone found in the valley. Woodstock derives its name from the wooden stocks, which still stand.

Oxford

No one should visit this county without seeing the "dreaming spires" of Oxford, one of England's most well known county towns and home of the famous University. It is a town of immense atmosphere, of quiet cloisters and narrow lanes full of the sounds of clattering cobbles and distant bells that set one to pondering on its past splendors. It was during the 12th century that Oxford became a meeting place for scholars and grew into the first established centre of learning in England. The earliest colleges to be founded were University College, Balliol and Merton and further colleges were built during the reign of the Tudors, as Oxford became a power in the kingdom. Christ Church chapel is now the cathedral of Oxford and a magnificent building with a deservedly famous choir.

OXFORDSHIRE GAZETEER

Areas of Outstanding Natural Beauty.
The North Wessex Downs. The Chiltern Hills. The Cotswolds.

Historic Houses and Castles

Ashdown House -- Nr. Lambourn
17th century built for Elizabeth of Bohemia, now contains portraits associated with her. Mansard roof has cupola with golden ball.

Blenheim Palace -- Woodstock
Sir John Vanbrugh's classical masterpiece. Garden designed by Vanbrugh and Henry Wise. Further work done by Capability Brown who created the lake. Collection of pictures and tapestries.

Broughton Castle -- Banbury
14th century mansion with moat -- interesting plasterwork, fine panelling and fireplaces.

Chasleton House -- Moreton-in-Marsh
17th century, good examples of plasterwork and panelling. Still has original furniture and tapestries, and topiary garden from 1700.

Greys Court -- Henley-on-Thames
16th century house containing 18th century plasterwork and furniture. Mediaeval ruins, Tudor donkey-wheel for raising water from well.

Mapledurham House -- Mapledurham
16th century Elizabethan house. Oak staircase, private chapel, paintings, original moulded ceilings. Watermill nearby.

Milton Manor House -- Nr. Abingdon
17th century house designed by Inigo Jones -- Georgian wings, walled garden, pleasure grounds.

Rousham House -- Steeple Ashton
17th century -- contains portraits and miniatures.

University of Oxford Colleges.

College	Date	College	Date
University college	1249	St. Edmund Hall	1270
Balliol	1263	Exeter	1314
Merton	1264	The Queen's	1340
Hertford	1284	Lincoln	1427
Oriel	1326	Magdalen	1458
New	1379	Corpus Christi	1516
All Souls	1438	Trinity	1554
Brasenose	1509	Jesus	1571
Christ Church	1546	Wadham	1610
St. John's	1555	Keble	1868
Pembroke	1624		
Worcester	1714		
Nuffield	1937		

Cathedrals and Churches

Abingdon (St. Helen)
14th-16th century perpendicular. Painted roof. Georgian stained and enamelled glass.

Burford (St. John the Baptist)
15th century. Sculptured table tombs in churchyard.

Chislehampton (St. Katherine)
18th century. Unspoilt interior of Georgian Period. Bellcote.

Dorchester (St. Peter & St. Paul)
13th century knight in stone effigy. Jesse window.

East Hagbourne (St. Andrew)
14th-15th century. Early glass, wooden roofs, 18th century tombs.

North Moreton (All Saints)
13th century with splendid 14th century chantry chapel -- tracery.

Oxford Cathedral
Smallest of our English cathedrals. Stone spire from 1230. Norman arcade has double arches, choir vault.

Ryecote (St. Michael and All Angels)
14th century benches and screen base. 17th century altar-piece and communion rails, old clear glass, good ceiling.

Stanton Harcourt (St. Michael)
Early English -- old stone and marble floor. Early screen with painting, monuments of 17th-19th century.

Yarnton (St. Bartholomew)
13th century -- late perpendicular additions. Jacobean screen, 15th century alabaster reredos.

Museums and Galleries

The Ashmolean Museum of Art and Archeology -- Oxford
British, European, Mediterranean, Egyptian and Near Eastern archeology. Oil paintings of Italian, Dutch, Flemish, French and English schools, Old Master, water colours, prints, drawings. Ceramics, silver, bronzes and sculptures. Chinese and Japanese porcelain, lacquer and painting. Tibetan, Islamic and Indian art.

Christ Church Picture Gallery -- Oxford
Old Master drawings and paintings.

Museum of Modern Art -- Oxford
Exhibitions of contemporary art.

Museum of Oxford
Many exhibits depicting the history of Oxford and its University.

The Rotunda -- Oxford
Privately owned collection of dolls' houses 1700-1900, with contents such as furniture, china, silver, dolls, etc.

Oxford University Museum
Entomological, Zoological, geological and mineralogical collections.

Pendon Museum of Miniture Landscape and Transport -- Abingdon
Showing in miniature the countryside and its means of transport in the thirties, with trains and thatched village. Railway relics.

Town Museum -- Abingdon
17th century building exhibiting fossil, archeological items, and collection of charters and documents.

Tolsey Museum -- Burford
Seals, maces, charters and bygones -- replica of Regency room with period furnishings and clothing.

Historic Monuments

Uffington Castle and White Horse -- Uffington
White horse cut into the chalk -- iron age hill fort.

Rollright Stones -- Nr. Chipping Norton
77 stones placed in circle -- an isolated King's stone and nearby an ancient burial chamber.

Minster Lovell House -- Minster Lovell
15th century mediaeval house -- ruins.

Deddington Castle -- Deddington

OXFORDSHIRE
Recommended roadside restaurants

043	A43	Weston on the Green, Oxon 6 miles north of Oxford
049	A423	Dorchstor on Thames, Oxon 8 miles south of Oxford
188	A41	Bicester Oxon ¼ mile east of Bicester
194	A423	Shipton-on-Cherwell Oxon 1 mile north of Kidlington
206	A34/ A43	Oxford Service Area, Oxon 2 miles north of Oxford
250	A34	Chipping Norton, Oxfordshire 18 miles north of Oxford
300	A40	Eynsham (Eastbound) Oxon 4 miles west of Oxford
301	A40	Eynsham (Westbound) Oxon 4 miles west of Oxford

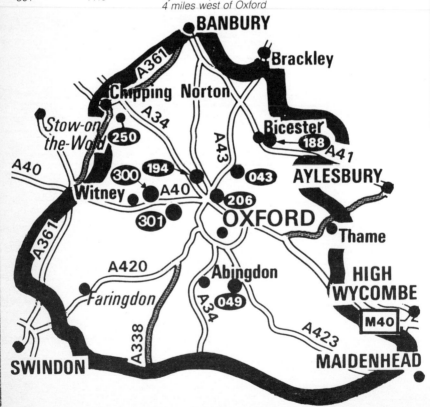

Oxfordshire

			minimum per person	children taken	evening meals available	animals taken
Mrs A.Y. Crowther **Fallowfields** **Southmoor with** **Kingston Bagpuize** **Nr. Abingdon OX13 5BH** **Tel: (0865) 820416** **OPEN: APRIL-OCT**	Nearest Road A.420 Fallowfields, the former home of Begum Aga Khan, is an absolutely delightful 300 year old Gothic style manor house. Beautifully furnished with the emphasis on gracious elegance. The lounge and T.V. room are spacious and comfortable. The four pleasant bedrooms have ample wardrobe space, pretty linens and tea/coffee making facilities. The elegant dining room befits the super cuisine served. Guests are also encouraged to use the croquet lawn and the outdoor swimming pool. Children over 10 years.	£13.50	○	○	○
Mrs Mary Rouse **University Farm Guest House** **Lew** **Nr. Bampton OX8 2AU** **Tel: (0993) 850297** **OPEN: ALL YEAR**	Nearest Roads A.40 A.4095 A charming 17th century farmhouse standing in 216 acres. Heavily beamed throughout, with a huge inglenook fireplace in the lounge. Six prettily decorated bedrooms, all with bath or shower en-suite. A superb timbered dining room and a most attractive lounge with colour T.V. There is a large sun terrace for guests use. Situated in a small peaceful village, 3 miles from Witney, it is an ideal base for touring.	£19.00	○	○	■
Allan & Maggie Witherick **Feldon House** **Lower Brailes** **Banbury OX15 5HW** **Tel: (060885) 580** **OPEN: ALL YEAR**	Nearest Roads A.34 B.4035 Situated in the middle of the village close to the church, this delightful period house dates back to the 17th century and has exposed beams. Set in an attractive garden, the house offers 3 lovely rooms, tastefully furnished and very comfortable. Comfort, care and cuisine are the prerequisites of this country home. Mr & Mrs. Witherick are renowned for their cooking and both luncheon and dinner must be booked in advance.	£13.00	○	○	○
Mrs Rebecca Trace **Rectory Farm** **Sulgrave** **Banbury OX17 2SG** **Tel: (029576) 261** **OPEN: ALL YEAR**	Nearest Road B.4525 Enjoy a country break in this delightful 17th century thatched farmhouse, on a small-holding of 6 acres. Rectory Farm overlooks Sulgrave Manor, the ancestral home of George Washington and is convenient for the Cotswolds, Oxford, Silverstone, Stratford and the Canals. Five bedrooms available, with children well provided for. Lounge and garden for guests use. Licensed.	£10.00	○	○	○
Malcolm and Gwynneth Hearne **Easington House** **50 Oxford Road** **Banbury OX16 9AN** **Tel: (0295) 59395** **OPEN: ALL YEAR**	Nearest Road A.41 Easington House is a family run, listed 16th century farmhouse located only 300 yards from Banbury Cross, the town centre and shops. Accommodation is in a choice of 12 rooms with modern amenities, T.V. and tea/coffee making facilities. A residents' lounge is also available. This makes a good base from which to tour Oxford and the Cotswolds.	£14.00	○	○	○

○ yes ■ no

187

	minimum per person	children taken	evening meals available	animals taken
P.J. & R.J. Oxford **Chadlington House Hotel** Chadlington OX7 3LZ Tel: (060876) 437 **OPEN: MAR-DEC** Nearest Roads A.34 A.361 A delightful country house dating back some 300 years, offering ten comfortable rooms with modern amenities. Situated in a tiny village and off the beaten track, it makes the ideal base for touring Oxford and the Cotswolds, so here one gets the best of both worlds. Lovely views from the house of the Evenlode Valley. Good home cooking and pleasant service.	£18.00	O	O	■
John Milligan **The Falkland Arms** Great Tew OX7 4DB Tel: (060883) 653 **OPEN: ALL YEAR** Nearest Road A.34 The Falkland Arms stands in enchanting Great Tew, a peaceful Oxfordshire village of honey-coloured thatched cottages and quiet lanes. This splendid pub accommodates guests in three bedrooms in traditional "olde worlde" style with comfortable iron beds and antique furniture. Expect cheerful and friendly service here, while enjoying the real ales, country wines, and rich atmosphere. Good bar lunches available.	£12.00	O	■	O
Mrs Aileen Buff **Kings Farm House** **Townsend** Harwell OX11 0DX Tel: (0235) 832833 **OPEN: ALL YEAR** Nearest Road A.34 A former 18th century farmhouse with a wealth of period features and character. Exposed beams, open fireplaces etc. All the rooms are comfortably and attractively furnished and decorated with paintings and objets d'art from all over the world. The same tender loving care is extended to guests. Four bedrooms with modern facilities. Riding and golf locally. Children over 10	£15.00	O	O	■
Mr & Mrs J.M. Riley **Slaters Farm** **Church Lane** **Rotherfield Peppard** **Henley-on-Thames RG9 5JL** Tel: (04917) 675 **OPEN: ALL YEAR** **(EXCEPT REGATTA WEEKS)** Nearest Roads A.423 B.481 A lovely old house dated 1765, now no longer a farmhouse, standing in 1 acre of grounds, fronting onto village green and opposite the village school. It has a very pleasant lounge with enormous open fireplace; logs burn cheerfully in winter. Centrally heated throughout, 3 very nice bedrooms, one single, two twin, all with basins, sharing a bathroom etc. Excellent village pub across the common, serves home cooked dinners. Hard tennis court in grounds, golf and riding nearby. Close to Henley, Oxford, Windsor, Blenheim and Heathrow.	£10.00	O	■	■
Mr & Mrs R. Ovey **Hernes** Henley-on-Thames RG9 4NT Tel: (0491) 573245 Nearest Road A.423 Set among trees and lawns, with croquet, tennis, and swimming facilities. This established family home offers spacious comfortable, centrally heated Georgian, Victorian and original 16th century rooms, with private or en-suite bathrooms, radios, tea/coffee making. Guests dine on home produced meat, game and vegetables. For relaxation or a touring base, with 30 minutes Heathrow, 60 minutes Gatwick. Hernes is waiting to welcome you.	£20.00	■	O	■

O yes ■ no

	minimum per person	children taken	evening meals available	animals taken
Ginnie & Peter Johnston **Chessall Shaw** **Newnham Hill** **Nettlebed RG9 5TN** **Tel: (0491) 641311** **OPEN: ALL YEAR** Nearest Road A.423 Chessall Shaw is delightfully located, 10 minutes from Henley-on-Thames, standing in the peaceful, idyllic Oxfordshire countryside. This pleasant south facing house, offers super views across meadows and woodland. Accommodation is in two comfortable rooms with private bath, phone, T.V./radio, and tea/coffee making facilities. A colour T.V. lounge, garden and swimming pool are also for guests' use. Delicious Cordon Bleu cuisine, using fresh home grown produce whenever possible. No single occupancy.	£20.00	○	○	○
Sue Fulford-Dobson **"Shepherds"** **Shepherds Green** **Rotherfield Greys** **Henley-on-Thames RG9 4QL** **Tel: (04917) 413** **OPEN: ALL YEAR** **(EXCL. XMAS)** Nearest Roads A.423 B.481 A most attractive house dating back to the 18th century, standing on the village green in a lovely 2 acre garden, covered in wisteria, honeysuckle, jasmin, clematis and roses. Two large, pleasant and comfortable twin rooms are offered to guests. Both rooms have private bathrooms. This house with its wood burning stoves and log fires has a delightful drawing room, enhanced with antiques, where guests can relax. Super evening meals are available.	£19.00	■	○	■
Mrs P.M. Evans **Holly House** **Station Road** **Lower Shiplake** **Henley-on-Thames RG9 3JP** **Tel: (073522) 3182** **OPEN: ALL YEAR** Nearest Road A.4155 A lovely large Edwardian country house with many period features and furnished with antiques, set in 2 acres of secluded gardens, 2 miles from Henley. Two twin rooms are available with their own bathroom, radio, and tea/coffee making facilities. Lounge with colour T.V., games room and large heated outdoor pool, all available to visitors. Heathrow is only 35 minutes away.	£15.00	○	■	■
Mr & Mrs G.J. Morris **"Pickwicks"** **17 London Road** **Headington OX3 7SP** **Tel: (0865) 750487** **OPEN: ALL YEAR** Nearest Road "Pickwicks" is a large Edwardian style red brick house. Recently renovated, it now caters for the comfort and convenience of visitors, whether on a business trip or holiday. There is a choice of 8 bedrooms, 6 with en-suite facilities, all with modern amenities and T.V. Tea/coffee are available on request. There is a residents' lounge available. This makes a good base for touring the historic centre of Oxford.	£12.00	○	○	○
Mr K.A. Naylor **Bowood House Hotel** **238 Oxford Road** **Kidlington OX5 1EB** **Tel: (08675) 2839** **OPEN: ALL YEAR** Nearest Road A.423 Expect a warm welcome in this small family hotel. Very comfortable accommodation is in nine bedrooms with modern furnishings and T.V., five with bath/shower. There is a bar and T.V. lounge and a pleasant garden with a patio and outdoor heated pool. Evening meals are very good value. The hotel is close to the city centre.	£14.00	○	○	■

○ yes ■ no

189

	minimum per person	children taken	evening meals available	animals taken

Mr & Mrs P. Morris **Pine Castle** **290 Iffley Road** **Oxford OX4 1AE** **Tel: (0865) 241497** **OPEN: ALL YEAR**	Nearest Road A.423 Comfortable, Edwardian guest house and restaurant, offering very pleasant accommodation with good amenities. The restaurant attached offers a good whole-some choice. Situated in the city, it is obviously a good base from which to explore this famous area. Cots are provided, T.V. and tea/coffee making facilities in all rooms.	£12.00	○	○	○
Mrs Catherine Tong **'Courtfield' Guest House** **367 Iffley Road** **Oxford OX4 4BP** **Tel: (0865) 242991** **OPEN: ALL YEAR**	Nearest Road 'Courtfield' Guest House has been recently refurbished to provide accommodation for guests in six rooms, most with en-suite facilities. A lounge and the garden are also available for visitors to relax in. Ample parking in mews style forecourt. Situated on good bus route, 1½ miles from the centre of Oxford. Children over 3 years. No single availability.	£12.00	○	■	■
Martin & Catherine Jelfs **Newton House** **82-84 Abingdon Road** **Oxford OX1 4PL** **Tel: (0865) 240561** **OPEN: ALL YEAR**	Nearest Roads A.34 A.4144 A pleasant and comfortable Victorian house, offering good accommodation with modern facilities and a warm welcome. Apart from the joys of Oxford itself there are many places of interest in the surrounding area. Blenheim Palace, Wytham Abbey and also the lovely village of Woodstock to name but three. Reasonably priced restaurant on the premises.	£8.00	○	○	■
Mr & Mrs L.S. Price **Portland House** **338 Banbury Road** **Oxford OX2 7PR** **Tel: (0865) 52076** **OPEN: ALL YEAR**	Nearest Roads A.34 A.423 Expect the best attention in this attractive family run Edwardian house, situated in one of the best parts of Oxford. Close to parks, the river, and the city centre with its colleges, restaurants and shops. The house is large and light and accommodates visitors in five rooms with modern facilities, T.V. and tea/coffee making. Excellent base for visiting the Cotswolds, Stratford and London.	£11.00	○	■	○
Mrs N. Reynish **Willow Reaches Hotel** **1 Wytham Street** **Oxford OX1 4SU** **Tel: (0865) 721545** **OPEN: ALL YEAR**	Nearest Road A.4144 A very comfortable small private hotel situated in a quiet street, just 1 mile from the city centre. All rooms have modern amenities, some have bathroom en-suite. There is a visitors' lounge with bar and colour T.V. The proprietress serves good dinners as well as traditional English breakfast.	£14.00	○	○	■

○ yes ■ no

	minimum per person	children taken	evening meals available	animals taken
Anna Kovac **Falcon Guest House** **88-90 Abingdon Road** **Oxford OX1 4PX** **Tel: (0865) 722995** **OPEN: 15 JAN-15 DEC** Nearest Road A.34 A pleasant modernised Victorian house offering ten comfortable rooms for visitors, 2 with private showers. Situated within a few minutes of the city centre, with all the superb historic buildings, lovely colleges and museums. There are many places of great interest in the surrounding countryside. Blenheim Palace, Broughton Castle and the Cotswolds. Cots are provided.	£11.50	○	■	■
Marie & Richard Jelfs **Becket House** **5 Becket Street** **Oxford** **Tel: (0865) 724675** **OPEN: ALL YEAR** Nearest Road An attractive and friendly Victorian town-house, offering six pleasant and comfortable rooms for visitors with modern facilities. Centrally situated, only 10 minutes walk to the city centre. It makes an excellent base for visitors wanting to take advantage of the sights of the city, of which there are many. Cots are provided. Animals taken only in special circumstances. Marie & Richard really aim to please.	£10.00	○	■	○
Mrs C.A. Jelfs **Green Gables** **326 Abingdon Road** **Oxford OX1 4TE** **Tel: (0865) 725870** **OPEN: ALL YEAR** Nearest Roads A.34 A.4144 Built in 1914, this substantial house is set well back from the main road in a mature garden. It offers eight very comfortable and pleasantly decorated rooms, three with en-suite bath. Every modern amenity and comfort. There is one room on the ground floor suitable for disabled guests. Mrs. Jelfs makes all her guests most welcome and provides very good evening meals from Tuesday to Saturday. Oxford offers so many wonderful places to visit and the countryside is very pretty.	£10.00	○	■	■
The Roundabout House **415 Banbury Road** **Oxford** **Tel: (0865) 513045** **OPEN: ALL YEAR** Nearest Roads A.40 A.34 A small friendly house, situated only 3 miles from the city centre, offering two well decorated and comfortable rooms, both with bath en-suite. There is one room on the ground floor which is suitable for disabled guests. A comfortable lounge with T.V. Oxford has so much to offer the visitor and the countryside is delightful with small villages and rivers. A day's drive will take visitors to the Cotswolds and its charming villages.	£11.00	○	■	■
Mrs B.A. Brown **Brown's Guest House** **281 Iffley Road** **Oxford OX4 4AQ** **Tel: (0865) 246822** **OPEN: ALL YEAR** Nearest Road A warm welcome awaits you at this well established family run guest house, within walking distance of Oxford's dreaming spires and all essential amenities close by. Six bedrooms with modern amenities, T.V. and tea/coffee making facilities. Children are well provided for. Residents' lounge is available for guests and full English breakfast is served, with Continental alternative if requested.	£10.00	○	■	○

○ yes ■ no

		minimum per person	children taken	evening meals available	animals taken
Philippa Neilson **Highfield House** 91 Rose Hill Oxford OX4 4HT Tel: (0865) 774083 **OPEN: ALL YEAR**	Nearest Road A.34 A pleasing quiet house, yet good access to the city centre. 5 large rooms, 4 with private facilities. Central heating throughout. Razor points, T.V, and coffee making in all rooms. Attractive lounge with T.V. The breakfast room overlooks a large landscaped garden. A short walk brings you to the old attractive village of Iffley, where there are good pubs with nice atmosphere, traditional English ales and food.	£12.00	O	■	O
Mr & Mrs Cotmore **The Lawns** 12 Manor Road South Hinksey Oxford OX1 5AS Tel: (0865) 739980 **OPEN: MAR-DEC**	Nearest Road Derek & Audrey will welcome you to their attractive modern home, quietly situated in charming South Hinksey on the doorstep of the city of Oxford. Every comfort has been provided here. Three centrally heated ground floor rooms with T.V. and tea/coffee making facilities. Lounge, garden and swimming pool for guests' use. Children are well provided for. Horse riding nearby.	£11.00	O	■	■
Alan & Pat Crawford **The Well House** 30-40 High Street Watlington OX9 5PY Tel: (049161) 3333 **OPEN: ALL YEAR**	Nearest Road M.40 This is a small hotel/restaurant with six rooms, three en-suite. A most fascinating and unusual 400 year old street house. It retains much of its original character, having a wealth of exposed oak beams. The original well can now be found in the cocktail bar. The accommodation is pleasant and comfortable. Vegetarian cooking can be arranged. The whole area is full of interesting things to see and do. Cots are provided.	£23.00	O	O	■
Mr & Mrs W.J. Burton **Church Mill Farm** **The Downs** Standlake Witney OX8 7ST Tel: (086731) 524 **OPEN: ALL YEAR**	Nearest Roads A.40 A.420 A very attractive 17th century mill house, standing on the banks of the River Windrush with a working water mill. Two charming rooms, with modern amenities, overlooking the mill stream and pond. Fishing is available. Situated off the main road it is a perfect peaceful retreat but not isolated. Easy walking distance to the village. From here Oxford, Stratford and the Cotswold villages can be visited. Mrs. Burton warmly welcomes all her guests and endeavours to make their stay a happy one.	£10.00	O	■	■
Mrs Stella Pickering **Hawthorn Farm** Calais Lane Standlake Witney OX8 7QU Tel: (086731) 211 **OPEN: APRIL-OCT**	Nearest Road A.415 A friendly North country welcome awaits you on this small holding. The farmhouse, originally Victorian, has been extensively modernised to provide comfortable accommodation. The farm is within easy reach of the Cotswolds and makes an ideal centre for visiting Oxford, Abingdon, Woodstock, Blenheim and the Berkshire Downs.	£9.00	O	■	O

O yes ■ no

192

	minimum per person	children taken	evening meals available	animals taken
Liz & John Simpson **Field View** **Wood Green** **Witney OX8 6DE** **Tel: (0993) 5485** **OPEN: ALL YEAR** Nearest Roads A.40 A.4095 Field View is situated in picturesque Wood Green, midway between Oxford University and the Cotswolds. It is an ideal centre for touring yet only 8 minutes walk from the centre of this lively Oxfordshire market town. Good home cooking and a warm welcome await you in this spacious Cotswold stone house. Accommodation is in two comfortable rooms with modern amenities and tea/coffee making facilities. A colour T.V. lounge is also available.	£10.00	O	O	■
Mrs A. Lastovka-Simpson **10 Crecy Walk** **Woodstock OX7 1UW** **Tel: (0993) 811115** **OPEN: ALL YEAR** Nearest Road A.34 A warm, homely atmosphere awaits the visitor to this private house. It is situated directly opposite Blenheim Palace and is within walking distance of the centre of Woodstock. Offering 2 bedrooms, bathroom and lounge with T.V. Within easy reach are Oxford, Stratford-upon-Avon and the Cotswolds.	£11.50	O	■	■
Mrs Pauline Jerrams **Cedar Gable** **46 Green Lane** **Woodstock OX7 1JZ** **Tel: (0993) 812231** **OPEN: ALL YEAR** Nearest Road A.34 Delightfully situated on the fringe of the Cotswolds in the Glyme Valley. A modern bungalow in a quiet secluded position overlooking open countryside. Accommodation is in 2 double rooms which can be turned into family rooms, with modern amenities and use of lounge. It is only a short walk to Blenheim Palace and the Park.	£12.00	O	O	■
Mr & Mrs A.R. Naylor **Essex House** **Chinnor Road** **Thame OX9 3LS** **Tel: (084421) 5145** **OPEN: ALL YEAR** Nearest Roads M.40 B.4445 Essex House was built in 1870 and offers comfortable accommodation in four pleasant rooms, three with en-suite facilities. A television lounge and garden for guests. Thame is an old market town and is a perfect base for visiting Oxford, Windsor, London and parts of the Cotswolds. A warm and friendly welcome await visitors and the Naylor's will do their best to ensure you have a pleasant stay.	£14.50	O	■	■
Mr & Mrs E.H. Aitken **Upper Green Farm** **Manor Road** **Towersey OX9 3QR** **Tel: (084421) 2496** **OPEN: ALL YEAR** Nearest Road A.4129 Lovely thatched 15th century timber framed farmhouse beside a large pond in 7 acres of beautiful countryside. Well restored, the house retains all its character, with beamed ceilings, priest's hole, old bread oven and Victorian kitchen range. 3 guest rooms with central heating and T.V. Guests' lounge. Close to Thame with large choice of eating places. Car essential. Non-smokers please.	£12.00	■	■	■

	minimum per person	children taken	evening meals available	animals taken
Carol Wadsworth **The Craven** **Fernham Road** **Uffington SN7 7RD** **Tel: (036782) 449** **OPEN: ALL YEAR**	Nearest Roads B.4507 A.420 An extremely attractive 17th century thatched farmhouse, with exposed beams and open log-burning fire. Accommodation is very comfortable in 6 bedrooms, 1 with 4-poster bed and private bathroom. Good home cooking with fresh local produce. The Craven offers a friendly relaxed atmosphere. The perfect base for touring this fascinating area.	£10.00	○	○	○
Mr & Mrs R. Harrison **Walltree House Farm** **Steane** **Brackley NN13 5NS** **Tel: (0295) 811235** **OPEN: ALL YEAR**	Nearest Road A.422 This large Victorian farm house has been recently restored and now provides guests with spacious comfortable accommodation with delightful woodland, and a garden to relax in. Offering a choice of seven bedrooms, some with private facilities, T.V. and radio. This makes an ideal base for touring the Cotswolds, Oxford, Blenheim and Stratford-on-Avon.	£12.00	○	○	○

○ yes ■ no

194

SHROPSHIRE

This county has had a very turbulent history giving it a very particular flavour - no other county is quite like it. It is a border land in all senses - physically is straddles the highlands and lowlands with border mountains to the west, glacial plains, uplands, moorlands, fertile valleys and is almost cut in two by the great river Severn. It has been quarrelled and fought over by rulers and Kings from earliest times. The English, the Romans and the Welsh all wanted to hold Shropshire because of its unique situation. The ruined castles and fortifications dotted across the county bear witness to its troubled life - the most impressive of all these defences being Offa's Dyke. This was a truly enormous undertaking intended to be a permanent frontier between England and Wales. In recent years there has been a walking trail built along the course of the Dyke so that it is possible to follow the line of the Dyke, including some of the most interesting places along the way, and enabling the walkers to enjoy the magnificent scenery.

Castles and Historic Houses

The great castles of Shrewsbury and Ludlow still serve as vivid reminders of the political importance attached to Shropshire. It was the axiom of the period that whoever held Shropshire held Wales - but many Kings put the castles under the control of trusted followers who then turned against the Crown. Before that the Romans had their troubles with the Welsh. The town of Shrewsbury was and is encircled almost completely by the River Severn, making it into a virtual island. At the only gap the great castle was built, sealing off the town completely, In this way comings and goings could be absolutely controlled. In the 18th century two classical bridges were built to carry the increasing traffic to the town - but it still remains England's finest Tudor city.

Ludlow was a Royal Castle, the home of Kings and Queens through the ages, especially the two little Princes who were later taken to the Tower of London where they met a horrible death.

A Festival of Art, Music and Drama is held annually in Ludlow and each year the numbers of patrons increase - people come from across the world to enjoy, for example, a Shakespearean play performed under the night sky at the Castle. Or concerts by distinguished musicians, given in a fine church or country house. By day they take the opportunity of visiting the ancient towns and village to admire our black and white Tudor Houses, or the timber-framed Yeoman houses. Large or small, they are all impressive and quite beautiful to our modern eyes. The White House at Aston Munslow is a mediaeval site with a Norman Dovecote and a Cruck Hall. Upton Cressett in Bridgnorth is an Elizabethan Manor House with fine plaster work and brick work. Stokesay Castle at Craven Arms is a moated, fortified Manor House from the 13th century with an Elizabethan Gatehouse - perfectly preserved.

Gardens

The world famous English Gardens flourish in this county. At Hodnet Hall near Market Drayton the grounds cover 60 acres and the landscaping includes lakes and pools, fine trees, shrubs and flowers in profusion, so that there is a colourful display at all times of the year. At Western Park the landscaping was by Capability Brown, designed to echo the beauty of this elegant house of the restoration period. It has a splendid collection of pictures, lovely furniture, priceless tapestries by Gobelin and Aubusson - all gracing a noble residence. The most extraordinary thing about the house is the fact it was designed by the Lady Wilbraham in 1671 without any professional help, apart from that given by her skilled stone-mason, Sam Grice. It stands as a monument to her skill, ingenuity and foresight.

The Industrial Revolution

Gradually, as order came out of chaos, the county settled to improving itself and became the cradle of the Industrial Revolution. It was here that Abraham Darby discovered how to use coke (from the locally mined coal) to smelt iron. There was more iron produced here in the 18th century than in any other county. Of course, the coal mining and the iron smelting industry laid the foundation of many fortunes, none of them due to patronage of church or state as previously. As a consequence men were free to develop new ideas in many directions and a variety of great industries sprang up. In 1781 the world's first iron bridge was opened to traffic.

SHROPSHIRE GAZETEER

Areas of Outstanding Natural Beauty
The Shropshire Hills.

Historic Houses and Castles

Stokesay Castle -- Craven Arms
13th century fortified manor house. Still occupied -- wonderful setting -- extremely well preserved. Fine timbered gatehouse.

Weston Park -- Nr. Shifnal
17th century -- fine example of Restoration period -- landscaping by Capability Brown. Superb collection of pictures.

Shrewsbury Castle -- Shrewsbury
Built in Norman era -- interior decorations -- painted boudoir.

Benthall Hall -- Much Wenlock
16th century. Stone House -- mullioned windows. Fine wooden staircase -- splendid plaster ceilings.

Shipton Hall -- Much Wenlock
Elizabethan. Manor House -- walled garden -- mediaeval dovecote.

Upton Cressett Hall -- Bridgnorth
Elizabethan. Manor House & Gatehouse. Excellent plasterwork. 14th century great hall.

Cathedrals and Churches

Ludlow (St. Lawrence)
14th century nave & transepts. 15th century pinnacled tower. Restored extensively in 19th century. Carved choir stalls, perpendicular chancel -- original glass. Monuments.

Shrewsbury (St. Mary)
14th, 15th, 16th century glass. Norman origins.

Stottesdon (St. Mary)
12th century carvings. Norman font. Fine decoration with columns and tracery.

Lydbury North (St. Michael)
14th century transept, 15th century nave roof, 17th century box pews and altar rails. Norman font.

Longor (St. Mary the Virgin)
13th century having an outer staircase to West gallery.

Cheswardine (St. Swithun)
13th century chapel -- largely early English. 19th century glass and old brasses. Fine sculpture.

Tong (St. Mary the Virgin with St. Bartholomew)
15th century. Golden chapel of 1515, stencilled walls, remains of paintings on screens, gilt fan vaulted ceiling. Effigies, fine monuments.

Museums and Galleries

Clive House -- Shrewsbury
Fine Georgian House -- collection of Shropshire ceramics. Regimental museum of 1st Queen's Dragroon Guards.

Rowley's House Museum -- Shrewsbury
Roman material from Viroconium and prehistoric.

Coleham Pumping Station -- Old Coleham
Preserved beam engines.

Acton Scott Working Farm Museum -- Nr. Church Stretton
Site showing agricultural practice before the advent of mechanization.

Ironbridge Gorge Museum -- Telford
Series of industrial sites in the Severn Gorge.

Coalbrookdale Museum and Furnace Site
Showing Abraham Darby's blast furnace history. Ironbridge Information centre is next to the world's first iron bridge.

Mortimer Forest Museum -- Nr. Ludlow
Forest industries of today and yesterday. Ecology of the forest.

Whitehouse Museum of Buildings & Country Life -- Aston Munslow
4 houses together in one, drawing from every century 13th to 18th, together with utensils and implements of the time.

The Buttercross Museum -- Ludlow
Geology, local and natural history of the district, local armour.

Reader's House -- Ludlow
Splendid example of 16th century town house. 3-storied porch.

Much Wenlock Museum -- Much Wenlock
Geology, natural and local history of area.

Clun Town Museum -- Clun
Pre-history earthworks, rights of way, commons & footpaths, local history, photographs.

Historic Monuments

Acton Burnell Castle -- Shrewsbury
13th century fortified manor house -- ruins only.

Boscobel House -- Shifnal
17th century house.

Bear Steps -- Shrewsbury
Half timbered buildings. Mediaeval.

Abbot's House -- Shrewsbury
15th century half-timbered.

Buildwas Abbey -- Nr. Telford
12th century -- Savignac Abbey -- ruins. The church is nearly complete with 14 Norman arches.

Haughmond Abbey -- Shrewsbury
12th century -- remains of house of Augustinian canons.

Wenlock Priory -- Much Wenlock
13th century abbey -- ruins.

Roman Town -- Wroxeter
2nd century -- remains of town of Viroconium including public baths and colonnade.

Moreton Corbet Castle -- Moreton Corbet
13th century keep, Elizabethan features -- gatehouse altered 1519.

Lilleshall Abbey
12th century -- completed 13th century. West front has noable doorway.

Bridgnorth Castle -- Bridgenorth
Ruins of Norman castle whose angle of incline is greater than Pisa.

Whiteladies Priory -- Boscobel
12th century cruciform church -- ruins.

Old Oswestry -- Oswestry
Iron age hill fort covering 68 acres; five ramparts and having an elaborate western portal.

SHROPSHIRE
Recommended roadside restaurants

038	A5	Whittington Nr Oswestry, Shropshire 3 miles east of Oswestry
042	A49	Leebotwood Church Stretton, Shropshire 4 miles north of Church Stretton
054	A49	Prees Heath, Whitchurch, Shropshire 4 miles south of Whitchurch (Southbound)
060	A442	Quatford Nr Bridgnorth, Shropshire 3 miles south of Bridgnorth

Shropshire

		minimum per person	children taken	evening meals available	animals taken
Mrs Carole Llewellyn **Dudgeley Mill** **All Stretton** **Church Stretton SY6 7JL** Tel: (0694) 723461 **OPEN: ALL YEAR**	Nearest Roads A.49 B.4370 A superb old water mill and farmhouse with many old beams and open log fires, makes this a most attractive base for visitors. Mrs. Llewellyn offers a warm welcome to guests in 7 delightful rooms with modern amenities, including tea making facilities. Excellent home cooking and informal atmosphere. The house is surrounded by marvellous countryside and has lovely views all around. 'Fun' trout fishing is available in the mill stream. It is an ideal centre for walking, riding or gliding. Golf courses are close by.	£12.00	○	○	■
Don & Rita Rogers **Belvedere Guest House** **Burway Road** **Church Stretton SY6 6DP** Tel: (0694) 722232 **OPEN: ALL YEAR**	Nearest Road A.49 A comfortable, relaxed atmosphere prevails in this centrally heated house, set on the slopes of the Long Mynd in the delightful village of Church Stretton. It is an ideal base for exploring Shropshire and the borders on foot or by car. All bedrooms have tea making facilities and two lounges are available to guests. Cots and packed lunches are available and there is a drinks license.	£10.50	○	○	○
H.C. Bovill **Batchcott Hall** **Church Stretton SY6 6NP** Tel: (06945) 234 **OPEN: APRIL-OCT**	Nearest Road A.49 Bathcott Hall is a large stock farm set 900 feet above sea level, on the north-east side of the Long Mynd with fantastic views. Guests are accommodated in three rooms, two double and one twin. Residents' lounge available to guests. Golf nearby at Church Stretton (18 holes). Riding and private fishing. Children over 10 years.	£8.00	○	■	■
Mrs J.A. Davies **Rectory Farm** **Woolstaston** **Leebotwood** **Church Stretton SY6 6NN** Tel: (06945) 306 **OPEN: MAR-NOV**	Nearest Road A.49 An extremely attractive half-timbered farmhouse dating back to 1600, offering three charming rooms all with bath en-suite. Situated on the edge of the National Trust Long Mynd Hills, it has marvellous views and superb walking right from the door. There is much for the sportsman here: golf, riding, fishing and gliding. Many historic houses and wonderful beauty spots are within a short drive.	£9.00	■	■	■
Mrs Avis Ades **Birches Mill** **Clun** **Craven Arms SY7 8NL** Tel: (05884) 409 **OPEN: ALL YEAR**	Nearest Road A.488 Visitors are made welcome in this happy and beautiful environment. Built around 1605 on the river bank, the house was a water mill, now converted to the highest standards, yet retaining its exposed beams and inglenook fireplaces. 2 guest rooms. Lounge and lovely waterside garden. Fly fishing available. Extensive organic vegetable garden providing for the table, where meals are the highest quality. Children welcome.	£9.75	○	○	○

○ yes ■ no

199

	minimum per person	children taken	evening meals available	animals taken
Martin Pool & Caroline Denham **Old Post Office** **9 The Square** **Clun** **Nr.Craven Arms SY7 0MG** Tel: (05884) 687 **OPEN: ALL YEAR** **(EXCL. FEBRUARY)** Nearest Road A.49 The Old Post Office has been carefully restored and converted from the original Victorian post office into a small French style, family run restaurant with accommodation. The three rooms are comfortable and pleasantly decorated with antiques and oil paintings. The food here is delicious, all the ingredients are fresh. Breakfast includes local smoked bacon, locally made bread, home-made marmalade and jams. There is also a well stocked bar.	£14.50	O	O	■
Mr & Mrs P. Hutton **The Grange** **Grange Road** **Ellesmere SY12 9DE** Tel: (069171) 3495 or 2735 **OPEN: ALL YEAR** Nearest Road A.5 A delightful 18th century Georgian country house standing in 10 acres of grounds. The Grange offers excellent accommodation in fifteen comfortable rooms all with private facilities, telephone, radio, T.V. and tea/coffee makers. In the grounds are hard tennis courts, croquet and putting greens. The Grange has an enviable reputation for good food using their own fresh produce - really good value. Superb countryside and historic sites make this an ideal base for touring.	£18.00	O	O	O
Pamela Allcock-Brown **Wadboro Thatch** **Haytons Bent** **Ludlow SY8 2AU** Tel: (058475) 249 **OPEN: APRIL-OCT** Nearest Road A.49 A delightful quaint 16th century thatched cottage with latticed windows, oak beams, antique furniture and large inglenook fire. Full of charm and comfort, the guest accommodation consists of 2 double bedrooms with private bathrooms and tea-making facilities. Sitting room and terrace leading onto gardens. Good English food a speciality with fresh garden produce. Beautiful secluded position. Ludlow 5 minutes drive.	£9.50	■	■	■
N.A. & J.L. Cooke **"Bromfield Manor"** **Bromfield** **Nr. Ludlow SY8 2JU** Tel: (058477) 279 **OPEN: ALL YEAR** Nearest Road A.49 A superb ancient house, possibly a hunting lodge of King Henry VIII, offering 7 delightful rooms with modern facilities. This is an ideal place for the traveller looking for a friendly relaxed atmosphere. Standing in its own large grounds, offering superb countryside all around with excellent walking and fishing. Croft Castle, Ludlow Castle, Stokesay Castle and Eye Manor are just a few of the fabulous places to visit. Cots and highchairs.	£9.50	O	O	O
Hilary M. Ward **Perry Farm** **Whittington** **Oswestry SY11 4PF** Tel: (0691) 662330 **OPEN: APRIL-OCT** Nearest Road A.5 A warm welcome awaits you at this 1820 Georgian farmhouse, in gardens running down to the River Perry. Accommodation is in one twin and one family room with modern amenities. Oak beamed lounge with colour T.V. and toby jug collection, also quiet lounge. Guests can choose to dine privately, but are encouraged to join the family for meals in the farmhouse kitchen.	£9.00	O	O	■

O yes ■ no

200

	Nearest Road / Description	minimum per person	children taken	evening meals available	animals taken
Mrs Doreen Davies **Pen-Y-Byrn Farm** **Llangedwyn** **Oswestry SY10 9LB** **Tel: (069189) 275** **OPEN: EASTER-OCT**	Nearest Road B.4396 A charming farmhouse dating back to 1750 offering two lovely rooms and a marvellous atmosphere. The house is situated right on the border of Shropshire, Clwyd and Powys, so the tours of countryside and historic sights are countless. One has the best of three worlds here. The countryside differs depending on which direction you wish to travel, but it is all superb. Excellent walking, riding and fishing. Evening meals are super.	£7.50	O	O	O
Mrs Brenda M. Jones **Bwlch-Y-Rhiw** **Llansilin** **Oswestry SY10 7PT** **Tel: (069170) 261** **OPEN: APRIL-OCT**	Nearest Road Mrs Brenda Jones extends a friendly invitation to visitors to her home; a comfortable, characterful farmhouse. Three spacious en-suite bedrooms with tea-making facilities have splendid views of the valley and surrounding hills. Dining room with open beams, slate floor and inglenook fireplace. Guests welcome to explore the sheep farm which is half in England, half in Wales. Fly fishing. Children over 8 years.	£10.00	O	■	O
Roy & Sylvia Anderson **Tankerville Lodge** **Stiperstones** **Nr. Minsterley** **Shrewsbury SY5 0NB** **Tel: (0743) 791401** **OPEN: ALL YEAR**	Nearest Road A.488 Tankerville is situated in the heart of the Shropshire hills in a National Nature Reserve. Offering four bedrooms with modern amenities, a lounge with colour T.V. and a dining room serving good food. There is also plenty of good walking with beautiful surrounding countryside.	£10.00	O	O	■
K.A. & H.M. Fox **Hawkstone Cottage** **Weston-under-Redcastle** **Shrewsbury SY4 5UZ** **Tel: (093924) 298** **OPEN: ALL YEAR**	Nearest Roads A.49 A.442 Hawkstone Cottage is a delightful house standing in a most attractive country garden. Set in a peaceful and pretty little village, this house offers a friendly and relaxed atmosphere. Accommodation is in two recently refurbished and modernised bedrooms, one en-suite room, both with T.V. and tea/coffee making facilities. The house is furnished throughout with antiques and there is a comfortable colour T.V. lounge available. Excellent home-cooked food. Own produce includes jam, marmalade and home-baked rolls.	£8.50	O	O	O
Mrs Marjorie Gilbride **Paradise House** **Coalbrookdale** **Telford TF8 7NR** **Tel: (095245) 3379** **OPEN: MAR-OCT**	Nearest Road A.5 A large detached house dating from the 17th century offering very comfortable accommodation in 3 light and airy rooms, with modern amenities and tea-making facilities. Situated in large grounds with lovely views over the wooded valley of Coalbrookdale. It offers peaceful surroundings with plenty of interesting places to visit including the Ironbridge Gorge Museum, and the houses associated with the hiding of Charles II after the Battle of Worcester.	£9.50	O	■	■

O yes ■ no

SOMERSET

Somerset people are rightly proud to claim their county is unique. From the rich local dialect and fabulous legends to the charming villages and marvellous 15th century church towers; from the superb landscape to the glory of Wells Cathedral, the county is in many ways outstanding.

The essence of Somerset lies in history and myth. The county has witnessed the unfolding of the Arthurian story, the role of the dark lake of Mere and its peoples, the Roman occupation, the rebellion against James II, the cruel retribution of "Bloody Judge Jeffries" and the fury of civil war.

Village Splendours

Somerset is a county of villages and small towns too numerous to detail here. Built in glorious local stone there is none that cannot boast a splendid church, a historic site or architectural treasure. Bearing gorgeous place names like Midsomer Norton, Kingsbury Episcopi and Temple Cloud, they are clustered in valleys and coombes. Village names carry a hidden code of meaning, Shillington, Limington and White Lackington all carry the Saxon "ington" suffix which marks the path of invasion and settlement across the country, whilst Shepton Mallet was a sheep market and Avalon itself means the "land of apples". The wealth of domestic architecture is unsurpassed. Martock is built of Ham Hill stone, mellowed to a lovely soft golden tint and like so many Somerset villages is crowned by a splendid 15th century church with characteristic timber roof and craftsman carved panels. Dunster is also unspoilt with a broad main street lined with buildings of brick, timber, stone, tile and thatch, few more recent than the 18th century. The mediaeval Castle which dominates the village rises from a plinth of close set trees and is the subject of a Turner painting. There is much to discover in every village, a water mill and wheel, an ancient packhorse bridge, a detail of carving or stained glass in churches and Stately Homes. Montacute House, for instance, is a magnificent Elizabethan mansion of Ham Stone, home of the Phelips Family. It is a treasurehouse of fine heraldic glass, tapestries, furniture and contains exhibitions of Elizabethan and Jacobean portraits.

The Legendary Vale of Avalon

In spring the apple orchards of the Vale of Taunton spread a carpet of pink blossom across the landscape and by autumn the pastures are under a cobble pavement of red and green wind- shaken apples. A mug of golden cider can be enjoyed with a pub lunch at inns throughout the county; where better to pause and ponder than Glastonbury. No ancient site in the world is so steeped in legend and conjecture, in myth and historic fact than the "Island Valley of Avalon - deep meadowed, happy, fair with orchard lawns and bowery hollows, crowned with summer sea". According to Tennyson it is here that Arthur staggered from Cadbury Castle after his last great battle to "heal me of my grievous wound".

Archeological fact lends support to the conjecture that Glastonbury with its famous Tor was an island in an ancient lake, across which Arthur's barge "dark as a funeral scarf from stem to stern" moved silently through the mists to the magic island.

Country Sights and Country Towns

To the north, the limestone hills of Mendip are honeycombed with spectacular caves and gorges, some with neolithic remains, as at Wookey Hole and Cheddar Gorge. Hard by is Wells, so named because of the multitude of natural springs. Although a city in name, Wells is at most a small town with a magnificent Cathedral set amongst spacious lawns and trees. The west front is one of the glories of English architecture with rank upon rank of sculptured figures and soaring arches which support the weight of the central tower. A spectacular feature is the Wells astronomical clock It is the workmanship of the 14th century monk Peter Lightfoot.

The intricate face tells the hours, minutes, days of the month and phases of the moon - on the hour four mounted knights charge forth and knock one another from their horses. The work of mediaeval craftsmen abounds throughout the cathedral; the careful observer can find in the detail of stained glass, wood and stone, a picture of everyday mediaeval life

SOMERSET GAZETEER

Area of Outstanding Natural Beauty
Mendip Hills -- Quantock Hills. National Park -- Exmoor.

Historic Houses and Castles

Abbot's Fish House -- Meare
14th century house.

Barrington Court -- Illminster
16th century house & gardens.

Brympton D'Evercy -- Nr. Yeovil
Mansion with 17th century front and Tudor west front. Adjacent is 13th century priests house and church. Formal gardens and Vineyard.

Dodington Hall -- Nether Stowey
14th and 15th century Hall with minstrels' gallery.

Dunster Castle -- Dunster
13th century castle with fine 17th century staircase and ceilings.

East Lambrook Manor -- South Petherton
15th century house with good panelling.

Gaulden Manor -- Tolland
12th century Manor. Great Hall having unique plaster ceiling and oak screen. Antique furniture.

Halsway Manor -- Crowcombe
14th century House with fine panelling.

Hatch Court -- Hatch Beauchamp
Georgian house in the Palladian style with China room.

King John's Hunting Lodge -- Axbridge
Early Tudor merchant's house.

Lytes Carry -- Somerton
14th and 15th century manor house with a chapel & formal garden.

Montacute House -- Yeovil
Elizabethan house with fine examples of Heraldic Glass, Tapestries, Panelling and furniture. Portrait gallery of Elizabethan & Jacobean paintings.

Tintinhull House -- Yeovil
17th century house with beautiful gardens.

Cathedrals and Churches

Axbridge (St. John)
1636 plaster ceiling and panelled roofs.

Bishop's Lydeard (St. Mary)
15th century. Notable tower, rood screen and glass.

Bruton (St. Mary)
Fine 2 towered church 15th century. Georgain chancel, tie beam roof, Georgian reredors, Jacobean screen, 15th century embroidery.

Chewton Mendip (St. Mary Magdalene)
12th century with later additions. 12 century doorway, 15th cenutury bench ends, magnificent 16th century tower and 17th century lecturn.

Crewkerne (St. Bartholomew)
Magnificent West front and roofs. 15th & 16th century. South doorway dating from 13th century. wonderful 15th century painted glass and 18th century chandeliers.

East Brent (St. Mary)
Mainly 15th century. Plaster ceiling, painted glass and carved bench ends.

Glastonbury (St. John)
One of the finest examples of perpendicular towers. Tie beam roof, late mediaeval painted glass,
mediaeval vestment and early 16th century altar tomb.

High Ham (St. Andrew)
Sumptuous roofs and vaulted rood screen. Carved bench ends. Jacobean lecturn mediaeval painted
glass. Norman font.

Kingsbury Episcopi (St. Martin)
14th-15th century. Good tower with fan vaulting. Late mediaeval painted glass.

Long Sutton (Holy Trinity)
15th century with noble tower and magnificent tie beam roof. 15th century pulpit and rood screen, tower
vaulting.

Martock (All Saints)
13th century chancel. Nave with tie beam roof outstanding of its kind. 17th century paintings of Apostles.

North Cadbury (St Michael)
Fine chancel. 15th century roofs, parclose and portion of cope, fragments of mediaval painted glass.

Pilton (St. John)
12th century with arcades. 15th century roofs.

Taunton (St. Mary Magdalene)
Highest towers in the county. Fine nave roof, fragments of mediaeval painted glass.

Trull (All Saints)
15th century with many mediaeval art treasures and 15th century glass

Wells Cathedral
Magnificent West Front with carved figures. Splendid tower. Early English arcade of nave and transepts. 60
fine misericords c. 1330 Lady chapel with rich glass and star vault. Chapter House and BishopsPalace.

Weston Zoyland (St. Mary)
15th century bench ends. 16th century heraldic glass. Jacobean pulpit.

Museums and Galleries

Admiral Blake Museum -- Bridgewater
Exhibits relating to Battle of Sedgemoor, Archaeology.

Burdon Manor -- Washford
14th century manor house with Saxon fireplace & cockpit.

Borough museum -- Hendford Manor Hall, Yeovil
Archaeology, Firearms Collections and Bailward Costume Collection.

Glastonbury Lake Village Museum -- Glastonbury
Late prehistoric antiquities.

Gough's Cave Museum -- Cheddar
Upper Paleolithic remains, Skeleton, flints, amber and engraved stones.

Wookey Hole Cave Museum -- Wookey Hole
Remains form Pliocene period. Relics of Celtic and Roman civilization. Exhibition of handmade paper-
making.

Historic Monuments

Cleeve Abbey -- Cleeve
Ruined 13th century house, with timber roof and wall paintings.

Farleigh Castle -- Farleigh Hungerford
14th century remains -- museum in chapel.

Glastonbury Abbey -- Glastonbury
12th & 13th century ruins. St. Joseph's chapel and Abbot's kitchen.

Muchelney Abbey -- Muchelney
15th century ruins of Benedictine abbey.

SOMERSET/DORSET
Recommended roadside restaurants

051	A35	Winterbourne Abbas Dorchester, Dorset 6 miles west of Dorchester
074	A31	St Leonards, Ringwood, Dorset 4 miles west of Ringwood (North-eastbound)
146	A31	Tricketts Cross Nr Ringwood, Dorset 9 miles east of Wimbourne 5 miles south-west of Ringwood (South-westbound)
240	A31	Wimborne, Dorset 2 miles west of Wimborne Opening May '84
265	A303	Sparkford, Somerset 1 mile west of Sparkford

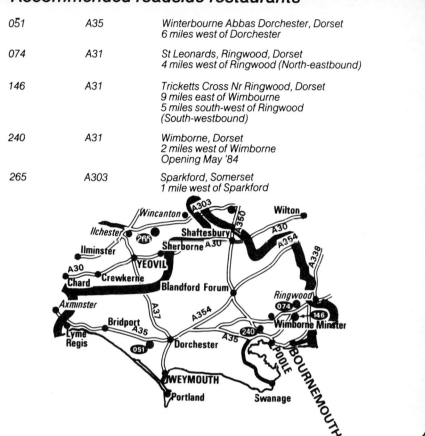

Somerset

Mrs M. Tingey **Greinton House** **Greinton** **Nr. Bridgwater** **Tel: (0458) 210307** **OPEN: ALL YEAR**	Nearest Road A.361 A fine 16th century rectory set on the southern slopes of the Polden Hills. Retaining its original oak panelling, galleried hall and elegant curving staircase, it provides very comfortable accommodation in three rooms, one en-suite, each with private sitting room. T.V. is also available. Guests may also use the swimming pool, tennis court and croquet lawns. Not suitable for young children. Strictly no smoking.	£10.00	■	■	■
Maria Blagg **Bincombe House** **Bincombe** **Overstowey** **Bridgwater TA5 1EZ** **Tel: (0278) 732386** **OPEN: ALL YEAR**	Nearest Road A.39 This is a lovely 200 year old farmhouse nestling in the partially wooded combe at the foot of the Quantock Hills. The house has been beautifully restored and is pleasantly furnished. Accommodation is in two comfortable rooms with modern amenities and wonderful views. A guests' T.V. lounge and dining room are also available. The meals are very good, using home and local produce, and catering for vegetarian diets with reasonable notice. The area is one of outstanding natural beauty. Jacobs sheep, ducks, geese and bees kept.	£11.50	○	○	■
Douglas Young & **John Blagrove** **"Little Barn"** **Rodney Stoke** **Nr. Cheddar BS27 3XB** **Tel: (0749870) 230** **OPEN: ALL YEAR**	Nearest Road A.371 "Little Barn" is a delightful 16th century country cottage set amid strawberry fields at the foot of the Mendip Hills. Three delightful rooms with wonderful views. The house has lots of charm and oak beams. The food is cooked with loving care and you are given the warmest of welcomes. A number of pubs nearby serving good food. Excellent base for touring the area.	£7.50	○	■	■
Mrs V.B. Moore **Conduit House** **Wells Road** **Rodney Stoke** **Nr. Cheddar BS27 3UU** **Tel: (0749) 870231** **OPEN: APRIL-OCT**	Nearest Roads A.38 A.371 Conduit House is a large modern house standing in an elevated position overlooking the village of Rodney Stoke. There are fabulous views of the Mendip Hills right across the Vale of Wedmore to the distant Quantock Hills. Accommodation is in three pleasant bedrooms with modern amenities and tea/coffee making facilities. A T.V. lounge is also available. Guests may also use the beautiful flowering garden	£7.50	○	■	○
Sue Blakeney-Edwards **Fairlands House** **Church Street** **Cheddar BS27 3RH** **Tel: (0934) 742629** **OPEN: ALL YEAR**	Nearest Roads A.371 A.38 A delightful Georgian house with parts dating back 400 years, offering excellent accommodation in five charming and comfortable rooms with modern amenities. It has inglenook fireplaces and flagstone floors and masses of atmosphere. They also have holiday cottages in a converted old property which also has excellent facilities and is comfortable. Croquet on the lawn. Cats and a pony.	£9.00	○	■	■

○ yes ■ no

		minimum per person	children taken	evening meals available	animals taken
Mr & Mrs B.D. Bishop **Church Farm Guest House** **School Lane** **Compton Dundon** **Nr. Somerton TA11 6PE** **Tel: (0458) 72927** **OPEN: ALL YEAR**	Nearest Roads B.3151 A.39 A superb thatched cottage over 400 years old, offering six delightful rooms with comfortable accommodation. In the legendary Vale of Avalon - King Arthur's Country, nestling below St.Andrews church in a lovely village. It is an ideal base to tour the delights of the West Country. From here one can visit the coast and the countryside, enjoying the rolling hills and marvellous views.	£12.50	O	O	O
Mrs Marion Fish **Tudor Cottage** **Broadway** **Nr. Ilminster TA19 9RB** **Tel: (04605) 2889** **OPEN: ALL YEAR**	Nearest Roads A.303 A.358 A tranquil and unhurried atmosphere is found at Tudor Cottage. A delightful wisteria-covered 16th century thatched house, it retains all its original character. Lovely oak beams, oak panelling, huge inglenook fireplaces and a pretty English garden for guests to explore. Ideally located for touring this picturesque and interesting part of England.	£10.00	O	■	O
Mrs Jennifer Firmin **Beauchamp House** **Shepton Beauchamp** **Nr. Ilminster TA19 0LQ** **Tel: (0460) 41447** **OPEN: ALL YEAR**	Nearest Road A303 Beauchamp House built of local Hamstone with mullioned windows, stands in an old orchard admid a profusion of lovely beeches and oaks. Beyond is a sheep meadow and a copse with woodpeckers. A warm and friendly welcome to guests in this peaceful and quiet atmosphere. One single and twin bedroom available with modern facilities radio, TV, tea/coffee making. Children over 5 welcome. National Trust Property surrounds with many gardens, forests and countryside walks.	£10.50	O	■	■
S.C. Carr **The Moorings** **Long Load** **Langport TA10 9JZ** **Tel: (045824) 303** **OPEN: ALL YEAR**	Nearest Road A303 The Moorings is a welcoming family home with spacious rooms and a pleasant, flower-filled garden situated in a quiet rural setting on the edge of the Somerset Levels. One twin and two single bedrooms available with modern amenities. Tea/coffee making facilities. Colour TV in residents lounge. Children can be provided with cots and high-chairs. Village of Long Load ¼ mile away.	£8.50	O	■	O
Robin & Philippa Watson **Old Stowey Farm** **Wheddon Cross** **Minehead TA24 7BT** **Tel: (064384) 268** **OPEN: ALL YEAR**	Nearest Roads M.5 A.39 Old Stowey is a 16th century farmhouse set in 80 acres in a sheltered wooded valley within Exmoor National Park. There are four rooms all with shower or bath en-suite. Rooms are charming and most comfortable with lovely views. The house has log fires and a woodburning stove. Food here is excellent with fresh vegetables and game in season. They offer super accommodation for horses, with hunting 6 days a week, rough shooting, a croquet lawn and hard tennis court. Fishing is close by. National Winners Kelloggs Award 1985.	£16.00	O	O	O

O yes ■ no

207

		minimum per person	children taken	evening meals available	animals taken
Paul Foss **Long House Hotel** **Pylle Road** **Pilton** **Nr.Shepton Mallet BA4 4BP** **Tel: (074 989) 701** **OPEN: 15 FEB-15 DEC**	Nearest Road A.361 A warm, friendly welcome is assured for the visitor to this 17th century hotel situated in a most attractive village. The 7 bedrooms are pleasant and comfortable, all are en-suite. There's a comfortably furnished lounge and a well stocked bar. The food is excellent and they prepare picnics as well. Special diets can be catered for. This is a perfect base for a touring holiday.	£16.00	O	O	O
Mrs Peggy Vaux **Rydon Farm** **Compton Durville** **South Petherton** **Somerset TA13 5ER** **Tel: (0460) 40468** **OPEN: ALL YEAR**	Nearest Road A.303 M.5 Large lounge with colour TV. Central for N and S coasts (Wild Life Park) among local attractions. Local fresh meat and own fruit and veg are used. Good home cooking, and cider served with evening meal. There are four rooms all with tea making facilities.	£10.00	O	O	■
Mrs Jose Pullin **"Midway House"** **Ston Easton** **Nr. Bath BA3 4DQ** **Tel: (076121) 280** **OPEN: ALL YEAR**	Nearest Road A.37 Excellent accommodation in an elegant 18th century country house standing in a walled and well-tended garden, just twenty minutes south of Bath. Three rooms are available for treble, double or single bookings, each with modern facilities, radio, TV and Tea/coffee making facilities. Breakfast is served in a well-furnished dining room and there is a lounge for guests' use. Bath, Wells and Cheddar nearby. Many interesting local pubs and restaurants for meals. Tennis, riding, golf locally.	£16.00	O	■	■
Eileen Holloway **Manor Farm** **Chiselborough** **Stoke-sub-Hamdon TR14 6TQ** **Tel: (093 588) 203** **OPEN: APRIL-OCT**	Nearest Roads A.303 B.3165 Manor Farm, in the heart of rural Somerset, stands in 450 acres. A most attractive Victorian Hamstone house offering four charming, comfortable rooms with modern amenities. A sitting room with colour T.V. for guests as well as a garden and games room. Marvellous evening meals using local fresh produce, home-baked rolls and a jug of cider. Imaginative cuisine and great value. Mrs. Holloway welcomes all her guests most warmly.	£9.50	O	O	■
Mrs Claire Mitchem **Whittles Farm** **Beercrocombe** **Taunton TA3 6AH** **Tel: (0823) 480 301** **OPEN: MAR-APR**	Nearest Road A.258 Guests at Whittles Farm can be sure of a high standard of accomodation and service. A superior 16th century farmhouse set in 200 acres of pasture land. It is luxuriously carpeted and furnished in traditional style. Inglenook fireplaces and log-burners. Five bedrooms with en-suite facilities individually furnished. TV, tea/coffee making. Excellent farmhouse food using own meat, eggs and vegetables and local Cheddar cheese and butter. Table license. Children over 12.	£12.50	■	O	■

O yes ■ no

	Nearest Road / Description	minimum per person	children taken	evening meals available	animals taken
Mr & Mrs. William Beaumont **Higher House** **West Bagborough** **Taunton TA4 3EF** **Tel: (0823) 432996** **OPEN: ALL YEAR**	Nearest Road A.358 A delightful 17th century farmhouse set in six acres of garden and paddocks. Higher House offers spacious and comfortable accommodation. The seven bedrooms all have modern amenities and spectacular views across the countryside. There is a beautifully proportioned drawing room with open log fire and French windows leading onto the lawn. A morning room with colour T.V. In the dining room a full English breakfast is served between 8am and 10am. Home cooking is a speciality and dinner is a delicious four-course meal with wine and spirits available.	£10.00	O	O	O
Mrs Margaret Davey **The Lodge** **Creech Heathfield** **Creech St. Michael** **Taunton TA3 5EG** **Tel: (0823) 443282** **OPEN: MAR-NOV**	Nearest Roads A.38 A.361 M.5 Exit 25 Country hospitality, comfortable surroundings and a relaxing time await the visitor to The Lodge. This spacious, period house set in an unspoilt village offers a choice of 4 rooms. A comfortable, beautifully furnished drawing room, dining room and a separate lounge with colour TV. Good country food is served using fresh produce. Delightful gardens. Fishing and riding nearby.	£10.00	O	O	■
Mrs Rosemary H. Rollason **Close House** **Hatch Beauchamp** **Nr. Taunton TA3 6AE** **Tel: (0823) 480424** **OPEN: ALL YEAR**	Nearest Roads A.358 A.303 Delightful 17th century manor house, ideally situated between the Bristol Channel and South Coast. Personal attention is assured in this family run establishment standing in six acres of secluded parkland. Eight rooms available to guests, with modern facilities, radio, TV, tea/coffee making. Single availability. Spacious and elegant period lounge and dining room serving English and International cuisine. Tennis courts, fishing available.	£15.00	O	O	O
Mrs M. Garner-Richards **Watercombe House** **Huish Champflower** **Wiveliscombe** **Nr. Taunton TA4 2EE** **Tel: (0984) 23725** **OPEN: APRIL-OCT**	Nearest Road A.361 A warm welcome awaits you at this charming country home with river frontage in a quiet beauty spot in a fold of the Brendon Hills. Friendly personal service will ensure a happy relaxing stay. One double, one twin room, with modern amenities. The house is well appointed but retains its "olde worlde" charm. Log fires, good home cooking with local produce. Private fishing, deep freeze available. Sailing and surfing 2 miles away. Easy access to Exmoor.	£10.00	■	O	■

O yes ■ no

	minimum per person	children taken	evening meals available	animals taken
John & Sarah Fox **Jews Farm House** **Huish Champflower** **Wiveliscombe** **Taunton TA4 2HL** **Tel: (0984) 24218** **OPEN: ALL YEAR** Nearest Road A.361 A lovely house dating from 1248, which stands high in the Brendon Hills commanding fine views of Exmoor. Guests are made very welcome and have full run of their own drawing room and dining room where excellent food is served. Three bedrooms, two with private facilities, and brass beds, tea/coffee making. Beautiful surrounding countryside for walking, riding and bird-watching. Fishing in trout ponds and reservoirs. Many historic places of interest nearby. Children over 10.	£19.50	O	O	O
Mrs Maureen Fewings **Higher Dipford Farm** **Trull** **Taunton TA3 7NU** **Tel: (0823) 75770** **OPEN: MAR-DEC** Nearest Road This delightful 14th century traditional Somerset long house stands in the beautiful Vale of Taunton Deane. This charming farmhouse with its elm beams and inglenook fireplace offers excellent accommodation in four bedrooms with bathroom en-suite, T.V. and tea/coffee making facilities. The food is excellent using fresh farm produce including home-cured hams, spring lamb, local salmon, farmhouse Cheddar, clotted cream and fresh milk. A jug of cider is also served with your meal. Nearby is golf, riding, and shooting.	£15.00	O	O	■
Mrs V.A. Cole **Frog Street Farm** **Beercrocombe** **Taunton TA3 6AF** **Tel: (0823) 480430** **OPEN: ALL YEAR** Nearest Road A.358 A delightful 15th century farmhouse retaining all its charm and character with its original beams, Jacobean panelling, and inglenook fireplaces. Located in a truly rural setting with a trout stream running through the meadows and an abundance of wildlife. A tranquil relaxing time will be had here. A swimming pool is set in the lovely garden. Specialising in home-produced food of a very high standard.	£11.00	O	O	■
Mrs Diana Frayne **Rushlands Farm** **Knowle Lane** **Wookey** **Nr. Wells BA5 1LD** **Tel: (0749) 73181** **OPEN: APR-OCT** Nearest Road A.371 A very friendly atmosphere awaits guests at Ruslands Farm. Situated down a quiet lane with open views, it is only five minutes from the village of Wookey. Six pleasant rooms with modern amenities. A lounge and garden for guests. Home cooking. Only one and half miles from the famous Wookey Hole Caves and two miles from beautiful Wells with its stuning Cathedral. Glastonbury is five miles. Within twenty miles are Bath, Bristol, Taunton and Longleat House plus sandy beaches.	£7.75	O	O	■

O yes ■ no

		minimum per person	children taken	evening meals available	animals taken
Anthony & Alison Grimstead **Burcott Mill** **Burcott** **Wells BA5 1NJ** **Tel: (0749) 73118** **OPEN: ALL YEAR**	Nearest Road A.39 Burcott Mill is a family run house where a free and easy atmosphere combines with polite, personal service. The house is "olde worlde" in very good decorative order, attached to any old water mill being converted to a crafts centre, and stands in 1½ acres with lots of pet animals: dogs, cats, goats, hens and ducks. Six bedrooms available to guests and children are very welcome. Good home cooked food. T.V. lounge, and games room. Riding.	£9.00	O	O	■
Mrs Pat Higgs **Home Farm** **Stoppers Lane** **Coxley** **Wells BA5 1QS** **Tel: (0749) 72434** **OPEN: ALL YEAR EXCL. XMAS**	Nearest Road A.39 Home Farm is set in the peace and quiet of the Somerset countryside where guests can enjoy a relaxing holiday. Offering accommodation in choice of seven rooms all with modern amenities and most with lovely views of the Mendip Hills. A colour T.V. lounge and garden are also available. Nearby are Wells, Bath, Cheddar Gorge and Wookey Hole Caves.	£8.50	O	O	O
Mrs Pauline Grimwade **Briscoe** **Wellington TA21 9NY** **Tel: (082347) 2073** **OPEN: ALL YEAR**	Nearest Road A.38 M.5 A fine Georgian house standing in beautiful grounds, with a delightful miniature formal garden, at the foot of the Blackdown Hills. There are lovely views across the moors - heather, bracken beeches and rhododendrons growing in profusion. There are three spacious, vey comfortable bedrooms one with private bath all with modern amenities and tea/coffee making facilities. There is also a lounge and garden for guests use. Mrs. Grimwade is a delightful hostess and goes out of her way to make her guests' feel at home. This makes an excellent base for touring as Devon is only one hours drive	£14.00	O	■	O
Tony & Karen Tilden **Penscot Farmhouse Hotel** **Shipham** **Winscombe BS25 1TW** **Tel: (093484) 2659** **OPEN: FEB-NOV**	Nearest Roads A.38 M.5 Exit 21 This charming 15th century farmhouse set in a quiet village, retains much of its original character with oak beams and log fires. The accommodation is very pleasant and comfortable and the food is good too. This is excellent walking and riding country. Lake fishing is also available. Close by is Wells with its great Cathedral, Glastonbury with its Abbey and Tor, Georgian Bath and Bristol.	£12.50	O	O	O
Mrs. A.L. Teague **Lower Church Farm** **Charlton Musgrove** **Wincanton BA9 8ES** **Tel: (0963) 32307** **OPEN: APR-OCT**	Nearest Road A.303 Lovely countryside surrounds this 18th century farmhouse and its sixty acres of dairy pasture. A pleasant, homely atmosphere prevails in the house with its beams and inglenooks. Three bedrooms are available to guests, with modern amenities, tea/coffee making facilities. Children are well provided for with cots, high-chairs, babysitting. No single availability. There is a lounge with colour T.V., and guests have use of the garden.	£8.50	O	O	O

O yes ■ no

		minimum per person	children taken	evening meals available	animals taken
Mrs M. Tucker **Carents Farm** **Yeovil Marsh** **Yeovil BA21 3QE** **Tel: (0935) 76622** **OPEN: FEB-NOV**	Nearest Road A.87 A handsome 16th/17th century hamstone house on a working arable and cattle farm. The house is full of oak beams and inglenooks and is set in a attractive garden in a quiet situation; an ideal base for touring and walking. Three bedrooms are available with modern amenities and antique furniture, one with a brass bed. Good food served here. Guests will enjoy the homely atmosphere in this pleasant house.	£9.00	O	O	

O yes ■ no

All the establishments in this book
are members of the
**WORLDWIDE BED & BREAKFAST
ASSOCIATION**

Look for this symbol

SUFFOLK

This is the county of men like Constable and Gainsborough, Admiral Lord Nelson and Benjamin Britten. It produces men of vision; the appreciation of beauty borne of long association with this gentle, dreaming land, and its unspoilt coastline. The small towns and villages are typical of an area with long seafaring traditions and inland they look comfortable and prosperous and conjure up pictures of a secure and confident people.

West Suffolk was famous for its wool trade back in the Middle Ages and the merchants gave thanks for their good fortune by building magnificent "wool" churches. Lavenham, which must surely be the most photographed of any English town, was the centre of the manufacturing trade and there the splendid houses and streets were built for the merchants - fine black and white Tudor buildings, still intact and lived in today.

County Town

Ipswich was granted the first Charter by King John in 1200, but had long been a trading community of seafaring people.

It's history can be read from the names of the streets, such as Buttermarket, Friars Street, Cornhill, Dial Lane and Tavern Street. The latter holds the famous Great White Horse Hotel mentioned by Charles Dickens in Pickwick Papers. Sadly, not many ancient buildings remain, but the mediaeval street pattern and the churches make a very interesting trail to follow for those who are searching for the origins of the town.

The Market town of Bury St. Edmunds is really quite charming and has much of its architectural heritage still surviving, with examples from past periods, from the Norman Cornhill to a fine Queen Anne house. The Abbey was at one time sold and the owner then proceeded to sell off the very stones with which it was built. What has been left to us is a strange mixture - 12th century and mediaeval mixed with the ancient building. However, Suffolk has some very fine churches, such as those at Mildenhall, Lakenheath, Framlingham, Lavenham and Stoke-by-Nayland, to mention but a very few of the many.

Countryside

The evident prosperity of this county in past times is marked by the large number of wonderful houses and great Halls which abound, and which contain a treasury of art in all its forms.

They were most lavishly furnished and decorated by brilliant designers and craftsmen, but not least, they were lovingly cared for by their owners and in many cases are still so today. They are for the most part open to public inspection and visiting them is the greatest pleasure, not to say privilege, for here is the rich tapestry of English life. The continuity of association with the same families throughout the centuries brings history into focus and gives us a true picture of the glories of England.

The land is green and fertile and highly productive, the low rainfall making it very suitable for arable crops. The hedgerows shelter some of our prettiest wild flowers, and the narrow country lanes are a pure delight - even though they can be very hazardous when the harvesting machines are about their work. The most memorable aspect is the ever changing skies. They appear much higher and wider than anywhere else in England making the landscape quite minor, and they attract painters from a wide background, all trying to capture them on canvas.

There is a great deal of heathland - probably the best known is Newmarket Heath where the racing and training of horses has been the local industry for some hundreds of years. The town of Newmarket was very popular with James I and Charles II; there was a royal palace there which burned down in a fire which destroyed most of the town but spared Nell Gwynne's cottage. The coast vies with the country as to which is the more interesting. The busy port of Felixstowe has an Edwardian air which endears it to many but others are much attracted to Aldeburgh or Thorpenses. Each small coastal town and village has something different to offer, but all are most charming. The beaches tend to be of pebbles and there is a constant whispering sound as they are turned about by the water.

SUFFOLK GAZETEER

Areas of Outstanding Natural Beauty.
Suffolk Coast. Heathlands. Dedham Vale.

Historic Houses and Castles

Euston Hall -- Thetford
18th century house with fine collection of pictures. Gardens and 17th century Parish Church nearby.

Christchurch Mansion -- Ipswich
16th century mansion built on site of 12th century Augustinian Priory. Gables and dormers added in 17th century and other alteration and additions made in 17th & 18th centuries.

Gainsborough's House -- Sudbury
Birthplace of Gainsborough, well funished, collection of paintings.

The Guildhall -- Hadleigh
15th century.

Glemham Hall -- Nr. Woodbridge
Elizabethan house of red brick -- 18th century alterations. Fine stair, panelled rooms with Queen Annefurniture.

Haughley Park -- Nr. Stowmarket
Jacobean Manor House.

Heveningham Hall -- Nr. Halesworth
Georgian mansion -- English Palladian -- Interior in Neo-Classical style. Garden by Capability Brown.

Ickworth -- Nr. Bury St. Edmunds
Mixed architectural styles -- late Regency and 18th century. French furniture, pictures and superb silver. Gardens with orangery.

Kentwell Hall. -- Long Melford
Elizabethan mansion in red brick, built in E plan surrounded by moat.

Little Hall -- Lavenham
15th century hall house, collection of furniture, pictures, china, etc.

Melford Hall -- Nr. Sudbury
16th century -- fine pictures, Chinese porcelain, furniture. Garden with gazebo.

Somerleyton Hall -- Nr. Lowestoft
Dating from 16th century -- additional work in 19th century. Carvings by Grinling Gibbons. Tapestries, library, pictures.

Cathedrals and Churches

Bury St. Edmunds (St. Mary)
15th century. Hammer Beam roof in nave, wagon roof in chancel. Boret monument 1467.

Bramfield (St. Andrew)
Early circular tower. Fine screen and vaulting. Renaissance effigy.

Bacton (St. Mary)
15th century timbered roof. East Anglian stone and flintwork.

Dennington (St. Mary)
15th century alabaster monuments and bench ends. Aisle and Parclose screens with lofts and parapets. 17th and 18th century pulpit, box pews.

Earl Stonhay (St. Mary)
14th century -- rebuilt with fine hammer roof and 17th century pulpit with four hour-glasses.

Euston (St. Genevieve)
17th century. Fine panelling, reredos may be Grinling Gibbons.

Framlingham (St. Michael)
15th century nave and west tower, hammer beam roof in false vaulting. Chancel was rebuilt in 16th century for the tombs of the Howard family, monumental art treasures. Thamar organ. 1674.

Fressingfield (St. Peter & St. Paul)
15th century woodwork -- very fine.

Lavenham (St. Peter & St. Paul)
15th century. Perpendicular. Fine towers. 14th century chancel screen. 17th century monument in alabaster.

Long Melford (Holy Trinity)
15th century Lady chapel, Splendid brasses. 15th century glass of note. Chantry chapel with fine roof. Like cathedral in proportions.

Stoke-by-Nayland (St. Mary)
16th to 17th century library, great tower. Fine nave and arcades. Good brasses and monuments.

Ufford (St. Mary)
Mediaeval font cover -- glorious.

Museums and Galleries

Christchurch Mansion -- Ipswich
Country house, collection of furniture, pictures, bygones, ceramics of 18th century. Paintings by Gainsborough, Constable and modern artists.

Ipswich Museum -- Ipswich
Natural History; prehistory, geology and archeololgy to mediaeval period.

Moyse's Hall Museum -- Bury St. Edmunds
12th century dwelling house with local antiquities and natural history.

Abbot's Hall Museum of Rural Life -- Stowmarket
Collections describing agriculture, crafts and domestic utensils.

Gershom-Parkington Collection -- Bury St. Edmunds
Queen Anne House containing collection of watches and clocks.

Dunwich Museum -- Dunwich
Flora and fauna; local history

Historic Monuments

The Abbey -- Bury St. Edmunds
Only West end now standing.

Framlingham Castle
12th and 13th centuries -- Tudor almshouses.

Bungay Castle -- Bungay
12th century. Restored 13th century Drawbridge and gatehouse.

Burgh Castle Roman Fort -- Burgh
Coastal defences -- 3rd century.

Herringfleet Priory -- Herringfleet
13th century -- remains of small Augustinian priory.

Leiston Abbey -- Leiston
14th century -- remains of cloisters, choir and transepts.

Orford Castle -- Orford
12th century -- 18 sided keep -- three towers.

SUFFOLK
Recommended roadside restaurants

185	A45	Kentford (South) Suffolk (Westbound) Kentford Filling Station 6 miles east of Newmarket
186	A45	Kentford (North) Suffolk (Eastbound) Kentford Filling Station 6 miles east of Newmarket
280	A45	Stowmarket Suffolk 2 miles west of Stowmarket
297	A12	Capel St Mary (North) Suffolk 3 miles south of Ipswich
298	A12	Capel St Mary (South) Suffolk 3 miles south of Ipswich

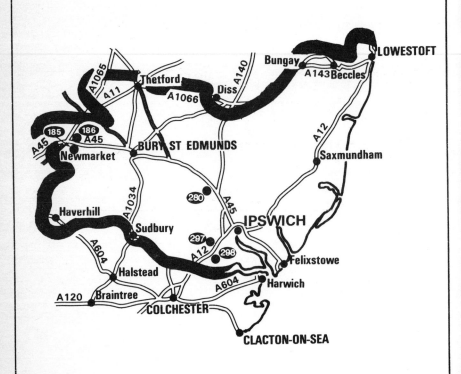

		minimum per person	children taken	evening meals available	animals taken
Ann & Roy Dakin "Dunston Guest House/Hotel" 8 Springfield Road Bury St.Edmunds IP33 3AN Tel: (0284) 67981 **OPEN: ALL YEAR**	Nearest Road A.45 A 19th century house, full of character, with a warm, friendly atmosphere. 17 rooms all very comfortable, plus T.V. lounge and a ground floor room available for handicapped guests. They also have a license. Situated in the centre of East Anglia, it is an ideal base for touring the region, with lovely towns and villages plus coastline.	£14.00	O	O	■
Mrs M.C. Ferguson 34 Guildhall Street Bury St.Edmunds IP33 1QF Tel: (0284) 703677 **OPEN: ALL YEAR**	Nearest Road A.45 Mrs Ferguson offers pleasant bed and breakfast accommodation in her pink 16th century timber-framed town house in Bury St. Edmunds. Three bedrooms are available with modern amenities, T.V. tea/coffee making facilities. Residents' lounge. Children are welcome, with cots provided and babysitting can be arranged. The house is in a conservation area.	£9.50	O	■	■
Joseph Thompson The Swan Inn Woolpit Bury St.Edmunds IP30 9QN Tel:(0359) 40482 **OPEN: ALL YEAR**	Nearest Road A.45 A very attractive 17th century inn situated between Bury St. Edmunds and Stowmarket. 40 mins from Felixstowe Ferries. The accommodation is in a comfortable modernised annexe to the rear of the main building and looks out onto a lovely walled garden, providing quiet secluded lodgings. 2 doubles one en-suite, 1 twin and 1 single. Colour T.V. and tea/coffee facilities in each room. Meals available some evenings.	£12.00	O	O	■
Mr & Mrs Avery The Four Horseshoes Country Inn and Hotel Thornham Magna IP23 7HD Nr. Eye Tel: (037971) 777 **OPEN: ALL YEAR**	Nearest Road A.140 A lovely long, low thatched 12th century black and white country inn, in the village of Thornham Magna. Superior bed and breakfast here. The eight guest rooms all have private bathrooms, telephones, colour T.V., central heating, tea/coffee making facilities. The restaurant has a reputation for good value-for-money meals, and of course, is licensed. Bar meals of great variety also available.	£25.50	O	O	O
Mike & Lise Hilton Otley House Otley Ipswich IP6 9NR Tel:(047339) 253 **OPEN: FEB-DEC**	Nearest Roads A.12 A.140 A.45 A magnificent 17th century house standing in its own spacious grounds, surrounded by mature trees with two small lakes, croquet lawn and putting green. Accommodation is in three luxuriously furnished bedrooms all with private facilities. Evening meals are a delight and served in the Regency dining room. There is also a billiard room, T.V. and drawing room for guests' use. Ideally located for visiting Woodbridge, Oxford, Dunwich, Southwold and fine cities of Norfolk and Cambridge. Nearby is golf, sailing and riding. Rates are two people. No single accommodation available.	£26.00	O	O	■

O yes ■ nò

		minimum per person	children taken	evening meals available	animals taken
Mrs Merryn Tyrrell **Cowslip Farm** **Witnesham** **Nr. Ipswich IP6 9JA** **Tel: (047385) 267** **OPEN: ALL YEAR**	Nearest Roads A.12 A.45 B.1077 A truly delightful 16th century Suffolk farmhouse standing in 140 acres of arable land, overlooking the Fynn Valley. Two completely self-contained apartments, each with a double bedroom, bathroom and sitting room. Also T.V. and tea/coffee makers. There is a lovely garden and games room for guests. An ideal base for touring, with river estuaries, the coast from Felixstowe to Southwold and Norfolk all within an hour. Many beautiful walks in the nearby forests. Numerous country houses, bird sanctuaries and pretty villages. Golf, riding, tennis	£10.00	O	■	■
Raewyn & Anthony **Hackett-Jones** **Pipps Ford** **Norwich Road Roundabout** **Needham Market** **IP6 8LJ** **Tel: (044979) 208** **OPEN: MID JAN-MID DEC**	Nearest Roads A.45 A.140 A beautiful black and white 16th century farmhouse in a delightful old fashioned garden and 8 acres, by the River Gipping in an area of outstanding beauty. Six very attractive bedrooms have private bedrooms and tea/coffee making facilities. A very extensive breakfast menu and delicious evening meals are served in the delightful conservatory. T.V. lounge, all-weather tennis court and swimming pool.	£11.50	O	O	O

Mrs Diana Ridsdale
Cherry Tree Farm
Mendlesham Green
Stowmarket IP14 5RQ
Tel: (04494) 376
  Changing to: (0449) 766376
  (Sometime in 1987)
 	
OPEN: ALL YEAR
	Nearest Road A.140
	
	Traditional timber-framed farmhouse, standing in ¾ acre of garden with orchard and duck ponds in peaceful Suffolk village. 2 bedrooms, spacious and comfortable lounge, ingleook fireplace with log fire. Hearty English breakfasts served in the oak-beamed dining room. Home-baked bread, own preserves and honey. Imaginative evening meals with garden and local produce, good cheeses and fine English wines.
		£10.00	O	O	■

Mr & Mrs W.F. Ardley **Queens Cottage** **Hacheston** **Woodbridge IP13 0DS** **Tel: (0728) 746273** **OPEN: MAY-SEPT**	Nearest Roads A.12 B.1116 A delighful whitewashed thatched and timber-framed house built 1400-1450. It has an inglenook fireplace and many exposed beams. Three charming rooms with modern amenities. Tea/coffee making facilities in each room and residents' lounge with colour T.V. A most friendly atmosphere. Mr & Mrs Ardley winners of the Kelloggs Regional Award for 1985, take pleasure in introducing guests to the historic area and help with itineraries. French spoken. No children under 12 please.	£10.50	O	■	■
Mrs Joan Hall **Cherry Tree House** **Hacheston** **Woodbridge IP13 0DR** **Tel: (0728) 746371** **OPEN: ALL YEAR**	Nearest Road A.12 A pretty, early 17th century house with oak beams, standing in a large garden. There are three guest rooms at Cherry Tree House, all with modern facilities. T.V. and tea/coffee making facilities, full central heating. Lounge available to residents. Framlingham Castle is close by and the coast is within easy reach, as are Aldeburgh, Minsmere, and Havergate Island. Pony trekking and golf is nearby.	£10.50	O	O	■

O yes ■ no

SURREY

One of the home counties - including a large area of London - south of the Thames. Quite a small county, rather hilly, blessed with great parks, fine landscaping, open heaths and downs and despite vast urban development it maintains some lovely countryside which, fortunately, is conserved and protected by the "Green Belt".

Geography and History

The land, geographically, is chalk sandwiched in clay and it was probably the lack of handy building material which was responsible for the area remaining virtually an uninhabited wilderness for centuries. The North Downs were a considerable barrier to cross, and the few gaps, created by the rivers, became the main routes and gradually people settled along them in small village communities.

There were fortified settlements during the Iron Age, a glass industry in the 13th century but when the timber for heating the furnaces ran out, so the industries died. Wool, was for a time quite valuable but on the whole it has little of great interest historically - or even architecturally.

The Romans built Stane Street following the gap cut by the River Mole to carry their traffic from Chichester to London and this encouraged the development of small towns. Others sprang up from the passage of the River Wey, such as Guildford and Weybridge, where it joins the Thames. The Wey Gap allows the Pilgrims Way to cross the foot of the downs, east to west, still a main road to and from London. Reigate, Dorking, Guildford and Farnham lie along the route.

Patronage of the Church - especially the Bishop of Chichester and wealthy families such as the de Warennis, established manors which grew and developed over the years but little happened to disturb the rural tranquility of the region. It has very little mention in the Domesday Book and when in the 17th century, assessments of wealth were made to extract "Ship Money", very little was raised in Surrey. As a county it has made little history - rather it has reflected the passing times. Arguably, its most important event was the signing of Magna Carta at Egham in 1215. However, its nearness to London and Royal patronage began to influence the area and improve the conditions then existing. The buildings of that period onwards shows this very clearly. It is said that when the Royal Palaces were built at Hampton Court and Richmond and also the great houses such as Loseley, stone for their building was taken from monasteries closed during the Reformation.

Royal Parks

It became a Royal playground over the centuries. The Norman Kings enjoyed the countryside for its hunting. The heathlands proved to be ideal for riding and horses became part of the landscape and the life of the people. Who has not heard of Epsom Downs racecourse? Then the Tudor Kings came along and built themselves very fine castles and stocked and enclosed huge deer parks. Richmond, the finest of these, was described as "the finest village in the British Dominions". Now, unhappily it is beset by 20th century traffic and consequent problems. However it is still a wonderful park and a most interesting area. Built on a slope overlooking the Thames, it has retained some superb buildings, such as Trumpeters House and Asgill House amongst others. The terraces and gardens give an air of great space and elegance in this overcrowded age. The riverside has some lovely stretches for walking and the park, first enclosed by Charles 1st., serves a place of leisure and recreation still for untold numbers of Londoners.

Other parts of the county, such as Bagshot and Purbright commons have wide areas of open heathland and there are wonderful views of woods and parkland from the North Downs.

All through the ages there had been very little growth in agriculture, apart from the fertile Thames Valley. This meant that vast areas were available for building land when the population began to increase, as it did dramatically in the 19th and 20th centuries. The proximity to London, which demanded more and more workers and the coming of the railway and the car have made commuting a way of life for hundreds of thousands of people.

SURREY GAZETEER

Historic Houses and Castles

Albury Park -- Albury, Nr. Guildford
A delightful country mansion designed by Pugin.

Clandon Park -- Guildford
A fine house in the Palladian style by Leoni. A good collection of furniture and pictures. The house boasts some fine plastework.

Claremont -- Esher
A superb Palladian house with interesting interior.

Detillens -- Limpsfield
A fine 15th century house with inglenook fireplaces and mediaeval furniture. A large, pleasant garden.

Greathed Manor -- Lingfield
An imposing Victorian manor house.

Hatchlands -- East Clandon
A National Trust property of the 18th century with a fine Adam interior.

Loseley House -- Guildford
A very fine Elizabethan masion with superb panelling furniture and paintings.

Polesden Lacy -- Dorking
A Regency villa housing the Greville collection of tapestries, pictures and furnishings. Extensive gardens.

Cathedrals and Churches

Compton (St. Nicholas)
The only surviving 2-storey sanctuary in the country. A fine 17th century pulpit.

Esher (St. George)
A fine Altar-piece and marble monument.

Hascombe (St. Peter)
A rich interior with much gilding and painted reredos and roofs.

Lingfield (St. Peter & St. Paul)
15th century. Holding a chained bible.

Ockham (St. Mary & All Saints)
Early church with 13th century east window.

Stoke D'Abernon (St. Mary)
Dating back to Pre-conquest time with additions from the 12th-15th centuries. A fine 13th century painting. Early brasses.

Museums and Galleries

Charterhouse School Museum -- Godalming
Peruvian pottery, Greek pottery, archaeology and natural history.

Chertsey Museum -- Chertsey
18th -- 19th century costume and furnishing displayed and local history.

Guildford House -- Guildford
The house is 17th century and of architectural interest housing monthly exhibitions.

Guildford Museum -- Guildford
A fine needleword collection and plenty on local history.

Old Kiln Agricultural -- Tilford
A very interesting collections of old farm implements.

Watermill Museum -- Haxted
A restored 17th century mill with working water wheels and machinery.

Weybridge Museum -- Weybridge
Good archaelogical exhibition plus costume and local history.

SURREY
Recommended roadside restaurants

001	A30	Camberley Surrey London Road 1 mile west of Camberley
010	A3	Milford Godalming Surrey 6 miles south of Guildford
020	A31	Hogs Back, Farnham, Surrey 2 miles east of Farnham
058	A3	Bramshott Chase Nr Hindhead, Surrey 1½ miles south of Hindhead
142	A217	Hookwood Horley, Surrey Reigate Road 5 miles south of Reigate
204	A22	Godstone Surrey Eastbourne Road 7 miles north of East Grinstead
258	A30	Ashford, Surrey 2 miles north of Staines
290	M3	Fleet Service Area Hants Between Junctions 4 & 5

Surrey

	minimum per person	children taken	evening meals available	animals taken
Mrs G.M. Hill **Bulmer Farm** Holmbury St. Mary Dorking RH5 6LG Tel: (0306) 730210 OPEN: ALL YEAR Nearest Roads A.25 B.2126 A warm welcome is assured in a really delighful farmhouse with many beams and an inglenook fireplace. Built around a courtyard, it offers 3 charming rooms. Situated in a picturesque, quiet village, it is convenient for London, Gatwick, Heathrow and the Surrey and Sussex countryside. A pleasant touring base. Farm produce and home-made marmalade are provided. Good pub meals nearby.	£8.50	■	■	■
Mrs Susan Anderton **Springfield House** Westcott Street Westcott RH4 3LU Nr. Dorking Tel: (0306) 889691 OPEN: ALL YEAR Nearest Road A.25 Springfield is a lovely, isolated Regency country house built for a French aristocrat. Wisteria-clad, it looks over extensive gardens and fields. Superb views of the Moor Downs. Three double bedrooms with all modern facilities radio/T.V., tea/coffee making facilities. Heated outdoor pool in courtyard garden. Children over 4 welcome. London 40 mins by train. Gatwick 30 mins by car.	£14.00	O	O	■
Mrs M. Carmichael **Deerfell** Blackdown Park Fernden Lane Haslemere GU27 3 LA Tel: (0428) 53409 OPEN: ALL YEAR Nearest Roads A.286 Deerfell is a family home, once the coach house to 16th century Blackdown House where Cromwell lived. Very quiet and comfortable accommodation is offered here in two bedrooms, one with private facilities. Children are welcome and well provided for. Spectacular views towards the Sussex Downs. Gatwick and Heathrow are both one hour away.	£9.00	O	O	O
Mr & Mrs K. Beartup **Felcourt Guest House** 79 Massetts Road Horley RH6 7EB Tel: (0293) 782651 OPEN: ALL YEAR Nearest Roads A.23 A well situated, comfortable guest house only three minutes from Gatwick airport. Six comfortable rooms with modern amenities. Rooms all have colour T.V. and tea/coffee makers. A television lounge and a garden. This is, of course, an ideal stopover for travellers going to Gatwick. Early breakfasts are no problem and Mr & Mrs Beartup will get you away to your place in plenty of time. They will even take you to the airport and pick you up there.	£14.50	O	■	■
Miss S. Vora **Beechwood Guest House** 39 Hatchlands Road Redhill RH1 6AP Tel: (0737) 61444 OPEN: ALL YEAR Nearest Road A.25 A warm welcome is assured in this select, pleasant Victorian house which stands in its own grounds. The accommodation is comfortable with modern amenities, T.V. lounge, tea/coffee making facilities. A full English breakfast is served. Evening meals and packed lunches are also available. This is an excellent base for touring. London is only 20 minutes by train, Gatwick 15 minutes. Nearby are Hampton Court, Kew Gardens, Brighton Pavilion, Chartwell and Polesdon Lacey. The establishment is licensed. Families are especially welcome.	£15.00	O	O	■

O yes ■ no

		minimum per person	children taken	evening meals available	animals taken

Christiane & David Ricketts
32 West Street
Reigate RH2 9BX
Tel: (07372) 41819

OPEN: ALL YEAR

Nearest Road A.25/M.25

A Victorian style house conveniently located in a residential area of Reigate. Accommodation is in a choice of five rooms with modern amenities, T.V. and tea/coffee making facilities. Gatwick airport is very easily accessible from here, as are the bus and train stations. Within easy driving distance are Chartwell and Epsom race course. One mile to the M.25

£15.00 — ○ ■ ○

Mr & Mrs Bussandri
Cranleigh Hotel
41 West Street
Relgate RH2 9BL
Tel:(07372) 40600/43468

OPEN: ALL YEAR

Nearest Roads A.25/M.25

The Cranleigh Hotel has a reputation for comfort, cleanliness and hospitality. Its modern facilities include hair dryers, T.V. a pleasant bar and lounge etc. Comfortable accommodation in pleasant rooms. ¾ of an hour from central London and a few minutes from Gatwick airport, the hotel stands in lovely gardens which provides flowers and fresh food for the table. They also offer a large heated pool for guests. Very convenient for travellers to the South West. Ideal for first or last night of travel.

£22.00 — ○ ○ ○

Dick & Mary Norminton
Priors Mead
Blanford Road
Reigate
Tel: (07372) 48776

OPEN: ALL YEAR

Nearest Road A.25

A most pleasant large house offering nine comfortable rooms with modern amenities. Situated in a very pleasant area there is much to visit locally or within a short drive. Epsom racecourse is not far away, neither is Chartwell - Churchill's home. It is conveniently placed for Gatwick Airport. Cots are provided.

£15.00 — ○ ■ ■

Mrs S.M. Preger
Aberford Guest House
53 Mount Ararat Road
Richmond
Tel: (01) 940 0040

OPEN: ALL YEAR

Nearest Road

Richmond is surrounded by places of interest, but without the noise and bustle of Central London. Kew Gardens, Hampton Court, Ham House, rugby at Twickenham, race course all nearby. Convenient for Heathrow and Gatwick. Quiet and comfortable the house offers five bedrooms all with private facilities, most en-suite with colour T.V., tea/coffee making facilities. Continental breakfast served.

£18.00 — ○ ■ ■

○ yes ■ no

Please mention **BEST BED & BREAKFAST IN THE WORLD** *when booking your accommodation.*

SUSSEX

Geologically, Sussex is almost a mirror image of neighbouring Kent. The South Downs stretch some eight miles along the coast reflecting the North Downs on the far side of the vast stretches of the Weald. It has a sheltered coastal plain in the south west and shingle beaches in the east with magnificent chalk cliffs in between. History has given Sussex its own distinctive character and there is a wealth of fascinating places to see today. The landscape of the Weald ranges from bracken covered heathlands, where deer still roam in the north west to the deep woodland stretches of the Ashdown Forest, eventually giving way to soft undulating hills and valleys, patterned with hop fields, small meadows, oast houses, windmills and fruit orchards. These hills terminate abruptly at the cliffs of Hastings and the ridges end at Rye and Winchelsea above the great Romney Marshes, stretching out to the sea. Originally the whole Weald was covered by dense forest. Villages like Midhurst and Wadhurst hold the Saxon suffix "hurst" meaning wood and must have grown up still surrounded by trees. Gradually the forests were cleared as agriculture changed the landscape and evidence of the county's Saxon farming heritage can still be found in place names like Boscham and Stedham, whose suffix "ham" means homestead or farm. Traditional timbered Priests Houses can be found at Itchingfield and Ewhurst. The latter village is not far from Bodiam castle, built in 1583 as defense against the French. It stands in a beautiful setting encircled by a lily covered moat. The South Downs stretch from the dramatic Beachy Head at Eastbourne along the coast to Chichester. Like the North Downs, they are traversed by an ancient trackway, developed first as the easiest route across country and becoming eventually an important trading route. There is much evidence of pre-historic settlement in the downs. Mount Caburn, east of Lewes, is crowned by an iron age fort and Cissbury Ring is archaeologically one of the most important sites in England. Covering about eighty acres it is the largest earthwork in Sussex and must have held a strategic defensive position. Above Brighton, Hollingbury Fort carved into the hillside and the Trundle, meaning circle, was constructed in 300-250 B.C. at an existing neolithic settlement. The view from these hillforts is magnificent and it is intriguing to speculate about the people who built them. The Long Man of Wilmington probably the most famous pre-historic site in Sussex stands 226 feet high, holding a staff in either hand and is believed to be Nordic, possibly representing Woden the god of war. Only two towns are located on the downs but they are both of considerable interest. Lewes lies in a hollow in the downs and still retains much of its mediaeval past. It has a fascinating folk museum in Ann of Cleves House, which itself is partly 16th century. Arundel lies on the other side of downs between Brighton and Chichester. As well as a fascinating mixture of architectural styles, it has a superb park with a lake, magnificent beech trees and an unrivalled view of the Arun valley.

Coastal Towns

Sussex has an extensive coastline and there is considerable variety in its coastal towns. At the western end stands Chichester with its magnificent cathedral. The harbour stretches deep into the coastal plain below and is rich in archaeological remains. The extensive creeks and mud flats also make it an excellent place for the birdwatcher. Brighton is probably the most famous of the Sussex seaside resorts with its pier, the promenades above the beaches, the oriental "folly" of George IV's Royal Pavilion and its superb Regency architecture. It also has "the lanes" a maze of narrow alleys and small squares full of fascinating shops, a thriving antique trade and some excellent pubs. Further east along the coast are Hastings, Winchelsea and Rye, members of the Cinque Ports Confederation, established in the 15th century to protect England's major trading ports against invasion from the Continent. Hasting "old town" with its narrow alleys and timbered houses still nestles below the cliffs and fishing boats still draw up on the shingle beaches drying their nets in curious tall thin timber net stores. Further along the coast the ancient town of Winchlesea stands on top of a hill, where it was rebuilt in the 13th century by Edward 1st. when the original town was engulfed by the sea. A thriving port for several centuries, it eventually contracted when the sea again receded in the 15th century. One of the three original town gates which still stand is now some distance from the town. Although smaller than the original settlement, Winchelsea is a beautiful town with an excellent museum in the Town Hall, a fine Norman church and many pretty houses. Across the Romney Marshes on the next hill stands Rye, its profile dominated by the church whose "quarter boys" still strike the quarter hours. Its is a fascinating town set amidst the marshes, with timbered houses along cobbled streets running down the hill from Church Square to the Strand Quay.

SUSSEX GAZETEER

Areas of Outstanding Natural Beauty.
The Sussex Downs. Chichester Harbour.

Historic Houses and Castles

Arundel Castle -- Arundel
18th century rebuilding of ancient castle, fine portraits, 15th century furniture.

Cuckfield Park -- Cuckfield
Elizabethan Manor House, gatehouse. Very fine panelling & ceilings.

Danny -- Hurstpierpoint
16th century -- Elizabethan & shaped house.

Goodwood House -- Chichester
18th century -- Jacobean house -- Fine Sussex flintwork, paintings by Van Dyck, Canaletto & Stubbs, English and French furniture, tapestries and porcelain.

Newtimber Place -- Newtimber
Moated house -- Etruscan style wall paintings.

Purham -- Pulborough
Elizabethan house containing important collection of Elizabethan, Jacobean and Georgian portraits, alsofine furniture.

Petworth House -- Petworth
17th century -- landscaped by Capability Brown -- important paintings. 14th century chapel.

St. Mary's -- Bramber
15th century timber framed house -- rare panelling.

Tanyard -- Sharpthorne
Mediaeval tannery -- 16th & 17th century additions.

The Thatched Cottage -- Lindfield
Close-studded weald house -- reputedly Henry VII hunting lodge.

Uppark -- Petersfield.
17th century -- 18th century interior decorations remain unaltered.

Alfriston Clergy House -- Nr. Seaford
14th century parish priest's house -- pre-reformation.

Battle Abbey -- Battle
Founded by William the Conqueror.

Charleston Manor -- Westdean
Norman, Tudor and Georgian architectural styles -- Romanesque window in the Norman wing.

Bull House -- Lewes
15th century half timbered house -- was home of Tom Paine.

Bateman's -- Burwash
17th century -- watermill-- home of Rudyard Kipling.

Bodiam Castle -- Nr. Hawksurst
14th century -- noted example of mediaeval moated military architecture.

Great Dixter -- Northiam.
15th century half timbered manor house -- great hall -- Lutyens gardens.

Glynde Place -- Nr. Lewes
16th century flint and brick -- built around courtyard-collection of paintings by Rubens, Hoppner, Kneller, Lely, Zoffany.

Michelham Priory -- Upper Dicker -- Nr. Hailsham
13th century Augustinian Priory -- became Tudor farmhouse -- working watermill, ancient stained glass, etc., enclosed by moat.

Royal Pavilion -- Brighton
Built for the Prince Regent by Nash upon classical villa by Holland. Exotic Building -- has superb original works of art lent by H.M. The Queen. Collections of Regency furniture also Art Nouveau and Art Deco in the Art Gallery and Museum.

Sheffield Park -- Nr. Uckfield
Beautiful Tudor House -- 18th century alterations -- splendid staircase.

Cathedrals and Churches

Alfriston (St. Andrew)
14th century -- transition from decorated style to perpendicular, Easter sepulchre.

Boxgrove (St. Mary & St. Blaise)
13th century choir with 16th century painted decoration on vaulting. Relic of Benedictine priory. 16th century chantry. Much decoration.

Chichester Cathedral
Norman and earliest Gothic. Large Romanesque relief sculptures in south choir aisle.

Etchingham (St. Mary & St. Nicholas)
14th century. Old glass, brasses, screen, carved stalls.

Hardham (St. Botolph)
11th century -- 12th century wall paintings.

Rotherfield (St. Denys)
16th century font cover, 17th century canopied pulpit, glass by Burne-Jones, Wall paintings, Georgian Royal Arms.

Sompting (St. Mary)
11th century Saxon tower -- Rhenish Helm Spire -- quite unique.

Worth (St. Nicholas)
10th century -- chancel arch is the largest Saxon arch in England. German carved pulpit c. 1500 together with altar rails.

Winchelsea (St. Thomas the Apostle)
14th century -- choir and aisles only. Canopied sedilia and piscina.

Museums and Galleries

Barbican House Museum -- Lewes
Collection relating to pre-historic, Romano-British and mediaeval antiquities of the area. Prints and water-colours of district.

Battle Museum -- Battle
Roman-British remains from archeological sites in area. Diorama of Battle of Hastings.

Bignor Roman Villa Collection -- Bignor
4th century mosaics, Samian pottery, hypocaust etc.

Brighton Museum and Art Gallery -- Brighton
Old Master Paintings, watercolours, ceramics, furniture. Surrealist paintings, Art Nouveau and Art Deco applied art, musical insturments and many other exhibits.

Marlipins Museum -- Shoreham
12th century building housing collections of ship models, photographs, old maps, geological specimens, etc.

Royal National Lifeboat Institution Museum -- Eastbourne
Lifeboats of all types used from earliest times to present.

Tower 73 -- Eastbourne
Martello tower restored to display the history of these forts. Exhibition of equipment, uniforms and weapons of the times.

The Toy Museum -- Rottingdean -- Brighton
Toys and playthings from many countries -- children's delight

SUSSEX
Recommended roadside restaurants

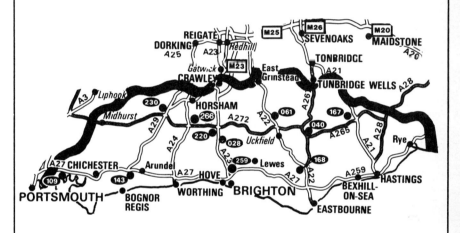

Sussex

	minimum per person	children taken	evening meals available	animals taken
Eunice & Jack Hutchinson **Bridge House & Cottage** **18 Queen Street** **Arundel BN18 9JG** **Tel: (0903) 882142/882779** **OPEN: ALL YEAR** Nearest Road A.27 A large house, built in 1772 and a 16th century cottage situated in the centre of picturesque Arundel and ideal centre for exploring beautiful Sussex. Four miles from sandy beaches and the harbour at Littlehampton. A number of ancestral homes and Roman ruins a short car ride away. The Castle and Wild Fowl Reserve a few minutes walk. A warm welcome and very pleasant rooms await visitors.	£12.00	O	■	O
Mrs June Ive **Moonshill Farm** **The Green** **Ninfield** **Battle TN33 9LH** **Tel: (0424) 892645** **OPEN: JAN-NOV** Nearest Road A.271 A most comfortable and welcoming modernised farmhouse set in ten acres with orchard and stables, at the heart of '1066' country, in charming village of Ninfield. Six rooms, three with private bathrooms, all centrally heated with tea/coffee making facilities, radio, some with T.V. Large cosy lounge. Children very welcome. Substantial breakfasts and country-fresh home-cooked evening meals. Guest may bring own wine.	£8.00	O	O	O
Mrs J.E. Tapping **Chantry Close Hotel** **13 Hastings Road** **Bexhill-on-Sea** **TN40 2HJ** **Tel: (0424) 222024** **OPEN: ALL YEAR** Nearest Road A.259 An imposing mock-Tudor house with panelled hall and beams. Situated in the old town close to a Norman church. Seven most comfortable rooms, five with private facilities, tea/coffee makers. A T.V. lounge and garden for guests. Mrs Tapping is well known for making her guests welcome and comfortable and her cooking is excellent. This is a sportsman's region with golf, sailing, riding and rambling close by. The area also has wonderful countryside and many historic houses, castle and museums.	£12.00	O	O	■
Mrs B.M. Hashfield **Taplow Cottage** **81 Nyewood Lane** **Bognor Regis** **PO21 2UE** **Tel: (0243) 821398** **OPEN: ALL YEAR** Nearest Road B.2166 A warm welcome is offered at this cottage-style house which has three most pleasant rooms all with modern facilities. They have a T.V. lounge. It is nicely placed for visiting the South Downs, the coast, Arundel Castle, Goodwood racecourse. The sea is only 600 yards from the house. Animals by arrangement.	£9.50	O	■	O
Laurie & Joseph Buttigieg **Marina House Hotel** **8 Charlotte Street** **Marine Parade** **Brighton BN2 1AG** **Tel: (0273) 605349** **OPEN: ALL YEAR** Nearest Road - Marine Parade A very pleasant Regency style house offering a warm welcome and ten comfortable rooms with modern facilities. Many of the rooms with private showers. Situated close to the sea, it is highly suitable for families. It is well known for its good cooking, specialising in Continental cuisine at its best, using only fresh produce. There is a host of places to visit locally with many historic sites and houses.	£10.50	O	O	O

O yes ■ no

	minimum per person	children taken	evening meals available	animals taken
Barry John Green **Downlands Hotel** **19 Charlotte St** **Brighton** **Tel: (0273) 601203** **OPEN: ALL YEAR** Nearest Road M.25 Downlands is a 14 bedroomed Regency private hotel, in a quiet street just 100 yards from the sea where you will always find a welcome. Close to the town and all local amenities. Cleanliness, friendliness, good food and service are the by-words here. All rooms have modern amenities: telephone, T.V./radio, tea/coffee making facilities etc. and are tastefully decorated.	£9.00	O	■	O
Mr C.B. Gregory **Braemar Guest House** **Steyning Road** **Rottingdean** **Brighton BN2 7GA** **Tel: (0273) 34263** **OPEN: ALL YEAR** Nearest Road A.259 A charming house - family run - offering fourteen pleasant, comfortable rooms with modern facilities. The proprietors really go out of their way to make their guests' stay a memorable one. From here Rudyard Kipling's house is only 2 minutes walk. The town is a famous smuggling place with many ancient buildings and a Saxon church. There is a multitude of places to discover in the area.	£9.00	O	■	O
Susan & Antony Trotman **White Barn** **Crede Lane** **Bosham** **Chichester PO18 8NX** **Tel: (0243) 573113** **OPEN: ALL YEAR** Nearest Road A.27 An outstanding modern open plan house, with heavily timbered interior in an attractive setting. Five lovely rooms, three en-suite, with tea/coffee makers. A charming sitting room with colour T.V. and log fire on chilly evenings. Breakfast is served overlooking the delightfully colourful garden. Evening meals are memorable. Every care is taken by the hosts to ensure your comfort and you can be sure of a warm welcome. Bosham is an original Saxon harbour village of great beauty.	£14.00	O	O	■
Mrs Mary Waller **Hatpins** **Bosham Lane** **Old Bosham** **Chichester PO18 8HG** **Tel: (0243) 572644** **OPEN: ALL YEAR** Nearest Road A.27 This unique property was designed and built by the Waller family. Located in the picturesque sailing village of Bosham it makes a lovely base for a relaxing holiday. Accommodation is in three very comfortable rooms, two with en-suite facilities. There is also a Victorian brass bed with French bed linen. English breakfast is taken in the conservarory overlooking the charming garden. A guests' T.V. lounge and garden are also available. The city of Chichester is nearby.	£13.00	O	■	■
Mrs C.M. Hartley **Easton House** **Chidham Lane** **Chidham** **Chichester PO18 8TF** **Tel: (0243) 572514** **OPEN: ALL YEAR** Nearest Road A.27 Easton House offers a peaceful and relaxed holiday. Built in 1580 this half timbered former Elizabethan farmhouse is situated on the Chidham peninsula of Chichester Harbour. Three delightful rooms, one with bath en-suite. Every modern comfort including tea/coffee making facilities in each room. A charming lounge and garden for guests' enjoyment. The house is within easy reach of Chichester, Portsmouth, The Downs & Goodwood. Delightful harbourside walks.	£10.50	O	■	O

O yes ■ no

	minimum per person	children taken	evening meals available	animals taken
Theo & Myrtle Hellier "Willowaye" **60 Manor Road** Selsey **Chichester PO20 0SF** Tel: (0243) 602472 **OPEN: ALL YEAR** — Nearest Road A.27/B.2145. A small attractive country house set in ¼ acre of garden. Located in the fishing village of Selsey, it is only half kilometer from the sea. Accommodation is in 3 rooms, with modern amenities, morning tea trays served. Within easy reach are Fisbourne Roman Palace, Chichester Cathedral, Goodwood racecourse.	£9.00	■	■	■
Mrs A.M. Blencowe The Old Rectory **Chidham** Nr.Chichester PO18 8TA Tel: (0243) 572088 **OPEN: ALL YEAR** — Nearest Road A.27. A friendly, relaxing stay is assured at the Old Rectory. This large, comfortable country house is set in its own pleasant garden in quiet surroundings. Four very pleasant rooms with modern amenities plus tea/coffee makers. A comfortable lounge and garden for guests' use. Also an outdoor swimming pool. The village has a Saxon church, a nice pub with good evening meals. The house is within walking distance of Chichester harbour. A lovely base for discovering this historic area with its many Roman sites and great houses, plus all the attractive villages along the coast.	£10.00	○	■	○
Mrs Marjorie Setchfield Chimneys **Ifield Wood** Nr. Crawley RH11 0LE Tel: (0293) 21312 **OPEN: ALL YEAR** — Nearest Road A.23. A charming Georgian country cottage dating back over 200 years, situated in a peaceful rural area. Three pleasant and comfortable rooms with modern amenities. Rooms have radio. Tea/coffee facilities are downstairs. A most comfortable and attractive lounge with colour T.V. Guests may use the garden. Very conveniently situated for Gatwick Airport - only 10 minutes away. Brighton, Redhill, Reigate are all easily accessible from here. A warm welcome awaits all visitors. The owners will take you or pick you up from Gatwick Airport free.	£17.50	○	■	■
Mr & Mrs K. Hambleton Southcroft Private Hotel **15 South Cliff Avenue** Meads **Eastbourne BN20 7AH** Tel: (0323) 29071 **OPEN: JAN-NOV** — Nearest Roads A.22 A.27. A pleasant hotel offering seven comfortable rooms with all modern facilities. Situated in a quiet residential area within easy reach of the beach, shopping centre and theatres. The area offers lovely walks through Friston Forest and the Cuckmere Valley. Plenty for everyone around here. Tea/coffee making facilities in all rooms. Licensed. Friendly atmosphere.	£12.00	○	○	■

○ yes ■ no

230

	Nearest Roads	minimum per person	children taken	evening meals available	animals taken
Denis & Jean Lloyd **Racehorse Cottage** **Nepcote** **Findon BN14 0SN** **Tel: (090671) 3783** **OPEN: ALL YEAR** **(EXCL. XMAS)**	Nearest Roads A.24 A.27 Comfortable cottage in historic and peaceful downland village sheltering under Cissbury Ring. An excellent base for exploring the South and South East. Ideal for walking and horse lovers. Four miles from the South coast and easily accessible by car, train or bus from Gatwick, Brighton, Arundel, Chichester and London. Two twin bedded rooms with downland views, tea making facilities and guests' own bathroom. Visitors have full use of house, sun room, garden and T.V. Evening meals with home-baking and garden produce by arrangement.	£10.00	O	O	O
Mrs M.T. Holden & Family **Cleavers Lyng** **Church Road** **Herstmonceux** **Hailsham BN27 1QJ** **Tel: (0323) 833131** **OPEN: FEB-DEC**	Nearest Road A.271 A delightful 16th century country hotel offering eight pleasant, comfortable rooms for visitors. Here one finds age blackened beams, inglenook fireplaces and a warm welcome. Situated adjacent to Herstmonceux Castle it is an ideal base for touring the county as there are many historic sites and houses, museums and galleries plus superb villages within a short drive.	£11.25	O	O	O
Christine & David Cooper **Bolebroke Mill** **Perry Hill** **Edenbridge Road** **Hartfield TN7 4JP** **Tel:(089277) 425** **OPEN: ALL YEAR**	Nearest Road A.22 An ancient watermill, recorded in Domesday Book 1086, still containing corn-grinding machinery, now charmingly converted into delightful accommodation of unspoil character. Secluded romantic woodland setting overlooking duck pond. 2 bedrooms both en-suite with T.V. tea/coffee making facilities. Groups of 4/6 have exclusive use of entire mill. Stairs are steep and unsuitable for disabled elderly people and young children. No single availability. Reductions for groups of 5-6.	£12.50	O	■	O
Mrs B.M. Chittenden **Little Lankhurst** **Stonestile Lane** **Nr. Westfield** **Hastings TN35 4PH** **Tel: (0424) 751138** **OPEN: ALL YEAR**	Nearest Road A.21 Little Lankhurst is a small country house set in 1 acre of garden and surrounded by lovely countryside. Accommodation is in two comfortable bedrooms with radio. Delightful views. One room has en-suite facilities plus patio. Guests have a separate entrance to their accommodation so they may come and go as they please. This makes a good base for touring. Battle and Hastings are within easy driving distance.	£10.50	■	O	■
Barbara Pettitt **Mattagami** **61 Franklynn Road** **Haywards Heath RH16 4DS** **Tel: (0444) 453506** **OPEN: JAN-OCT**	Nearest Road A.23 Personal service is offered here, in a private family home close to the shops and restaurants of Haywards Heath, handy for Gatwick Airport, by car or rail and surrounded by the beautiful Sussex countryside, Bluebell Railway, Sheffield Park etc. A choice fo five bedrooms with modern amenities, T.V. Children welcome. Full English breakfast served.	£12.50	O	■	■

O yes ■ no

		minimum per person	children taken	evening meals available	animals taken
Mrs M. Wilkin **Great Wapses Farm** **Wineham** **Henfield BN5 9BJ** **Tel: (0273) 492544** **OPEN: ALL YEAR**	Nearest Roads A.23 B.2116 An attractive Tudor/Georgian farmhouse set in rural and peaceful surroundings with horses, calves, chickens, etc. Offering three rooms all en-suite, one with 4-poster bed. T.V. and tea/coffee making facilities. Locally there are plenty of nice pubs and restaurants serving good food. Within easy reach of Brighton and Gatwick.	£14.00	O	■	O
Mrs J. Forbes **Little Oreham Farm** **Henfield BN5 9SB** **Nr. Woodsmill** **Tel: (0273) 492931** **OPEN: APR-OCT**	Nearest Road A beautiful 300 year-old farmhouse set in lovely gardens with roses and a dove cote in a quiet rural position. Five guest rooms are available, most with private bathrooms all well-equipped with radio, T.V. tea/coffee making facilities. Children catered for. Games room available. Many delightful walks. Nature reserve adjacent. Convenient for Brighton, Gatwick, Goodwood and Hickstead.	£15.00	O	O	O
Mrs Sylvia Fowler **Frylands** **Wineham** **Henfield BN5 9BP** **Tel: (0403)710214** **OPEN: ALL YEAR** **(EXCL. XMAS WEEK)**	Nearest Road A.272 A relaxed atmosphere is to be found at Frylands, a beautiful creeper-clad timber framed Tudor farmhouse in a secluded setting of farmland, woods and river. Three lovely bedrooms with modern amenities, private sitting room with T.V. and telephone, heated swimming pool and large garden. Fishing available. Children welcome. Evening meals optional-excellent food available locally. Nearest village 4 miles. Gatwick, Brighton 20 mins.	£9.00	O	■	■
Mr & Mrs John Walby **Winterpick Corner** **Winterpit Lane** **Mannings Heath** **Horsham RH13 6LZ** **Tel:(0403) 53882** **OPEN: ALL YEAR**	Nearest Roads A.281 A.279 A lovely tile hung country house set in secluded grounds overlooking St. Leonards Forest and golf course. Four charming and pretty rooms with modern amenities and tea/coffee makers. An attractive lounge with colour T.V. and a lovely garden with putting green and outdoor pool. A really super base with Gatwick Airport 15 minutes. Brighton 30 minutes. Marvellous countryside and delightful villages to discover. A very friendly welcome is extended to all guests.	£15.00	O	■	■
Mrs Kathleen Ticktum **Westlands** **Brighton Road** **Monks Gate RH13 6JD** **Nr. Horsham.** **Tel: (040376) 383** **OPEN: ALL YEAR**	Nearest Road A.281 A most pleasant large Victorian house maintained to a high standard with accommodation for guests in three bedrooms with modern amenities, radio/T.V. Residents' lounge. An acre of garden to stroll and relax in, mostly laid to lawns surrounded by trees and shrubs. Good access to Gatwick, Horsham, Brighton and the coast, Leonard's Lee gardens and Nymans.	£14.50	O	■	■

O yes ■ no

	Nearest Road	minimum per person	children taken	evening meals available	animals taken
Mrs J.M. McMullen **Little Broomhall** **Warnham** **Horsham RH12 3PA** **Tel: (0403) 64922** **OPEN: APR-OCT**	Nearest Road A.24 Little Broomhall is part of a large typical 17th century Sussex country house with open log fires, beams and panelling providing a welcoming atmosphere. Timber-framed drawing room dates from earlier period. An attractively laid-out garden with trees, shrubs and pond. Guests, limited to one or two at any time, receive personal attention and are made to feel part of the family.	£19.00	■	O	■
Mrs Elizabeth Cox **Glebe End** **Church Street** **Warnham RH12 3QW** **Tel: (0403) 61711** **OPEN: ALL YEAR**	Nearest Road A.24 Glebe End is a fascinating tile, wood and stone, part medieval house standing in its own beautifully tended walled garden. Located in a pretty Sussex village in the rolling countryside. The accommodation is in two pleasant bedrooms with own bathroom, radio, T.V. and tea/coffee making facilities. There is also a colour T.V. lounge with open fireplace and delightful Tudor dining room with log burning stove. Mrs. Cox is an excellent cook and meals are delicious. Tennis and golf nearby. Health centre/gymnasium-/sauna next door. 20 minutes from Gatwick without the noise.	£10.00	O	O	■
Mr & Mrs J.R. Field **Mill Farm** **Trotton** **Midhurst GU31 5EL** **Tel: (073081) 3080** **OPEN: ALL YEAR**	Nearest Road A.272 A pretty tile-hung Sussex farmhouse set in 15 acres of pasture with a large garden, offering delightful accommodation in four pleasant rooms. With superb views over the South Downs. Offering lovely walks, this is an ideal location to have a holiday base. Places of interest include Chichester Cathedral, Theatre and Roman Palace, Goodwood House and Racecourse, Arundel Castle, Petworth House, Cowdray Park and polo, attractive town of Midhurst just 3 miles away.	£10.00	O	O	■
Mr & Mrs I Marsden **The Almshouses** **Tillington GU28 0RA** **Nr. Petworth** **Tel: (0798) 43432** **OPEN: ALL YEAR**	Nearest Road A.272 The Almshouses built in 1840 have been converted into a comfortable lovely home with wonderful view where June and Ian look forward to welcome guests. Four bedrooms, most with private facilities, all with T.V./radio, tea/coffee making facilities. Electric blankets on request. Pay-phone available. One self-contained double suite for family/friends. Plenty of excellent inns and restaurants nearby. Good walking, swimming, riding and golf.	£10.00	O	■	O

O yes ■ no

		minimum per person	children taken	evening meals available	animals taken
John Rabone **Stringers Hall** **East Street** **Petworth GU28 0AB** **Tel: (0798) 43179** **OPEN: ALL YEAR**	Nearest Road A.283 Stringers Hall is a large and elegant listed building restored in 1654. It stands in the centre of Petworth in a large and lovely garden. Accommodation is in one single or twin room wtih private bathroom, tea/coffee making facilities. Lounge and garden available for guests. Petworth is rich in inns, restaurants, wine bars for dining out, also setting for numerous antique shops dealing in quality period pieces and collectors' items and three galleries.	£11.00	■	■	■
A.M. Steele **New House Farm** **Broadford Bridge Road** **West Chiltington** **Nr.Pulborough RH20 2LA** **Tel: (07983) 2215** **OPEN: JAN-NOV**	Nearest Road A.29 A lovely 15th century house with oak beams, and inglenook fireplaces situated in the village with a 12th century church. Four delightful rooms, two en-suite with modern amenities, T.V. and tea/coffee makers. A pleasant lounge with T.V. and a lovely garden. Evening meals by arrangement. Gatwick Airport is easily reached. Parham Gardens, W. Sussex golf course. Amberley Wild Brooks, Arundel Castle, Petworth House. Polo at Cowdray Park. Children over 10 years accepted.	£12.00	○	○	■
Mrs L.C. Shiner **Coldharbour Farm** **Sutton** **Pulborough RH20 1PR** **Tel: (07987) 200** **OPEN: MAR-OCT**	Nearest Road A.285 A delightful 16th century black and white farmhouse, offering a warm welcome and three very comfortable rooms for visitors, one with private bathroom. Sitting room with colour T.V. Situated in a beautiful, quiet position on the northside of the South Downs with pretty walks including the South Downs Way. A drive of 20 minutes to Chichester, Arundel, Petworth. Two miles from Bignor Roman Villa and twelve miles from the sea. Rates are for two people.	£22.00	○	○	■
Mr Ron Dellar **Western House** **113 Winchelsea Road** **Rye** **Tel: (0797) 223419** **OPEN: ALL YEAR**	Nearest Road A.259 The proprietors of this delightful 18th century house are artists and antique dealers, this being reflected throughout the premises. Three rooms available to guests, two with private bathroom, all with modern facilities, and interesting books. The house has its own grounds at the foot of historic, fascinating Rye, backs onto the Brede Valley. Children over 5, please. Ideal for country, sea or town.	£12.00	○	■	○

Why not use our fast efficient
RESERVATION SERVICE
to book all your accommodation.

234

	minimum per person	children taken	evening meals available	animals taken
Robert & Geraldine Bromley **Little Orchard House** **West Street** **Rye TN31 7ES** **Tel: (0797) 223831** **OPEN: ALL YEAR**	Nearest Roads A.259 A.268 Rye is the most complete small mediaeval hill town in Britain and this charming Georgian town house with its traditional walled garden is a delightful surprise right at the heart of the ancient town's cobbled streets. It is a perfect touring base for visiting the historic and beautiful South East with its castles, gardens and country houses. Guests are assured of the Bromley's personal attention and their generous country breakfasts are something of a social occasion, when the days plans are discussed. Three bedrooms, with colour T.V. and drinks tray, and each room has its own bathroom. Five outstanding restaurants within a few minutes stroll.	£17.00	■	■	■
Pauline Willis **Newbarn** **Wards Lane** **Wadhurst TN5 6MP** **Tel; (089288) 2042** **OPEN: ALL YEAR**	Nearest Road B.2099 A friendly and helpful family welcome is assured for guests at this 18th century farmhouse. Full of beams and with a inglenook fireplace, the house stands by a lovely old barn and twin out houses in secluded beautiful gardens and countryside, overlooking Bewl Water and trout fishery. Well placed for castles, gardens of West Sussex, the coast. London 55 minutes by rail from Wadhurst.	£12.50	○	■	○
Mr & Mrs R.J. Price **Wolsey Hotel** **179-181 Brighton Road** **Worthing BN11 2EX** **Tel: (0903) 36149** **OPEN: ALL YEAR**	Nearest Roads A.27 A.259 A very pleasant and well modernised Victorian house offering a warm welcome and good accommodation in fourteen comfortable rooms, all with modern amenities, tea/coffee makers and televisions. This friendly, family run hotel has a happy and relaxed atmosphere. A good sized lounge with colour T.V. and large garden. Uninterrupted sea views from the house. It is only half a mile form the town centre. Also close to the aquarena and bowling greens. Mr & Mrs Price do everything they can to ensure a happy stay for visitors.	£13.50	○	○	○

○ yes ■ no

ADVANCE RESERVATIONS

Don't be disappointed. Book ahead.
Use our fast efficient
RESERVATION SERVICE

WARWICKSHIRE

This is the heart of England. Shakespeare's country which millions of people have visited over the centuries to pay tribute to his memory at his birthplace in Stratford-on-Avon, and to walk the streets of the villages and towns he knew and loved. But it is a county of contrasts and contradictions. Here rural tranquility surrounds industrial towns, there are working canals and meandering rivers, mediaeval castles and Regency towns, such as the lovely Leamington Spa.

The Romans left their mark here, building great roads on their march through England and we still follow those same roads today, using the same names - Watling Street, Icknield Way and Fosse Way. But the Romans found little of value like silver or lead so they used the county simply as a passage to other areas, as folk did before and after. When the Romans left Britain in the 4th century other invaders came and went each leaving a trace of their visit. Several kingdoms were created, one of them being the Kingdom of Mercia which, in the fullness of time, became Warwickshire, King Offa of Mercia left us his own very particular mark - a coin which bore the imprint of his likeness his "pen" and this became our penny! Another Earl of Mercia, Leofric, was begged by his wife to repeal a tax he had levied upon the people, but he was a hard man and challenged her to ride naked through the streets of Coventry as the price of her request. Knowning that her long hair would cover her nakedness, the Lady Godiva made the ride and the people, who loved her, stayed indoors with closed windows - with one exception - Peeping Tom. She is still remembered and blessed for her generosity to the poor and to the religious foundations of the time. This was the beginning of the charming little village churches which are scattered across the county. Each one of these is a historical record in itself through its architectural form, brasses and monuments. The Parish Church of St. Mary in Warwick has some wonderful effigies in the Beauchamp Chapel dating from 1443. This chapel was built by the family who built the fortified Castle of Warwick, standing high on a rock above the town, where defence works had stood from earliest times. Canaletto painted a picture of the Castle in all its glory. Kenilworth Castle - now a majestic ruin - was built in the 12th century by Geoffrey de Clinton, who was Treasurer to Henry I.

Developement of Industry

Warwickshire, though blessed with fine rivers, is landlocked, and it was due to the ingenuity of James Brindley, at the behest of the Duke of Bridgewater, that the canal system was built in order to bring coal to the industrial towns and carry their products back to the sea ports from where they were sent all around the world.

The canal barges, "narrow boats", are still in use and the people who live in them and work the canal trade are a fascinating part of the living traditions linking them to the industrial revolution. One of the most colourful traditions is the charming paintings of roses and castles with which they decorate the boats and water cans, etc. With shining brass, painted wood-work and snowy white lace and linens, their cabin homes are quite delightful.

Coventry has long enjoyed a reputation as a thriving and prosperous city, being noted for its weaving of silks and ribbons; learned from the refugee Hugenots. But, inevitably, progress brought powered looms and the beginning of the factory based industries, making watches among other things. Then when the age of mechanised travel arrived, Coventry was the foremost in manufacturing bicycles and cars which became the mainstay of the city. Unhappily, the city of Coventry suffered grievously from aerial bombardment in the war and lost innumerable ancient and treasured buildings, including the cathedral - however, now a magnificent new Cathedral stands beside the shell of the old and is already world renowned for its architecture. So the link continues - from the 8th century when the King of Mercia gave land for a monastery up to the present time.

Heritage

The 15th, 16th and 17th centuries were the heyday of fine building and some of the most gracious and lovely homes to be seen in the County date back to that era. Compton Wynyates, for example, is built of rosy pink bricks, is battlemented and moated, has twisted chimney stacks, a yew garden, and lies amongst green hills presenting an unforgettable, romantic pictures of a perfect Tudor House.

WARWICKSHIRE GAZETEER

Areas of Outstanding Natural Beauty.
The Edge Hills.

Historic Houses and Castles

Arbury Hall -- Nuneaton
 18th century Gothic mansion -- made famous by George Elliot as øheverel Manor -- paintings, period funishings, etc.

Compton Wynyates
 15th century -- famous Tudor House -- pink brick, twisted chimneys battlemented walls. Interior almost untouched -- period furnishing.

Coughton Court -- Alcester.
 15th century -- Elizabethan half-timbered wings. Holds Jacobite relics.

Harvard House -- Stratford-on-Avon
 16th century -- home of mother of John Harvard, University Founder.

Hornington Hall -- Shipston-on-Stour
 17th century with fine 18th century plasterwork.

Packwood House -- Hockley Heath
 Tudor timber framed house -- 17th century additions. Famous yew garden.

Ragley Hall   Aloootor
 17th century Palladian -- magnificent house with fine collection of porcelain, paintings, furniture etc. and a valuable library.

Shakespeare's Birthplace Trust Properties -- Stratford-upon-Avon

 Anne Hathaway's Cottage -- Shottery
 The thatched cottage home of Anne Hathaway.

Hall's Croft. Old Town
 Tudor house where Shakespeare's daughter Susanna lived.

Mary Arden's House -- Wilmcote
 Tudor farmhouse with dovecote. Home of Shakespeare's mother.

New Place -- Chapel Street
 Shakespeare's last home -- the foundations of this house are preserved in Elizabethan garden.

Birthplace of Shakespeare -- Henley Street
 Many rare Shakespeare relics exhibited in this half timbered house.

Lord Leycester Hospital -- Warwick
 16th century timber framed group around courtyard -- hospital for oor persons in the mediaeval guilds.

Upton House -- Edge Hill
 Dating from James II reign -- contains Brussels Tapestries, Sevres porcelain, Chelsea Figurines, 18th century furniture and other works of art, including old Masters.

Warwick Castle -- Warwick
 Splendid mediaeval castle -- site was originally fortified more than a thousand, years ago. Present castle 14th century. Armoury.

Cathedrals and Churches

Astley (St. Mary the Virgin)
 17th century -- has remains of 14th century collegiate church. 15th century painted stalls.

Beaudesert (St. Nicholas)
 Norman with fine arches in chancel.

Brailes (St. George)
 15th century -- decorated nave and aisles -- 14th century font, 15th century carved oak chest.

Compton Wynyates
Church of Restoration period having painted ceiling.

Lapworth (St. Mary)
13th and 14th century -- steeple and north aisle connected by passage.

Preston-on-Stour (The Blessed Virgin Mary).
18th century. Gilded ceiling, 17th century glass.

Tredington (St. Gregory)
Saxon walls in nave -- largely 14th century, 17th century pulpit. Fine spire.

Warwick (St. Mary)
15th century Beauchamp Chapel, vaulted choir, some 17th century Gothic.

Wooton Wawen (St. Peter)
Saxon, with remanants of mediaeval wall painting. 15th century screens and pulpit: Small 17th century chained library.

Museums and Galleries

The Royal Shakespeare Theatre Picture Gallery -- Stratford-upon-Avon.
Original designs and paintings, portraits of famous actors, etc.

Motor Museum -- Stratford-upon-Avon
Collection of cars, racing, vintage, exotic, replica of 1930 garage. Fashions etc. of 20's.

Leamington Spa Art Gallery & Museum -- Leamington Spa.
Dutch and Flemish masters, English 20th century oils and watercolours, pottery and porcelain collection, also glass.

Nuneaton Museum and Art Gallery -- Nuneaton
Archeology, geology, anthropology, ethnography, local history, George Elliot memorabilia.

St. John's House -- Warwick
Bygones, period costumes and furniture of district. Military museum.

Warwickshire Museum -- Warwick
Geology, archeology, history of Warwickshire. Wild life of area.

Historic Monuments

Kenilworth Castle -- Kenilworth
Majestic sandstone castle ruins.

WARWICKSHIRE
Recommended roadside restaurants

Warwickshire

	minimum per person	children taken	evening meals available	animals taken
Mr. D. Mason **Fosbroke House** **4 High Stree** **Bidford on Avon** **B50 4BU** **Tel: (0789) 772327** **OPEN: ALL YEAR** Nearest Road A.439 A warm welcome and friendly atmosphere awaits you at this enchanting Georgian country house, in a historic riverside village. Four nicely furnished rooms with modern amenities, radio, colour T.V., tea/coffee making facilities, central heating. Wide choice of breakfast menu; evening meal by arrangement served in elegant dining room. Licensed. Lovely old English garden. Evesham and Stratford 6 miles.	£10.00	■	○	■
Francis & Doreen Bromilow **Woodside** **Langley Road** **Claverdon CV35 8PJ** **Tel: (092684) 2446** **OPEN: ALL YEAR** Nearest Road B.4095 Woodside is a quiet and secluded family home where guests receive a warm and friendly reception. The house is set in a large, attractive wooded garden strewn with hundreds of daffodils. Offering four comfortable bedrooms all with modern amenities and tea/coffee making facilities some with T.V. The pleasant colour T.V. lounge/dining room with open log burning fireplace is furnished with antique and period pieces. Delicious home cooking is a speciality.	£9.00	○	○	○
Charles & **Barbara Robinson** **Northanger House** **35 Westminster Road** **Coventry CV1 3GB** **Tel: (0203) 26780** **OPEN: ALL YEAR** Nearest Roads M.6 A.45 A very pleasant house offering nine most comfortable rooms with modern facilities. A warm welcome from the hospitable proprietors who offer coffee and tea at all times without charge. Within five minutes walk of the marvellous city centre with its cathedral, museums and galleries. There are a tremendous number of places of interest to visit around here.	£9.50	○	■	○
Mr F. Garcia & Mr C. Eades **Ashleigh House** **Whitley Hill** **Henley-in-Arden** **B95 5DL** **Tel: (05642) 2315** **OPEN: ALL YEAR** Nearest Road A.34 A spacious and elegant Edwardian house set in its own lovely grounds with magnificent views towards the Cotswold Hills. Beautifully decorated with many antiques. There are 11 delightful rooms, 9 with bath en-suite and televisions. An attractive lounge with colour T.V. and a garden for guests to enjoy. Excellent breakfast. Very convenient for Stratford on Avon - only 7 miles, the National Exhibition Centre and numerous other attractions.	£15.00	○	■	○
Mrs Christopher Cooper **Impsley Farm** **Henley-in-Arden** **B45 5QH** **Tel: (05642) 2300** **OPEN: ALL YEAR** Nearest Road A.34 Ancient, heavily-timbered, surrounded by the fields of leafy Warwichshire, Impsley Farm is totally peaceful, yet offers easy access to Warwich, Stratford, The Cotswold and the National Exhibition Centre. Modern comforts are concealed within and have not spoiled the character of this delightful old house. Luxuriously appointed accommodation is in four rooms, all en-suite, which can become 2 self catering flats if preferred. A timbered rickyard cottage ajoining the house sleeps 4/6. Central heating electric blankets and T.V. Large garden.	£12.50	○	■	■

○ yes ■ no

	minimum per person	children taken	evening meals available	animals taken
Mrs E. Mitchell **Ferndale Guest House** **45 Priory Road** **Kenilworth CV8 1LL** **Tel: (0926) 53214** **OPEN: ALL YEAR** Nearest Road A.46 Situated in a tree lined road, near to the centre of town, this excellent guest house offers seven comfortable rooms with modern amenities. In this large Victorian house you can be assured of a warm welcome. Many places of great interest around here including the Royal Agricultural Show Grounds, Stratford on Avon and Coventry. German spoken.	£10.00	O	■	■
Deborah Lea **Crandon House** **Avon Dassett** **Leamington Spa CV33 0AA** **Tel: (029577) 652** **OPEN: ALL YEAR** Nearest Road A.41 Crandon House is a comfortable well equiped farmhouse standing in 20 acres of beautiful countryside. Accommodation is in three rooms with modern amenities, and T.V. A colour T.V. lounge and garden are also available. The small working farm has cows, sheep and poultry which provide the fresh produce used in the excellent farmhouse fare	£10.00	O	O	O
Sue Hutsby **Nolands Farm** **Oxhill CV35 0RJ** **Tel: (0926) 640309** **OPEN: JAN-NOV** Nearest Road A.422 A delightful period farmhouse situated in a tranquil valley. All bedrooms in annex over looking quiet stableyard. Two bedrooms en-suite and colour T.V. One luxury cottage with every facility. Use of drawing-room and large open plan garden with croquet, well-stocked lake, woods, wildlife, family ponies and pets. Dinner includes home-grown pheasant, duck and vegetables.	£7.00	O	O	■
Pamela Barnacle **Ambleside Guest House** **41 Grove Road** **Stratford on Avon** **CV37 6PB** **Tel: (0789) 297239/295670** **OPEN: ALL YEAR** Nearest Roads A.439 A.34 A small homely guest house with seven pleasant rooms - two have private showers. All rooms have the usual modern amenities including tea/coffee makers and colour T.V. Situated opposite a park, Ambleside is a good base for visitors to this historic town. The hosts Stratfordians, Ron and Pam are very happy to help visitors with tour planning.	£9.50	O	■	O
Mr & Mrs I. Castelli **Minola Guest House** **25 Evesham Place** **Stratford upon Avon** **CV37 6HT** **Tel: (0789) 293573** **OPEN: ALL YEAR** Nearest Road A.439 A comfortable house with a relaxed atmosphere offering good accommodation and modern amenities. Straford offers a myriad of delights for the visitor including the Royal Shakespeare Theatre, set by the River Avon this makes a lovely place for a picnic lunch or early evening meal before the performance. Cots are provided. Italian and French spoken.	£10.00	O	■	■

O yes ■ no

	minimum per person	children taken	evening meals available	animals taken
Mr John Monk **Hunters Moon Guest House** 150 Alcester Road Stratford upon Avon CV37 9DR Tel: (0789) 292888 OPEN: ALL YEAR Nearest Road A.422 This pleasant guest house offers ten comfortable rooms with modern facilities, five rooms are en-suite, all have tea/coffee makers and hair dryers. It has a very good reputation built up over 25 years. Situated close to Anne Hathaways Cottage it is an ideal base for touring Stratford and the surrounding area. Will collect from station.	£10.00	○	■	○
Meg Morton **Grove Farm** Ettington Nr.Stratford-upon-Avon CV37 7NX Tel: (0789) 740228 OPEN: ALL YEAR Nearest Road A.422 A very warm and friendly welcome await guests at Grove Farm. This lovely old house with its flag-stoned kitchen, log burning fires and antiques, is a super place for a holiday. The three comfortable spacious bedrooms all have private facilities, T.V. and tea/coffee making facilities and spectacular views over the countryside. There are lovely walks through the farm and woodland. Plenty of fallow and roe deer, muntjac and other wildlife are found in the woods. On the farm are chickens, Labrador dog and an old horse in the orchard.	£9.00	○	■	○
Mr & Mrs P.W Savage **Kawartha Guest House** 39 Grove Road Stratford-upon-Avon CV37 6PB Tel: (0789) 204469 OPEN: ALL YEAR (EXCL. XMAS) Nearest Road A.439 An excellent house offering very comfortable accommodation in six pleasant rooms with modern facilities. Stratford offers so much in the way of historic houses and, of course, the superb theatre. They do not do evening meals but Mrs Savage's friend owns a 400 year pub just five minutes away, with super food.	£10.00	○	■	○
Jill & Ernie Coulson **"Hardwick House"** 1 Avenue Road Stratford-upon-Avon CV37 6UY Tel: (0789) 204307 OPEN: ALL YEAR (EXCL. XMAS) Nearest Road A.46 You will be welcomed to Hardwick House, an impressive Victorian home in a quiet area, yet just five minutes walk to the town centre and the theatre. A choice of fourteen spacious and comfortable bedrooms, many with private facilities, all with T.V. and tea/coffee making facilities. Residents' lounge, parking space. Enjoy its friendly atmosphere and home-cooked breakfasts. Golf, swimming nearby.	£11.50	○	■	■
Pauline Rush **Parkfield Guest House** 3 Broad Walk Stratford-upon-Avon CV37 6HS Tel: (0789) 293313 OPEN: ALL YEAR Nearest Road A.439 An attractive Victorian house, in a quiet situation just 5 minutes walk to the town centre and the Royal Shakespeare Theatre. Ideally situated for touring the Cotswold, Warwick Castle etc. Seven spacious and comfortable rooms, all with full central heating, colour T.V. and tea/coffee making facilities. Lots of tourist information. Guests can be collected from the station.	£10.00	○	■	○

○ yes ■ no

	minimum per person	children taken	evening meals available	animals taken
Mr & Mrs W.J. Giles **Craig House** **69 Shipston Road** **Stratford-upon-Avon** **CV37 7LW** **Tel: (0789) 297473** **OPEN: ALL YEAR** **(EXCL. XMAS)** Nearest Road A.34 A most hospitable house offering five excellent rooms with comfortable accommodation and modern amenities. A very good base for visiting this most historic town with its superb theatre and Shakespeare connections. Many museums and galleries in the area and lovely countryside. Cots and highchairs provided. Warm welcome assured.	£9.00	O	■	■
Patricia Ann Andrews **The Croft** **49 Shipston Road** **Stratford-upon-Avon** **CV37 7LN** **Tel: (0789) 293419** **OPEN: ALL YEAR** Nearest Road A.34 The Croft is a small family run guest house, situated about 200 yards from the Clopton Bridge spanning the River Avon. Nine pleasant rooms with modern amenities, some en-suite. Rooms have T.V. and tea/coffee making facilities. Close to the theatre, gardens, river boats and shopping centre. This is a good base for touring Warwick and Coventry, the Cotswold and numerous historic houses.	£11.00	O	O	O
Mrs M.S. Spencer **Moonraker House** **40 Alcester Road** **Stratford-on-Avon** **CV37 9DB** **Tel: (0789) 67115** **OPEN: ALL YEAR** Nearest Road A.422 A charming house offering home-from-home atmosphere with superb facilities in fifteen rooms all with bath en-suite. Centrally heated, tea/coffee makers, colour T.V. and hair dryers. Perfect centre for exploring the Cotswolds, Vale of Evesham, Warwick and Kenilworth Castles, Blenheim Palace and Shakespeare's country. Rates are for two people.	£20.00	O	■	O
Keith & June Childs **All Seasons** **51 Grove Road** **Stratford-upon-Avon** **CV37 6PB** **Tel: (0789) 293404** **OPEN: ALL YEAR** Nearest Road A.439 A warm welcome awaits guest to this modernised spacious Victorian house. Offering guests a choice of five comfortable rooms with modern amenities and tea/coffee making facilities. A residents' colour T.V. lounge is also available throughout the day. Located close to the town centre with good access for rail and coach stations. The Shakespeare Centre and Theatre are also close by. This makes a good base from which to tour this historic area.	£9.00	O	■	O
Philip & Jean Evans **Sequoia House Hotel** **51 Shipston Road** **Stratford-upon-Avon** **CV37 7LN** **Tel: (0789) 68852** **OPEN: ALL YEAR** Nearest Road A.34 Superbly situated across the river Avon from the theatre, recently renovated to a high standard, Sequoia House offers charmingly appointed accommodation with friendly personal attention. Most bedrooms have private facilities. All have colour T.V., tea/coffee making facilities. Large car park and delightful gardens in which stands the Sequoia tree. Short garden walk to Shakespeare Theatre, riverside gardens, shops and leisure centre.	£12.50	O	O	O

O yes ■ no

		minimum per person	children taken	evening meals available	animals taken
Mrs A. Cross **Lemarquand** **186 Evesham Road** **Stratford-upon-Avon** **CV37 9BS** **Tel: (0789) 204164** **OPEN: ALL YEAR**	Nearest Road A.439 A friendly welcome and home-from-home atmosphere await you in this modern, private, detached house. Accommodation is in 2 rooms with modern amenities. Within easy walking distance of Anne Hathaway's Cottage. Warwick Castle - 9 miles. National Exhibition Centre 20 mins by car.	£8.00	O	■	O
Mrs Betty Walker **"The Riding"** **254 Alcester Road** **Stratford-upon-Avon** **CV37 5JQ** **Tel: (0789) 66015** **OPEN: JAN-NOV**	Nearest Road A.422 The Riding is a welcoming modern detached home with pleasant lawned gardens and good parking within a mile of the town centre. Four bedrooms are available with modern amenities, radio/T.V., lounge and garden for guests use. English or continental breakfast served. Children over 8 welcome. Anne Hathaway's cottage within walking distance.	£10.00	O	■	■
Mrs Marian J. Walters **Church Farm** **Dorsington** **Stratford-on-Avon** **CV37 8AX** **Tel: (0789) 720471** **OPEN: ALL YEAR**	Nearest Road A.439 A warm, friendly welcome await you at this Georgian farmhouse with its open fires and central heating, situated in beautiful countryside within easy driving distance of Stratford-on-Avon, Warwick, the Cotswolds and the Vale of Evesham. Guests are free to explore the farm with its cattle and horses. Three rooms are available with modern amenities and children are well provided for. Good home cooking using fresh produce.	£11.00	O	O	■
Mrs I. Vernon Miller **Alderminster Farm** **Alderminster** **Stratford-upon-Avon** **CV37 8BP** **Tel: (078987) 296** **OPEN: ALL YEAR**	Nearest Road A.34 Alderminster farmhouse is an attractive Georgian house standing on a 250 acre sheep/arable farm. It is located in an attractive, rural setting overlooking the river Stour. Accommodation is in three rooms with modern amenities T.V. and a residents' T.V. lounge. This makes a pleasant base for a touring holiday as Stratford-upon-Avon is only 3 miles and Shipston-on-Stour 6 miles away. An enjoyable and restful spot for a lovely base.	£12.00	O	■	O
Mrs Diane Smith **The White House** **Kings Lane** **Bishopton** **Stratford-on-Avon** **CV37 0RD** **Tel:(0789) 294296** **OPEN: APR-OCT**	Nearest Road A.34 An elegant, welcoming Edwardian home, in a rural setting yet only 1½ miles from the centre of Stratford upon Avon. Laura Ashley interior. Four attractive bedrooms all ensuite or private facilities, T.V. and tea/coffee making facilities. Breakfast to suit both the hearty and the healthy appetite, using free range eggs, local honey etc. Pre-theatre meals by arrangement.	£10.00	■	O	O

O yes ■ no

	minimum per person	children taken	evening meals available	animals taken
Mrs Rebecca Mawle **Lower Farm Barn** **Great Wolford** **Shipston-on-Stour** **CV36 5NG** **Tel: (0608) 74435** **OPEN: MAR-OCT** Nearest Road A.429 This lovely 100 year old converted barn stands in the small, peaceful Warwickshire village of Great Wolford. The property retains much of its original form including exposed beams and ancient stone work. Now tastefully modernised, it makes a very comfortable home. The accommodation is in two beautifully furnished double rooms, one en-suite.	£9.00	O	■	O
A. & T.W. Pendleton **Church Farm** **Tysoe** **Warwick CU35 0SF** **Tel: (029588) 385** **OPEN: ALL YEAR** Nearest Road A.422 Tysoe village is mainly built of local stone and nestles at the foot of Edge Hill. A family run farm. This most attractive house, built in 1617, offers very comfortable accommodation in five pretty rooms with modern amenities and tea making facilities. A guest lounge with colour T.V. Wonderful evening meals using home-grown produce and excellent value too. Superbly situated in a delightful old village, it is a marvellous base for touring the Cotswold. Shakespear's country, Oxford, Stratford upon Avon and Warwick Castle. Wonderful walks in the vicinity of the house.	£7.50	O	O	O
Carolyn Howard **Willowbrook House** **Lighthorne Road** **Kineton CV35 0JL** **Tel: (0926) 640475** **OPEN: MAR-OCT** Nearest Road A.41 Willowbrook is a peaceful house with charming views, standing in 4 acres of garden and paddocks. It has two attractive twin rooms with modern amenities and tea/coffee makers. Guests have own very comfortable sitting room with colour T.V. and cosy log fire for chilly evenings. Imaginative evening meals available on request using own produce. Excellent base for Stratford, Warwick and the Cotswold villages. Children very welcome. Mrs Howard makes all her guests most welcome.	£8.50	O	O	O

O yes ■ no

Don't be disappointed. Book ahead.
Use our fast efficient
RESERVATION SERVICE
Reservation forms & Reservation Bureau
Be sure of your accommodation
Book Now!!
01-370 7099 *Call us on* **01-370 7099**

245

WILTSHIRE

Wiltshire is a county of rolling chalk downs, small towns, charming villages, fine churches and great country houses. It is a pastoral landscape of lush grasslands dappled with the chasing shadows of summer clouds and crowned with islands of beech trees. The expanse of Salisbury Plain is divided by the beautiful valleys of Nadder, Wylye, Ebble and Avon, each with a string of villages characterised by ancient churches and thatched cottages. At its centre stands the historic town of Salisbury dominated by the soaring tower and spire of the 13th century cathedral. Built in a period of only 38 years it is an unrivalled classic of pure early English architecture. Ancient trackways cross the landscape clinging to the chalk escarpments along which King Alfred marched to rout the forces of the invading Danes near Westbury. The site is identified by the giant form of a white horse carved in the chalk hillside.

Prehistoric Wiltshire

No other county is so rich in archaeological sites. The stark forms of ancient hill forts and long barrows stand on the skyline as evidence of the occupation of the chalk uplands by early man. Many of these prehistoric monuments are at once magnificent and mysterious. The massive stone arches and monoliths of Stonehenge have long been regarded as the centre of Celtic ritual. Some claim the Druid priests were responsible for its construction but it almost certainly pre-dates them. It was built over a period of five hundred years, some of the stones were transported a great distance, from north Wales. There are extraordinary astronomical alignments most notably at midsummer sunrise. Recent suggestions are that the monument acted as a huge stone calendar and enabled the priesthood to predict eclipses of the moon and sun. Another ritual monument at Avebury is equally mysterious and the small village is completely encircled by standing stones and the massive bank and ditch earthwork. Throughout the county there are iron age hill forts and burial mounds, many of which have been excavated and offer indications of a high degree of social organisation. Bush Barrow for example, yielded fine bronze and gold daggers and a stone sceptre-head similar to one found at Mycenae in Greece. Others, like the huge man made hill at Silbury remain a mystery.

Villages, Churches and Towns

Just outside Salisbury is the deserted city of Old Sarum. Although deserted in favour of modern Salisbury in the 13th century, this "rotten borough" nevertheless managed to regularly return two M.P.'s to Parliament, including the famous statesman William Pitt, until the passing of the Reform Bill in 1832. The modern city came into being with the laying of the foundation stone of the Cathedral in 1220. Supported by the prosperous wool trade the place grew rapidly and the streets around the Close form a superb setting. It is flanked by a variety of brick and stone buildings, some with elegant Georgian facades, some picturesquely gabled. Nearby there are mediaeval guildhalls, almshouses, coaching inns and the fine houses of wool merchants clustered in the historic city centre. On a smaller scale the countyholds many delightful villages. One of the most attractive is the unspoilt village of Lacock where the twisting steets hold examples of buildings ranging from mediaeval half timbered houses to Tudor and Georgian. The 13th century Abbey was the home of Fox Talbot, a pioneer of early photography whose work is commemorated in the Abbey museum. Nearby, Castle Coombe was a cloth weaving centre with typical stone cottages clustered around the market cross and perpendicular style church. To the west of the county the Avon flows through a deep wooded valley of great beauty passing through the fascinating old town of Bradford on Avon, which boasts many splendid buildings of mellow Bath stone. The most notable is the church of St. Lawerence, which is a rare example of an almost perfect Saxon church, dating from around 900. Other Saxon work can be seen in the pretty villages of Britford and Burcombe. There is an interesting Saxon sculpture at Codford St. Peter and Malmesbury Abbey offers some fine Norman carvings which are nothing short of works of art. The village of Farley can boast an unusual brick church probably designed by Sir Christopher Wren and Rodbourne has stained glass designed in the 1870's by William Morris. In this county the list of notable churches is even longer than the list of pleasing villages.

WILTSHIRE GAZETEER

Areas of Outstanding Natural Beauty.
The Cotswolds and the North Wessex Downs.

Historic Houses and Castles

Corsham Court -- Chippenham
16th and 17th centuries from Elizabethan and Georgian periods. 18th century furniture, British, Flemish and Italian Old Masters, Gardens by Capability Brown.

Great Chalfield Manor -- Melksham
15th century manor house -- moated.

Church House -- Salisbury
15th century house.

Chalcot House -- Westbury
17th century small house in Palladian manner.

Lacock Abbey -- Nr. Chippenham
13th century abbey. In 1540 converted into house -- 18th century alterations. Mediaevel cloisters andbrewery.

Longleat House. -- Warminster
16th century -- early Renaissance, alterations in early 1800s. 19th century Italian Renaissance decorations. Splendid state rooms, pictures, books, furniture. Victorian kitchens -- game reserve.

Littlecote -- Nr. Hungerford
15th century Tudor manor. Panelled rooms, moulded plaster ceilings.

Luckington Court -- Luckington
Queen Anne for the most part -- fine ancient buildings.

Malmesbury House -- Salisbury
Queen Ann house -- part 14th century. Rococo plasterwork.

Newhouse -- Redlynch
17th century brick Jocobean rinity house -- two Georgian wings.

Phillips House -- Dinton
1816 Classical house.

Sheldon Manor -- Chippenham
13th century porch & 15th century chapel in this Plantagenet manor.

Stourhead -- Stourton
18th century Palladian house with famed landscape gardens.

Westwoood Manor -- Bradford-on-Avon
15th century manor house -- alterations in 16th & 17th centuries.

Wardour Castle -- Tisbury
18th century house in Palladian manner.

Wilton House -- Salisbury
17th century -- work of Inigo Jones and later of James Wyatt in 1810. Paintings, Kent and Chippendale funiture.

Avebury Manor -- Nr. Malborough
Elizabethan Manor house -- beautiful plasterwork, panelling and furniture. Gardens with topiary.

Bowood -- Calne
18th century -- work of several famous architects. Gardens by Capability Brown -- famous beechwoods. Doric Temple. Cascade.

Mompesson House -- Salisbury
Queen Anne town house -- Georgian plasterwork.

Cathedrals and Churches

Salisbury Cathedral
  13th century -- decorated tower with stone spire. Part of original stone pulpitum is perserved. Beautiful large decorated cloisters. Exterior mostly early English.

Salisbury (St. Thomas of Canterbury)
  15thcentury rebuilding -- 12th century font, 14th & 15th century glass, 17th century monuments. 'Doom' painting over chancel and murals in south chapel.

Amesbury (St. Mary & St. Melor)
  13th century -- refashioned 15th and restored in 19th century. Splendid timber roofs, stone vaulting over chapel of north transept, mediaeval painted glass, 15th century screen, Norman font.

Bishops Cannings (St. Mary the Virgin)
  13th -- 15th centuries. Fine arcading in transept -- fine porch doorway -- 17th century almsbox, Jacobean Holy table.

Bradford-on-Avon (St. Lawerence)
  Best known of all Saxon churches in England.

Cricklade (St. Sampson)
  12th to 16th century. Tudor central tower vault, 15th century chapel.

Inglesham (St. John the Baptist)
  Mediaeval wall paintings, high pews, clear glass, remains of painted screens.

Malmesbury (St. Mary)
  Norman -- 12th century arcades, refashioning in 14th century with clerestory, 15th century stone pulpitum added. Fine sculpture.

Tisbury (St. John the Baptist)
  14th -- 15th centuries. 15th -- 17th century roofing to nave & aisles. Two storeyed porch and chancel.

Potterne (St. Mary)
  13th, 14th, 15th centuries. Inscribed Norman tub font. Wooden pulpit.

Museums and Galleries

Salisbury and South Wiltshire Museum -- Salisbury
  Collections showing history of the area in all periods. Models of Stonehenge and Old Sarum -- archeologically important collection.

Devizes Museum -- Devizes
  Unique archeological and geological collections, including Sir Richard Colt-Hoare's Stourhead collection of prehistoric material.

Alexander Keiller Museum -- Avebury
  Collection of items from the Neolithic and Bronze ages and from excavations in district.

Athelstan Museum -- Malmesbury
  Collection of articles referring to the town -- household, coin, etc.

Bedwyn Stone Museum -- Great Bedwyn
  Open-air museum showing where Stonehenge was carved.

Lydiard Park - Lydiard Tregoze
  Parish church of St. Mary and a splendid Georgian mansion standing in park -- memorials -- also permanent and travelling exhibitions.

Borough of Thamesdown Museum and Art Gallery -- Swindon
  Natural History and Geology of Wiltshire, Bygones, coins, etc. 20th century British art and ceramic collection.

Great Western Railway Museum -- Swindon
  Historic locomotives.

Historic Monuments

Stonehenge -- Nr. Amesbury
Prehistoric monument -- encircling bank and ditch and Augrey holes are Neolithic. Stone circles possibly early Bronze age.

Avebury
Relics of enormous circular gathering place B.C. 2700 -- 1700.

Old Sarum -- Nr. Salisbury
Possibly first Iron age camp, later Roman area, then Norman castle.

Silbury Hill -- Nr. Avebury
Mound -- conical in shape -- probably a memorial c.3000-2000 B.C.

Windmill Hill -- Nr. Avebury
Causewayed camp c. 3000-2300 B.C.

Bratton Camp & White Horse -- Bratton
Hill fort standing above White Horse.

West Kennet Long Barrow
Burial place c. 4000-2500 B.C.

Ludgershall Castle -- Ludgershall
Motte and bailey of Norman castle, earthworks, also flint walling from later castle.

WILTSHIRE
Recommended roadside restaurants

039	A303	West Knoyle Nr Mere, Wilts 20 miles west of Amesbury 4 miles east of Mere
079	A303	Chicklade Nr Hindon, Wilts 7 miles east of Mere
244	A30	Winterslow, Wilts 5 miles north east of Salisbury
273	A350	Melksham Wiltshire 1 mile south of Melksham

Wiltshire

Column headers (diagonal):
- minimum per person
- children taken
- evening meals available
- animals taken

		minimum per person	children taken	evening meals available	animals taken
Major & Mrs P.B. Hartland **2 Cove House** **Ashton Keynes SN6 6NS** **Tel: (0285) 861221** **OPEN: ALL YEAR**	Nearest Road A.419 Peter and Elizabeth will welcome you warmly to their historic Cotswold manor house with invitation to dinner at the family table. The house, containing antiques and paintings, stands in 1½ acres of secluded garden and offers accommodation in five single or double bedrooms, most with private facilities. Good home cooking using seasonal produce from the garden. Fishing, windsurfing, sailing and riding close by and your hosts are enthusiastic tennis and squash players, pleased to arrange a game.	£10.00	O	O	O
Dr & Mrs John Dilley **Chilvester Hill House** **Calne SN11 0LP** **Tel: (0249) 813981/815785** **OPEN: ALL YEAR**	Nearest Road A.4 A delightful Georgian country house elegantly furnished with many antiques and paintings. This superb house offers three delightful rooms with modern amenities, all overlooking the Downs. Each room offers television and private bathroom. They accept prior bookings ONLY. It is an excellent base for touring Laycock, Castle Combe, Avebury, Silbury Hill and Bath. All rooms have tea/coffee making facilities, outdoor heated pool. Riding, golf nearby. Children over 12 years accepted.	£25.00	■	O	■
Gloria Steed **The Cottage** **Westbrook** **Bromham** **Nr.Chippenham SN15 2EE** **Tel: (0380) 850255** **OPEN: ALL YEAR**	Nearest Roads A.3102 M.4 This delightful cottage is reputed to have been a coaching inn and dates back to 1450. There are three charming bedrooms, most with private bath, T.V. and tea/coffee makers in a beautifully converted barn. Many exposed beams that were ship's timbers. Breakfast is served in the old beamed dining room. A comfortable lounge and lovely garden. They also have a badminton court. This lovely house is an ideal centre for visiting Bath, Bristol, Devizes, Marleborough, Avebury, Stonehenge, Longleat, Castle Combe and Lacock.	£12.00	O	■	O
Doug Webb & Sandie Nash **The Neeld Arms Inn** **The Street** **Grittleton** **Chippenham SN14 6AP** **Tel: (0249) 782470** **OPEN: ALL YEAR**	Nearest Road M.4 The Neeld Arms is a 17th century coaching inn with accommodation in 4 guest rooms, set in the unspoilt village of Grittleton. The bedrooms, some with en-suite facilities, all with T.V. and tea/coffee makers, are comfortable and cosy in keeping with the rest of the inn. The restaurant offers a large range of dishes from steaks to seafood and vegetarian and vegans can be catered for. A fine range of wines, spirits and traditional ales are available in the bar.	£15.00	O	O	O

O yes ■ no

251

	Nearest Road	minimum per person	children taken	evening meals available	animals taken
Anna T. Moore **Church House** Grittleton Nr.Chippenham SN14 6AP Tel: (0249) 782562 OPEN: ALL YEAR	Nearest Road M.4 Church House, a huge and beautiful Georgian rectory, stands on lawns among immense copper beeches, an orchard, walled garden, fields of sheep and a well heated swimming pool. Visitors, treated as house guests may be entertained to musical evenings or with visits to the Royal Shakespeare Theatre followed by a champagne picnic. Anna, Cordon Bleu trained, produces imaginative meals. Four twin bedrooms, furnished with antiques with all modern amenities. Handsome sitting and dining rooms. Children over 12 years.	£17.50	■	○	■
Mrs Margaret Addison **The Old Rectory** Lacock Nr.Chippenham SN15 2JZ Tel: (024973) 335 OPEN: JAN-NOV	Nearest Road A.4 Situated in the mediaeval village of Lacock. The Old Rectory built in 1866, is a fine example of Victorian gothic architecture with creeper-clad walls and mullioned windows. It stands in 12 acres of its own carefully tended grounds which include a tennis court and croquet lawn. It offers four comfortable bedrooms, 2 with private bath.	£12.50	○	■	○
Mr & Mrs Woods **King John's Hunting Lodge** 21 Church Street Lacock Chippenham SN15 2LB Tel: (024973) 313 OPEN: ALL YEAR	Nearest Road A.350 King John's Hunting Lodge was built circa 1200 and is the oldest house in Lacock, which is an unspoilt National Trust village, still resembling a medieval town. The atmosphere is very quiet and casual and breakfast will be served at anytime to suit. Two romantic bedrooms, one with 4-poster bed. Children are accommodated. The house combines a most pleasant teashop and there is a garden for guests use.	£20.00	○	■	○
Major & Mrs Malcolm Firth **Eastcott Manor** Easterton Devizes SN10 4PL Tel: (038081) 3313 OPEN: ALL YEAR	Nearest Road A.3098 An interesting 16th century, Grade II listed Elizabethan manor house, formerly part of Edington Priory with later 18/19th century additions. It offers guests a choice of 4 pleasant and comfortable rooms. The area is rich in historical interest. An ideal centre for visiting Stonehenge, Avebury Ring, Longleat and Dodington. The Ridgeway runs close by so there is fine walking. Children over 10 years accepted.	£12.50	○	○	○
Mrs E.M. Thomas **Swiss Cottage** Roundway Devizes SW10 2JA Tel: (0380) 3716 OPEN: ALL YEAR	Nearest Road A.361 This 150 year old gamekeeper's cottage is situated in 6 acres of woodland, built to resemble a Swiss chalet. It offers two comfortable rooms. The views from the cottage are glorious. Excellent walking country and a great place for those who like peace and quiet. Devizes is only 2 miles away.	£10.00	■	○	○

○ yes ■ no

	Nearest Road / Description	minimum per person	children taken	evening meals available	animals taken
Mrs J. Edwards Stonehill Farm Charlton Nr.Malmesbury SN16 9DY Tel: (06662) 3310 (Early 87: (0666) 823310 OPEN: MAR-OCT	Nearest Road B.4040 A warm welcome is yours at Stonehill, a 500 year old Cotswold stone farmhouse on 200 acres of dairy and sheep farm. In a quiet location but only 15 miles from the M.4 (junctions 16 or 17), it is ideally situated for days out in Bath, the Cotswold, Stratford, Salisbury and Stonehenge. Two bedrooms available, one with en-suite facilities and children (and dogs) are welcome and will enjoy the homely atmosphere.	£10.00	O	■	O
Mrs Lyn Frost Chetcombe House Hotel Salisbury Road Mere BA12 6AZ Tel: (0747) 860219 OPEN: ALL YEAR	Nearest Road A.303 This is a delightful small country house hotel, standing in an acre of lovely gardens just off the approach road to picturesque Mere, which dates from Saxon times. The four bedrooms are very pleasant and well decorated and have south facing views. Children are well provided for. Stourhead and Longleat are close by and Stonehenge, Salisbury, Wilton and Shaftsbury are within 20 mile radius. Traditional English fare. Residential license.	£13.00	O	O	O
Mr & Mrs E.J. Curley Holmhurst Guest House Downton Road Salisbury SP2 8AR Tel: (0722) 23164 OPEN: ALL YEAR	Nearest Road A.338 A large, well appointed guest house, situated a few minutes walk from Salisbury Cathedral, the city centre and pleasant riverside and country walks. Ample car parking on the premises. Eight bedrooms, most having en-suite facilities, two are on the ground floor. Places of historical interest around Salisbury include Stonehenge, Avebury, Rockbourne. Bath and Winchester a drive away.	£13.00	O	■	■
David and Sandra Loader Richburn Guest House 23/25 Estcourt Road Salisbury SP1 3AP Tel: (0722) 25189 OPEN: ALL YEAR	Nearest Road A.30 A renovated Victorian house with large and comfortable rooms, just five minutes walk from the city centre and all amenities. A selection of ten rooms available to guests, some with bath and shower en-suite, and children are well provided for. Residents' lounge with colour T.V. for weary travellers to relax in a pleasant atmosphere.	£12.00	O	■	■
Mr & Mrs Marks Hayburn Wyke 72 Castle Road Salisbury SP1 3RL Tel: (0722) 24141 OPEN: ALL YEAR	Nearest Road A.345 A spacious home, situated next to Victoria Park, just outside the city centre. Offering six pleasant rooms, all with modern facilities, one with private bath. A T.V. lounge for guests, plus car parking. Mr. & Mrs. Marks will arrange car hire for guests and also tours of this historic area. Apart from the beautiful city with its famous cathedral, Stonehenge and Avebury are easily visited from here.	£9.50	O	■	■

O yes ■ no

253

	minimum per person	children taken	evening meals available	animals taken
Mrs Gillian Rodwell **'Farthings'** **9 Swayne's Close** **Salisbury SP1 3AE** **Tel: (0722) 330749** **OPEN: ALL YEAR** Nearest Road A.30 'Farthings' is a comfortable Victorian house with a pleasant garden in a quiet street, but conveniently close to Salisbury's market square and its many excellent restaurants. Four bedrooms are available to guests with modern amenities and tea/coffee makers. Residents' lounge with colour T.V. Children can be provided with cots and high chairs.	£9.00	○	■	■
Mr & Mrs N.N. Castle **Byways Guest House** **31 Fowlers Road** **Milford Hill** **Salisbury SP1 2QP** **Tel: (0722) 28364** **OPEN: ALL YEAR** Nearest Roads A.36 A.30 A comfortable Victorian house with a quiet walled garden and a coach house. The proprietors offer a very warm welcome to visitors and have pleasant rooms, ten en-suite. Situated only 10 minutes walk from the cathedral and the market place, the city restaurants and pubs. Grovely Woods, which are famous for miles of beech trees, make superb walking. Cots are provided for young children.	£10.50	○	■	■
Mrs Jill Bayly **Stratford Lodge** **4 Park Lane** **Victoria Park** **Salisbury SP1 3NP** **Tel: (072) 25177** **OPEN: FEB-NOV** Nearest Road A.345 An excellent Victorian house, offering four very pleasant rooms with comfortable accommodation, all rooms with en-suite facilities. Delightfully furnished to a high standard with antiques and pictures. The house specialises in really imaginative cuisine using their own produce. From here one can visit numerous places - lovely villages such as Castle Combe, Amesbury and Salisbury itself offers an enormous amount of history. Price shown for two people.	£26.00	○	○	■
Mr & Mrs Peter Higgins **Saint Marie's Grange** **Alderbury** **Salisbury SP5 3DJ** **Tel: (0722) 710351** **OPEN: ALL YEAR** Nearest Road A.36 Pleasant hosts here are offering true English hospitality in an unusual interesting house, the first home of Augustus Pugin, co-architect of the Houses of Parliament. Set in beautiful grounds beside the Avon, with fine view across the water meadow. The house offers three comfortable rooms to guests, with modern amenities, radio, tea/coffee makers. Exceptional food is on offer, using fresh garden vegetables and visitors can be met by vintage car. Children welcome.	£15.00	○	○	■
Mr P. Morris **White Lodge** **68 London Road** **Salisbury** **Tel (0722) 27991** **OPEN: ALL YEAR** Nearest Road A.303 White Lodge is an attractive brick-gabled house opposite St. Mark's Church, with a greenhouse the entrance through trailing vines and potted geraniums. The house is furnished with nice old pieces blended with modern comforts. Six pleasant bedrooms are available with modern amenities, tea/coffee making facilities, and there is a T.V. lounge for guests. Plenty of car parking space. Children over 5 please.	£10.00	○	○	○

○ yes ■ no

254

	minimum per person	children taken	evening meals available	animals taken
Diana Gifford Mead **The Mill House** **Berwick St. James** **Nr. Salisbury** **Tel: (0722) 790331** **OPEN: ALL YEAR** Nearest Roads A.303 A.36 B.3083 The lovely rooms of Mill House, built in 1785, view the river Till running through beautiful old-fashioned rose gardens and acres of water-meadows rich with birds and wild flowers. The Old Mill, still working, straddles ¼ mile of dry fly-fishing. Stonehenge is within walking distance and numerous stately homes, historic sites, pubs and eating places are nearby. Diana offers the warmest of welcomes.	£14.00	○	■	■
Mrs Carol Plant **Dinton Lodge** **St.Marys Lane** **Dinton** **Nr. Salisbury** **SP3 5HH** **Tel: (072276) 216** **OPEN: ALL YEAR** Nearest Roads A.30 A.303 Dinton Lodge is a beautiful 200 year old house with stone mullioned windows standing in a quiet pretty village opposite a Norman Church. Three rooms are available to guests all large and beautifully decorated and furnished. Tea or coffee can be served in bed if requested. Meals can be taken in the lovely dinning room with its antiques and silver. Guests have use of the garden.	£15.00	■	○	■
Mrs Janice L. Hyde **Milton Farn** **East Knoyle** **Salisbury SP3 6BG** **Tel: (074783) 247** **OPEN APR-OCT** Nearest Roads A.303 A.350 A picturesque Queen Anne house with oak beams and inglenook fireplace. Accommodation is very comfortable. Decorated in Laura Ashley and Sanderson fabrics and enhanced by the lovely fresh flowers and displays of silver. Offering 3 comfortalbe bedrooms one with shower and others with bath. Candlelit dinners served in front of log fire. Cordon bleu cooking.	£13.00	○	○	■
Mary Tucker **1 Riverside Close** **Laverstock** **Salisbury SP1 1QW** **Tel: (0722) 20287** **OPEN: ALL YEAR** Nearest Road A.30 An executive's home in a quiet area one and a half miles from Salisbury Cathedral. A tastefully furnished ground floor suite comprising private shower room, a double and single room with patio door opening onto a beautiful flower arrangers garden, in addition guests have their own colour T.V and tea/coffee making facilities. An excellent base for those visiting this historic city.	£12.50	○	■	■
Mrs Elva Randall **Cape Cottage** **Lower Woodford** **Salisbury SP4 6NQ** **OPEN: ALL YEAR** Nearest Road A.345 A charming hostess waits to welcome you to her pretty cottage with its attractive garden and countryside views. Situated in the beautiful Woodford valley close to the Village Inn. The three lovely bedrooms have modern amenities, T.V. and china tea-sets. Children are well provided for with cots and high chairs and babysitting arranged. Residents lounge. An ideal base for seeing Salisbury with its cathedral, or visiting Stonehenge.	£10.00	○	■	○

○ yes ■ no

255

	minimum per person	children taken	evening meals available	animals taken
Jean & Tony Poat **Glen Lyn** **6 Bellamy Lane** **Milford Hill** **Salisbury SP1 2SP** **Tel: (0722) 27880** **OPEN: ALL YEAR** Nearest Roads A.30 A.36 A warm welcome and friendly hosts are found at Glen Lyn. A large comfortably furnished Victorian house located in a quiet cul-de-sac conveniently situated for several good restaurants and the city centre. Accommodation is in five rooms, two with en-suite facilities, all with tea/coffee making facilities. A residents colour T.V. lounge is also available throughout the day. This makes a good base for touring this wonderful cathedral city	£10.00	○	■	■
Jean Dewbury **Newton Farm Guest House** **Southampton Rd** **Whiteparish** **Salisbury SP5 2QL** **Tel: (07948) 416** **OPEN: ALL YEAR** Nearest Road - On A.36 A warm and friendly welcome awaits guests at this delighful family run 16th century farmhouse, with its original flagstone floors and oak beams. Five rooms for guests, all charmingly furnished and very comfortable with en-suite facilities and tea/coffee making facilities. Colour T.V. lounge, outdoor swimming pool and acres of garden. The house, which was part of the Trafalgar Estate gifted to Lord Nelson, makes a marvellous centre for touring.	£10.00	○	■	○
Philip & Liz Young **Clanfield House** **Amesbury Road** **Shrewton SP3 4DB** **Tel: (0980) 620234** **OPEN: FEB-DEC** Nearest Road A.303 A most attractive large 19th century house offering two pleasant rooms, all with modern amenities. A comfortable lounge with colour T.V. and a garden for guests. Mr. & Mrs. Young make all visitors most welcome and will help plan tours of this historic area. The prehistoric stone circle of Stonehenge is only two and a half miles from the house. Easily accessible from here is the New Forest, Longleat, the beautiful city of Bath.	£10.00	○	■	■
Mrs Margaret Stacey **62b Paxcroft Cottage** **Devizes Road** **Hilperton** **Trowbridge BA14 0RB** **Tel: (02214) 65838** **OPEN: ALL YEAR** Nearest Road A.361 Friendly hosts and a welcoming atmosphere are found at Paxcroft Cottage. Set in open countryside with magnificent views all around this makes a tranquil and peaceful base from which to tour the region. Accommodation is in three rooms with modern amenities. Morning tea is provided. A residents T.V. lounge is also available for guests use as is the garden. Mrs. Stacey will go out of her way to ensure you have a memorable stay. No smoking please.	£9.00	■	■	■
Mr & Mrs Cronan **Welham House** **Bratton Road** **West Ashton** **Trowbridge BA14 6AZ** **Tel: (02214) 5908** **OPEN: ALL YEAR** Nearest Road A.350 Welham House was built in 1840 and is a fine example of Gothic architecture. Wonderful stained glass in hall windows. This charming house has five lovely rooms, one with en-suite facilities. Rooms have pretty views over the garden. An attractive lounge with colour T.V. and garden for guests to enjoy. Standing in an acre of garden there is a marvellous view of the famous Westbury White Horse. An excellent base for visiting Lacock, Bradford-upon-Avon,	£9.00	○	■	■

○ yes ■ no

YORKSHIRE

Yorkshire is the "most renown'd of shires" according to Drayton, writing in the 1600's and certainly this largest county has much to offer the modern visitor. As its centre is the historic City of York, graced by its magnificent cathedral and mediaeval city walls. To the west lies the incomparable scenery of the dales and to the north is the wild splendour of moors, ablaze with a purple fire of heather in autumn. The tranquility of Yorkshire villages belies the county's turbulent history. There are ruined abbeys like Rievaulx, Fountains and Bolton Priory, still elegant in pastoral settings; there are spendid stately homes such as Temple Newsam and exceptional churches at Ripon and Beverly. The county has an extensive coastline with many secluded fishing ports including the attractive port of Whitby. Overlooked by the ruins of the cliff top abbey the small town tumbles in red roofed tiers down to the busy harbour from which Captain James Cook sailed.

The Dales

The Yorkshire Dales form one of the finest landscapes in England. These deep Pennine valleys were once the home of remote farming communities and today they remain unspoilt. The beautiful rivers of the Dales begin as small trickles in the windswept moors but the waters gather into torrents forced down the narrow gorges of the high valleys. However, the spectacular waterfalls give way to a gentler landscape of broad river, wide green valleys which are enclosed by steeply rising fells. The landscape is covered by a network of drystone walls, some as ancient as the stone built villages but those which climb the valley sides to the high moors are the product of the 18th century enclosures and a good wall builder in those days would cover about 7 metres a day. Each of the Dales has a distinctive character. The upper reaches of Airedale hold the remarkable limestone cliffs of Malham cove.

Wildest of all is Swaledale, its entrance guarded by the superb Norman Castle and tower at Richmond which is a charming market town. Wensleydale holds Bolton Castle where Mary, Queen of Scots was held captive. The ruins of the once great Bolton Priory are set amongst the woods and meadows of Wharfedale in some the most enchanting scenery to be found in England.

Bronte Country

The Bronte Sisters produced much of their writing in Haworth, a plain Yorkshire village of strong character with a steep cobbled main street and cottages of millstone grit. The parsonage where the sisters lived, is a simple two storey Georgian building which is now the Bronte Society Museum with the rooms arranged as they were when the Bronte family lived there. But it is beyond the village and the waterfall that the real flavour of the bronte country can be found, up towards the "distant, dreamy, dim blue chain of mountains circling every side" which Emily Bronte describes in "Wuthering Heights". Fine local houses remain, just as described in the Bronte novels. Charlotte's description of Oakwell Hall is almost a guide book to the building. Kirklees is "Nunnely" of the novel "Shirley" and Shibden Hall is featured in "Wuthering Heights".

Mediaeval York

York is the finest mediaeval city in England. It is encircled by the cream coloured ribbon of limestone from whichthe massive city walls are built,pierced by four Great Gates which were the only entrances to the city. Within these walls there is a jumbled roof line, dog leg streets and the sudden courtyards of a mediaeval city.

Half timbered buildings with over-sailing upper stories jostle with Georgian brick houses along the network of narrow streets around King Edward Square and The Shambles. Street names reveal ancient trades of the people of the city. Coppergate, curiously, is the street of the joiners; Spurriergate the street of spur makers, Stone gate and Petergate follow the line of the Via Praetoria, laid some 16 centuries ago when the city was a Roman Garrison town. Excavations have revealed signs of occupation and settlement by the Vikings, and a reconstruction of the Viking village of Jorvik is open to the public. The Minster stands at the heart of this ancient city and is the finest mediaeval cathedral in Northern Europe.

YORKSHIRE GAZETEER.

Areas of Outstanding Natural Beauty.
The Peak District. The North Yorkshire Moors and The Yorkshire Dales.

Historic Houses and Castles

Carlton Towers
17th century, remodelled in later centuries. Paintings, silver, furniture, pictures. Carved woodwork, painted decorations, examples of Victorian craftsmanship.

Castle Howard -- Nr. York
18th century -- celebrated architect, Sir John Vanbrugh -- paintings, costumes, furniture by Chippendale, Sheraton, Adam. Not to be missed.

East Riddlesden Hall-- Keighley
17th century manor house with fishponds and historic barns, one of which is regarded as very fine example of mediaeval tithe barns.

Newby Hall -- Ripon
17th century Wren style extended by Robert Adam. Gobelins tapestry, Chippendale furniture, sculpture galleries with Roman rotunda, statuary.

Nostell Priory -- Wakefield
18th century, Georgain mansion, Chippendale furniture, paintings.

Burton Constable Hall -- Hull
16th century, Elizabethan, remodelled in Georgian period. Stained glass, Hepplewhite furniture, gardens by Capability Brown.

Ripley Castle -- Harrogate
14th century, parts dating during 16th and 18th centuries. Priest hole, armour and weapons, beautiful ceilings.

The Treasurer's House -- York
17th & 18th centuries, splendid interiors, furniture, pictures.

Harewood House -- Leeds
18th century -- Robert Adam design, Chippendale furniture, Italian and English paintings, Sevres and Chinese porcelain.

Benningbrough Hall -- York
18th century. Highly decorative woodwork, oak staircase, friezes etc. Splendid hall.

Markenfield Hall -- Ripon
14th to 16th century -- fine Manor house surrounded by moat.

Heath Hall -- Wakefield
18th century, palladian. Fine woodwork and plasterwork, rococo ceilings, excellent furniture, paintings and porcelain.

Bishops House -- Sheffield
16th century. Only complete timber framed yeoman farmhouse surviving. Vernacular architecture. Superb.

Cathedrals and Churches

York Minster
13th century. Greatest Gothic Cathedral North of the Alps. Imposing grandeur -- superb Chapter house, contains half of the medieval stained glass of England. Outstandingly beautiful.

York (All Saints, North Street)
15th century roofing in parts -- 18th century pulpit wonderful mediaeval glass.

Ripon Cathedral
12th century -- though in some parts Saxon in origin. Decorated choir stalls -- gables buttresses. Church of 672 preserved in crypt, as remains, Caxton Book, ecclesiastic treasures.

Bolton Percy (All Saints)
15th century. Maintains original glass in east window. Jacobean font cover. Georgian pulpit. Interesting monuments.

Rievaulx Abbey
12th century, masterpiece of Early English architecture. One of three great Cistercian Abbeys built inYorkshire. Impressive ruins.

Campsall (St. Mary Magdalene)
Fine Norman tower -- 15th century rood screen, carved & painted stone altar.

Fountains Abbey -- Ripon
Ruins of Englands greatest mediaeval abbey -- surrounded by wonderful landscaped gardens. Enormous tower, vaulted cellar 300 feet long.

Whitby (St. Mary)
12th century tower and doorway. 18th century remodelling -- box pews much interior woodwork painted -- galleries. High pulpit. Table tombs.

Whitby Abbey -- Whitby (St. Hilda)
7th century superb ruin -- venue of Synod of 664. Destroyed by Vikings, restored 1078 -- magnificent north transept.

Halifax (St. John The Baptist)
12th century orgins, showing work from each succeeding century -- heraldic ceilings, Cromwell glass.

Beverley Minster -- Beverley
14th century. Fine Gothic Minster -- remarkable medieval effigies of musicians playing instruments. Founded as monastery in 700.

Museums and Galleries

Aldborough Roman Museum -- Boroughbridge
Remnants of Roman period of the town -- coins, glass, pottery etc.

Great Ayton
Home of Captain Cook, explorer & seaman. Exhibits of maps, etc.

Art Gallery -- City of York
Modern paintings, old masters, watercolours, prints, ceramics.

Lotherton Hall Nr. Leeds
Museum with furniture, paintings, silver, works of art from the Leeds collection and oriental art gallery.

National Railway Museum -- York
Devoted to railway engineering and its development.

York Castle Museum
The Kirk Collection of bygones including cobbled streets, shops, costumes, toys, household and farm equipment, -- fascinating collection.

Cannon Hall Art Gallery -- Barnsley
18th century house with fine furniture and glass etc. Flemish & Dutch paintings. Also houses museum of the 13/18 Royal Hussars.

Mappin Art Gallery - Sheffield
Works from 18th, 19th and 20th century painters and sculptors. Contemporary exhibitions.

Graves Art Gallery - Sheffield
British portraiture. European works, and examples of Asian and African art. Loan exhibitions are heldthere.

Royal Pump Room Museum. -- Harrogate
Original sulphur well used in the Victorian Spa. Local history costume and pottery etc.

Bolling Hall -- Bradford
A period house with mixture of styles -- collections of 17th century oak furniture, domestic utensils,toys and bygones.

Georgian Theatre -- Richmond
Oldest theatre in the country -- interesting theatrical memorabilia.

Jorvik Viking Centre -- York
Recently excavated site in centre of York showing hundreds of artifacts dating from the Viking period. One of the most important archeological discoveries this century

Abbey House Museum -- Kirkstall, Leeds
Illustrates past 300 years of Yorkshire life. Shows 3 full streets from 19th century with houses, shops and workplaces.

Piece Hall -- Halifax
 Remarkable building -- constructed around huge quadrangle -- now Textile Industrial museum, Art galleryand has craft & antique shops.

Historic Monuments

Conisborough Castle -- Doncaster
 12th century -- curtain walls, solid round towers, circular six buttressed keep. Built by a Plantagenet. Setting for fivanhoe·

Scarborough Castle -- Scarborough
 12th century castle. Suffered damage in Civil War and First World War.

Stanwick Oppidum -- Stanwick
 Area of defences of the Brigantian capital in 1st. century.

Knaresborough Castle -- Knaresborough
 14th century -- remains of stronghold showing keep, baileys and gatehouse.

Aldborough
 Roman town -- boundary wall -- 2 tessellated pavements.

Pontefract Castle -- Pontefract
 Ruins of stronghold -- Norman cloverleaf keep, chapel and dungeons.

Devil's Arrows -- Boroughbridge.
 Three Bronze age monoliths.

Richmond castle -- Richmond
 Huge Norman keep dominating the market town below -- superb setting. 100 foot high rectangular keep --one of oldest in England.

YORKSHIRE/HUMBERSIDE
Recommended roadside restaurants

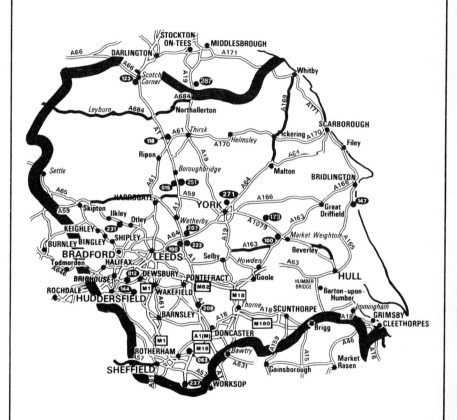

Yorkshire

		minimum per person	children taken	evening meals available	animals taken
Edith Lillie **Elmfield House** Arrathorne Bedale DL8 1NE Tel: (0677) 50558 **OPEN: ALL YEAR**	Nearest Road A.1 A very enjoyable home-from-home atmosphere will be found at Elmfield House, an excellent base for visiting the Yorkshire Dales, Richmond, James Heriot Country, York, Fountains and Rievaulx Abbeys. This luxury home offers three rooms to guests, two with private facilities, and very spacious. Families are well provided for. Lovely home-cooked meals. Everything arranged for guests comfort.	£9.00	O	O	O
John & Carol Regan **The Triton Inn** Sledmere Nr.Driffield YO25 0XQ Tel: (0377) 86644 **OPEN: ALL YEAR**	Nearest Road A.166 A family run old coaching inn in an unspoilt wolds village, offering charm, character and comfort. Six rooms for guests with modern amenities, telephone, radio/T.V., tea/coffee making facilities. Children all well provided for. Residents' lounge, games room. Excellent home cooking with a wide variety of food. Traditional hand-pulled beers served in a fine old bar with real log fire.	£10.50	O	O	O
Mrs S.M. Arnett **Windross House** Windross Square Market Place Easingwold YO6 3AG Tel: (0347) 21293 **OPEN: ALL YEAR**	Nearest Road A.19 Windross House is a fine Georgian property where guests will enjoy a comfortable, homely and family atmosphere. Four bedrooms are available, with a lounge and garden to relax in. Central for all services which surround. A picturesque market square in Easingwold, gateway to the Dales, the North Yorkshire Moors and the North East coastal resorts. Numerous sporting facilities in the area.	£.9.00	O	■	O
Rachel Ritchie **The Old Rectory** Thormanby Easingwold YO6 3NN Tel: (0845) 401417 **OPEN: ALL YEAR**	Nearest Road A.19 A beautiful and interesting Georgian rectory dating back to 1737, with many of its original features including a record of all previous owners. Three delightful rooms, all with modern amenities. A charming lounge with colour T.V. and a large mature garden. This is an excellent base and is in the centre of 'Herriot country'. The Yorkshire moors and dales are easily accessible and there are many historic houses and monuments in this area. York itself is only 17 miles. Many pubs and restaurants locally.	£9.50	O	■	O
Rowena Naish **Prospect Farm** Grafton York YO5 9QJ Tel: (09012) 2045 **OPEN: ALL YEAR**	Nearest Road A.1 Bed and breakfast in an 15th century farmhouse on a working arable farm, with spectacular views. Three bedrooms available to guests with modern amenities, T.V., tea/coffee making facilities. Children are well provided for. Residents' lounge and garden. Fishing available. Easy access to York, Harrogate, the dales, moors and the coast.	£9.00	O	■	■

O yes ■ no

		minimum per person	children taken	evening meals available	animals taken
Mr & Mrs N.H. Bloom **Manor House Farm** **Ingleby Greenhow** **Great Ayton TS9 6RB** **Tel: (0642) 722384** **OPEN: ALL YEAR**	Nearest Roads A.19 B.1257 A charming old farm in idyllic surroundings at the foot of the Cleveland Hills in the North York Moors National Park. Set in park and woodland, this lovely house with beams and open fires has three delightful rooms with modern amenities. A pretty lounge with T.V. for guests and also a garden. Very friendly and personal service and wonderful cooking; wining and dining by candlelight. Packed lunches can be arranged. Horse riding and golf locally, plus stabling if you can bring your own mount. A wonderful base for touring.	£12.50	O	O	O
Marilyn J. Bateson **Alexa House Hotel &** ** Stable Cottages** **26 Ripon Road** **Harrogate HG2 2JJ** **Tel: (0423) 501988** **OPEN: ALL YEAR**	Nearest Road A.61 Built in 1830 for Baron de Ferrier and now a warm and welcoming small hotel. Marilyn and Peter have taken great care in the creation of supremely comfortable and charming bedrooms, all en-suite, with every attention to guests' needs. There is a happy family atmosphere and good food is the pride of the establishment, with the dining room regarded as the hub of the home. Marilyn and Peter were delighted to receive their Regional Award for Best Bed and Breakfast 1986.	£13.50	O	O	■
Sylvia & Frank Johnson **Daryl House** **42 Dragon Parade** **Harrogate HG1 5DA** **Tel: (0423) 502775** **OPEN: ALL YEAR** **(EXCL. XMAS & N. YEARS DAY**	Nearest Road A.59 A small, friendly, family run house offering excellent accommodation in six most pleasant rooms with every modern comfort. Tea/coffee makers and T.V. in all rooms. An attractive lounge with colour T.V. and a garden for guests' enjoyment. Home-cooked food and personal attention are the hallmarks of Daryl House. Close to the town centre with its conference facilities. A very warm welcome awaits all visitors from Sylvia & Frank.	£10.00	O	O	■
Mrs Sheila McNamara **Abbey Lodge Guest House** **31 Ripon Road** **Harrogate HG61 2JL** **Tel: (0423) 69712** **OPEN: ALL YEAR**	Nearest Road A.61 Abbey Lodge is a large, detached Victorian house set well back from the main Harrogate to Ripon road, close to the town centre. Mrs. McNamara offers 15 very comfortable rooms, seven with en-suite facilities. Rooms all have radio and tea/coffee makers and there is a T.V. if required. A pleasant T.V. lounge and garden for guests' use. The hostess has a fine reputation for her excellent cooking. Ideally situated for touring the Dales and the many interesting sites in the region.	£12.00	O	O	■

O yes ■ no

	minimum per person	children taken	evening meals available	animals taken
Mrs Susan Pearcey **Knox Mill House** **Knox Mill Lane** **Harrogate HG3 2AE** **Tel: (0423) 60650** **OPEN: ALL YEAR** Nearest Road A.61 Built in 1785, this lovely old millhouse stands on the banks of a stream in a quiet rural setting, yet only one and a half miles from the centre of Harrogate. Beautifully renovated, it still retains all its original features: oak beams, inglenook fireplace and stone arches. There are three delightful rooms attractively and comfortably furnished, all having modern amenities and tea/coffee makers, with views over the stream and fields. A delightful lounge with colour T.V. and garden for guests' enjoyment. Mrs. Pearcey will help plan tours of the area.	£12.50	○	■	■
Mr & Mrs N. Gill **Gillmore Hotel** **98/100 Kings Road** **Harrogate HG1 5HH** **Tel: (0423) 503699/507122** **OPEN: ALL YEAR** Nearest Road A.1 A pleasant hotel offering excellent, comfortable accommodation in twenty-eight rooms with modern facilities. There is a bar lounge and a T.V. lounge. From here one can visit the Bronte country, Knaresborough Castle, Mother Shipton's Well and Harewood House, to name but a few. An ideal base. Evening meals are good value.	£12.50	○	○	○
G.W. & B.C. Cargill **Stoney Lea** **13 Spring Grove** **Springfield Avenue** **Harrogate HG1 2HS** **Tel: (0423) 501524** **OPEN: ALL YEAR** Nearest Roads A.61 A.1 An interesting house of mellow stone with part Tudor gabling. Situated in a quiet area offering six excellent rooms with modern amenities and a very warm welcome. Only 2 minutes from the centre of the city, it is a perfect base for visiting the historic buildings, Roman baths, and superb countryside with its wealth of historic houses. Tea making facilities in all rooms. Food excellent value.	£16.00	○	○	■
Mrs G. Bendtson **The Woodhouse** **7 Spring Grove** **Harrogate HG1 2HS** **Tel: (0423) 60081** **OPEN: ALL YEAR** **(EXCL. XMAS/NEW YEAR)** Nearest Road A warm welcome awaits you at this privately owned, family-run, attractive Victorian guest house in a quiet cul-de-sac in the heart of Harrogate. Nine attractive and tastefully decorated bedrooms, mostly en-suite, all with radio/T.V., tea/coffee makers. Very comfortable and relaxing lounge. A high standard of service is offered and exceptional home cooking to enjoy. Scandinavian languages spoken.	£11.00	○	○	■
Cliff & Mary Matthews **Arden House Hotel** **69/71 Franklin Road** **Harrogate HG1 5EH** **Tel: (0423) 509224** **OPEN: ALL YEAR** Nearest Road A.61 A.59 Very friendly service will be found here. Arden House is a small luxury family hotel with all the comforts of home, accommodating guests in a selection of 12 bedrooms, all with private bathroom facilities: telephone, radio/T.V., tea/coffee making facilities. Lounge for residents. Licensed. Children are well provided for. Good home-cooked meals.	£14.50	○	○	■

○ yes ■ no

		minimum per person	children taken	evening meals available	animals taken
Susan & Brian Jutsum **Rookhurst Georgian Country** **House** **Gayle** **Hawes DL8 3RT** **Tel: (09697) 454** **OPEN: ALL YEAR**	Nearest Road A.65 Susan and Brian welcome you to their unique Dales country house. The six bedrooms are very comfortable, furnished with antiques. Some rooms are heavily beamed, others are very spacious. Some have lovely 4-poster beds and most have en-suite or private facilities. All have radio., T.V. & tea/cofee makers. The bridal suite is superb. The delightful dining room offers a delicious menu which is changed daily, candlelight dinners and fine wines. Fresh produce is used whenever possible.	£18.00	○	○	■
Mrs N.W. Nelson **"Springfield"** **Cragg Vale** **Hebden Bridge HX7 5SR** **Tel: (0422) 882029** **OPEN: ALL YEAR**	Nearest Road A.646 "Springfield" is a modern, stone built, split level house in an acre of garden on a hillside in a picturesque valley in the South Pennine Park. Open views of woods and moorland. Three rooms, centrally heated and comfortably furnished with adjacent bath/shower rooms, I.V. Lounge, sauna and garden for guests' use. The breakfasts are delicious and highly recommended.	£8.50	○	■	■
Mrs Mollie Bell **"Langber Country** **Guest House"** **Ingleton** **(via Carnforth) LA6 3DT** **Tel: (0468) 41587** **OPEN: ALL YEAR** **(EXCL. XMAS)**	Nearest Road A.65 A large Victorian house set in 37 acres of its own garden and paddock. Surrounded by lovely countryside, the house has wonderful views. Offering six rooms, all very nicely furnished with modern amenities. A lounge, with colour T.V. and dining room. Children have a special play area with swings, see-saw and games. Ideal for rambling, bird watching and climbing.	£8.00	○	○	○
Mrs Dorothy C. Holme **"Eastfield Lodge"** **Leyburn DL8 5EL** **Tel: (0969) 23196** **OPEN: ALL YEAR**	Nearest Road A.1 A warm welcome awaits you at Eastfield Lodge, a family run business in beautiful Wensleydale - "James Herriot" country. This Victorian house is a few seconds from Leyburn market square with its well-stocked shops and friendly local people. Ten bedrooms with modern facilities. T.V. Morning tea served on request. Varied meal-time menus, morning coffee and cream teas available. Licensed.	£10.00	○	○	○
Douglas & Marjorie Maughan **Lynnwood House** **18 Alexandra Road** **Upper Moor** **Pudsey** **Leeds LS28 8BY** **Tel: (0532) 571117** **OPEN: ALL YEAR**	Nearest Roads A.647 B.6154 This comfortable, centrally heated home has a friendly atmosphere. Only 15 mins. from the airport and city centres, with rail station and buses nearby. Good shopping and theatre as well as stately homes, castles and the Industrial Heritage of Northern England. There is a kingsize airbath to relax in after local walking, tennis, swimming or dancing. Two golf clubs locally. Also cricket and football in their season and bowls can be enjoyed in the park.	£18.00	■	○	○

○ yes ■ no

	minimum per person	children taken	evening meals available	animals taken
David & Angela Wilcock **The White Horse** **Farm Hotel** **Rosedale Abbey** **Nr.Pickering YO18 8SE** **Tel: (07515) 239** **OPEN: ALL YEAR** Nearest Road A.170 A delightful house dating back before 1700, in an idyllic setting overlooking Rosedale village and surrounding dales and moors. An ideal base for touring being in the heart of the North York Moors National Park and only 15 miles from Yorkshire's Heritage coast. Character bar and dining room noted for good, interesting English country cooking, real ale and friendly staff. Bargain breaks all year.	£21.50	O	O	O
J.M.B. Brenkley **Merrifield Farm** **Scurragh Lane** **Skeeby** **Richmond DL10 5EF** **Tel: (0748) 2391** **OPEN: ALL YEAR** Nearest Road A.1 Enjoy the homely and peaceful atmosphere at Merrifield, a small sheep farm in the Dales. A pleasing, modern, stone built house with three comfortable rooms for guests, full central heating, T.V. lounge. Good home-cooked meals, lovely countryside views from the garden. Children welcome. An ideal base for touring Richmond and the Dales. ¼ mile from A.1 with easy access North and South.	£10.00	O	O	O
Ian & Angela Close **The Old Hall** **Jervaulx Abbey** **Ripon H64 4PH** **Tel: (0677) 60313** **OPEN: ALL YEAR** Nearest Road A.1 A mellow old stone house in four acres of courtyards, stabling and grazing sheep. This friendly Yorkshire home welcomes your visit. Period pieces decorate the interior. All bedrooms have en-suite bathrooms and are very well appointed. Tea/coffee making facilities, ample car parking. Children are well provided for. Golf, riding, fishing, locally. Delicious home-cooked meals. A lovely Wensleydale base for touring North Yorkshire.	£18.00	O	O	O
Mr P.J. Gill & **Mr A. Van Der Horst** **Bank Villa** **Masham** **Ripon HG4 4DB** **Tel: (0765) 89605** **OPEN: MAR-OCT** Nearest Road A.6108 A fine Georgian house overlooking the River Ure in large, terraced gardens offering a fine welcome and delightful accommodation in seven comfortable double roooms with modern amenities. It is a super base for visiting the Druids Temple, Jervaulx Abbey, Middleham Castle and the wonderful James Herriot country. Dutch is spoken. Meals are excellent value. T.V. and quiet lounge. Children under 5 not accommodated.	£13.50	O	O	O
T.S. & J.E. Whitaker **Cottage Leas Country Hotel** **Nova Lane** **Middleton** **Pickering YO18 8PN** **Tel: (0751) 72129** **OPEN: ALL YEAR** Nearest Road A.170 A delightful 18th century converted farmhouse offering a warm welcome and really confortable accommodation in delightful rooms, 7 have private bath. Set in two acres of garden and surrounded by farmland with fine views over the Vale of Pickering, it is the perfect touring base. They offer a tennis court and bicycles for hire. The food here is scrumptious and excellent value.	£17.00	O	O	O

O yes ■ no

266

Roger & Margaret Callan **Woodlands** **The Mains** **Giggleswick** **Settle BD24 0AX** **Tel: (07292) 2576** **OPEN: ALL YEAR** **(EXCL. XMAS/NEW YEAR)**	Nearest Road A.65 A really handsome Georgian country house with superb views over the Ribble Valley. It offers nine well appointed, comfortable rooms with delightful views and modern amenities. This is an excellent base for touring this fascinating region. Ribblsdale and the Forest of Bowland, the Fountains Fell and Pennines are all easily accessible from here. Children under twelve cannot be accommodated.	£17.00	■	○	■
Ruth and Ken Horsman **Ivy Cottage** **Buckden** **Nr.Skipton BD23 5JA** **Tel: (075676) 827** **OPEN: ALL YEAR**	Nearest Roads A.59 A.65 An ancient small country manaor house. Exposed beams and inglenook fireplace with plenty of atmosphere. Three charming comfortable rooms with modern amenities. A beamed lounge with colour T.V. and a garden for guests to enjoy. A very good base for touring with Yorkshire Dales National Park, The Forest of Bowland, likely Moor, Haworth and Harrogate all easily accessible. Guest will enjoy the warm welcome and the good food here.	£9.00	○	■	○
John B. Fredrick & **Marjorie Forster** **The George Inn** **Kirk Gill** **Hubberholme** **Via Skipton** **BD23 5JE** **Tel: (075676) 223** **OPEN: ALL YEAR**	Nearest Road The George Inn is an ancient hostelry dated from 1600, situated in rural surroundings of great beauty and tranquility in the heart of the Yorkshire Dales. (J.B. Priestley's favourite pub. His ashes are in the Hubberholme Church). Four bedrooms are available with modern facilities, tea/coffee makers. Lounge and garden for guests use. Good walking country. Riding and fishing nearby. Children over 8 welcome.	£12.00	○	○	○
Mr & Mrs R.T. Shelmerdine **Eshton Grange** **Gargrave** **Nr. Skipton BD23 3QE** **Tel: (075678) 383** **OPEN: ALL YEAR**	Nearest Road A.65 A recently modernized attractive, 18th century listed farmhouse. It's a 20 acre working stock farm and Shetland pony stud. Situated in the Yorkshire Dales National Park. It is close to many beauty spots with walking, potholing and pony trekking nearby. It offers 5 bedrooms. A drying room for walking gear. A lovely walled garden with beautiful views.	£9.00	○	○	■
Mrs M.A. Flaving **Kirk Syke Hotel** **High Street** **Gargrave** **Skipton BD23 3RA** **Tel: (075678) 356** **OPEN: ALL YEAR**	Nearest Road A.65 Kirk Syke is a small, licensed family run hotel in the heart of the Yorkshire Dales, offering comfortable and pleasant accommodation. 9 modern guest rooms are available, on ground level all with private bathroom and tea making facilities, some with television. Garden and lounge for guests use. 18 hole golf course at Skipton. Pennine way nearby and good access to Dales and Moors. Children welcome.	£12.00	○	○	○

○ yes ■ no

	minimum per person	children taken	evening meals available	animals taken
Paul & Jean Dolan **Park Bottom Guest House** **and Licensed Restaurant** **Litton** **Nr. Skipton** **Tel: (075677) 235** **OPEN: MAR-NOV** Nearest Road A.59 A recently built architect-designed house situated in a quiet hamlet in the unspoilt valley of Littondale, in the heart of the Yorkshire Dales. Offering very pleasant accommodation. Seven bedrooms are available, well-furnished and with en-suite facilities, central heating, tea/coffee makers. There is an open log fire in the lounge. Traditional or vegetarian menu of very good freshly prepared food.	£14.00	O	O	O
Gwyneth Dover **"Harrow Ings"** **Mitton Lane** **Lothersdale** **Nr.Skipton BD20 8HR** **Tel: (0535) 36658** **OPEN: ALL YEAR** Nearest Road A.629 Charming old Yorkshire farmhouse in beautiful historic village of Lothersdale. Set in 2 arces of garden and surrounded by the rolling hills of the dales, enjoying panoramic views. Excellent sightseeing, walking, golf. Five guest bedrooms, 2 with private bathroom, all with modern amenities, radio/T.V., tea/coffee making facilities. Good home cooking and a very warm welcome. No smoking. Children over 5.	£9.50	O	O	■
Mr & Mrs D. Sugars **"Sevenford House"** **Thorgill** **Rosedale Abbey** **Pickering YO18 8SE** **Tel: (07515) 283** **OPEN: ALL YEAR** Nearest Road A.170 Originally a vicarage and built from the stones of Rosedale Abbey. "Sevenford House" stands in four acres in the heart of the beautiful Yorkshire Moors National Park. Five well decorated comfortable rooms all with modern amenities and lovely views. There is a garden for guests' use. This beautiful country house is an excellent base for exploring the region. Riding and golf locally. Ryedale Folk Museum, ruined abbeys, Roman roads, steam railways, the beautiful coastline and pretty fishing towns, forests and moors.	£9.00	O	■	■
F.P. & C.W. Fell **The Hall Country Guest House** **Slingsbuy** **Nr.York YO6 7AL** **Tel: (065382) 375** **OPEN: APR-OCT** Nearest Roads A.64 B.1257 A regency house of character set in five acres of gardens with croquet lawn and stream. Situated in a real English village with a ruined castle. Eight lovely rooms, one en-suite, attractively furnished and comfortable with modern facilities and T.V. A pleasant colour T.V. lounge and garden for guests. Fine evening meals here and excellent value. Castle Howard three miles away. Convenient for York and the moors. The house offers a relaxed atmosphere and very personal attention.	£10.00	■	O	■

O yes ■ no

Legend columns (diagonal headers): minimum per person | children taken | evening meals available | animals taken

Entry	Nearest Roads / Description	minimum per person	children taken	evening meals available	animals taken
Patricia Cowell Ringtree Cottage Hillam Square Hillam South Milford LS25 5HF Tel: (0977) 682247 OPEN: ALL YEAR	Nearest Roads A.63 A.1 M.62 Ringtree Cottage a delightfully located in the village square overlooking a beautiful flowering chestnut tree. This 16th century cottage retains much of its original character including low beamed celings and antique fireplace. Accommodation is in five rooms with colour T.V. lounge. The walled garden is a wonderful spot to relax in. Fairburn Ings Nature Reserve is only 3 miles and York 20 miles. This is also an ideal stopover for those travelling to or from Scotland.	£8.00	O	O	■
Paul Ross The Glen Smelthouses Nr. Summerbridge Harrogate HG3 4DJ Tel: (0423) 780328 OPEN: APRIL-OCT	Nearest Roads A.61 B.6165 Pleasant house in traditional style. Warm welcome. Two double and one twin bedroom, all with hand basins. Excellent breakfast here. Good restaurant/pub nearby. This house was a flax mill in the 18th century and retains the mill pond. Lovely walks and has associations with Fountains Abbey. Take marked road, watch out for The Glen on sharp bend. Drive into courtyard. Children over 12.	£15.00	O	■	■
Mrs E. Ogleby St.James House 36 St.James Green Thirsk YO7 1AQ Tel: (0845) 22676 OPEN: APR-OCT	Nearest Roads A.63 A.19 St.James House is a delightful 18th century building standing on the green and only 2 minutes walk from the market place. Beautifully furnished with antiques throughout. Mrs. Ogleby offers six lovely rooms with modern amenities and tea/coffee makers. A comfortable lounge with colour T.V. is available for guests - also a portable T.V. The garden may be used by visitors. No smoking in the house. This is James Herriot's town.	£12.00	O	■	■
Miss B. Estill Tudor Mead Thorpe Lane Robin Hood's Bay Whitby YO22 4RN Tel: (0947) 880368 OPEN: APRIL-OCT	Nearest Road A.171 A warm welcome in this comfortable house with excellent accommodation and modern facilities. Tudor Mead is situated at the top of the most fascinating old fishing village of Robin Hood's Bay, surrounded by moors and glorious scenery. Sandy beach and rock pools, coastal walks to Whitby or Ravenscar. Pubs, tea-shops and restaurants in the village.	£7.80	■	■	■
Jean & David Cockburn Moorview Guest House 104 Skipton Road Ilkley LS29 9HE Tel: (0943) 600156 OPEN: MAR-NOV	Nearest Road A.65 A very warm welcome awaits the visitor to Moorview. A fully refurbished, tastefully furnished and decorated Victorian villa, offering 11 rooms, 5 with private bath. All have lovely views and modern amenities including tea/coffee making facilities, many with T.V. A guests' lounge with colour T.V. Ideally situated for touring the Yorkshire Dales. Nearby are Bolton Abbey and Barden Towers.	£18.00	O	O	■

O yes ■ no

	minimum per person	children taken	evening meals available	animals taken
Chas & Susan Bruce **The Blossoms** **28 Clifton** **York YO3 6AE** **Tel: (0904) 652391** **OPEN: ALL YEAR** Nearest Road A.19 A fine Georgian town house which is ideally situated only a few minutes away from the town centre. Twelve most charming rooms that are well decorated and furnished to a high standard. Seven rooms have en-suite facilities. There is a large lounge for guests and tea/coffee are always available here. Plenty for everyone in historic York. The City Walls are only 15 minutes away. A warm welcome is guaranteed. Rate is for two people.	£16.00	○	■	○
Judy & Rod Slip **Annjoa House** **34/36 Millfield Road** **Scarcroft Road** **York YO2 1NQ** **Tel:(0904) 653731** **OPEN: ALL YEAR** Nearest Road A.64 Small family run licensed hotel, quietly located close to railway station. Offering guests a choice of eleven rooms all with modern amenities, tea/coffee and some with T.V. There's a residents' colour T.V. lounge and a comfortable bar to relax in. Conveniently located for the city centre and racecourse, making this a good base from which to explore the historic city of York with its fine Minster and many interesting museums and ancient Roman and Viking sites.	£10.00	○	○	■
Mr & Mrs Earp **Acer Guest House** **52 Scarcroft Hill** **The Mount** **York YO2 1DE** **Tel: (0904) 53839** **OPEN: ALL YEAR** Nearest Roads A.64 A.1 A pleasant Victorian house offering five comfortable rooms with all modern amenities and laundry facilities. Situated in a quiet area adjoining the Knavesmore race course and parkland, the city centre is only 10-15 minutes walk away. The dales, North Yorkshire moors and the coast are all easily accessible. The warm welcome offered by the proprietors ensures a happy and memorable stay. Ideal for long weekends, walking and touring holidays.	£8.50	○	○	○
Keith Jackman **Dairy Wholefood** ** Guest House** **3 Scarcroft Road** **York YO2 1ND** **Tel: (0904) 39367** **OPEN: FEB-NOV** Nearest Roads A.19 A.64 The Dairy is a tastefully renovated Victorian house within walking distance of the city centre and just 200 yards from the mediaeval city walls. Decorated and furnished in the styles of Habitat, Sandersons and Laura Ashley with the emphasis on pine and plants. Six bedrooms with modern amenities, T.V., hot drink facilities and extensive information on York and Yorkshire. One room is on the ground floor, some are en-suite. There is a lovely enclosed courtyard. Breakfast choice ranges from tranditional English to wholefood vegetarian.	£9.50	○	■	○

○ yes ■ no

		minimum per person	children taken	evening meals available	animals taken
Liz & Malcolm Greaves **Carlton House Hotel** **134 The Mount** **York YO2 2AS** **Tel: (0904) 22265** **OPEN: ALL YEAR**	Nearest Road A.40 Each and every guest will receive a warm and friendly welcome from proprietors Liz & Malcolm Greaves. This pleasant family run hotel offers guests a choice of fifteen rooms all with colour T.V. and radio. Some have private facilities. The two spacious lounges are comfortable and pleasantly furnished. A traditional English is cooked to order each morning and served in the dining room. Light refreshments are available at most times throughout the day. Nearby are York race course, the Minster museums.	£12.50	O	■	■
Russell & **Cherry Whitbourn-Hammond** **Nunmill House** **85 Bishopthorpe Road** **York YO2 1NX** **Tel: (0904) 34047** **OPEN: MAR-OCT**	Nearest Roads A.64 A.59 A splendid late Victorian residence tastefully restored to enhance the architectural features. Accommodation in comfortable rooms with modern facilities. It is very close to the race course. From here one can discover the joys of the city and the delightful countryside with its lovely villages and old buildings. Conveniently located only 10 minutes walk from York city centre.	£10.00	O	O	■
Mrs P Foster **The Abbingdon** **60 Bootham Crescent** **York YO3 7AH** **Tel: (0904) 21761** **OPEN: JAN-NOV**	Nearest Road A.19 Friendly service and all the comforts expected of a small hotel will be found at the Abbingdon. Beautifully appointed throughout, the house offers a choice of seven rooms, most with private bathroom facilities. Remote control T.V., hair dryers and irons. A hearty English breakfast is served, with Continental alternative or other dietary considerations. Residents lounge. Within easy walking distance of The Minster.	£9.00	O	■	■
Miss W. Peacock **The Manor Country** **Guest House** **Acaster Malbis** **York YO2 1UL** **Tel: (0904) 706723** **OPEN: ALL YEAR**	Nearest Road A.64 A modernised country house by the River Ouse, set in 6 acres of beautiful grounds with woodlands, lake and small island. Offering 12 bedrooms, some with shower only, all with modern amenities, tea/coffee making facilities. Comfortable lounge with open coal fire and dining room. Central for visiting York, Moors and the dales. Please send S.A.E. or for Internatioanl reply coupons for illustrated brochure with maps.	£10.50	O	O	O
Mrs A.J. Robinson **Sandwith Lodge** **Bilbrough** **York YO2 3PQ** **Tel: (0937) 834928** **OPEN: ALL YEAR**	Nearest Road A.64 An individual and most attractive modern farmhouse in lovely, peaceful countryside where an excellent welcome, privacy and comfort are assured. Spacious accommodation is in two rooms, a double, which can be used as a family room, and a twin. It is traditionally furnished, has private facilities., T.V. tea/coffee makers, and a large balcony with superb views of open and wooded countryside. Tennis court, riding and shooting available.	£9.00	O	O	O

O yes ■ no

	minimum per person	children taken	evening meals available	animals taken
Joan Tree **Inglewood Guest House** **7 Clifton Green** **Clifton** **York YO3 6LH** **Tel: (0904) 653523** **OPEN: ALL YEAR** Nearest Road A.19 In this charming Victorian house guests will instantly feel completely at home. The friendliness and warmth of your host will ensure an enjoyable and relaxing stay. Accommodation is in six comfortable bedrooms some with en-suite facilities, all with colour T.V. and modern amenities. The first class breakfast is served in the attractive dinning room. This makes an ideal base from which to visit the many attractions in and around York city.	£14.00	O	■	■
C.E.H. & S.A. Roberts **Avenue Guest House** **6 The Avenue** **Clifton** **York YO3 6AS** **Tel: (0904) 20575** **OPEN: ALL YEAR** Nearest Road A.19 A warm welcome is offered to guests here in this comfortable house with very good accommodation. Modern amenities and good food, all excellent rates. Apart from the joys of York with its historic buildings, great cathedral and city walls there is much to see in the surrounding area - Benningbrough Hall and Castle Howard being just two of the superb places to visit. T.V. in all rooms.	£9.50	O	O	■
Mrs K. Jackson **Townend Farm** **Great Ouseburn** **York YO5 9RG** **Tel: (0901) 30200** **OPEN: ALL YEAR** Nearest Roads A.1. A.59 A well furnished 18th century farmhouse with open fires in an inglenook fireplace. The house, in a village setting within easy reach of York, Harrogate, the dales and the moors, has 3 comfortable bedrooms with modern amenities including tea/coffee makers, and there is a large and lovely secluded garden. Fresh farm produce is served. Golf within 2 miles.	£9.00	O	■	O
Mr & Mrs J.C. Welch **Turnbridge House** **York Road** **Moor Monkton** **YO5 8JZ** **Tel: (090483) 387** **OPEN: FEB-DEC** Nearest Road A.59 Turnbridge House is set in an acre of attractive gardens, surrounded on all sides by rolling countryside. 4 miles n.w. of York, with easy access to the Yorkshire moors and dales. Ideal touring centre. Accommodation is in four bedrooms with modern facilities, T.V. and comfortable lounges and dining room. Excellent home cooked meals. Children over 7. Friendly and helpful host.	£13.00	O	O	O
S.T. & D. Butler **Rangers House** **The Park** **Sheriff Hutton** **YO6 1RH** **Tel: (03477) 397** **OPEN: ALL YEAR** Nearest Road A.64 Built in 1639 and situated in the centre of the park, this excellent house with its lovely dove cote offers the perfect base for tourists. Beautifully decorated it offers delightful rooms with modern amenities. The whole house is extensively furnished with antiques and panelling with many old beams. It would be hard to find a more perfect spot. Wonderful evening meals. Lots to see locally.	£19.00	O	O	■

O yes ■ no

		minimum per person	children taken	evening meals available	animals taken
Mr & Mrs M. McNab **Horseshoe House** **York Road** **Dunnington YO1 5QJ** **Tel: (0904) 489369** **OPEN: ALL YEAR**	Nearest Road A.1079 Guests are welcomed into a warm friendly family atmosphere at Horseshoe House. Delightfully located on the edge of an attractive village with views across open countryside, yet only 3½ miles from York city. Accommodation in four bedrooms, two with private bathrooms, all with modern ammenities tea/coffee making facilities. A comfortable colour T.V. lounge and breakfast room are also available. An ideal base for touring. Convenient for the racecoure and golf club. No single occupancy.	£8.00	O	■	O
Hilary Maltman **The Grange** **Harewood Road** **Collingham LS22 5BL** **Tel: (0937) 72752** **OPEN: ALL YEAR**	Nearest Road A.659 A warm welcome and a friendly host await guests at The Grange. Located only 12 miles from York City, this comfortable house offers guests accommodation in a choice of 4 rooms with modern amenities. Some with en suite bath or shower, radio and tea/coffee making facilities. A T.V. lounge and large garden are also available. Ideally situated for touring "Herriot Country", the dales and York. Village inns and restaurants close by. Children over 7, please.	£14.00	O	■	■
Mr & Mrs A.C. Bell **Village Farm** **Raskelf YO6 3LF** **Tel: (0347) 21463** **OPEN: APR-OCT**	Nearest Road A.19 Village Farm is an attractive modern farmhouse with splendid views, whose guests can relax and enjoy the peace and quiet of the beautiful Yorkshire countryside. Accommodation is in two rooms with guests shower and bathroom. A T.V. lounge and delighful garden are also available. Close by are good pubs and restaurants. An excellent base for visiting York 12 miles, and touring the dales and North Yorkshire.	£10.00	O	■	■

O yes ■ no

SCOTLAND

Scottish people are immensely proud of the unique character of their country - and with reason. Itsculture and traditions, its glorious landscape, its history and literature, its architecture, the accent of its people and even the wildlife set it apart from the rest of Britain.

The fierce tradition of Scottish independence goes back to pre-Roman times and the landscape still holds evidence of early settlement like the huge megalithic tombs at Maes Howe in Orkney, the numerous Iron Age round towers called Brochs. The Roman legions never over-ran the warlike tribes of Scotland but preferred to keep them at bay with the spectacular defenses of Hadrians Wall which traverses the Border country from Carlisle to Newcastle. Much of Scotland's history is concerned with the struggle to retain independence from England. Romance and historic fact surround the glittering characters of history. Robert the Bruce drove the English from the land having scaled the heights of Edinburgh Castle to take the city and later routed the enemy forces at Bannockburn. Mary, Queen of Scots, a beautiful but tragic figure, spent much of her life imprisoned by Elizabeth 1 and most famous of all, Bonnie Prince Charlie (Edward Charles Stuart) led the Jacobite Rebellion which ended in the terrible defeat at Culloden.

The events of this turbulent history are recorded today in the folklore and national songs of Scotland. The colourful Border Gatherings, Common Ridings and festivals are more than a chance to wear national dress, they are reminders that Scotland's proud history is not forgotten. Highland Games are held throughout the country and are quite unique. Local and national champions compete inthe unusual events from tossing the caber, requiring incredible strength, piping contests and elegant sword dances and flings, the speciality of small boys and young men wearing the full dress tartan of their clan.

Scotland's landscape is one of variety and contrast from the rugged scenery of the Highlands to the lush pastureland of Lothian and the Central Valley, from the rounded hills of the border country to the far flung island of Hebrides, Orkney, and Shetland. It provides mountains for the climber, beautiful hill country for walking and riding and excellent sport for the hunter and fisherman. There are beautiful lochs and glens biting deep into the mountains and a marvellous coastline with superb beaches. The bounty of the land can also furnish the elements for a fine cuisine. Aberdeen Angus provides perhaps the world's best beef; salmon, sea trout and game are plentiful and Scotland's most famous export, whisky, is available in a confusing variety of distinctive pure malts.

The Borders, Dumfries & Galloway

The borderlands with England form a countryside of rounded hills and beautiful rivers. Itis a landscape of subtle colours from the purple foothills of the Cheviot hills to the dark green valley of the River Tweed. There are rich farmlands, broad heather covered moors and a rocky coastline holding romantic villages and little harbours like Port William, Rockliffe and St. Abbs. To the west, the Galloway Forest Park some 250 square miles offers a magnificent landscape of moors,lochs and forest, perfect for touring and walking. The borderlands have been fought over from Romantimes until mid 17th century and there is scarcely a square yard that does not hold a story of battle, feud, legend or romance. Sweetheart Abbey derives it's name from the story of it's founder who carried her husband's heart in a casket for many years and it now lies with her in the grave within the Abbey. The peaceful village of Coldstream is sited by a ford over the Tweed. Here Edward 1 crossed in 1296 on his way to sack Berwick; here James IV led the young "flowers" of Scotland to the battle of Flodden from which they were never to return.

The years of destructive border warfare has left a scatter of ruined towers, abbeys and castles throughout the country. Roxburgh for instance, near Kelso, was once a Royal Castle and James II waskilled here during a siege. Now there are only the shattered remains of massive stone walls. Others escaped destruction; Boswell is probably the finest 13th century castle in Scotland and Culzean is a good example of the 18th century work of Robert Adam. Threave Castle is a stern Douglas Tower standing on an island in the River Dee and was the last local stronghold to resist therising power of the Scottish monarchy until it fell to James II in 1455. Smailholm, Hume and Greenknowe are also worthy of a visit.

In the heart of the border country near Melrose, lies the beautiful estate of Abbotsford where Sir Walter Scott lived and worked. One of the great literary men of Scotland he perhaps did more than any other to reveal the beauty and culture of Scotland to the world at large. A prolific poet and novelist his most famous works are the Waverley novels written around 1800. He died at Abbotsford in 1832 and the house holds many of the possessions that Scott himself gathered including an excellent collection of armour. The place known as Scott's View is one of the best vantage points in the borderlands offering a prospect of the silvery Tweed and the three distinctive summits of theEildon Hills.

This is Scotland's horse country and has been so since the time of the maurauding mediaeval raiders and freebooters. Today horse breeding, sales and races are still continued and pony trekking has become a popular activity. The common ridings and gatherings attract many riders to follow the ancient tradition of patrolling the town boundaries to prevent encroach-ment. The area is also famous for knitwear and woven cloth, the main centres being at Berwick and Galashiels and there is awool textile museum at Walkerburn.

There is a wealth of beautiful buildings including the enchanting ruined abbeys of Jedburgh, Kelso, Dryburgh and the beautiful red sandstone ruins at Melrose. The ancient Kingdom of Galloway is the cradle of Christianity in Scotland. The first church was built by St. Ninian at Whitehorn in 400 ona site now occupied by the 13th century priory. The spread of Christianity is marked by the early Christian memorial stones including the Latinus stone at Whitehorn and the 18th century stone cross at Ruthwell near Dumfries. In contrast there are the gracious stately homes of Mammerscales, an elegant Georgian building and Manderston, near Dows, considered to be the best example of an Edwardian country house in Scotland. Traquair House, reputed to be the oldest inhabited stately home in the country, locked its main gates after a visit from Bonnie Prince Charlie in 1745 never tobe re-opened until a Stuart King comes to the throne. Mallerstain House, near Gordon, dates from 1770 and has a wonderful interior designed by Robert Adam.

Central Lothian and Strathclyde.

The heartland of Scotland holds an astonishing variety of landscape and places to visit from peaceful lochs and lonely mountains, to bustling coastal towns and the greatly contrasting cities of Edinburgh and Glasgow. The Firth of Clyde ranks amongst the best sailing waters in Europeand its shoreline is dotted with many pleasant resort. To the north the romantic reaches of Loch Lomond lead towards the highland country of the Trossachs which offer a magnificent landscape of mountains, lochs and forest. The seaside towns of Dunoon, Rothesay and Oban are set close to the dramatic scenery of the Argyll I lighlands with its long sea lochs cutting deep inland. Oban is a good base for visiting the Islands of the Inner Hebrides, Mull, Islay and Iona where the quiet cloisters of the Abbey of St. Columba retain an atmosphere of timeless tranquility.

It is evident at first sight that Edinburgh is Scotland's capital city. It has earned a reputation as one of Europe's finest cities both through its architecture and its history. The "Athens of the North" is crowned by Edinburgh Castle. Perched high on a craggy rock it is linked to the city by the long tail of historic buildings and streets known as the Royal Mile. A network of streets, courts, closes, wynds, passageways and gaunt tenements cling to the ridge of "the Mile" and form theheart of the old city. Within this maze is the house of John Knox whose fiery sermons of 1559 sparked off the destruction of the monastries. Nearby is the well restored building of Canongate Tolbooth dating from 1591. The fine Gothic architecture of Parliament Hill is found amongst these streets and rising above the rooftops is the great tower of St. Giles Cathedral. The Royal Mile leads to the Palace of Holyrood House which was the home of Mary, Queen of Scots for several years. She returned here from France, a widow at 19 and strikingly beautiful. In this house she was harrassed by John Knox, here her favourite, David Rizzio was dragged from her side and murdered and here was the scene of her hasty marriage to Bothwell. The Palace has many magnificent rooms and offers and intimate glimpse into the tragic life of Mary. The old town is associated with a famous group of literary figures, including James Boswell, Sir Walter Scott and Robert Louis Stevenson.

It is thought that Stevenson based his story of "Dr Jekyll & Mr Hyde" on the character of notorious Deacon Brodie who was a respected town councillor by day but a daring thief by night. Brodie Squareis named after this infamous character. The cultural traditions of Edin-burgh are alive and well andat their most flamboyant in August and September during the Edinburgh Festival. Beside the famous military tatoo there is drama, film, music and fringe events which combine to make the greatest artsfestival in Great Britain.

Glasgow is quite different. It is robust Victorian city noted more for the vitality of its people than for its historic buildings. However, John Betjeman has drawn attention to the fact that Glasgow is "the finest Victorian city in Britain" and the municipal buildings in George Street are agood illustration of his point. From an earlier period the city Cathedral is a perfect example of English Gothic architecture and in this century, the Glasgow School of art in Renfrew Street is an outstanding piece of work by Charles Rennie Machintosh. By and large the history and achievement ofGlasgow has an industrial base. The city has long been famous for engineering and shipbuilding which is reflected today in the comprehensive model collection at Kelvingrove museum.

Robert Burns is undoubtedly Scotland's greatest and best loved poet and "Burns Night" is widely celebrated. The region of Strathclyde shares with Dumfries and Galloway the distinguished title of "Burns Country". The son of a peasant farmer, Burns lived in poverty for much of his life and the little village of Alloway near Ayr retains the simple house where he was born. The village church still stands where Tam O'Shanter "saw an unco sight/Warlocks and witches in a dance". In the town of Ayr is the Auld Kirk where Burns was baptised and the footbridge immortalised in the poem "The Brigs of Ayr" is still in use. The famous Tam O'Shanter Inn is now a Burns museum but it retains its thatched roof and simple fittings. The "Burns Trail" leads on to Mauchline, many of the buildings described by the poet are gone but Possie Nansie's Inn remains. At Tarbolton the NationalTrust now care for the old house where Burns founded the "Batchelors Club" debating society. Burns later moved to Dumfries and the small red sandstone house in Burns Street where he lived in his latter years is now a museum.

Fife, Grampian and Tayside.

North of Edinburgh across the Firth of Forth lies the ancient kingdom of Fife and still further north are Tayside, Grampian and the granite city of Aberdeen. It is spacious and magnificent country from the towering mountain peaks of the Grampian highlands to the great shimmering lochs of Tummel, Rannoch and Tay. It is a land of rivers, streams rise in the glacier scarred mountains of the north east and tumble down through steep glens and wooded hills to become broad swift rivers crossing the farmlands of the coastal plain. The coast harbours picturesque fishing villages like Crail, Elie and St. Monans and some really superb beaches. The coastal towns like Arbroath, Montrose and Aberdeen itself, all have their individual character and are unmistakably Scottish.

It is a paradise for the golfer. St. Andrews, one of the historic towns of Scotland, is best known as the home of golf but with its university, cathedral ruins, fine buildings and splendid location it has more to offer. There are the world famous courses at Gleneagles and at Carnoustie and over 30 other excellent courses often set in magnificent scenery as at Crieff and Blairgowrie. Here are the fairy tale castles of Scotland. Their clusters of towers and turrets, battlements and conical roofs look pretty but their defenses are real enough and many have been put to the test in the violent struggles of the past. You can find them everywhere, perched on clifftops, guarding towns and glens and in beautiful country estates. Many are a kind of hybrid, half house, half castle, fortheir purposes were domestic as well as military. Doune Castle near Stirling provides one of the best restored examples dating from the 14th century. Grampian holds a number of fine castles notably along Deeside and Donside. Especially well known are Balmoral, home of the Royal Family during shooting season and Blair Atholl, a white turreted castle and traditional home of the Dukes of Athol. It has the distinction of being the last castle in Britain to be besieged and it houses atreasure trove of antiquities including portraits, furniture and one of the finest arms collections in the world. Glamis is an imposing castle of turrets and battlemented parapets and was the childhood home of the Queen Mother. King Malcolm was murdered here and it is easy to see why Shakespeare based Macbeth in its echoing rooms -- it is reputed to be the most haunted place in Britain. Nearby are the ruins of the castle of Dunsinane, where according to Shakespeare, Macbeth met his fate.

The countryside is also rich in history. In the pass of Killiecrankie a single standing stone marksthe spot where the highlanders charged barefoot to overwhelm the redcoat soldies of General MacKay. Despite its gory history the deep wooded gorge is a strikingly beautiful location. Elgin is one ofthe most pleasant towns in Scotland and is traditionally a centre of the Jacobite cult. Just to thesouth at Culloden over 1,000 highlanders fell and hopes for a Stuart restoration were ended. The Duke of Cumberland earned the hatred of the Scots by killing all the wounded and systematically massacreing the clansmen throughout the area.

The two worldwide symbols of Scotland, Whisky and the tartan can both be found here. The Spey Valley is dotted with world famous distilleries which can be found every few miles from Grantown-on-Spey to Aberdeen. Braemar, north of Aberdeen is the scene of the famous Highland Gatherings. Each clan has its own distinctive tartan and good collections can be seen at the tartan museum in Comrieand at Blair Athol.

There are many old towns and pleasant villages throughout the region. Crieff and Pitlochry are attractive and an ideal base for exploring the Cannoch area where the bleak moorlands have been sanctuary for many a hunted highlander in times gone by. The village of Ceves has much to commend it, including the Fife Folk Museum and Falkland Palace and nearby the mediaeval town of Culross has been well restored and offers a living glimpse into history.

Highlands & Islands

The northern Highlands are divided from the rest of Scotland by the dramatic valley of the Great Glen. From Fort William to Inverness, sea lochs, canals and the mysterious waters of LochNess form a chain of waterways that link both coasts. Visitors to the north come for the wide open spaces and the scenery for here lies the grandeur of the true highlands and the last untouched landscape of Britain. There are wild, picturesque glens, soft moorlands, dark forests and dramatic coastline fretted by sea lochs extending their salty fingers many miles inland.

To the north of Loch Ness are the remnants of the ancient Caledonian Forests which once covered the country and an unsurpassed wealth of wildlife. Red deer and magnificent stags are a common sight onthe hills but there are rarer species including the peregrine falcon, the osprey and the king of theskies, the golden eagle. The Scottish wildcat is a rare sight even in the excellent wildlife parks of Kincraig. The wonderful colours of spring and autumn attract many visitors and both summer and winter sports facilities can be found at the Aviemore Centre and at the towns and villages in the valley.

The valleys were once the home of crofting communities and the clansmen who went forth in support ofthe Jacobite cause. The wild and rugged scenery of Glencoe is a favourite haunt of climbers and walkers but it has a tragic tale. Its name literally means the "glen of weeping" and refers to the massacre of the Macdonald clansmen in 1692 when the royal troops who had been received as guests treacherously attacked their sleeping hosts at dawn. The valleys are largely empty today as a result of the infamous highland clearances in the 19th century when the landowners turned out the tenant farmers in order to introduce the more profitable cheviot sheep. The emigration of many Scots to the U.S.A. and British Colonies resulted from these events.

North of Fort William the landscape is at its most majestic and Ben Nevis, Britain's highest peak and the ranges of the Sutherland Mountains form a magnificent vista from Loch Linnhe. The region isnot all mountain and moor and the coasts of Moray offer fine beaches as do the islands of the outerHebrides. The islands each have their own attractions, Shetland Orkney have a strong Scandinavian influence and the Norse festival of "Up Hellu Aa" is still cele-brated in Lerwick with much pageantry. Indeed Shetland and Orkney were not part of Scotland until the 15th century, when they formed part of the dowry of a Scandinavian princess. It never really gets dark here during mid summer and the northern lights flicker in the night sky. There is much evidence of early settlementhere, Jarlshof is an excavated Bronze Age village on Sheltand and Skara Brae village and the Maes Howe burial mound of Orkney date from the Stone Age.

The Kyle of Lochalsh is a good base for Skye and the Isles of Harris, Lewis and a visit to the outerHebrides. Skye is a beautiful mountainous island characterised by soft sea mists and lingering sunsets. There are tiny villages and crofting communities and a wealth of historic sites. In the outer Hebrides the Gaelic culture and language still flourish and islands are famous for their excellent tweed cloth and the standing stones of Callanish form the most eleborate and complete prehistoric site in Britain. The variety and romance of the islands is endless. From rugged fishing villages to tales of Bonnie Prince Charlie, from Viking settle-ments to ruined castles and abbeys, the islands once visited will not be forgotten.

SCOTLAND GAZETEER

It would be invidious, not to say almost impossible, to choose any particular area of Scotland as having a more beautiful aspect than another -- the entire country is a joy to the traveller. The Rugged Highlands, the great glens, tumbling waters, tranquil lochs -- the deep countryside or the wild coastline -- simply come and choose your own piece of paradise.

Historic Houses and Castles

Bowhill -- Nr. Selkirk
18th-19th century -- home of the Duke of Bucceleugh and Queensberry. Has an outstanding collection of pictures by Canaletto, Claude, Gainsborough, Guardi, Reynolds and Leonardo da Vinci. Also superb silver, porcelain and furniture. 16th-17th century miniatures.

Floors Castle -- Kelso
18th century -- home of the Duke and Duchess of Roxburgh. One the borders overlooking the River Tweed. Collection of paintings by Canaletto, Gainsborough, Lely, and Reynolds -- also porcelain.

Traquair House -- Innerleithen
A unique and ancient house being the oldest inhabited home in Scotland. It is rich in associations with every form of political history and after Bonnie Prince Charlie passed through its main gates in 1745 no other visitor has been allowed to use them. There are tresures in the house dating from 12th century, and it has an 18th century library and a priest's room with secret stairs.

Linlithgow Palace -- Linlithgow
The birth place of Mary, Queen of Scots.

Stirling Castle -- Stirling
Royal Castle.

Drumlanrigg Castle -- Nr. Thornhill
17th century castle of pale pink stone -- romantic and historic -- wonderful art treasures including a magnificent Rembrandt and a huge silver chandelier. Beautiful garden setting.

Braemar Castle -- Braemar
17th century castle great historic interest. Has round central tower with spiral staircase giving it a fairy-tale appearence.

Drum Castle -- Nr. Aberdeen
Dating in part from 13th century, it has a great square tower.

Cawdor Castle -- Nairn
14th century fortress -- like castle -- Has always been the home of the Thanes of Cawdor -- background to Shakespeare's Macbeth.

Dunvegan Castle -- Isle of Skye
13th century -- has always been the home of the Chiefs of McLeod.

Hopetoun House -- South Queensferry
Very fine example of Adam architecture and has a fine collection of pictures and furniture. Splendid landscaped grounds.

Inverary Castle -- Argyll
Home of the Dukes of Argyll. 18th century -- Headquarters of Clan Campbell.

Burn's Cottage -- Alloway
Birthplace of Robert Burns -- 1659 -- thatched cottage -- museum of Burns' relics.

Bachelors' Club --Tarbolton
17th century house -- thatched -- where Burns and friends formed their club -- 1780.

Blair Castle -- Blair Atholl
Home of the Duke of Atholl. 13th century Baronial mansion -- collection of Jacobite relics, Armour, Paintings, China and many other items.

Glamis Castle -- Angus
17th century remodelling in Chateau style -- home of the Earl of Strathmore and Kinghorne. Very attractive castle -- lovely grounds by Capability Brown.

Scone Palace -- Perth
Has always been associated with seat of Government of Scotland from earliest times. The stone of Destiny was removed form the Palace in 1296 and taken to Westminster Abbey. Present palace rebuilt in early 1800's still incorporating parts of the old. Lovely gardens.

Edinburgh Castle
Fortess standing high over the town -- famous for military tattoo.

Cathedrals and Churches

Dunfermline Abbey -- Dunfermline
Norman remains of beautiful church. Modern east end and tower.

Edinburgh (church of the Holy Rood)
15th century -- was divided into two in 17th century and re-united 1938. Here Mary, Queen of Scots wascrowned.

Glasgow (St. Mungo)
12th-15th century cathedral -- 19th century interior. Central tower with spire.

Kirkwall (St. Magnus)
12th century cathedral with very fine nave.

Falkirk Old Parish Church -- Falkirk
The spotted appearance (faw) of the church (kirk) gave the town it's name. The site of the church has been used since 7th century, with succesive churches built upon it. The present church was much rebuilt in 19th century. Interesting historically.

Museums and Galleries

Angus Folk Museum -- Glamis
17th century cottages with stone slab roofs, restored by the National Trust for Scotland and houses a fine folk collection.

Mary, Queen of Scots House -- Jedburgh
Life and times of the Queen along with paintings etc.

Andrew Carnegie Birthplace -- Dunfermline
The cottage where he was born is now part of a museum showing his life's work.

Aberdeen Art Gallery & Museum -- Aberdeen
Sculpture, paintings, watercolours, prints and drawings. Applied arts. Maritime museum exhibits.

Provost Skene's House -- Aberdeen
17th century house now exhibiting local domestic life etc.

Highland Folk Museum -- Kingussie
Examples of craft work and tools -- furnished cottage with mill.

West Highland Museum -- Fort William
Natural and local history. Relics of Jacobites and exhibition of the '45 Rising.

Clan Macpherson House -- Newtonmore
Relics of the Clan.

Glasgow Art Gallery & Museum -- Glasgow
Archeology, technology, local and natural history. Old masters, tapestries, porcelain, glass & silver etc. Sculpture.

Scottish National Gallery -- Edingburgh
20th centruy collection -- paintings and sculpture -- Arp, Leger, Giacometti, Matisse, Picasso. Modern Scottish painting.

National Museum of Antiquities in Scotland -- Edinburgh
Collection from Stone Age to modern times -- Relics of Celtic Church, Stuart relics, Highland weapons, etc. etc.

Gladstone Court -- Biggar
Small indoor street of shops, a bank, schoolroom, library etc.

Burns' Cottage and Museum -- Alloway
Relics of Robert Burns -- National Poet.

Inverness Museum & Art Gallery -- Inverness
Social History, archeology and cultural life of the Highlands. Display of the Life of the Clans -- good Highland silver -- crafts, etc.

Kirkintilloch -- Nr. Glassgow
Auld Kirk Museum. Local history including archeological speciments from the Antonine Wall (Roman). Local industries, exhibitions etc.

The foregoing are but a few of the many museums and galleries in Scotland -- further information is always freely availbable from the Tourist Information Bureaux.

Historic Monuments

Aberdour Castle -- Aberdour
14th century fortification -- part still roofed.

Balvenie Castle -- Dufton
15th century castle ruins.

Cambuskenneth Abbey -- Nr. Stirling
12th century abbey -- seat of Bruce's Parliament in 1326. Ruins.

Dryburgh Abbey -- Dryburgh
Remains of monastery.

Loch Leven Castle -- Port Glasgow
15th century ruined stronghold - once lived in by Mary, Queen of Scots.

Newark Castle -- Port Glasgow
16th century turreted castle.

Rothesay Castle -- Rothesay
13th century moated castle.

Elgin Cathedral -- Elgin
13th century cathedral -- Now ruins.

Rosslyn Castle -- Rosslyn
14th century castle -- ruins.

Tolquhon Castle -- Taves
15th century tower -- 16th century mansion, now roofless.

Haggs Castle -- Glasgow.
16th century castle now museum for children.

SCOTLAND
Recommended roadside restaurants

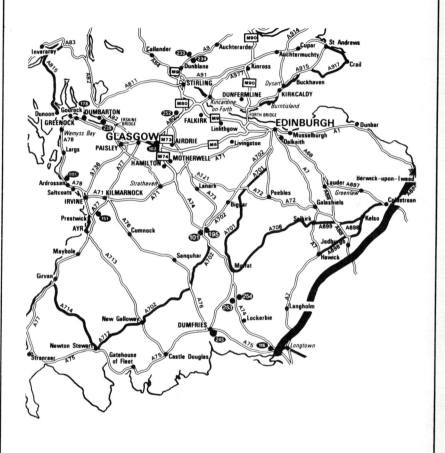

SCOTLAND
Recommended roadside restaurants

087	A96	Inverness Milburn Road 1 mile east of Inverness
090	A9	Killiecrankie Perth 3 miles north of Pitlochry
103	A92	Newtonhill Stonehaven, Kincardineshire 8 miles south of Aberdeen
174	A92	Claverhouse Dundee Abroath Road 3 miles east of Dundee
236	A94	Brechin Tayside 4 miles west of Brechin
279	A96	Forres Highland 1 mile west of Forres

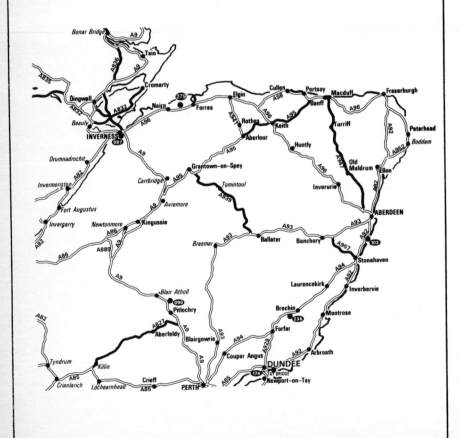

Scotland
Aberdeen

Mrs J.B. Ramsey **Klibreck Guest House** **410 Great Western Road** **Aberdeen AB1 6NR** **Tel: (0224) 316115** **OPEN: ALL YEAR**	Nearest Roads A.93 A.92 A.96 A solid, comfortable house offering a very warm welcome to visitors in six charming, well decorated rooms with modern amenities. Also a T.V. lounge. This is an ideal base for touring both North and South. Situated within 10 minutes of the city centre, with plenty of interesting museums and galleries.	£11.50	○	○	■
Angie & Colin Campbell **Hazlehurst Lodge** **Ballater Road** **Aboyne AB3 5HY** **Tel: (0339) 2921/2** **OPEN: APRIL-OCT**	Nearest Road A.93 A delightful 105 year old converted coachman's house built in attractive pink granite. The accommodation is super. Offering four very comfortable bedrooms, one with private shower. Fresh flowers, nice soap, tissues, tea/coffee making facilities in each room, guests' sitting room and dining room serving delicious food at times convenient to guests. An excellent base for a holiday.	£9.00	○	○	○

Argyll

C.W. & B. Phillips **Abbots Brae Hotel** **West Bay** **Dunoon PA23 7QJ** **Tel: (0369) 5021** **OPEN: FEB-NOV**	Nearest Road A.885 An attractive hotel, situated in four acres of partially wooded grounds adjacent to the beauty spot Morag's Fairy Glen, with beautiful views over the hills and Firth of Clyde. It offers 7 most comfortable rooms, several with private bath or shower, radio, colour T.V. and tea making facilities. Situated opposite beach with town centre 10 minutes. Riding and trekking, fishing and golf in the area. Perfect for families.	£13.50	○	○	○
Mrs Mary Trybis **Glenrigh Private Hotel** **Esplanade** **Oban PA34 5AQ** **Tel: (0631) 62991** **OPEN: MAR-OCT**	Nearest Road A warm welcome and friendly hosts await the visitor to Glenrigh. This is a traditional, Scottish Victorian house built of local granite stone. Centrally located on the esplanade offering beautiful sea views from the dining room and lounge. Accommodation is in 12 rooms with modern amenities. There is also a T.V. lounge available for guests' use.	£9.20	○	○	○

Ayrshire

John & Sarah Gracie **Arran View** **9 St. Ninian's Road** **Prestwick KA9 1SL** **Tel: (0292) 77221** **OPEN: ALL YEAR**	Nearest Road A.78 A.77 A pleasing cottage style house offering a warm welcome in 5 comfortable rooms all with modern facilities. A guests' lounge is also offered. Situated opposite a golf course and the Firth of Clyde with the Isle of Arran in the distance. Only 3 minutes from an excellent beach and many historic sites and houses plus sporting facilities in the locality. Tea/coffee making facilities in all rooms.	£8.50	○	■	○

○ yes ■ no   **283**

Caithness

		minimum per person	children taken	evening meals available	animals taken

E. Davidson
37 Durness Street
Thurso KW14 8BQ
Tel: (0847) 63069

OPEN: ALL YEAR

Nearest Road A.9

Mrs Davidson offers two bedrooms, one double, one twin, to guests at her home in Durness Street, a quiet residential area with an uninterrupted view over Thurso Bay, the Orkney Isles in the distance. Thurso Town Centre, just 3 minutes, car parking no problem. Mr Davidson is a piper and welcomes visitors to join him in his interests in Scottish entertainment.

£8.00 ○ ■ ■

Dumbartonshire

Mrs K.J. Wylie
Greenbank Guest House
  and Licensed Restaurant
Main Street
Arrochar G83 7AA
Tel: (03012) 305

OPEN: ALL YEAR

Nearest Road A.83

A pretty house with a licensed restaurant attached. A lovely rockery at the front and well cared for garden at the rear. Four pleasant modern rooms all with shower ensuite plus T.V. and tea/coffee makers. Mrs. Wylie offers good food in her restaurant and excellent Scottish breakfast. All types of diets catered for. Situated on the shore of the loch with mountain views, it is an ideal base for touring, walking, riding, and fishing. A very warm welcome awaits all visitors here.

£10.00 ○ ○ ○

Dumfriesshire

Jean & Derrick Ainsworth
Cavens House
Kirkbean by Dumfries
DG2 BAA
Tel: (038788) 234

OPEN: ALL YEAR

Nearest Road A.710

Formerly an old mansion, this charming guest house offers 5 really comfortable rooms with modern facilities including private bath or shower. Tea making facilities in each room. Standing in 11 acres of mature gardens and woodland, it makes a perfect base for those wishing to explore the joys of the Solway Coast with its beautiful scenery and excellent beaches. Sailing, fishing, walking, golfing and riding all local. Excellent cuisine here. Special facilities for the disabled. Friendly atmosphere and good value.

£15.00 ○ ○ ○

Robert & Elizabeth Drummond
Hartfell House
Hartfell Crescent
Moffat DG10 9AL
Tel: (0683) 20153

OPEN: MAR-NOV

Nearest Road A.74

A really superb 19th century house renowned for its fine interior woodwork, with nine delightful comfortable rooms with every modern amenity. This country house is set in magnificent scenery offering an ideal base for visitors. Salmon fishing, sailing, walking, riding, deer stalking all locally and Traquair House is not far away. Evening meals here are excellent and very food value. The Drummond's really make all their guests feel 'at home' and help plan tours etc. Private fishing and shooting rights. Riding and golf at Moffat can be arranged for visitors.

£9.50 ○ ○ ○

	minimum per person	children taken	evening meals available	animals taken
Mrs Vera G. Waugh **Cabana Guest House** **Ballplay Road** **Moffat DJ10 9JX** **Tel: (0683) 20400** **OPEN: ALL YEAR** Nearest Roads A.74 A.701 A.708 A beautifully maintained large chalet bungalow in a quiet residential area with fine views of the Moffat Hills. Fully central heated. 4 designer-decorated rooms with all modern amenities. T.V. lounge/dining room and separate residents' lounge. Good home cooking tastefully presented with true Scottish hospitality. Private parking. Ideal stopover to and from the Highlands or for touring the Borders and Lowlands. Fishing, golf, tennis, bowling horse-riding, boating available locally.	£9.50	O	O	O
Brenda Ptolomey **Comlongon Castle** **Clarencefield** **Dumfries DG1 4NA** **Tel: (038787) 283** **OPEN: MAR-DEC** Nearest Road A.75 Excellent food and superb accommodation awaits guests at this 15th century castle. Set in 30 acres of private grounds, this super mediaeval castle retains all its original features including the dungeon, chapel, laird's hall and concealed rooms within its 13 foot thick walls. Guests are accommodated in the elegant Edwardian apartments of the adjoining mansion. There's a choice of seven very comfortable bedrooms, most with 4-poster beds and private bathrooms. After a delicious dinner guests are invited to join a candlelit tour of the ancient castle. No single occupancy available.	£20.00	O	O	■

Edinburgh

	minimum per person	children taken	evening meals available	animals taken
Mrs Esther G. Riley **Teviotdale House** **53 Grange Loan** **Edinburgh E49 2ER** **Tel: (031) 6674376** **OPEN: ALL YEAR** Nearest Road A.7 Teviotdale House is situated in a quiet residential conservation area of south Edinburgh, 1½ miles from Princes Street close to A.7, A.68, and A.702 and has unlimited street parking. The house is beautifully restored and tastefully decorted and offers splendid accommodation. Most rooms have private facilities, centrally heated, colour T.V. and tea/coffee making facilities. Breakfasts are delicious.	£15.50	O	■	O
Mrs H. Donaldson **Invermark** **60 Polwarth Terrace** **Edinburgh EH11 1NJ** **Tel: (031 337) 1066** **OPEN: ALL YEAR** Nearest Roads A.702 A.70 Invermark is a Georgian semi-detached villa situated in quiet suburbs on a main bus route to the city, only five minutes away. Three comfortable and well decorated rooms all with modern facilities. It is well situated for all the amenities of this lovely capital city. Museums, galleries, Holyrood Palace, the Castle, sports centre and superb countryside. Mrs. Donaldson warmly welcomes all her guests.	£9.00	O	■	O

O yes ■ no

285

	Nearest Road / Description	minimum per person	children taken	evening meals available	animals taken
Bob & Helen Cowan **Buchan Private Hotel** **3 Coates Gardens** **Edinburgh EH12 5LG** **Tel: (031337) 1045/8047** **OPEN: ALL YEAR**	Nearest Road A.8 A small happy family run hotel very centrally situated, where the emphasis is on making guests really comfortable. Nine pleasant rooms all with modern amenities, and T.V. is available in rooms if required. Tea/coffee always available. A comfortable lounge with colour T.V. Evening meals are good value here. Only minutes away from Princes Street, the Castle and wonderful antique shops. A warm welcome awaits all visitors.	£12.00	O	O	O
Mr & Mrs Franzese **Clarin Guest House** **4 East Mayfield** **Edinburgh EH9 1SD** **Tel: (031667) 2433** **OPEN: ALL YEAR**	Nearest Road A charming Victorian terraced town house offering seven very pleasant comfortable rooms with modern facilities. Bedrooms beautifully decorated with tea/coffee making facilities and T.V. in each room. The house is being restored back to its original style so it offers a superb atmosphere. Well situated for discovering the joys of the city and countryside.	£10.00	O	■	O
John & Gill Hamilton **Hamilton House** ** Guest House** **12 Moston Terrace** **Newington** **Edinburgh EH9 2DE** **Tel: (031667) 2540** **OPEN: ALL YEAR**	Nearest Roads A.70 A.7 A elegant and comfortable Victorian villa quietly situated yet convenient for the city centre. Service to their guests is John & Gill's priority and children are especially well catered for here. The house has a pleasant homely atmosphere and unusual ornate ceilings. Only 1 mile form the Castle, Holyrood Palace and the Royal Mile.	£11.00	O	O	■
Sheila & Robert Clark **Galloway** **22 Dean Park Crescent** **Edinburgh EH4 1PH** **Tel: (031) 3323672** **OPEN: ALL YEAR**	Nearest Road A.9 A Victorian town house situated a mile from Princes Street. This well known house offers first class accomodation in charming, comfortable rooms, some having private shower. The very warm welcome and the delightul atmosphere of the house are what so many people are looking for. Evening meals are excellent. Apart from the joys of Edinburgh itself visitors can explore Holyrood Park, Arthurs Seat and the Royal Botanic Gardens. Evening meals in off-season only. 7 nights for the price of 6 all year. Also Oct-Apr (excl. Easter) 4 nights for price of 3.	£12.00	O	O	O
Mr & Mrs William Wright **Salisbury Hotel** **45 Salisbury Road** **Edinburgh EH16 5AA** **Tel: (031) 6671264** **OPEN: ALL YEAR**	Nearest Roads A.7 A.68 Under personal supervision of resident proprietors, Brenda and William Wright, who offer real Scottish hospitality in a well maintained Georgian townhouse quietly situated one mile from city centre, convenient for main bus routes. Light, airy comfortably furnished rooms with tea/coffee makers. Single rooms and private facilities available.	£11.00	O	■	O

O yes ■ no

	minimum per person	children taken	evening meals available	animals taken
Mrs Helen Hall 'Woodlands' 55 Barnton Avenue Davidson's Mains Edinburgh EH4 6JJ Tel: (031) 3361685 — OPEN: ALL YEAR	£18.00	O	■	O
Wilma & Bill Hogg Kingsley Guest House 30 Craigmillar Park Newington Edinburgh EH16 5PS Tel: (031) 6678439 — OPEN: ALL YEAR	£9.00	O	■	O
John A. Buchanan Tankard Guest House 40 East Claremont Street Edinburgh EH7 4JR Tel: (031) 5564218 — OPEN: ALL YEAR	11.00		■	O
Mr & Mrs Simpson Greenside Hotel 9 Royal Terrace Edinburgh EH7 5AB Tel: (031) 5570022 — OPEN: JAN-OCT	£18.40	O	■	■
Mrs S. McLellan Allison House Hotel 15-17 Mayfield Gardens Edinburgh EH9 2AX Tel: (031) 6678049 — OPEN: ALL YEAR	£12.00	O	■	■

Mrs Helen Hall
'Woodlands'
55 Barnton Avenue
Davidson's Mains
Edinburgh EH4 6JJ
Tel: (031) 3361685

OPEN: ALL YEAR

Nearest Road A.90

A small mansion house offering three very pleasant, comfortable rooms with modern amenities. Set in 2 acres of lawns and woodland next to the Royal Burgess golf course. It is ideal as a tranquil base yet is very close to the city. Whilst the city itself holds a wealth of interest the surronding countryside should not be overlooked. One mile from Lauriston Castle.

Wilma & Bill Hogg
Kingsley Guest House
30 Craigmillar Park
Newington
Edinburgh EH16 5PS
Tel: (031) 6678439

OPEN: ALL YEAR

Nearest Road A.7

A pleasing Victorian terraced villa offering seven charming, comfortable rooms, and tea making facilities. All with modern amenities. Personal attention and a warm welcome await the visitor here. It is most conveniently situated for the city centre and the marvellous countryside. It also offers reduced rates for families and Senior Citizens. A really good base for everyone. Cots are provided.

John A. Buchanan
Tankard Guest House
40 East Claremont Street
Edinburgh EH7 4JR
Tel: (031) 5564218

OPEN: ALL YEAR

Nearest Road A.1

A warm and friendly welcome awaits guests to Tankard Guest House. Conveniently located for the many attractions of Edinburgh, it offers very pleasant accommodation in a choice of seven rooms all with modern amenities, radio and T.V. Keys are provided so guests are free to come and go as they please. A full breakfast is served each morning 7.30am and 9am. Mr Buchanan is happy to book tours and shows for his guests.

Mr & Mrs Simpson
Greenside Hotel
9 Royal Terrace
Edinburgh EH7 5AB
Tel: (031) 5570022

OPEN: JAN-OCT

Nearest Road A.1

The Greenside Hotel is situated in a Georgian Terrace, about 15 minutes walk from Edinburgh City Centre. The hotel has 12 spacious, comfortable rooms all with modern amenities and fully centrally heated. A large lounge with T.V. and a piano for guests use. A hearty breakfast is served between 8-9am and coffee is served in the lounge each evening around 9.30pm. Mr and Mrs Simpson will make you most welcome. U.S. visitors have made many repeat visits.

Mrs S. McLellan
Allison House Hotel
15-17 Mayfield Gardens
Edinburgh EH9 2AX
Tel: (031) 6678049

OPEN: ALL YEAR

Nearest Road A.7

A very attractive terrace of villas offering 24 well decorated, comfortable rooms, with central heating, colour T.V., tea/coffee making facilities. Most rooms have private facilities. Situated only 5 mintues from the Royal Commonwealth Swimming Pool and very good sports centre. It is a good base for both touring the city and for those who enjoy sports. The Royal Mile is easily accessible from here as are the craft centres, museums and galleries.

O yes ■ no

	minimum per person	children taken	evening meals available	animals taken

Mrs Anne Saunders
The Studio
11 McDonald Rd
EH7 4LX
Tel: (031) 5563434

OPEN: APR-OCT

Nearest Roads A.7 A.1

Mrs Saunders offers a very warm welcome and pleasant, comfortable accommodation in a central and conveniently located house. Within easy walking distance of all the main areas of interest in Edinburgh including Princess Street. This makes the perfect base for touring. Accommodation is in a choice of three rooms all with modern amenities, tea/coffee and chocolate making facilities. A babysitting service is also available. A super Scottish breakfast is served every morning and a brunch breakfast is also available.

£12.00 ○ ■ ■

Alan & Angela Vidler
Rowan Guest House
13 Glenorchy Terrace
Edinburgh EH9 2DQ
Tel: (031) 6672463

OPEN: ALL YEAR

Nearest Roads A.7 A.68

A fine Victorian house of character situated in a quiet residential area. You will find comfortable rooms and a warm welcome from the proprietors here. Nine bedrooms available, with modern amenities. Childern well provided for. Full Scottish breakfast. Tea, coffee and biscuits at anytime in the T.V. lounge. Unrestricted parking and good bus service into town only a short ride away.

£10.00 ○ ■ ○

Mrs A. Dunlop
O'Airlie
63 Glasgow Road
Corstorphine
Edinburgh EH12 8LL
Tel: (031) 3342306

OPEN:

Nearest Roads M.8 A.8

A very attractive bungalow offering, 2 well decorated, most comfortable guest rooms with modern facilities. Situated in an interesting area it offers the best of both worlds, the numerous atractions of the city itself and the joys of the superb countryside with many historic houses and sites. Excellent sporting facilities including golf and riding available within a few miles.

£9.00 ○ ■ ■

Mr & Mrs Roscilli
Tania Guest House
19 Minto Street
Edinburgh EH9 1RQ
Tel: (031) 4144

OPEN: ALL YEAR

Nearest Road A.7

Tania Guest House is a semi-detached Georgian house with a well-maintanined front garden. Located on the South side of Edinburgh. Offering six bedrooms are available all with modern amenities tea/coffee making facilities, some with T.V. and all on the first floor. There is a lounge with colour T.V. for guests use and the premises has a table licence. Car parking space available.

£10.00 ○ ○ ○

Mrs A Gallo
Rosedene Guest House
4 Queen's Crescent
Edinburgh EH9 2AZ
Tel: (031) 6675806

OPEN: APR-OCT

Nearest Roads A.68 A.7

Rosedene is a pleasant detached villa in a select residential area away from the main road, approximately 1½ miles from Princes Street. Parking spaces available. Nine bedrooms for guests with modern amenities, televison, tea/coffee making facilities. Three rooms are on the ground floor. Full Scottish breakfast served.

£10.00 ○ ■ ■

○ yes ■ no

288

	minimum per person	children taken	evening meals available	animals taken
Mr C Marrocco **Lorne Villa Guest House** **9 East Mayfield** **Edinburgh EH9 1SD** Tel: (031) 667 7159 **OPEN: ALL YEAR** Nearest Road A.7 Lorne Villa is a pleasant Victorian house offering accommodation in 6 rooms with modern amenities, most with T.V. and tea/coffee making facilities. A residents' T.V. lounge is available for guests' use. The house is centrally situated with easy access to the city centre.	£13.00	O	■	O
Mrs M Dewar **'Glenesk'** **Delta Place/Smeaton Grove** **Inveresk** **Musselburgh EH21 7TP** Tel: (031) 6653217 **OPEN: APR-SEP** Nearest Road A.1 Quietly situated in picturesque and historic village of Inveresk, 'Glenesk' is a spacious detached villa. It is convenient for all the scenic beauties, beaches and sporting activities of the East Coast, while only 7 miles from centre of Edinburgh, one mile from busy shopping centre of Musselburgh. All 3 bedrooms have private shower rooms or bathrooms, colour T.V. and tea/coffee making facilities. Comfortable lounge. Parking space. No signs displayed — conservation area.	£14.00	O	■	■

Fifeshire

	minimum per person	children taken	evening meals available	animals taken
Mrs May Grant **Greigston Farm** **Peat Inn** **Cupar KY15 5LF** Tel: (033) 484284 **OPEN: APR-OCT** Nearest Roads B.941 B.940 A.915 A truly delightful stone house built in the 18th century offering 2 absolutely charming, comfortable guest rooms with modern facilities. Here the welcome is very warm and the cooking is superb. Standing in a sheltered position with lawns and trees it is the ideal base for touring. There are marvellous beaches, wildlife reserves, superb golf at Carnoustie, Gleneagles and St. Andrews.	£9.50	O	O	O
Mrs E. MacGeachy **"The Dykes"** **69 Pittenweem Road** **Anstruther KY10 3DT** Tel: (0333) 310537 **OPEN: MAR-OCT** Nearest Road A.917 A delightful modern bungalow offering 2 comfortable guest rooms with modern facilities. Situated overlooking the golf course and the sea, this is an ideal base for families and tourists to this lovely region. There are many historic houses and golf courses locally and the walking and riding are excellent. Only 9 miles from St. Andrews.	£8.00	O	■	■

Inverness-shire

	minimum per person	children taken	evening meals available	animals taken
Mrs Lyn Williamson **Alvie Manse** **Aviemore PH22 1QB** Tel: (0479) 810248 **OPEN: FEB-NOV** Nearest Road A.9 An impressive Scottish house situated by a small church on a picturesque site by on Loch Alvie on a large Highland estate. The guest accommodation is in three rooms on the top floor, having views over the loch and the Monadlith hills. Children welcome. Fishing on the spey. Shooting, tennis available on the estate.	£12.50	O	O	■

O yes ■ no

		minimum per person	children taken	evening meals available	animals taken
Mrs E. Munro **Tomich House** **Beauly** **Tel: (0463) 2225** **OPEN: MAR-OCT**	Nearest Roads A.9 A.862 A delightful Georgian house of great charm and character. Built in 1805, it stands in 900 acres of farmland. There are 4 very well decorated, comfortable rooms with modern amenities and kept to every high standard. The landscape and scenic beauty are outstanding. Many sporting activities are available locally. Ideal touring base for the North and West.	.9.00	O	■	■
Peter & Penny Rawson **The Keeper's House** **Private Hotel** **Carrbridge PH23 3AT** **Tel: (047984) 621** **OPEN: DEC-OCT**	Nearest Road A.9 A charming old gamekeeper's cottage and coach house, with very comfortable accommodation in five rooms which are decorated to a very high standard, one en-suite. All rooms have tea/coffee makers. A cosy cottage atmosphere with pretty lounge and courtyard garden for guests. Superb home cooking with fresh produce from the garden. Beautiful views from the house of the Cairngorms and Spey Valley. Fishing, golf and hill-walking.	£9.00	O	O	O
Mrs M.E. Pottie **Easter Dalziel Farmhouse** **Daicross** **Inverness IV1 2JL** **Tel: (0667) 62213** **OPEN: EASTER-OCT**	Nearest Roads A.96 B.9039 A warm welcome and a family atmosphere await the visitor to beautiful Easter Dalziel Farm. A 200 acre working farm with cows and barley. Accommodation is in two very comfortable bedrooms. Plenty of good farmhouse food, lovely garden for guests. An ideal centre for touring. Within a short drive: Cawdor Castle, Loch Ness, Fort George and beautiful sandy beaches at Nairn.	£9.00	O	O	O
Commander & Mrs **I.A.S. Wedderburn** **Dunlichity Lodge** **Farr IV1 2AN** **Tel: (08083) 282** **OPEN: APR-OCT**	Nearest Road A.9 A charming country house situated in two acres offering a very warm welcome and Highland hospitality. Four delightful rooms, two have private bath en-suite. The house has superb food. Situated in a peaceful area with easy access to Loch Ness & Culloden. Private fishing, golfing and walking are all superb locally. Commander and Mrs Wedderburn will advise on places of interest locally and do everything to make their guests' stay a happy one.	£12.50	■	O	O
Mr & Mrs J. Rosie **Gulsachan Guest House** **Alma Road** **Fort William PH33 6HA** **Tel: (0397) 3797** **OPEN: ALL YEAR**	Nearest Road A.82 A friendly Scottish welcome awaits the visitor to Guisachan Guest House. Accommodation is in fifteen rooms, some with private facilities, all with modern amenities and tea/coffee making equipment. A residents' colour T.V. lounge is available throughout the day. Vegetarian diets can be catered for with advance notice. This makes a good base for touring the Fort William area.	£9.00	O	O	■

O yes ■ no

Mrs Margaret Cairns **Invergloy House** **Spean Bridge** **PH34 4DY** **Tel: (039781) 681** **OPEN: ALL YEAR**	Nearest Road A.82 A really interesting Scottish coach house dating back 110 years, offering 3 charming, comfortable rooms with modern facilities; 2 bathrooms. Situated 5 miles north of the village of Spean Bridge towards Inverness, it is signposted on the left along a wooded drive. Guests have use of own sitting room, overlooking Loch Lochy in 50 acres of superb woodland of rhododendron and azaleas. Fishing from the private beach and rowing boats, hard tennis court. Children over 8 welcome.	£9.00	○	○	■
The MacLean Family **Innseagan Guest House** **Achintore Road** **Fort William PH33 6RW** **Tel: (0397) 2452** **OPEN: APR-OCT**	Nearest Road A.82 A delightful guest house dating back over 100 years offering a wonderful atmosphere and great hospitality. 26 very comfortable guest rooms with every modern amenity, many rooms having private bath en-suite. Standing on the shores of Loch Linnhe offering magnificent views with mountains all around. The proprietors offer tour-planning assistance which is vital as there is so much to see. Great care is taken to ensure a memorable holiday. The rate shown includes dinner.	£14.00	○	○	■
Mrs C. Baillie **Victoria Guest House** **1 Victoria Terrace** **Inverness** **Tel: (0463) 237682** **OPEN: ALL YEAR**	Nearest Road A.9 A pleasant Victorian terraced house offering four pleasant, comfortable rooms with modern facilities, with private shower. Situated near the site of King Duncan's Castle, it is a good base for touring the region. Clava Stones, a Druid burial ground, is well worth visiting. Cots and highchairs provided	£9.00	○	■	■
Mr & Mrs M. Macarthur **Crownleigh Guest House** **6 Midmills Road** **Inverness IV2 3NX** **Tel: (0463) 220316** **OPEN: ALL YEAR**	Nearest Road A.9 A pleasant Victorian terraced house in the old residential area of historic Inverness. Five comfortable rooms with modern amenities and tea/coffee making facilities in all rooms. A T.V. lounge is available for guests' use. A baby listening service and cots provided. Packed lunches available on request. Mr & Mrs Macarthur warmly welcome all visitors and will help plan tours. An excellent base for touring.	£8.00	○	■	○
Mrs Jennifer Mackay **The Terrace Guest House** **3 Victoria Terrace** **Inverness IV2 3QA** **Tel: (0463) 225535** **OPEN: ALL YEAR**	Nearest Road A.9 The friendliest of welcomes awaits you at 'The Terrace', a guest house with a family atmosphere in a quiet and peaceful location with open views to the hills but only 5 minutes walking to the town centre. 4 bedrooms are available in this Victorian house, all centrally heated with modern facilities, T.V., tea/coffee making. Lounge and garden for guests' use. Children are welcome and well provided for.	£8.00	○	■	■

○ yes ■ no

		minimum per person	children taken	evening meals available	animals taken
Mr Hayes **Aberfeldy Lodge** **11 Southside Road** **Inverness IV2 3BG** **Tel: (0463) 231120** **OPEN: ALL YEAR**	Nearest Roads A.9 A warm and comfortable great house offering a high standard of accommodation. Mr & Mrs Hayes will be found most helpful regarding all aspects of travellers' needs. Ten rooms are available, five with private facilities, all with modern amenities, tea/coffee makers, some with T.V. Lounge and garden for guests' use. No single availability. Children over 4.	£10.00	O	O	■
Mrs C.M. Macleod **Glasdair** **42 Island Bank Road** **Inverness IV2 4QT** **Tel: (0463) 224692** **OPEN: ALL YEAR**	Nearest Road A.9 A charming period stone built house situated in a conservation area, one and a half miles from the town centre. Three very attractive and comfortable rooms. A pleasant lounge with colour T.V. Lovely gardens which run down to the edge of the River Ness. Packed lunches are available and vegetarian cooking on request. Permanent arrangements with the Inverness & Torveo Golf clubs for guests. Riding is also arranged for you and the house has its own fishing rights. Superb countryside.	£8.00	O	O	O
Mrs I. Donald **"Kerrisdale"** **4 Muirfield Road** **Inverness IV2 4AY** **Tel: (0463) 235489** **OPEN: ALL YEAR**	Nearest Road A.9 A spacious attractive Victorian house set in a large garden in a quiet residential area of Inverness, where you will be warmly welcomed and attended to. Three guest rooms are available, one double, one twin and one family room. Residents' lounge with T.V., and garden available to guests. Nearby is the theatre, the river walks and parks and the amenities of the city.	£9.00	O	O	■
Duncan & Pauline Reeves **The Osprey Hotel** **Kingussie** **Inverness PH21 1EN** **Tel: (05402) 510** **OPEN: JAN-OCT**	Nearest Road A.9 Food, wine, warm and friendly service are the cornerstones of this small, informal hotel, with guests returning from all over the world year after year. The cooking is exceptional and underlines the joy of pure, fresh, whole food. Delightful atmosphere in the hotel. Located in the lovely Spey Valley with plently to do and see and sports to play.	£13.00	O	O	O
Mr & Mrs P. Cruickshank **Sunny Brae Guest House** **Marine Road** **Nairn IV12 4EA** **Tel: (0667) 52309** **OPEN: APR-OCT**	Nearest Road A.96 A modern guest house offering ten very comfortable rooms with all the modern facilities. A warm welcome awaits vistors here. The proprietors offer a babysitting service. The region holds plenty of attractions for all ages and children will love the freedom of the area. Cots and highchairs are provided. The house has magnificent views over the Nairn Links and the Moray Firth to the mountains of Ross & Cromarty, Sutherland and Caithness. Less than 250 yards is a safe, sandy beach.	£12.50	O	O	O

O yes ■ no

	minimum per person	children taken	evening meals taken	animals taken	available

Phyllis & Roy Henderson
Glenquoich Guest House
Glen Road
Newtonmore PH20 1EB
Tel: (05403) 461

OPEN: ALL YEAR
(EXCL. XMAS)

Nearest Roads A.9 A.85

A charming old villa offering a very warm welcome and real Scottish hospitality. Six very pleasant, comfortable guest rooms with modern facilities. The house specialises in home cooking and baking; using fresh local produce it is all very good. The region offers plenty for all ages to discover: historic houses, sites and good sporting facilities. Cots and highchairs are provided.

£9.90 ○ ○ ○

Mr & Mrs G. Nottage
Coig Na Shee
Fort William Road
Newtonmore PH20 1DG
Tel: (05403) 216

OPEN: FEB-NOV

Nearest Road A.9

Coig Na Shee is a delightful large family house set in extensive gardens on the peaceful outskirts of Newtonmore. 7 very nice rooms with washing facilities and lovely views. All have tea/coffee makers. A warm welcome is given here and, delicious home cooked meals include home-made soups, pate and bread. Vegetarian diets catered for. Private riding arrangements can be made. Walking, fishing, canoeing, bowling and tennis. Aviemore is a short drive away. Log fires and drying room.

£10.50 ○ ○ ○

Lanarkshire

Mr S. Ansari
McLays Guest House
268/272 Renfrew Street
Charing Cross
Glasgow G3 6TT
Tel: (041) 3324796/3327798

OPEN: ALL YEAR

Nearest Road M.8

A pleasant hotel situated in the town centre with Sauchiehall Street only a minute away. There are twenty modern and very pleasant rooms, five with en-suite facilities. There is a tea/coffee maker in each room. A large lounge with T.V. for guests. The proprietors have a large map highlighting the superb amenities in the central Glasgow area and will help visitors plan excursions.

£12.00 ○ ○ ■

Phoebe Poole
Field End Guest House
The Loaning
Crawford ML12 6TN
Tel: (08642) 276

OPEN: ALL YEAR
(EXCL XMAS & NEW YEAR)

Nearest Road A.174

A warm Scottish welcome is always waiting for guests at Field End. This traditional stone built guest house offers accommodaton in a choice of five rooms, all with modern amenities and tea/coffee making facilities. T.V. is also available. There is a colour T.V. lounge for guests as well as 2 games rooms. Close by are facilities for riding/pony trekking, golf and tennis. The area has magnificent scenery and lots of opportunities for walking and hiking. Guests can be met at the railway station, ports or airports for a small additional fee.

£8.50 ○ ○ ■

○ yes ■ no

Lothian

		minimum per person	children taken	evening meals available	animals taken
Miss Roma C. Capaldi **Redan** **7 Hamilton Road** **North Berwick EH39 4NH** **Tel: (0620) 2533** **OPEN: MAY-OCT**	Nearest Road A.1 A pleasant, modernised Victorian stone villa offering 2 comfortable rooms to visitors. The area is superb with beaches accessible from here. Fishing and riding. Several historic sites in the area. An interesting area for ornithologists. Only 22 miles from Edinburgh, with excellent train and bus services. Top-class golfing centre including Muirfield.	£10.00	O	■	O
Lady Marioth Hay **Forbes Lodge** **Gifford** **Tel: (062081) 212** **OPEN: APR-OCT**	Nearest Road A.1 A handsome 18th century house with an accomplished hostess where involvement with entertainment music and gardening compliment the fine atmosphere. Three splendid rooms, all well appointed, one with private facilities and 4-poster bed. Lady Hay's family have lived in the area since the 1400's and their portraits are on the walls. 4-course dinner can be ordered in advance. Golf nearby at Muirfield and Gullane.	£25.00	■	O	■
Thomas B. Ovenstone **Marine Guest House** **7 Marine Road** **Dunbar EH42 1AR** **Tel: (0368) 63315** **OPEN: ALL YEAR**	Nearest Road A.1 A very comfortable house offering 10 pleasant, well decorated rooms with modern amenities. Most rooms have beautiful sea views. Beaches, which are safe and sandy, are close by. For the golfer there are several excellent courses in the area. Children will love it here. Cots and highchairs are provided.	£9.00	O	O	O

Isle of Mull

		minimum per person	children taken	evening meals available	animals taken
John & Ruth Wagstaff **Red Bay Cottage** **Deargphort** **Fionnphort** **Isle of Mull PA66 6BP** **Tel: (06817) 396** **OPEN: ALL YEAR**	Nearest Road A really warm welcome awaits the visitor to this charming modern house offering four very comfortable rooms with modern facilities. Situated only 20 metres from the sea and overlooking Iona Sound and the white sandy beaches on the Isle of Iona, this surely must be the ideal base. Mr & Mrs Wagstaff offer superb food. Half board rates are excellent.	£9.00	O	O	O

O yes ■ no

	minimum per person	children taken	evening meals available	animals taken
Phyllis & Michael Ingham **Lubnaig Hotel** **Leny Feus** **Callander FK17 8AS** **Tel: (0877) 30376** **OPEN: MAR-NOV** Nearest Road A.84 A very attractive,private luxury hotel offering ten delightful, quality bedrooms with private bath or shower en-suite. Situated in marvellous,secluded grounds it is a perfect base for visitors to this attractive region. Rugged mountains, pine forests, waterfalls, lochs, nature trails, excellent sporting facilities including golf, riding, water sports. The tranquility here is wonderful and the beauty unrivalled. Evening meals are really superb with food imaginatively prepared to gourmet standards. This lovely hotel offers excellent value for money and Mr & Mrs Ingham give their guests personal attention and the warmest of welcomes.	£17.00	O	O	O
Mrs Eslyn Craven **Highland House Hotel** **South Church Street** **Callander FK17 8BN** **Tel: (0877) 30269** **OPEN: APR-OCT** Nearest Road A.84 A most charming, white-painted Georgian terraced house with ten beautifully furnished and comfortable rooms. Three rooms have private shower and all have modern amenities. There are two lounges, one with colour T.V. and the other a small cocktail bar with log fire. Eslyn Craven is well known as a Cordon Bleu cook and her food is superb, including traditional Scottish dishes. Callander is an attractive town, standing on the river Teith. A wonderful area for golf, walking and touring the Trossachs. A warm welcome awaits.	£11.00	O	O	O
Roger McDonald **Allt-Chaorain House Hotel** **Crianlarich FK20 8RU** **Tel: (08383) 283** **OPEN: MAR-OCT** Nearest Road A.82 A delightful host and a welcoming atmosphere are found at Allt-Chaorain. Beautifully located in some of Scotland's most scenic countryside, Allt-Chaorain has the most wonderful views of Ben Morrand and Stob Binnion. Accommodation in 9 rooms, some with en-suite facilities, radio, and tea/coffee making. A residents' sun lounge and comfortable T.V. lounge are also available with log fires to relax by. This is a perfect base for touring Glen Coe, Rannoch Moor and Loch Lomond.	£13.00	O	O	O
Mr & Mrs Chisholm **The Riverside Guest House** **Tigh na Struith** **Crianlarich FK20 8RU** **Tel: (08383) 235** **OPEN: APR-OCT** Nearest Road A.82 Voted the best house in Britain by the Guild of Travel Writers in 1984, this superbly situated guest house comprises six luxurious bedrooms, each with unrestricted views of the surrounding hills and glens. A feature remarked upon by many of the guests is the abundance of oil paitings on the walls, and the comforts of T.V. and tea/coffee making facilities in every bedroom. Personally supervised by the owners, Janica and Sandy Chisholm, Tigh na Struith gives visitors a unique opportunity to relax and enjoy rural Scotland at its best. No single occupancy.	£9.00	O	■	O

O yes ■ no

○ yes ■ no

Ross-shire

		minimum per person	children taken	evening meals available	animals taken
D.A. Maclean **North West Hotel** **Main Street** **Kyle of Lochalsh** **IV40 8AB** **Tel: (0599) 4204** **OPEN: ALL YEAR**	Nearest Road North West Hotel is situated only a few minutes walk from some of Scotland's magnificent scenery. It is well situated for all the trains, ferries and boats that will take you to and from Kyle of Lochalsh. Accommodation is comfortable, in a choice of 34 bedrooms. There is a games room and lounge with T.V. for guests' use. Packed lunches are available and they have licensed premises.	£10.00	O	O	O
Mr & Mrs J.R. Waters **St. Katherine's** **Guest House** **Union Street** **Fortrose IV10 8TD** **Tel: (0381) 20949** **OPEN: APR-OCT**	Nearest Road A.9 An absolutely delightful 18th century house formely a residence for the Cannons of the Cathedral. Attractively located overlooking the ancient Cathedral ruins, this most interesting house offers extremely comfortable accommodation and great hospitality from the proprietors, John and Elizabeth. Although fully modernised, the house retains all its former character and atmosphere including Adam fireplaces, Oriel window and fine mouldings. The three bedrooms are very comfortable with modern amenities, radio, T.V. and tea/coffee making facilities. Large secluded walled garden well stocked with aromatic herbs. Excellent cuisine	£10.00	O	O	■

Roxburghshire

		minimum per person	children taken	evening meals available	animals taken
Mrs H.H. Irvine **Froylehurst** **The Friars** **Jedburgh** **Tel: (0835) 62477** **OPEN: APR-OCT**	Nearest Road A.68 An attractive Victorian house offering 4 comfortable guest rooms with modern amenities and a residents' lounge. Situated in a large garden overlooking the town in a quiet area. It offers great scope for touring. Edinburgh is only 1 hour. Golf, pony trekking, fishing and the sports centre all local. Tea and biscuits in the evening. Cots and highchairs are provided.	£8.50	O	■	O

Isle of Skye

		minimum per person	children taken	evening meals available	animals taken
Mr & Mrs D.D. Kemp **Craiglockhart Guest House** **Beaumont Crescent** **Portree** **Isle of Skye IV51 9DF** **Tel: (0478) 2233** **OPEN: JAN-NOV**	Nearest Roads A.850 A.87 A house of great architectural interest - a listed building which has been tastefully modernised, offering ten comfortable guest rooms with modern facilities. Everyone will love the area as there is much to discover here. Beaches, fishing, swimming, sea trips and riding all locally available. A warm welcome awaits the visitor here.	£11.50	O	O	O
Janice Macdonald **"Grianan"** **8 Glenbernisdale** **Skeabost Bridge** **by Portree IV51 9NP** **Tel: (047032) 387** **OPEN: MAY-SEP**	Nearest Road A.850 Grianan is a modern bungalow standing on croft land surrounded by open countryside, overlooking Loch Snizort. Accommodation is in a choice of three bedrooms. A colour T.V. lounge is available and tea/coffee are provided on request. Mrs Macdonald goes out of her way to ensure that her guests are comfortable and well looked after ensuring all visitors have a memorable holiday.	£7.00	O	O	O

O yes ■ no

WALES

To the west of England, surrounded by sea on three sides, is the small country of Wales. To the north it is a land of mountains, lakes and wide river estuaries, to the south there are gentler hills green valleys and a splendid coastline. It is a country where an ancient language is still spoken everyday and where history and folk lore are not forgotten.

It is a beautiful land of high moors, red with heather or under a golden blaze of summer gorse and craggy heights shrouded in mysterious mists. There are little farmhouses snug in green valleys and tiny fishing villages huddled in sandy coves. There are the great cities of Cardiff and Swansea andpleasant country towns still the home of regular livestock markets and country shows.

The changing skies of Wales have seen the settlement of early man from the Gower in the south to Anglesey in the north. Later occupation by the legions of Rome has left some impressive remains at Caerwent in the south but for the rest, occupation meant forts and military roads. As the Roman influence declined Christianity began to take firm hold. In a grassy hollow stands St Davids Cathedral, founded in the 6th century by Wales Patron Saint. Throughout the country there are abbeys, cathedrals and Christian memorial stones, all eloquent evidence from this age of faith.

Wales is a land of castles, over 100 of them, dating, mostly, from the Norman conquest. They dominate the landscape from spectacular rock outcrops guarding valleys and mountain passes, others are intimidating coastal fortresses such as Caernarfon and Harlech with soaring towers and fortifiedgateways. They are vivid testament to the resistance of the Welsh. At Caerphilly for example the complex land and water defenses mark one of Europes most impregnable castles and in the north Conwayhas no less than 21 towers.

From Taliesin in the 6th century to Dylan Thomas in modern times Wales has always inspired poetry and song. The legends of the western coasts speak of giants and princesses, of love, treason and revenge and of a lost land beneath the swirling waters of Cardigan Bay. The romance of the past is reflected today in the glorious landscape that is, and can only be, Wales.

South Wales

South Wales is a region of startling scenic variety. The little coves and wide sandy beaches of Pembrokeshire and the Gower Peninsular contrast sharply with the serene beauty of the wooded slopes of the Wye Valley and behind the charming villages and thatched cottages of the Vale of Glamorgan the land rises steeply to the high wild moorlands and hill farms of the Brecon Beacons National park. The area holds the capital city of Cardiff with its fine cathedral at Llandaff and there are tiny coastal villages like Bosherton near St. Govans Head is a tiny chapel hidden in a cleft in the massive limestone cliffs. There are seaside resort towns with brightly painted cottages and busy fishing harbours like Tenby and by contrast there are the south Wales valley town of Merthyr, Tonypandy and Rhymney, famous names from the heyday of coal mining.

Throughout this varied landscape there are constant reminders of the violent history of Wales. In ariverside village set amidst the beautiful woodlands of the Wye valley is the magnificent ruin of the Great Abbey of Tintern. Founded 1131 by the Cistercians, the abbey was active until the dissolution of the monasteries by Henry VIII in the 16th century. The ruins are hauntingly beautiful in the peaceful pastoral setting. At Caephilly there is a moated castle dating from the 13th century. This most impressive and virtually impregnable fortress has a leaning tower dating from the civil War when Cromwells troops tried to blow up the castle. The sweeping bays and sandy beaches were an attractive target for Norman invasion during the 11th century. The Normans successfully overran the coastlands from the sea and then defended their beachheads with a ring of castles on the landward side. As a result there are literally dozens of castles but perhaps the most notable are Pembroke Castle, birthplace of Henry VII and Kidwelly Castle.

From an earlier age the Preseli Hills of Pembrokeshire hold the massive prehistoric burial chambers Pentre Ifan and these same mountains provided the great blue-stones used at far-away Stonehenge in Southern England.

The folk museum at St Fagins just outside Cardiff has a fascinating collection reflecting traditional life in rural Wales. Set in the grounds of a fine old mansion, the museum contains manybuildings saved from demolition, rebuilt, stone by stone and carefully furnished to give a realisticimpression of the building forms and life styles throughout Welsh history.

The northern headland of St. Brides Bay is the most westerly point in the country and at the centre of a tiny village stands the Cathedral of St. David, the Patron Saint of Wales. The 12th century buildings is of local purple coloured stone and lies in a shallow valley out of sight of raiders andmaurauders. It was, at one time, the sole outpost of christianity in Britain and has been a place of pilgrimage for many centuries. Its rugged stonework blends perfectly with the green windswept countryside but belies the richly decorated interior.

Amongst the many villages and coastal towns is the picturesque village of Laugharne just outside Carmarthen. Here, Dylan Thomas lived and worked in what was a boathouse and is now a museum. The surrounding countryside and the village itself has been described in much of his work and his simplegrave is in the village churchyard.

Mid Wales

The limitless green hills of mid Wales form a truly rural landscape where there are almost three sheep to everyone person. It is a common sight to see a lone shepherd with his border collie move a flock of wayward sheep with a few whistles and hand gestures. This is the background for the craft of weaving which has been practised here for centuries. In the valley of the River Tefi and on an upper tributary of the Wye and the Irfon, there are a scatter of tiny riverbank millswhich produce the colourful Welsh plaid cloth from the raw wool. There is a timeless quality about mid Wales: places like Old Radnor, Knighton and Montgomery provide a picture of what country towns were like at the turn of the century. There are quiet market towns like Rhayader, Lampeter and Dolgellau where there are weekly sales of livestock and the annual agricultural shows, the largest is the national show at Builth Wells in July.

It has not always been quite so peaceful in mid Wales. The line of the border is followed by a hugeearthwork of bank and ditch known as Offa's Dyke. Offa was King of the ancient kingdom of Mercia, subject to incessant raids from across the Welsh border, so he constructed this massive fortification in a 750-800 A.D. to keep the Welsh at bay. It is now a long distance footpath and a walk along any stretch is a fine way to see the unsurpassed rolling countryside of the borders. Later the borders were defended by a chain of castles at Hay on Wye, Builth Wells, Welshpool and Chirk. Wales also suffered the loss of many fine buildings during the dissolution of the monastriesunder Henry VII. The ruins of the abbeys at Cymer -- near Dolgellau and Strata Frorida are the romantic remains of the superb buildings of the Cistercian monks. The area between Welshpool and Newtown are characterised by white and black half timbered buildings in villages and larger farmsteads but deeper into Wales the typical stone built houses predominate. However many remote parish churches can boast fine rood screens and soaring columns showing clearly the skills of mediaeval craftsmen.

To the north, on the borders of Snowdonia National Park the land rises to the scale of true mountains Mighty Cader Idris and the vast expenses of Plynlimon were once inaccessible to all but the shepherd and climber. Now they are popular centres for walking and ponytrekking and here as in many of the mid Wales beauty spots are excellent and well sign posted nature trails. To the west, the narrow coastal plain holds tiny towns and superb beaches.

Poetry and Legend

Cardigan Bay has been the inspiration of poets and the scene of legend for centuries. Taliesin the 6th century Celtic poet is reputed to be buried in the hamlet of Tre Taliesin and more recently Dylan Thomas has immortalised the little port of New Quay and its characters in "Under MilkWood". The earliest folk tales of Britain come from this coast including the tales of the mabinogion. The daughter of the Llyr tells of Welsh princess Branwen who was ill treated by her husband the King of Ireland. The giant Bendigied-fran goes to her rescue by wading across to Ireland and towing his fleet behind him. The Sarns are stone causeways that extend deep into Cardigan Bay from Harlech, Tywyn and Aberystwyth and lend some credence to the stories. Likewise, the lost cities of Cantre Gwaelod are reputed to be under the sea off the coast of Aberdovey. Whatever the truth of these legends the magnificent coastline offers a variety of water sports or an excursion into the hills on the delightful narrow gauge mountain railways. Tiny steam engines and stations have been beautifully restored and offer a unique way to see some of the most magnificent countryside in Britain.

North Wales

North Wales is chiefly renowed for the 850 miles of Snowdonia National Park. It is a land of mountains and lakes, cascading rivers and water falls, deep glacier valleys and high peaks. The superb scenery is justly popular with walkers and pony trekkers but the Snowdown mountain railway provides easy access to the summit of the highest mountain in the range with magnificent views across "the roof of Wales". Yet within a few miles of this wild, highland landscape is a superb coastline of smooth beaches, wide estuaries and little fishing villages.

Barmouth is a picturesque town with miles of golden sands, estuary walks and mountain scenery on itsdoorstep. Bangor and Llandudno are popular resort towns and Anglesey and the Lleyn peninsula are full of tiny bays and coastal villages, which are uncrowded and quite idyllic. The Lleyn peninsula, the long arm of north Wales, reaches west towards Ireland, and is an area of great charm. In mediaeval times pilgrims came from all over Britain to visit Bardsey, the Isle of 20,000 saints, just off Aberdaron, at the tip of the peninsula. The Isle of Anglesey also holds much for the visitor. It is linked to the mainland by the handsome Menai Straits suspension bridge. Certainly the town of Beaumaris with its 13th century castle is worth seeing as are many other fine buildings in the historic town centre.

Historically north Wales is a fiercely independent land where powerful local lords resisted first the Roman legions and later the armies of English kings. Armies clashed in the mountain passes in mediaeval times and the coastline is studded with magnificent 13th century castles. The dramatically sited fortress of Harlech commands the town and wide sweep of the coastline. The greatcitadel of Edward I at Caenarfon comprises both the castle and encircling town walls and is recognised as the finest castle in Britain. In 1969 it was the scene of the Investiture of His Royal Highness Prince Charles as Prince of Wales.

The areas holds elegant stately homes like Plas Newydd in Anglesey and the gentler countryside near Wrexham has Eriddig House. However, it is the variety of domestic architecture which is most charming. The timber frame buildings of the border country are seen at their best in the historic town of Ruthin set in the beautiful Vale of Clyd. Further west are the stone cottages of Snowdonia built of large stones and roofed with the distinctive blue and green local slate. Many of these hillside cottages are called "one-night houses" and are the result of the old custom of erectinga house on common land and lighting a fire in the hearth all in one night. The low, snow white cottages of Anglesey and the Lleyn peninsula are typical of the "Atlantic coast" architecture that can be found on all the coasts of western Europe. The houses are constructed of huge boulders with tiny windows and doors and are traditionally painted whlte. By contrast there is the marvellous architectural fantasy of Porthmeirion village. On a wooded peninsula betwen Harlech and Portmadog, Sir Clough Williams Ellis created a perfect Italianate village complete with pastel coloured buildings, a town hall and luxury hotel. It is a unique achievement and should be seen to be believed.

WALES GAZETEER

Areas of Outstanding Natural Beauty.
The Pembrokeshire Coast. The Brecon Beacons. Snowdonia. Gower.

Historic Houses and Castles

Cardiff Castle -- Cardiff
Built on a Roman site in the 11th century.

Caerphilly Castle -- Caerphilly
13th century fortress.

Chirk Castle -- Nr. Wrexham
14th century Border Castle. Lovely gardens.

Coity Castle -- Coity
Mediaeval stronghold -- Three storied round tower.

Gwydir Castle -- Nr. Lanrwst
Royal residence in past days -- wonderful Tudor furnishings. Gardens with peacocks.

Penrhyn Castle -- Bangor
Neo-Norman architecture 19th century -- large grounds with museum and exhibitions. Victorian garden.

Picton Castle -- Haverfordwest
12th century -- lived in by the same family continuously. Fine gardens.

Caernarfon Castle -- Caernarfon
13th century -- castle of great importance to Edward I.

Conway Castle -- Conwy
13th century -- one of Edward I's chain of castles.

Powis Castle -- Welshpool
14th century -- reconstruction work in 17th century. Murals, furnishings, tapestries and paintings, terraced gardens.

Pembroke Castle -- Pembroke
12th century Norman castle with huge keep and immense walls. Birthplace of Henry VII.

Plas Newydd -- Isle of Anglesey
18th century Gothic style house, home of the Marquis of Anglesey. Stands on the edge of the Menai Strait looking across to the Snowdonia Range. Famous for the Rex Whistler murals.

The Tudor Merchant's House -- Tenby
Built in 15th century.

Tretower Court and Castle -- Crickhowell
Mediaeval -- finest example in Wales.

Cathedrals and Churches

St. Asaph Cathedral
13th century -- 19th century restoration. Smallest of Cathedrals in England and Wales.

Holywell (St. Winifred)
15th century well chapel and chamber -- fine example.

St. Davids (St. David)
12th century cathedral -- spendid tower -- oak roof to nave.

Gwent (St. Woolos)
Norman Cathedral -- Gothic additions -- 19th century restoration.

Abergavenny (St. Mary)
14th century church of 12th century Benedictine priory.

Llanengan (St. Engan)
Mediaeval church -- very large with original roof and stalls 16th century tower.

Esyronen
17th century chapel, much original interior remaining.

Llandegley (St. Tegla)
18th century Quaker meeting house -- thatched roof -- simple structure divided into schoolroom and meeting room.

Llandaff Cathedral (St. Peter & St. Paul)
Founded in 6th century -- present building begun in 12th century. Great damage suffered in bombing during war, now restored with Epstein's famous figure of Christ.

Museums and Galleries

National Museum of Wales -- Cardiff. (Also Turner House)
Geology, archeology, zoology, botany, industry and art exhibitions.

Welsh Folk Museum -- St. Fagans Castle -- Cardiff
13th century walls curtaining a 16th century house -- now a most interesting and comprehensive folk museum.

County Museum -- Carmarthen
Roman jewellery, gold etc. Romano-British and Stone age relics.

National Library of Wales -- Aberystwth
Records of Wales and Celtic areas. Great historical interest.

University College of Wales Gallery -- Aberystwyth
Travelling exhibitions of painting and sculpture.

Newport Museum and Art Gallery -- Newport
Specialist collection of English watercolours -- natural history Roman remains, etc.

Legionary Museum -- Caerleon
Roman relics found on the site of legionary fortress at Isca.

Nelson Museum -- Monmouth
Interesting relics of Admiral Lord Nelson and Lady Hamilton.

Bangor Art Gallery -- Bangor
Exhibitions of contemporary paintings and sculpture.

Bangor Museum of Welsh Antiquities -- Bangor
History of North Wales is shown. Splendid exhibits of furniture, clothing, domestic objects, etc. etc. Also Roman antiquities.

Narrow Gauge Railway Museum -- Tywyn
Rolling stock and exhibitions of narrow gauge railways of U.K.

Museum of Childhood -- Menai Bridge.
Charming museum of dolls and toys and children's things.

Brecknock Museum -- Brecon
Natural history, archeology, agriculture, local history etc.

Glynn Vivian Art Gallery & Museum -- Swansea.
Ceramics, old and contemporary, British paintings and drawings, sculpture, loan exhibitions.

Stone Museum -- Margam
Carved stones and crosses from pre-historic times.

Plas Mawr -- Conwy
A beautiful Elizabethan town mansion house in its original condition. Now holds the Royal Cambrain Academy of Art.

Historic Monuments

Rhuddlan Castle -- Rhuddlan
13th century castle -- interesting diamond plan.

Valle Crucis Abbey -- Llangollen
13th century Cistercian Abbey Church.

WALES
Recommended roadside restaurants

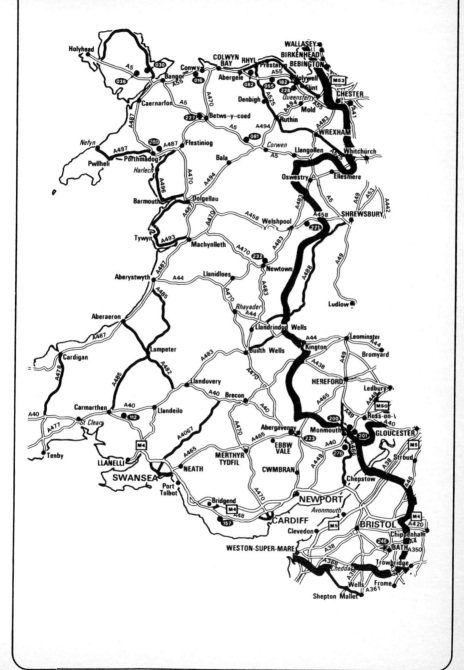

Wales
Clwyd

	minimum per person	children taken	evening meals available	animals taken

Mrs Gwyneth Webb
Plas Newydd Farm
Llanddulas LL22 8HH
Nr. Abergele
Tel: (0492) 516038

OPEN: ALL YEAR

Nearest Road A.55

A lovely, 400 year old Welsh farmhouse retaining its original character including lots of oak beams. Accommodation is in 2 pleasant bedrooms with modern amenities. An ideal base for touring as Snowdonia, Conway and Anglesey are within easy reach, also conveniently placed for the local beaches and outdoor activities.

£9.00 ○ ■ ■

Mrs E. Davies
Tyn-Y-Coed Farm
Llanellian
Colwyn Bay LL29 8YR
Tel: (0492) 516142

OPEN: APR-OCT

Nearest Road A.55

A pleasant and homely modern bungalow standing in 42 acres, offering two double rooms with modern amenities. Evening meals are excellent value - so is half board. A good base for families. There is much to discover in the town and the surrounding countryside. Three miles from beach. Overlooking Colwyn Bay and Clwydian Hills.

£7.00 ○ ○ ■

Frances Williams-Lee &
** Cedric B. Sumner**
Buck Farm
Hanmer SY14 7LX
Tel: (094874) 339

OPEN: ALL YEAR

Nearest Road A.525

An unspoiled, half timbered, Tudor farmhouse on the A.525 midway between Wrexham and Whitchurch. Ideal as a touring base for North Wales, Cheshire, Shropshire and the Potteries. Buck Farm offers warm hospitality, excellent country cooking with fresh local produce, organically grown whenever possible. Wholefood vegetarian and vegan meals and special diets are available on request and the wholemeal breads, granola, muesli and vegetable soups are but some of the specialites. No smoking. Yoga weekends.

£10.00 ○ ○ ■

Mrs Jen Spencer
Eyarth Station
Llanfair DC
Ruthin LL15 2EE
Tel: (082 42) 3643

OPEN: ALL YEAR

Nearest Road A.525

A warm and friendly reception awaits the visitor to Eyarth Station. A super converted former Railway Station located in the beautiful countryside of the Vale of Clwyd. A choice of six bedrooms all with private shower. There is a comfortable colour T.V. lounge and guests are welcome to use the garden and sun patio. Conveniently located for the many historic towns in the region including Conway, Caernafon and Ruthin Castle with medieval banquet 2 mins drive. The Roman town of Chester is also within driving distance. Price shown is for two people.

£22.00 ○ ○ ○

Mrs E.A. Parry
Llainwen Ucha
Pentre Celyn
Ruthin LL15 2HL
Tel: (097888) 253

OPEN: ALL YEAR

Nearest Road A.525

A very pleasant modern house where you can be assured of a warm welcome. The proprietors offer 2 pleasantly decorated, comfortable rooms with modern amenities. Overlooking the very beautiful Vale of Clwyd and the gateway to Snowdonia. It is an ideal base for touring this lovely region of North Wales. The local fishing is very good. Cots are provided.

£7.50 ○ ○ ■

---

		minimum per person	children taken	evening meals available	animals taken
C.M. Vaughton **Awel-Y-Grug** **Boncath SA37 0JP** **Tel: (023974) 260** **OPEN: ALL YEAR**	Nearest Road B.4332 Awel-Y-Grug is a small family run Guest House where guests are welcomed to a relaxed homely atmosphere. Good and plentiful home-cooked food is served using home grown fruit and vegetables when available and vegetarian meals are a speciality. Licensed. Three bedrooms, dinning room, T.V. lounge with log fires, games room and a large and pleasant garden. Children welcome.	£9.00	O	O	O
Sheila & P.T. Heard **Tregynon Farmhouse** **Pontfaen** **Nr. Fishguard SA65 9TU** **Tel: (0239) 820531** **OPEN: ALL YEAR**	Nearest Road B.4313 This is a traditional, beamed, 16th century family run farmhouse standing in acres of grounds by ancient oak woodlands overlooking the glorious Gwaun Valley in the Pembrokeshire Coast National Park. It is unique and of great natural beauty and still quite unspoiled. It offers five rooms, 2 with facilities on the ground floor for disabled guests. Traditional and special diets, wholefood and vegetarian specialities, using fresh home produce when possible, own trout. A good range of wine is also available. Own 200ft waterfall and iron age fort, abundant wildlife.	£10.00	O	O	O
Brenda & Tony Huxton **Siriole Guest House** **Quay Road** **Goodwick SA64 0BS** **Tel: (0348) 873203** **OPEN: ALL YEAR**	Nearest Road A.40 This pleasant house, once belonging to a sea captain, offers comfortable accommodation in six rooms with modern facilities. Situated on the edge of Fishguard Bay with the Precelli Hills in the distance, it is an ideal place for touring the region and for those using the port to Ireland. Children over 6 accepted.	£8.50	O	■	■
Mrs Peggy Evans **Maes-Y-Ffynnon** **Croesgoch** **Haverfordwest SA62 5JN** **Tel: (03483) 319** **OPEN: FEB-OCT**	Nearest Road A.487 A warm welcome and a friendly atmosphere are assured at Maes-Y-Ffynnon. Located on the edge of the beautiful National Coastal Park it is situated 1 mile from the coast with many unspoilt sandy beaches, coves and harbours nearby. The accommodation is in a choice of three bedrooms, two with modern amenities and radio. There is a colour T.V. lounge. Guests may also like to use the garden. This makes a good base for either a stopover or for a touring holiday.	£10.00	O	O	O
Mrs C. Disandolo **Villa House** **St. Thomas Green** **Haverfordwest SA61 1QN** **Tel: (0437) 2977** **OPEN: ALL YEAR**	Nearest Road A.484 A warm welcome awaits the visitor to this very pleasant house with three comfortable rooms all with modern facilities. Standing in its own grounds it makes an ideal base for touring the superb area with its excellent, coastline and lovely countryside. The house is known for its super Italian/English cooking.	£8.00	O	O	O

O yes ■ no

	minimum per person	children taken	evening meals available	animals taken

Mrs E.V. Evans
Heathfield Lodge Farm
Wiston
Haverfordwest SA62 4PT
Tel: (043782) 200

OPEN: APR-OCT

Nearest Road A.40

Heathfield Lodge is a modern farm bunga-low, surrounded by an attractive well main-tained garden and spacious lawns, with panoramic views across the open farmland. Accommodation is in four rooms with mod-ern amenities. A residents' lounge with col-our T.V. is also available throughout the day. Good farmhouse food is served daily using fresh farm produce. The farm is conveniently located for visiting Llys-Y-Fran reservoir which offers sailing, fishing and good pic-nicking areas. Close by are golf, pony trek-king and many beaches.

£9.00 | O | O | O

Mrs Bradley-Watson
Hurst House
East Marsh
Laugharne SA33 4RS
Tel: (099421) 235

OPEN: ALL YEAR

Nearest Roads A.40 A.4066

An elegant Georgian house literally 'Under Milk Wood'. 2 miles from Laugharne of Dylan Thomas fame, with numerous close beaches. The house was the principal farm house of the Broadway estate, situated be-side the Taf estuary with an abundance of wildlife. It has a double bedroom with a bathroom en-suite and a twin room, both with televisions. There is a separate drawing room. Additional facilities include an indoor badminton court, table tennis, a croquet lawn and a small swimming pool.

£9.00 | O | O | O

Glamorgan

Mrs J.E. Morgan
Penuchadre Farm
St.Brides Major
Bridgend
Mid Glamorgan CF32 0TE
Tel: (0656) 880313

OPEN: ALL YEAR

Nearest Roads A.48 B.4265 M.4

Dating back in part over 500 years, this pleasant farm is situated in 130 acres on the edge of the Heritage Coast. Well mod-ernised with central heating, all three rooms have washing facilities and are most com-fortable. A T.V. lounge is available for guests. The cooking is excellent with all pro-duce from the farm plus home-baked bread and cakes. It is an ideal centre for exploring the many beaches, the Brecon Beacons, the Dan-yr-Ogof Caves and the Welsh National Folk Museum. A delightful holiday base.

£8.50 | O | ■ | ■

Mr & Mrs Milosevic
Princes Guest House
10 Princes Street
Roath
Cardiff CF2 3PR
Tel: (0222) 491732/481394

OPEN: ALL YEAR

Nearest Roads A.48 M.4

A family run guest house with a homely atmosphere. Pleasant rooms with modern facilities. Colour T.V. lounge. A warm wel-come to visitors. Within walking distance of Roath Park and the boating lake. Swan-bridge and Penarth are only a few miles away. Roath Castle and the museum are within walking distance.

£9.00 | O | O | ■

O yes ■ no

306

		minimum per person	children taken	evening meals available	animals taken

Mrs J. Davies
The Croft
Heol-Y-Barna
Pontardulais
Swansea SA4 1HG
Tel: (0792) 883654

OPEN: ALL YEAR

Nearest Road A.48

A very pleasant farmhouse, standing on a five acre small holding, completely modernised, and offering three charming and comfortable rooms. Situated on a quiet country road with fine views of the surrounding countryside. Taking only 6 guests, the atmosphere is very informal and all visitors can be assured of a warm welcome and good food. All rooms have modern amenities. The comfortable lounge has a colour T.V. and is available to guests throughout the day. The Croft is ideally situated for visiting many parts of South Wales with easy access for the M.4

£8.00   O O O

Heather & Bruce Wearing
Parkway Hotel
253 Gower Road
Sketty
Swansea SA2 9JL
Tel: (0792) 201632

OPEN: ALL YEAR

Nearest Road A.4118

A small mansion style house in its own grounds offering pleasant, comfortable rooms with modern facilities, plus tea making equipment. This is an ideal base for touring the lovely Gower Peninsula and Swansea Bay. The city centre is easily accessible and is full of interest as are the many historic sites which abound in this region. Personal service and a warm welcome await all visitors. Friendly and relaxed atmosphere.

£12.50   O O O

Mr Paul &
Mrs Monica Renwick
Sant-Y-Nyll House
St.Brides-Super-Ely
CF5 6EZ
Tel: (0446) 760209

OPEN: ALL YEAR

Nearest Road M.4

You can be assured of a friendly welcome to Saint-Y-Nyll, a charming Georgian country residence in its own extensive grounds with spectacular views over the Vale of Glamorgan. 6 guest rooms with modern facilities, T.V., tea/coffee making, comfortable, warm and relaxing. Licensed. Children welcome. Cardiff just 7 miles. St. Fagans Welsh Folk Museum 2 miles.

£12.50   O O ■

Gwent

Mrs Kathleen Williams
Fairlea
24 Belmont Road
Abergavenny NP7 5HN
Tel: (0873) 6976

OPEN: FEB-OCT

Nearest Road A.40

Fairlea is a delightful and unusual Victorian black and white house. It stands in a quiet residential area with splendid views of the surrounding countryside. Accommodation in 4 very comfortable well furnished rooms with modern amenities, phone and T.V. An attractive colour T.V. lounge is also available. This makes an idea base for touring the area.

£10.00   O ■ ■

Mrs E.M. Davies
Crossways Farm
Llangattock
Lingoed
Abergavenny NP7 8RR
Tel: (087386) 395

OPEN: ALL YEAR

Nearest Road B.4521

A most comfortable modern bungalow, offering pleasant accommodation in two guest rooms, in a peaceful area with beautiful views. The region is excellent for touring with many historic sites and castles in the area. Museums and galleries are well worth visiting. The countryside offers superb walking and the coast is accessible. A car is essential. Golden Valley, Llanthony Valley, Offas Dyke. Pony trekking.

£8.00   O ■ ■

O yes ■ no

		min.	child.	meals	anim.
Mrs Priscilla Llewelyn **Penpergwm House** **Abergavenny NP7 9AP** **Tel (0873) 840267** **OPEN: ALL YEAR**	Nearest Road A.40 Priscilla and her family will welcome and cosset you in true country house tradition. This charming Georgian house, formerly a rectory, combines comfort and convenience. Accommodation is in four rooms, one en-suite and one with traditional 4-poster bed, all with modern amenities, tea/coffee making facilities and radio. Salmon and trout fishing are available on the River Usk. This is a pleasant base from which to explore this beautiful and little known area of the Welsh Hills. Guided tours. Fully inclusive mid-week mini-breaks.	£10.00	O	O	O
Mrs Dinah Price **"Great House"** **Isca Road** **Old Village** **Caerleon NP6 1QG** **Tel: (0633) 420216** **OPEN: ALL YEAR**	Nearest Road A.48 "Great House" is an attractive 17th century home located on the banks of the River Usk. Retaining much of its original characer, including beams and inglenook fireplaces, this delightful home offer very pretty accommodation in 3 rooms with T.V. and tea/coffee making facilities. An attractive T.V. lounge and pretty garden are also available for guests' use. Within easy reach are riding, golf, fishing and forest trials. Ideal as a stopover for those on the way to Wales.	£9.00	O	■	■
Amanda & Bruce Weatherill **Llanwenarth House** **Govilon** **Abergavenny NP7 9SF** **Tel: (0873) 830289** **OPEN: ALL YEAR** **(EXCL. FEB)**	Nearest Road A.465 A truly delightful 16th century manor house. Standing in its own beautiful grounds and surrounded by the tranquil scenic hills of the Brecon Beacons National Park. Amanda and Bruce provide the highest standards of comfort and convenience in their recently renovated house. Elegantly furnished, tastefully decorated and with superb views, this house is a real pleasure to visit. Dinner cooked by Amanda, a Cordon Bleu cook, is a delight. It is served by candlelight in the lovely dining room. Accommodation is in five rooms all with private facilities. Many sporting facilities are close by: fishing, riding, golf, climbing, walking, shooting.	£19.50	O	O	O
Mrs Rosemary Townsend **"Lugano"** **LLandogo** **Monmouth NP5 4TL** **Tel: (0594) 530496** **OPEN: ALL YEAR**	Nearest Road A.466 A warm welcome to the happy family atmosphere at Lugano, a modern dormer bungalow in pleasant grounds in the heart of the Wye Valley. Accommodation is in three tastefully furnished rooms with all amenities, one en-suite and with access to the garden. Comprehensive selection of literature on the area for guests to read. Many local inns and restaurants serving food.	£11.00	O	■	O

The diagonal column headers are: minimum per person, children taken, evening meals available, animals taken.

		Nearest Road	minimum per person	children taken	evening meals available	animals taken
Mrs C.T. Park **Brick House Farm** Redwick Newport NP6 3DX Tel: (0633) 880230 **OPEN: ALL YEAR**	Brick House Farm is a listed Georgian farmhouse dating from about 1765, but with up-to-date conveniences. Most bedrooms have either en-suite bathroom or wash hand basin. Full central heating and T.V. lounge complete guests' comfort. Brick House is ideally placed for touring South Wales and the Wye Valley, or as a stopping-off point just over the Severn Bridge.	Nearest Road M.4	£10.00	O	O	O

Gwynedd

		Nearest Road	minimum per person	children taken	evening meals available	animals taken
Mrs Jean E. Smith **Pen-Isar-Llan Farm Guest House & Riding Centre** Llanfor Bala LL23 TDW Tel: (0678) 520507 **OPEN: ALL YEAR**	A most attractive 300 year old farmhouse standing in its own grounds ½ a mile outside Bala. Accommodation is in seven pleasantly decorated bedrooms, with tea/coffee making facilities. The lounge is large and comfortable with cosy log fire, T.V., video and bar. There is also a games room with snooker and darts. Of special interest is the horse riding facility. Trekking for the less able, or for the more experienced longer rides are available. Lessons can also be arranged. If you prefer you can bring you own pony or horse. Close by are bird watching, canoeing, fishing, golf, sailing, walking, windsurfing.	Nearest Road A.494	£9.50	O	O	O
T. Glynn Jones **Frondderw Private Hotel** Stryd-y-Fron Bala LL23 7YD Tel: (0678) 520301 **OPEN: ALL YEAR**	A beautiful 17th century mansion offering eight delightful rooms, two en-suite. Colour T.V. lounge. Books and games for guests. Situated in parkland, it is a perfect base for visitors. There are many mountain walks and waterfalls close by. Roman remains and historic sites. Food here is excellent and good value. Excellent weekly terms.	Nearest Road A.5	£9.50	O	O	■
Mrs P.M. & Mr S.P. Strong **Glenwood** Betws-Y-Coed LL24 0BN Tel: (06902) 508 **OPEN: FEB-NOV**	A spacious house situated in its own lovely grounds near Gwydyr Forest. Cream teas are served in the garden overlooking the River Llugwy. 6 pleasant, comfortable rooms are available all with lovely views, and modern amenities. Walkers, climbers and riders will love it and it is ideal for families. Castles, lakes and rivers all around.	Nearest Road A.5	£15.00	O	■	■
Norman & Gwen Pritchard **Henllys (Old Court) Hotel** Betws-Y-Coed LL24 OAL Tel: (06902) 534 **OPEN: ALL YEAR**	A really charming hotel, in a class of its own, situated in waterside gardens on the banks of the River Conwy. Dine on superb cuisine, where magistrates once resided, in this converted courthouse. Several of the 11 excellent bedrooms have extra King size beds for extra comfort. There is a beamed lounge bar. Personally run by the friendly and most hospitable proprietors.	Nearest Road A.5	£13.50	O	O	O

O yes ■ no

	Nearest Road	minimum per person	children taken	evening meals available	animals taken
Jean & Graham Ball **Fairy Glen Hotel** **Betws-Y-Coed LL24 0SH** **Tel: (06902) 269** **OPEN: FEB-NOV**	Nearest Road A.5 Dating back over 300 years, this charming 17th century hotel offers accommodation in ten comfortable rooms with modern amenities. Situated by the Beaver Bridge on the Conway river it is an excellent base for touring this scenic and historic region. Fairy Glen beauty spot is only five minutes away. Conway Falls only a mile away.	£14.00	O	O	O
W. & J. Major **Mount Garmon Hotel** **Betws-y-Coed LL24 0AN** **Tel: (06902) 335** **OPEN: MAR-OCT**	Nearest Road on A.5 An early Victorian house, tastefully convered into a small family hotel with comfortable accommodation for guests. Five bedrooms, three en-suite, dining-room, television lounge and lounge bar, all pleasantly furnished and with a welcoming atmosphere. The food is good - traditional English breakfast and a home-cooked roast dinner complimented by a varied wine list. Children over 3 years.	£15.00	O	O	■
Catherine Booth **'Bron Celyn' Guest House** **Llanwrst Road** **Betws-Y-Coed LL24 0HD** **Tel: (06902) 333** **OPEN: JAN-NOV**	Nearest Road A.5 A small and friendly guest house with comfort and good food in a relaxed atmosphere. An ideal touring centre only 5 minutes walk to the village and overlooking a picturesque valley. Seven spacious rooms are available, some en-suite all with T.V. and tea/coffee making facilities. Lounge and garden. Children welcome. Golf and riding available nearby.	£9.00	O	O	O
Mrs Wendy Whalley **Rhiwafallen** **Llandwrog** **Caernarfon LL54 5SW** **Tel: (0286) 831237** **OPEN: ALL YEAR**	Nearest Road A.499 An early Victorian farmhouse, recently renovated to a high standard. Offering 3 very quiet and well furnished rooms, with modern amenities, tea/coffee makers. Set back from the Caenarfon-Pwllheli road, guests can enjoy the surrounding acreage of pasture and secluded woodland. Visitors are made most welcome and will find good beaches nearby and access to Snowdonia.	£9.00	O	■	O
Mrs R. Murray **Min-Y-Gaer Private Hotel** **Porthmadog Road** **Criccieth LL52 0HP** **Tel: (076671) 2151** **OPEN: APR-OCT**	Nearest Road A.497 A pleasant licensed house in a quiet residental area offering very good accommodation in ten comfortable rooms with tea/coffee makers. It is only 2 minutes walk to the safe sandy beach and fishing, golfing, tennis and pony trekking all close by. Ideal for touring Snowdonia. The hotel overlooks the esplanade and has commanding views of Cardigan Bay coastline. Children welcome.	£9.50	O	O	O

O yes ■ no

	minimum per person	children taken	evening meals available	animals taken

Jim & Betty Yuill
Castle Cottage Hotel
Pen Llech
Harlech LL46 2YL
Tel: (0766) 780479

OPEN: ALL YEAR

Nearest Roads A.496 B.4573

A delightful house dating back at least 200 years with many exposed beams offering five rooms of great character which are comfortable and have modern amenities. The restaurant is known for its good food. Only 200 yards from Harlech Castle. The beach and nature reserve are within five miles. An ideal base for touring this lovely region. Golf arrangements have been made for guests' to use Royal St. Davids. Garden for guests' enjoyment.

£13.50 | ○ | ○ | ○

Marion & Dio Jones
Penarwel Country House
Llanbedrog
Pwllheli LL53 7NN
Tel: (0758) 740719

OPEN: APR-OCT

Nearest Road A.499

An Edwardian country mansion with turreted tower and gargoyles where guests are made most welcome and comfortable. The house is peacefully situated in 4 acres of wooded gardens, yet only half a mile from the sea. Seven elegant bedrooms, three with private bathrooms, all with modern facilities, T.V. if requested and tea/coffee making. Meals are freshly cooked using local produce.

£11.00 | ○ | ○ | ■

Mike & Sue McGarry
The Beaulieu Hotel
6 Hill Terrace
Llandudno LL30 2LS
Tel: (0492) 77234

OPEN: MAR-DEC

Nearest Roads A.55 A.546

A small family run Victorian hotel which has fantastic views overlooking bays and the Conway Valley. There are ten very comfortable and well furnished rooms, five with private facilities. All rooms have modern amenities, tea/coffee makers and televisions are available in seven rooms. A large sunny lounge with colour T.V. for guests. Mike and Sue McGarry offer a homely atmosphere, good cooking and unlimited service. This is an ideal base for touring the beautiful coastline and countryside. Children are very welcome here.

£9.50 | ○ | ○ | ○

Eric & Hilda Beardmore
Puffin Lodge Hotel
Central Promenade
Llandudno LL30 1AT
Tel: (0492) 77713

OPEN: APR-OCT

Nearest Roads A.55 A.5

Approximately 100 years old, this pleasant house offers 14 comfortable rooms with modern facilities. With superb views of the countryside, the bay and Snowdonia, it is ideal for Conway Castle, Conway Valley and many historic sites and museums.

£10.50 | ○ | ○ | ■

Janet Jones
Tan-y-Fynwent
Aber
Llanfairfechan
LL33 0LB
Tel: (0248) 681521

OPEN: ALL YEAR

Nearest Road A.55

A large family home and garden on the edge of the Snowdonia National Park, close to the sea. Three spacious, comfortable bedrooms with tea/coffee making facilities, one with en-suite bathroom. The lounge has colour T.V. and log fires for chilly evenings. Plenty for the energetic to do in the area and also peaceful seclusion for those seeking a restful break in beautiful scenery.

£10.00 | ○ | ○ | ■

○ yes ■ no

311

	minimum per person	children taken	evening meals available	animals taken
Norman Terence Barker **Hafod House Hotel** **& Restaurant** **Trefriw LL27 0RQ** **Tel: (0492) 640029** **OPEN: ALL YEAR**	Nearest Road A.5 A most attractive 17th century traditional Welsh stone farmhouse in a peaceful setting on the edge of Trefriw in the beautiful Conway Valley, inside Snowdonia National Park. All 9 guest rooms are very well appointed, two having luxury status with designer decor, four poster beds and whirlpool baths. Your host is your chef serving first class dishes. Children over 6.	£12.50	O	O	■
Brian & Cynthia Elson **Greenfield Private Hotel** **& Restaurant** **High Street** **Tywyn LL36 9AD** **Tel: (0654) 710354** **OPEN: JAN-FEB**	Nearest Road A.493 An excellent private hotel offering 14 pleasant, comfortable rooms with modern facilities. A comfortable lounge and residents' bar. It is an ideal centre for discovering this area on the edge of Snowdonia. Sports locally include swimming, golf, bowling, tennis, putting and pony trekking. Very good half board terms. Safe, sandy beaches close by.	£10.75	O	O	■

Powys

	minimum per person	children taken	evening meals available	animals taken
C.M. Hammond **Querida** **43 Garth Road** **Builth Wells LD2 3AR** **Tel: (0982) 553642** **OPEN: ALL YEAR**	Nearest Road A.483 A pleasant stone-built guest house within easy reach of the town centre. Golf, fishing and 2 sports halls are nearby. There are excellent walks along the River Wye. The Brecon Beacons, Black Mountains and the Elan Valley are easily reached. Accommodation is in 3 rooms with modern amenities.	£7.50	O	O	O
Mrs Z.E. Hope **Caepandy Farm** **Garth Road** **Builth Wells LD2 3NS** **Tel: (0982) 553793** **OPEN: ALL YEAR**	Nearest Road A.483 A warm welcome awaits visitors to Caepandy Farm. This modernised 17th century farmhouse stands one mile outside Builth Wells and has magnificent views of the Irfon Valley and the surrounding countryside. There is a choice of 3 rooms, 2 double and 1 family room. Guest have the use of the T.V. lounge and the garden. This is a good base for exploring all of mid Wales.	£7.50	O	O	O
Mrs Valerie Powell **Dolfawr Farm** **Cwmdu** **Crickhowell NP8 1RT** **Tel: (0874) 730684** **OPEN: APR-OCT**	Nearest Road A.479 A very old, traditional long Welsh farmhouse iwith a log fire, thick walls and oak beams, set on a 170 acre mixed farm situated in the beautiful Brecon Beacons National Park. There are superb forest and mountain walks as well as pony trekking, tennis and golf. Accommodatiuon is in 3 bedrooms with modern amenities.	£7.50	O	■	O

O yes ■ no

312

	minimum per person	children taken	evening meals available	animals taken
Mr & Mrs J.H. Usborne **Glan-Nant** **Brecon Road** **Crickhowell** **Powys NP8 1DL** **Tel: (0873) 810631** **OPEN: APR-OCT** Nearest Road A.40 A substantial country family house, part Georgian, part Regency, with an attractive verandah, standing in peaceful grounds with superb views over the mountains and countryside. Three attractive rooms with modern facilities, one with bath en-suite. Tea/coffee makers provided. Situated in a marvellous area for touring and walking. Pony trekking and fishing locally. An excellent pub close by for evening meals. Mrs Usborne will make you very welcome. Children welcome over 8 years of age.	£10.00	O	■	O
Mrs C.H. Hood **Pilleth Court** **Whitton** **Knighton LD7 1NP** **Tel: (05476) 272** **OPEN: APR-OCT** Nearest Road A.488 An Eizabethan house with all the character and atmosphere retained. Offering 3 delightful, comfortable rooms with modern facilities. Set in 600 acres, it is surrounded by marvellous countryside. Close by are the ruins of a wooden castle, an early church and the site of the Battle of Pilleth. Presteigne is not far away and is a superb historic town. This must be the most ideal place to stay. Good home cooking with flair.	£9.00	O	O	■
Miss Sheila Like **& Mrs Sylvia Knott** **The Ffaldau Country House** **Llandegley** **LD1 5UD** **Tel: (059787) 421** **OPEN: ALL YEAR** Nearest Road A.44 The Ffaldau is a 17th century Welsh stone-built 'cruck' house set off the road, surrounded by fields and open hillside. Three bedrooms prettily decorated, with modern amenities. Morning 'cuppa' in bed. Oak beamed dining room with log fire where excellent home cooking is served. A la Carte menu using fresh produce and many little 'goodies'. No single availability.	£11.00	O	O	■
Wyn & Gwyneth Jones **Moat Farm** **Welshpool SY21 8SE** **Tel: (0938) 3179** **OPEN: APRIL-OCT** Nearest Road A.483 A very warm welcome and a friendly atmosphere are found at this delightful 16th century farmhouse. It is surrounded by the lovely Severn Valley countryside and is only a stone's throw away from the river itself. The house retains many of its original beams and open log-burning stone fireplaces. Moat Farm has a lovely family atmosphere where guests can really relax and enjoy themselves, taking an interest in farm activities or exploring the wonderful countryside. Accommodation is in 3 comfortable rooms with modern amenities and tea/coffee making facilities. There is also a guests' dining room and T.V. lounge.	£10.00	O	O	■

O yes ■ no

	minimum per person	children taken	evening meals available	animals taken

Mrs Freda Emberton
Tynllwyn Farm
Welshpool SY21 9BW
Tel: (0938) 3175/3054

OPEN: ALL YEAR

Nearest Road A.490

A friendly, informal family atmosphere exists at Tynllwyn Farm. This delightful 100 year old farmhouse stands on a hillside surrounded by 150 acres of its own dairy farmland. Accommodation is in 6 rooms with modern amenities and T.V. There is also a colour T.V. lounge for guests' to use. Good farmhouse food is served using local or own produce where possible. There is also a full bar license so guests can enjoy a relaxing drink. This makes a lovely base from which to explore the area. Guests are also welcome to wander around the farm. Welshpool is only 1 mile from here.

£10.00 ○ ○ ○

○ yes ■ no

314

Recommendations
& Complaints

Proprietors:_____

Address:_____

_____

Your Name & Address:_____

General Information:_____

_____

_____

✂

Proprietors:_____

Address:_____

_____

Your Name & Address:_____

General Information:_____

_____

_____

Reply to: W.W.B.B.A.

P.O.Box 134, 15 Gledhow Gardens,

London SW5 0TX. U.K.